The English District Saga

A Niche in the History of the
Evangelical Lutheran Church in North America

Rev. Dr. David P. Stechholz
Bishop Emeritus and Archivist

Foreword by Rev. Dr. Jamison J. Hardy
Bishop, English District of the LCMS

Angels' Portion Books

Text © 2021 by David P. Stechholz
Edited by Deborah Kunkel, Christopher I. Thoma, Brian P. Westgate, and Luke T. Zimmerman
Title Page Image: The Recessional in the Divine Service of Redeemer Evangelical Lutheran Church of
Fort Wayne, Indiana

SECOND EDITION

Angels' Portion Books
AngelsPortion.com

Cover design and layout: Angels' Portion Books
Cover Image: Michael Gaida
For more information, visit *https://EnglishDistrict.org*

    Stechholz, David P., 1948—
    The English District Saga
    ISBN-13: 978-1-7367051-3-1

Printed in the United States of America

ENDORSEMENTS

"The story of the English District of the Missouri Synod is a fascinating one, and Dr. David Stechholz has told it eloquently. People who are new to the Missouri Synod (or maybe not so new), often wonder why it has a district called 'English' when almost all the others are strictly geographical. Well, this book tells them. More importantly, the history of this non-geographical district provides a window into the challenges Lutherans in the United States have faced on account of the 'Americanization' process. They included a lot more than language, indeed, even some that were overtly theological. Dr. Stechholz explores them all as he tells the story of Lutherans who assimilated fully to America but also sought to remain fully Lutheran."

REV. DR. CAMERON MACKENZIE
Professor of Historical Theology
Concordia Theological Seminary, Fort Wayne, IN

"The ambition of Bishop David Stechholz in *The English District Saga* is to set the history of the English District firmly in the context not only of The Lutheran Church—Missouri Synod but also within the larger scope of American Lutheranism. He achieves this admirably, but of special interest is his reporting and documenting of the district's deep involvement in the controversies of the 1960s and 70s that led to the faculty walk out in 1974 from the St. Louis seminary and an eventual loss of 78 congregations from the English District. Some of what he reports in this book has never before been printed. There is no doubt therefore in my mind that *The English District Saga* will soon become essential reading for anyone seeking to understand what occurred in those dark and difficult days."

REV. DR. DAVID H. PETERSEN
Senior Pastor, Redeemer Lutheran Church, Fort Wayne, IN

"I don't know anyone who would be better qualified to prepare a history of the LCMS's English District than the Rev. Dr. David Stechholz. David is not only an emeritus President and Bishop of the District, he also has spent nearly all of his life in the District, has had wide personal interactions with countless English District pastors and lay persons, and has been both studying, living, and generally absorbing the District's history for decades. Add to all that this ingredient: he loves the District and the Synod. He is a respectful historian who loves his subject and works at putting 'the best construction' on the characters he discusses. I commend this insider's glimpse into a slice of the LCMS which has, at various times, played a critical role in the Synod's history."

REV. DR. LARRY VOGEL
Vacancy Pastor, Martin Luther Chapel, Pennsauken, NJ
Assoc. Exec. Director Emeritus, LCMS Commission on Theology and Church Relations

"*The English District Saga* by Bishop David Stechholz is well-written, historically accurate, evangelical in tone, balanced toward the contrarians, and provides to the church at large an important contribution to the body of knowledge. I heartily recommend it to all who care about the Church of Our Lord Jesus, and this 'little band,' as Luther would have called it, who fought the good fight far above its weight."

REV. FREDERIC W. BAUE
Pastor Emeritus
Author of *The Epistles of Herman Noodix*

CONTENTS

Contents

Contents

Contents

Prelude to a Saga

A SAGA IS a long, involved story. When writing about biblical history and the history of the Christian Church, one always returns to the Source, God Himself. The Lord God is the Author of Creation and has recorded His Word through the writings of the prophets, evangelists, and apostles. The story of salvation history of the Promised Messiah and Savior of the world, God the Son, our Lord Jesus Christ, continues after the conception and birth, life and ministry, suffering and death, and resurrection and ascension of our Lord. It has continued for two millennia in the present work of the Holy Spirit through God's Word in the hearts and lives of Christian believers gathered in Christian congregations around God's holy Word and Sacraments.

Millions, perhaps billions of Christians have walked the face of this earth and died in the Lord. They await the return of our blessed Savior and Redeemer and the resurrection of all flesh on the Last Day and the Church Triumphant, God's Kingdom of Glory in heaven. So when we look at the history of Christianity and view the English District of The Lutheran Church—Missouri Synod, we only view a small speck of history. Yet even a speck is a cherished moment of time in a believer's walk of faith in Christ in the Church catholic, the earthly Church Militant. A speck in the eye of an individual can be an irritant, at best. A speck in a drop of water, reminding us of the Sacrament of Holy Baptism, can become a beautiful prism of light. Specks are not unimportant.

The history of the English District-LCMS is but a speck, or niche, in the history of the Evangelical Lutheran Church in North America, now over 400 years old. You do not have to be a historian to understand and appreciate history. Yet historians and history get a bad rap. Perhaps that is because we historians too often report facts of the past to which people see no relevance for getting through life's daily challenges. It may also be that we historians get caught up in too many finite details, so as to leave a reader bored or frustrated. [Reader, please do not give up at this point!]

In embarking on the writing of this saga, this author began from a historian's love for detail, replete with endless footnotes and rabbit trail minutiae. Wiser loved ones and friends, including my dear wife, Janet, and Pastors in the Detroit Circuits of the English District urged me to forsake the minutiae. Much of that minutiae is still preserved in the endnotes at the end of this book.

I'm titling this history a saga because a saga can include details that are not necessarily good or pleasing. But a historian has a duty to reflect over the expanse of time and report the truth in as accurate a manner as possible.

The history of this non-geographic district of The Lutheran Church—Missouri Synod is fascinating, and yes, it involves details. Skip over what may seem too tedious. Thank you for your patience. I hope you find it an interesting saga. And as in all things in the Church Militant, Christ's Church on earth, *Soli Deo Gloria* (To God alone be the glory).

The Rev. Dr. David P. Stechholz

How to Read this Book

THIS IS NOT a novel. Nor is it a doctoral dissertation, though it is loaded with detail, especially with its plentiful endnotes and citations. Rather, it is a detailed history of a middle judicatory, the English District-LCMS and her antecedents. At times the English District will be referred to as "her" since the author has a deep affection for this district (or diocese), even though a small niche in Christendom. Other times, possession in the English District will be referred to as "its."

For most people who have not spent decades in a congregation of the English District or in some leadership position within The Lutheran Church—Missouri Synod, this book is best read by carefully reviewing the table of contents. Perhaps there is a time period that would especially interest you. Start there. You can then go back to other chapters or start from the beginning. Remember, it is a saga.

If you find some of the detail too tedious, simply skim over those chapters or sections. If interested, you can always come back to extensive detail later on.

Be aware that, while the book is chronological, not all the stories, details, and explanation follow exactly, year by year. In order to complete a thought, the book may follow through on a particular subject or train of thought and then come back to earlier dates, events, and people at a later point in the chapter.

The author is grateful that you are willing to undertake this exercise. Every effort has been made to write the history accurately and fairly. However, the period of the late 1960s and the 1970s may stir some deep hurt, passion, or concern. Those of us who lived through that era, including the author, saw families and friendships divided and separated. Even the most humble writer is not without his or her viewpoints and strong beliefs, feelings, and perspectives.

So, thank you for taking the time to invest in *The English District Saga*. The author is willing to listen to you and learn from your comments and suggestions.

Prayer

Lord God, Eternal Father, we thank and praise You for Your great love and mercy. Saved by Your grace through the Blood of Your beloved Son, Jesus Christ, on the altar of the Cross, You have brought us into His Body, the one holy catholic and apostolic Church to be the Bride of Christ. Bless Your Church throughout the world and across the ages. Help us in this little niche of the Evangelical Lutheran Church in North America called the English District of The Lutheran Church—Missouri Synod to boldly proclaim the saving Gospel of our Lord Jesus Christ and to cast wide the net to bring in the harvest of souls. Grant that this history of the English District and her antecedents may humbly remind us both of Your grace and the Lord's call to seek and find the lost for Him, the Savior of our lost and fallen race of humanity. To You, O Father, be all honor and glory with the Son and the Holy Spirit, one God, through all ages. Amen.

In Nomine Jesu

THE HISTORY OF the non-geographic English District of The Lutheran Church—Missouri Synod and its antecedent, The English Evangelical Lutheran Synod of Missouri and Other States, needs to be brought up to date. Though much has been written in the past, often in shorter articles, a complete, current, but easy-read historical look at the pilgrimage of this storied district of the LCMS needs to be penned. Most of the previous writings were articles by the author and by previous Bishops (District Presidents) of the English District, and especially Dr. H.P. Eckhardt's *The English District: A Historical Sketch*, published in 1945. Eckhardt served as the president of the "English Missouri Synod" when it became a district of the German Evangelical Lutheran Synod of Missouri, Ohio, and Other States in 1911, serving his whole ministry in the Synod and District.

This book is a saga of the now 110-year old English District-LCMS and the history that preceded its formation. That preceding history includes roots in the old Tennessee Synod (1820-1920) and its off-shoot, the English Missouri Synod (The English Evangelical Lutheran Synod of Missouri and Other States). The English Missouri Synod started to evolve and, on May 15, 1911, was affiliated with *Die Deutsche Evangelisch-Lutherische Synode von Missouri, Ohio, und andern Staaten* (The German Evangelical Lutheran Synod of Missouri, Ohio, and Other States). That affiliation finally occurred on May 15, 1911. The German Missouri Synod changed its title in 1917 just prior to the United States' entry into World

War I. The name of the church body from 1917 to 1947 was The Evangelical Lutheran Synod of Missouri, Ohio, and Other States. In 1947, the name was changed to The Lutheran Church—Missouri Synod, henceforth known as the LCMS. The name chosen was not a popular one, but it was the most acceptable in the 1947 (100th anniversary year) Convention of the Synod. This book, however, is more concerned about the English District-LCMS and its antecedents.

The English Evangelical Lutheran Synod of Missouri and Other States was known by a few different names, sometimes omitting "and Other States," sometimes omitting "Evangelical," and often being called the English Missouri Synod or the English Synod. The date of 1872 is prominent because of the August 16-20 meeting of Dr. C.F.W. Walther and representatives of English-speaking confessional Evangelical Lutherans at Zion Evangelical Lutheran Church of Gravelton, Missouri. Other dates prominent in that time period between 1872 and 1911 will be covered in various chapters in this book. Significant history prior to 1872 involving the Tennessee Synod and the Henkel family must be considered.

This book is truly about God and His grace in shielding a fledgling people on what was and still is a pilgrimage. With its rich liturgical history as a district in the LCMS, the worship of the blessed Trinity, Father, (✝) Son, and Holy Spirit, at the altar of the Lord has been central to the English Synod's and the English District's history and pilgrimage, along with its missionary zeal. That is why this is a saga.

In addition to Dr. Eckhardt's *The English District: A Historical Sketch*, other books, publications, and an essay of note are the following:

- *A Tree Grows in Missouri: An English District Centennial Publication*, Dr. John Baumgaertner, ed. (1975)
- *Amazing Comeback: Survey of English District History*, by Dr. Martin Mueller (1986)
- Numerous *Convention Proceedings* and *Workbooks* of the English District and her predecessors, the English Missouri Conference, the English Evangelical Lutheran Conference (later, Synod) of Missouri and Other States, and *"Minutes"* of Board of Directors' meetings
- *"The English District Story,"* 1961 reprints from the English District Supplement to *The Lutheran Witness*
- *My Life*, the autobiography of Dr. William Dallmann; *Lutherans in America*, by Dr. Mark Granquist; *Love, Hope, and Faith: Anecdotes*

from the Building Programs of Three Churches (all three being English District); and, *Concordia Historical Institute* (CHI) *Quarterly* article, *"Faith Driven—Future Focused: The English District Celebrates 100 Years,"* Spring, 2012.

Two PowerPoint presentations that I've shared with pastors and laity have also been useful for the writing of this saga. Please note the extensive bibliography for further research and study. The historic symbol of the English District is a double-trunked sycamore tree, pictured on the previous page. It will be explained in this volume. The 1975 book *A Tree Grows in Missouri* refers to the sycamore tree, though the book is a bit of a misnomer, since the English District dates properly to 1911, not 1872. It was the English Evangelical Lutheran Synod of Missouri and Other States and its antecedents that properly date to 1872 and the roots in the Tennessee Synod.

Many thanks go to family and friends in the writing of this history. First and foremost is thanks to my wife Janet and son Andrew for their great patience and encouragement. Our married daughters, Mary and Sarah, Lutheran school teachers, grew up in the three parishes of the English District where I served as Pastor and have provided encouragement. Second, I wish to thank my younger friends Rev. Luke Zimmerman, District Secretary, and Rev. Christopher Thoma. I'm thankful to Luke for his invaluable skill and discernment as well as his many long hours spent in editing this volume, and to Chris for many hours spent, as well as his excellent stylistic editing and handling of the layout. Special thanks also goes to Rev. Greg Musolf and Livonia Rotarian friends for their publishing skills, David and Mary Ellyn Lambert for their assistance, and to my dear fellow English District cohort, Dr. Larry Vogel, for his encouragement, editing, and insights. Thanks also goes to my eventual successor at the English Evangelical Lutheran Church of Our Redeemer, Oakmont, Pennsylvania, Rev. Brian Westgate, a fine historian, and to Dr. Martin Noland, Pastor of Grace Evangelical Lutheran Church, San Mateo, California, and previously Executive Director of the Concordia Historical Institute (CHI) at Concordia Seminary, St. Louis. Marty was the first who urged me to write this history.

Additional thanks goes to: my Bishop and successor, Dr. Jamison Hardy, Bishop and President of the English District-LCMS while also serving as Assistant Pastor of Peace Lutheran Church, McMurray, Pennsylvania. Dr. Hardy said to me, regarding the writing of this book, "Who better than you?" He was also very helpful in producing this book. Others who have provided details, help or encouragement include the following: brother pastors Drs. John Stieve, Frank Pies, Paul Bacon, Joe Fabry, Ron Farah, Jon Diefenthaler (Southeastern District President Emeritus), Charles McClean; pastors of the Detroit Circuits of the English District, including my own Pastor, Rev. Mark Braden, and Rev. Tim Halboth, who provided a lot of valuable details; the Staff at the English District Office in Farmington, Michigan, especially Peggy Oke and Sally Naglich; Rev. Dennis O'Neill; the Concordia Historical Institute Staff and its current Executive Director, Dr. Daniel Harmelink; Martha Wohlfeil at the Michigan District Office in Ann Arbor, Michigan; Tonya Perez at the LCMS Dept. of Rosters and Statistics; and notably, my predecessors in the office of Bishop and President, Bishop Emeriti of the English District, the late Rev. Dr. Roger Pittelko and the Rev. Dr. David Ritt, both of whom supplied helpful information; and last, but not least, the late Dr. Victor Halboth Jr., former Pastor at Grace Evangelical Lutheran Church, Redford Twp., Michigan. "Vic" was an encourager, a walking history book of the English District, and long-time Archivist of the English District-LCMS. Any shortcoming in this saga are my own. I humbly ask your pardon for any you might find.

Foreword

THE ACCOUNT OF the English District is not only a glimpse into the history of a member district of The Lutheran Church—Missouri Synod (LCMS), but it is a crossing of paths with the life of the Church of God throughout the ages.

An association of 167 congregations across twenty-two states and extending into the province of Ontario, Canada, the English District has experienced the ebbs and flows of Church life over the course of its 110-year history, most certainly demonstrating the sinner-saint realities along the way.

Bishop Emeritus Stechholz's volume, *The English District Saga*, captures this motion.

Stechholz provides a multifaceted recollection of significant events and most noteworthy struggles that have impacted the course of the English District and its member churches throughout its century of life. Most importantly, the events he has taken time to investigate and record reveal for the reader the impact of the English District's Gospel witness to Christ as the Savior of the world. This theme remains central as he mines the depths of the District's love for seeking and saving the lost. From coast to coast, from top to bottom, through the Spirit-driven muscle of countless congregations led by generations of faithful pastors and lay leaders, the proclamation of God's Word has been broadcast in the languages of the people, regardless of the shifting theological influences or the winds of cultural change.

Of course, much of the history of the English District has happened beneath the wing of its mother church, the LCMS. Blessed by Christ with such a joyful collegiality, both have remained rooted in the same confession of trust in the inerrant Word of God as the sole source and norm for all its efforts. The fruits of this Godly relationship have been clearly evident in the English District. Innumerable Christians have built countless facilities with wonderful Gospel-centered ministries, all the while enjoying fellowship with a larger Synod that both supported and emboldened a right confession of the faith, even as in certain contexts it became necessary to adapt to ever-changing landscapes filled with seemingly insurmountable challenges.

And yet, throughout its history the work of the English District has remained the same: to reach out with the everlasting message of forgiveness through faith in Jesus Christ, the Son of God.

I want to thank Bishop Emeritus David Stechholz for his faithful labors in producing this volume, and for all the lively accounts in the District over the years that he brings to life in its pages. The entirety of my career in the Church has been within the English District, and for that, I am equally thankful to God. My first call was to a wonderful parish just south of Pittsburgh. It was there that the Lord blessed me with the opportunity to learn from three veteran English District pastors in my circuit. It became clear to me early in my ministry that the English District was indeed a blessing. My hope is that this book will enlighten you with the same sense of appreciation.

Rev. Dr. Jamison J. Hardy
Bishop, English District of The Lutheran Church—Missouri Synod

Timeline

1483   Birth of Martin Luther, November 10th

1517   Luther's nailing of the 95 Theses in Wittenberg, Germany, October 31; Start of the Lutheran Reformation

1520   Luther's three great Treatises that defined the Reformation

1530   Presentation of the Augsburg Confession, June 25

1546   Death of Martin Luther, February 18

1580   Adoption of the Book of Concord, the Confessions of the Evangelical Lutheran Church

1619   First Lutheran Service in North America in Hudson Bay

1748   Henry Melchior Muhlenberg starts first Lutheran pastoral body in America, the Pennsylvania Ministerium

1772   Start of Koiner's Church, Coyners Store, Augusta County, Virginia, at one time the oldest congregation in the English Evangelical Lutheran Conference/Synod of Missouri and Other States

1792   Rev. Paul Henkel (born in North Carolina) ordained in Pennsylvania Ministerium

1803   North Carolina Synod organized

1818   Ohio Synod organized

1817   Initial Lutheran mission planting at Gravelton, Missouri, though Zion Congregation not officially formed until 1857

1820   First Lutheran church body organized, the Evangelical Lutheran General Synod of the United States under Rev. Samuel S. Schmucker and first Lutheran Seminary at Gettysburg

1820   Rev. Paul Henkel and others leave North Carolina Synod to start the Tennessee Synod as a confessional alternative to the "General Synod"

1847   Formation of the German Missouri Synod as *Die Deutsche Evangelisch-Lutherische Synode von Missouri, Ohio, und andern Staaten* in Chicago, April 26

1851   *Book of Concord* published by Henkel Press of New Market, Virginia, under Dr. Socrates Henkel

1857   "English District" of Joint Synod of Ohio organized, the third such to be organized in Ohio

Late 1850s Pastors from the German Missouri Synod and Tennessee Synod begin cordial meetings and explore doctrinal agreements

1861-1865 Civil War divides the United States and the Confederacy

1867   The General Council organized, splitting off of the General Synod

1872   Historic meeting of Tennessee & Holston Synod pastors and German Missouri Synod Dr. C.F. W. Walther and others at Zion Evangelical Lutheran Church, Gravelton, Missouri, August 16-20. Doctrinal agreement affirmed with adoption of Walther's 16 Theses

1872   A small English Lutheran Conference begins, holding annual meetings

1874   Rev. Frederick Kuegele (St. Louis graduate) called to Coyner's Store, Virginia

1875   The "Galesburg Rule" adopted by the General Council

1876   Concordia College, Conover, North Carolina, started

1885   First English preaching graduate from Concordia Seminary, St. Louis, to enter English work. (Second was William Dallmann in 1886.)

1887   Death of Dr. C.F.W. Walther, President of German Missouri Synod and one who championed confessional Lutheran English language mission work, May 7. First official attempt by English Lutheran Conference to seek union with German Missouri Synod

1888   Formation and first Convention of English Evangelical Lutheran Conference of Missouri and Other States as number of congregations grows

1889   English Missouri Conference receives *The Lutheran Witness* as its official publication

1891   Official name change of English Missouri Conference to the English Evangelical Lutheran Synod of Missouri and Other States

1893   English Missouri Synod milestone convention in receiving Concordia College, Conover, North Carolina, and St. John's College, Winfield, Kansas; the Common Service; English *Sunday School Hymnal*

1897   English Missouri Synod reports work at 24 localities in 13 states and District of Columbia

1899	First English Synod Extension loans granted to two Baltimore English Missouri Synod congregations, $100 each
1909	Seven points of understanding adopted by English Synod as articles for "union" with German Missouri Synod
1911	Union of English Missouri Synod into German Missouri Synod as the English District of *Die Deutsche Evangelisch-Lutherische Synode von Missouri, Ohio,und andern Staaten.* 53 congregations in English District. English Synod becomes English District at German Missouri Synod's Holy Cross Church, St. Louis, on May 15
1912	First English-language hymnal of German Missouri Synod, a gift from the English Missouri Synod. Also, English District begins mission work in Dallas, Texas, and all transactions reported as complete between English and German Missouri Synod, including *The Lutheran Witness*, Pittsburgh publishing business, and colleges. First English District Convention, held at Jackson Square Evangelical Lutheran Church in Baltimore, Maryland
1913	English District mission work begins in California and Oklahoma
1917	English District work begins in Lincoln, Nebraska. Eventually Redeemer Church, Lincoln, becomes strongest District financial supporter
1922	English District mission work continues to expand, spreading to Montana and into Canada with reception of St. John's Church, Toronto
1923	First request (by Western District) to dissolve English District and force congregations to amalgamate into geographic districts
1925	English District respectfully rejects request for amalgamation
1935	Closure of Concordia College, Conover, North Carolina, following major fire
1939	English District cedes 38 congregations (some of the oldest and largest), 28 pastors, and 3,500 communicants, along with some Eastern District congregations to form the Southeastern District-LCMS
1945	Request of two English District congregations to dissolve District and amalgamate into geographic districts declined, though a Committee on Amalgamation for study was approved. Amalgamation rejected in 1946
1947	Evangelical Lutheran Synod of Missouri, Ohio, and Other States renamed The Lutheran Church—Missouri Synod

13

1948   English District brings LCMS into the state of Arizona, establishing missions in Phoenix and Tucson

1949-1951 Three Montana English District congregations released to strengthen the new Montana District-LCMS

1952-1954 English District re-enters Georgia at Macon and Atlanta

1954   English District adopts a Board of Directors form of government

1956   English District-LCMS Office building completed at 23001 Grand River Avenue, Detroit, as business center. District President, however, still part-time and located where serving as parish pastor

1950s   Unofficial beginning of usage of "Bishop" nomenclature in English District, used informally

1959   English District begins English mission work in Montreal, Quebec

1960   English District congregations in Texas join Texas District-LCMS

1961   English District keeps a Golden Anniversary (50th year) by supporting student work at universities. Convention Jubilee Service held at Rockefeller Chapel of the University of Chicago[1]

1970   Rev. John Baumgaertner of Milwaukee elected first full-time president. President/Bishop's Office remains in Milwaukee

1973   New Orleans Convention of LCMS, as Synod heads toward a "split"

1974   Walk-out at Concordia Seminary and start of Seminex, St. Louis 1974 Election of Executive Secretary, Rev. Harold Hecht, as President of the English District-LCMS and recognition of 100 years since the 1872 Gravelton conference. Hecht first full-time President/Bishop in Detroit

1975-1976 Following Anaheim Convention of LCMS in the "LCMS Civil War," formation of Association of Evangelical Lutheran Churches (AELC) and English Synod of AELC. One-third of English District-LCMS congregations depart for the English Synod of the AELC

1976   President/Bishop Hecht removed from office by LCMS President J.A.O. Preus. Election of Dr. George Bornemann as President/Bishop of the English District-LCMS and beginning of the "come-back"

1977   Rev. Kenneth Lindsay called as Executive Secretary of the District. Subsidized ministries maintained; new missions started in late 1970s

1982-2020 Executive Staff additions and changes, beginning with Dr. Delphin "Bud" Schultz as Parish Services Counselor. Nomenclature of positions changes over the years

1983 Bishop/President Bornemann resigns. He retires, January 31, 1984. Rev. Donald Jung serves as Acting President/Bishop

1985-1989 Dr. Donald Jung elected as President/Bishop. A period of intense mission activity. Number of congregations and preaching stations increases from 139 to 170. "A District in Mission" (ADIM) raises $7.5 million in new investments in LCEF to fund new missions and existing congregations

1986 Death in office of Bishop Jung; First Vice President Dr. Roger Pittelko, previously serving as "regent" becomes Acting Bishop/President

1986 LCMS closes St. John's College, Winfield, Kansas

1987 Dr. Roger Pittelko elected as Bishop/President. Use of the term "President/Bishop" or "Bishop and President" comes into official usage in English District, along with the use of the historic term, "Circuit Visitors"

1995 District Office moved to building at 33100 Freedom Road, Farmington, Michigan

1997 Bishop-Emeritus George Bornemann dies in Oviedo, Florida. Mr. Ervin Henkelmann killed in a San Diego traffic accident; Mr. Ted Geheb assumes Parish Service Executive position

1997 Election of Dr. David Ritt as Bishop/President. District approves policy-based governance after three-year study of structure and governance

1999 English District begins Missions Alive $1.7 million campaign for advanced site loses; goal reached in pay-off to LCEF in 2001

2003 English District Board of Directors approve a mission-deployed staff structure

2004 Board of Directors approve and implement District-wide congregational visitation program, "Pray, Proclaim, Provide" (PPP)

2006 Election of Dr. David Stechholz as Bishop/President

2007-2012 English District involved in effort to save Concordia University, Ann Arbor, Michigan

2009   For the first time in several decades, English District Convention held at a District church: Hales Corners Lutheran, Hales Corners, Wisconsin

2011   Celebration of 100th Anniversary of English District, May 15, in St. Louis. English District Board of Directors provides $250,000 as the first of the four partner districts in a successful effort to help Concordia University, Ann Arbor, MI, survive and then thrive

2011-2012 100th Anniversary Year of the English District-LCMS. Commences with historic walk in St. Louis, MO, on May 15, 2011

2012   Climax of 100th Anniversary Year with District Convention in St. Louis with Divine Service at Concordia Seminary and visit to LCMS International Center

2012-2014 New mission congregations added in Nevada. English District becomes a "managing partner" of the Dominican Republic Lutheran Mission (DRLM)

2015   Election of Dr. Jamison Hardy as Bishop/President at District Convention, held at Concordia University, Ann Arbor, Michigan. English District stands as microcosm of Synod crossing four time zones working in over 20 languages and dialects of worship and praise to God

2016-2019 New mission congregations added in Washington and West Virginia

2020   COVID-19 (coronavirus) pandemic affects whole world. Most churches not able to worship face-to-face in America in large groupings for several months. Many go to live-streaming. Virus cases grow again in most U.S. states and several countries, even while re-openings of churches, business and industry, and social gatherings occurring. No COVID vaccine as of mid-September, 2020. Huge uncertainty in this election year, save hope in God's grace and mercy. Bishop Emeritus Pittelko dies, November 12.

2021   New Roger D. Pittelko "He Loved the Church" Award established.

PART ONE

THE PLANTING OF THE EVANGELICAL LUTHERAN CHURCH
IN THE ENGLISH LANGUAGE IN NORTH AMERICA

CHAPTER 1
The Evangelical Lutheran Church in North America

Historical Overview

Martin Luther and the Lutheran Reformation

R EV. ALFRED FAULSTICK wrote a fine article entitled "Martin Luther, His Life and Work." It is an appendix in the Small Catechism instruction book, *Catechetical Helps*, by Rev. Erwin Kurth, first published by Concordia Publishing House in 1941 but dating back to 1935. Many catechism class students were reared on *Catechetical Helps*. Both Faulstick and "King" Kurth (as he was nicknamed) served as pastors in the English District of The Lutheran Church—Missouri Synod.

In his article, Pastor Faulstick succinctly noted the formation of Christ's Church on earth and its subsequent "deformation."[2] In viewing the history of the English District, one must understand the need for the Lutheran Reformation and the work, under God's grace and guidance, of Dr. Martin Luther (1483-1546). Most Lutheran Christians are well aware of Luther's posting of his 95 Theses on All Hallows' Eve (Reformation Day), October 31, 1517. However, the larger Reformation insights come from Luther's treatises or tracts of 1519 and 1520: *The Blessed Sacrament of the Holy and True Body of Christ;* other writings on the Mass; *Address To the Christian Nobility of the German Nation; The Babylonian Captivity of the Church;* and *A Treatise on Christian Liberty (The Freedom of the Christian Man)*. The next year, Martin Luther made his great "Here I Stand" public defense before Emperor Charles V at the Diet (Parliament or Reichstag) of Worms on April 18, 1521. A couple weeks later in early May, he was spirited away to the Wartburg castle in a "friendly kidnapping" arranged by his protector, Elector Frederick the Wise. In 11 weeks during those ten-plus months of "captivity" (protection) in the Wartburg, the "Great Reformer" translated the New Testament from Biblical (Koine) Greek into German. What the Medieval papacy most feared, namely the Holy Scriptures in the common language of the people instead of the Latin Vulgate, had now become a reality.

Luther was not able to be present for the Presentation of the Augsburg Confession on June 25, 1530. Since he had been both excommunicated by the Pope and declared an outlaw by the Emperor, his right-hand man in the Reformation, Philip Melanchthon, performed the final revisions on what has come to be known as the Augsburg Confession. (In its "unaltered" form, the Augsburg Confession is known by the letters UAC, often found on Lutheran church cornerstones). The German princes then presented this document to the Emperor, and the Evangelical Lutheran Church declared its confessional stance. Luther died in 1546, having served till his death as Professor at Wittenberg University, lecturer, author, pastor, and confessor par excellence, and husband and father. While the German Schmalkaldic League of Reformation nobility suffered military defeat in 1547 (the year after Luther's death), at the hands of the Roman Catholic forces of the Emperor, the Reformation was not wiped out. During the period following Luther's death, the Church of the Reformation entered a period of disharmony and confusion with fractures or eight major theological controversies, which, God be praised, became resolved by 1580.[3]

A treaty signed in 1555, called the Peace of Augsburg, allowed Roman Catholics and Lutherans to coexist. However, the practice now would be that the "religion" of the ruler became the religion of the state (territory). This territorial principle was summed up in the Latin phrase *cuius regio, eius religio* ("whose region, his religion"). In 1580, the Evangelical Lutheran Church, under the guidance of the "second Martin," Martin Chemnitz, and other Lutheran reformers, adopted as its confessional standard the *Book of Concord* or *Concordia* (the Confessional writings of the Evangelical Lutheran Church). This was published by a joint resolution and order of the electors, princes, free cities, and other governmental entities of the Holy Roman Empire, definitively declaring what the Evangelical Lutheran Church believes, teaches, and confesses.[4]

The Latin masthead of the Reformation was VDMA (*Verbum Domini Manet in Aeternum*). Translated, it is the words of Isaiah 40 and I Peter 1, *"The Word of the Lord endures forever."* Lutheran churches, pastors, German states and countries that held to a full or *quia* subscription of the Book of Concord and not just the Three Ecumenical Creeds (Apostles, Nicene, and Athanasian) "because it is in agreement with the Word of God" were considered confessional Evangelical Lutherans. Rejected was a *quatenus* ("in so far as") subscription of the Confessions in whatever interpreted way they might agree with the Holy Scriptures. This becomes hugely significant in the New World as exploration and colonization of the Western Hemisphere expanded (1492-1600s).

The Evangelical Lutheran Church Enters the "New World"

The first Lutheran service conducted in North America by a Lutheran pastor, Rev. Rasmus Jensen, occurred in 1619. Danish explorers, seeking to find a "Northwest Passage" to the Pacific Ocean and the lucrative treasures, gems, and spices of China, eastern Asia, and the East Indies, had a Lutheran Service of worship in Hudson Bay in what is today northern Canada. However, the few Lutheran pastors who came to the New World in the next century either stayed just a short time or died. The New World's climate did not help with survival of many of the first pilgrim immigrants to the American colonies. As settlements gradually became established in Philadelphia, New Amsterdam (New York after 1664), along the Hudson River, and in Delaware, Lutheran pastors speaking their ethnic tongues came to the New World. There were no colleges, universities, or seminaries where future pastors might be trained. The orientation of Christian churches regardless of denomination was toward the Old World. The supply of pastors was very limited; they came from Europe. Many returned after a very short time.

Danish, Swedish, Dutch, and German Lutherans, often individual men, settled in very small communities from 1619 through 1720, speaking their native tongues. They were scattered throughout the New World with little or no communication between them. Though started by people from Lutheran lands, early colonial developments were not necessarily exclusively Lutheran during the period of 1720-1748. Lutheran pastors were rare. Colonial developments with Lutherans among the settlers were in Philadelphia and along the Delaware River, New Amsterdam (New York), Albany, and along the Hudson River, and in Georgia, the latter receiving Salzburg Lutherans after fleeing persecution in their Roman Catholic country of Austria. Swedish Lutherans in Delaware, New Jersey, and Philadelphia become Anglican (Episcopal) when Swedish pastors of the "state church" (Church of Sweden), were no longer sent to the New World. The Church of England (Anglican) and the Church of Sweden

(Lutheran) both had retained apostolic succession, that is, pastors ordained by a bishop in a line going back to St. Peter in Rome.

"The Church Being Planted"

With the arrival of Henry Melchior Muhlenberg in 1742 to Philadelphia, the Evangelical Lutheran Church was planted in the New World. Though influenced by Halle Pietism, Muhlenberg's confessionalism was an unqualified subscription to the entire Book of Concord, mixed with his own hierarchical tendencies.[5] Muhlenberg's congregation at The Trappe near Philadelphia became the seat for a first-ever Lutheran church body in the New World: the Pennsylvania Ministerium. This small, German-speaking church body was formed by Muhlenberg in 1748 with a limited confessional Lutheran emphasis. For this, Muhlenberg is often called "the Patriarch of the Evangelical Lutheran Church in North America."

The defining action in North America was the American Revolutionary War (1776-1781) and the winning of independence by the Thirteen Colonies from Great Britain. Gradually these Lutherans in America started speaking English, even though German persisted among those original Lutherans for many decades after 1781. Interestingly, before the July 4, 1776 signing of the Declaration of Independence and at the very outset of the Revolutionary War, Muhlenberg's eldest son, Rev. Peter Muhlenberg, opened up his ministerial garb during the Divine Service in front of his Woodstock, Virginia parishioners, revealing a military uniform of a Colonel. During the Revolutionary War, he rose to the rank of Major General under George Washington in the Continental Army of the United Colonies, distinguishing himself at the Battles of Brandywine, Germantown, Monmouth, and Yorktown from 1776 to 1781. Peter Muhlenberg also served in the United States Congress as Speaker of the House of Representatives.[6]

When Henry Muhlenberg formed the Pennsylvania Ministerium, the church body lacked a Constitution.[7] The Constitution for the Ministerium was completed in 1777. Muhlenberg is rightly credited for his description of missions for the Evangelical Lutheran Church under the Latin term *ecclesia plantanda* ("the Church that still has to be planted").[8] He also promoted Lutheran worship, vestments, and Lutheran practices. However, the Pennsylvania Ministerium and the later New York Ministerium, organized in 1792, both lacked a robust confessional basis and no subscription. But God was about to raise up new Lutheran leaders on the American continent in another multi-generational family of pastors, publishers, and synod leaders, the Henkel family.

Excursus: The Book of Concord

Following the death of Luther in 1546, a period of war, disharmony, and confusion ensued. Several divides occurred in the Evangelical Lutheran Church. The Lutheran princes and free cities that constituted the Smalcaldic League were defeated in battle by the armies of Charles V. Despite military losses, the Lutheran faith was not defeated; however, serious fractures arose as Lutheran theologians claiming the mantel of Luther diverged on several doctrinal positions, some even compromising key positions in an attempt to accommodate Rome. These fractures or eight major theological controversies were the Adiaphoristic Controversy (1548-1555), the Majoristic Controversy (1551-1562), the Synergistic Controversy (1555-1560), the Flacian Controversy (1560-1575), the Osiandrian Controversy and Stancarian Controversy (1549-1566), the Antinomian Controversy (1527-1556), and the Crypto-Calvinist Controversy (1560-1574).[9]

God be praised. Again, God, the Shield of His people, raised up faithful orthodox Lutherans under Martin Chemnitz ("the second Martin"), Jacob Andreae, Johann Brenz, and others. The controversies were finally settled with the production of the Epitome and Solid Declaration of the Formula of Concord in 1577. On the fiftieth anniversary of the (Unaltered) Augsburg Confession in 1580, the *Book of Concord* was published. The *Book of Concord*, also known by its Latin name *Concordia*, contains the confessional writing of the Evangelical Lutheran Church. This was published by a joint resolution and order of the electors, princes, free cities, and other governmental entities of the Holy Roman Empire, definitively declaring what Evangelical Lutherans believe, teach, and confess.

Contained in The Book of Concord are the following:

- The Three Universal or Ecumenical Creeds (the Apostles', Niceno-Constantinopolitan [Nicene], and Athanasian Creed)
- The Augsburg Confession (1530)
- The Apology (Defense) of the Augsburg Confession (1531)
- The Smalcald Articles (1537)
- The Power and Primacy of the Pope (1537)
- The Small Catechism of Martin Luther (1529)
- The Large Catechism of Martin Luther (1529)
- The Formula of Concord, Epitome (1577)
- The Formula of Concord, Solid Declaration (1577).

Confessional Lutherans down through the centuries have "subscribed" to the *Book of Concord* with a *quia* subscription. Simply put, this means that Lutheran clergy, church workers, and congregations in The Lutheran Church—Missouri Synod and other confessional Evangelical Lutheran Churches around the world accept the *Book of Concord* in all its parts because it is in agreement with the Word of God (Holy Scriptures), not "in so far" (a q*uatenus* subscription) as they are in agreement with Holy Scriptures. This was significant especially to Rev. Paul Henkel and his family of Lutheran pastors.

CHAPTER 2
The Roots: English-speaking Confessional Lutherans

THE AMERICAN RELIGIOUS scene of the early 1800s was one in which Lutheranism was a minority. This was even more so in the South where Baptist and Methodist denominations were rapidly gaining in membership. The families of Christian denominations also had a special bond with democratizing tendencies in American politics, tendencies that were transforming the American Christian landscape. Preachers in that era were often without formal theological education. They showed their leadership notably by organizing religious movements from the bottom up. This challenged the Evangelical Lutheran Church in early America: "In this context, Lutherans faced a series of choices that coalesced around two interrelated points: the Lutheran doctrine of the ministry and how mission work would be done."[10]

Servants of the Lord: The Reverends Paul & David Henkel, and the Tennessee Synod (1820-1920)

Henkel.

In the American South, the Lord God raised up Rev. Paul Henkel (1754-1825), his son, Rev. David Henkel, and a whole multi-generational clan, the Henkel family. Paul Henkel was a close friend of Rev. Peter Muhlenberg. He was ordained into the Holy Ministry in the Lutheran Ministerium of Pennsylvania in 1792, five years after the death of the founder of that Ministerium, Rev. Henry Melchior Muhlenberg.

The Henkels were a confessionally-Lutheran family, and the English District traces its roots back to them. With the organization of the North Carolina Synod (1803), the Ohio Synod (1818) and the Tennessee Synod (1820) under Paul Henkel and other pastors, English-speaking Evangelical Lutheran churches eventually began to be planted in the South and West. At this point of the early 1800s, the "West" was Tennessee, Missouri, Indiana, Kansas, Arkansas, and other states.

In the Henkel family coat of arms going back to their German roots, notice the prominent Anchor Cross in the form of a shield. The Triune God is sometimes humanly-depicted as a shield.

"Behold, O God, Our Shield" – Psalm 84:9

The early Lutherans on the East Coast were influenced by pietism and rationalism. Like chameleons, blending into their Protestant early American milieu, these Lutherans began to stray from their confessional Lutheran roots. With the continued prevailing laxity of doctrine and practice found among the older Lutheran synods of the East, the Henkels wanted a sound confessional basis, especially for the new Tennessee Synod. The Henkel Press, established in 1806 in New Market, Virginia, began publishing Luther's *Small Catechism*, first in German and later in English. The small "Tennessee Synod" resolved unanimously to translate [into English] and publish the entire *Book of Concord* (*Concordia*) containing all the confessional writings of the Evangelical Lutheran Church."[11]   The *Concordia* was finally published in 1851.

The organization of this church body was extremely significant. These Tennessee Synod pastors and parishioners moved westward into southern Missouri and became the spiritual forefathers of what later became the English Evangelical Lutheran Synod of Missouri and Other States. Dr. H.P. Eckhardt, the last president of the old English Evangelical Lutheran Synod of Missouri and Other States, serving from 1905 to May 15, 1911, and the first president of the English District of the German Evangelical Lutheran Synod of Missouri, Ohio, and Others States from 1911 to 1912, writes in his 1946 booklet, *The English District: A Historical Sketch*:

> The English Lutheran Church in America owes a debt of gratitude to Pastor Paul Henkel and the Henkel family... Paul Henkel came from a family that gave a large number of ministers and educators to the Lutheran Church in our country. The family was descended from one Anthony Jacob Henkel, 1663-1728, who had been Court Chaplain to Duke Maurice of Saxony, but was exiled when the duke became a Roman Catholic. He [Anthony Jacob Henkel] came to America in 1717

and is regarded as the founder of the old Lutheran churches in Philadelphia and Germantown. [This would be a couple decades before the arrival of Muhlenberg.] Paul was the grandson of Anthony Jacob. He was born in North Carolina in 1754. He was pastor at New Market, Va., Salisbury, N.C., and again at New Market...[12]

Dr. Eckhardt goes on to add:

> It was largely through Rev. Paul Henkel's influence and leadership that the Tennessee Synod was organized in 1820 by a number of pastors and their churches in Eastern Tennessee, the [Shenandoah] valley of Virginia, and Western North Carolina... The Tennessee Synod adopted a sound confessional basis, which is evident from the following paragraphs of its "Basis and Regulation": All teachings relative to the faith and all doctrines concerning Christian conduct as well as all books publicly used in the Church, the service or worship of God, shall be arranged and kept, as nearly as it is possible to do so, in accordance with the doctrines of the Holy Scriptures and the Augsburg Confession. And especially shall the young, and others who need it, be instructed in Luther's Small Catechism... This said Catechism shall always be the chief Catechism in our churches.[13]

Eckhardt further notes the Tennessee Synod's obligation of its pastors and teachers to hold a confessional subscription to the new standard set by the Synod and that they could not have connection with the General Synod, due to the doctrinal laxity of that American Lutheran church body. Still later, in 1866, the Tennessee Synod strengthened its doctrinal basis (confession) to affirm that the Old and New Testaments of Holy Scriptures "shall be the one rule and standard of doctrine and church discipline," and that the whole Book of Concord, including the Unaltered Augsburg Confession, be held "as a true and faithful exhibition of the doctrine of the Holy Scriptures in regard to matters of faith and practice..."[14] That is significant, for these are the roots from which the English Missouri Synod and English District sprang up. Theological terminology has changed somewhat over 150 years, but this was bold, clear reversal of the liberal theological directions of the General Synod and its earlier antecedent church bodies.

But how did Dr. Eckhardt know all this about the Henkels without some first-hand knowledge? Some knowledge he gained from a book he referenced, *Fifty Years in the Lutheran Ministry*, by J.G. Morris (1878).[15] He additionally cited Dr. Socrates Henkel's *History of the Evangelical Lutheran Tennessee Synod.*[16] Eckhardt was also a fellow pastor, close friend, and successor as president of the English Missouri Synod's first president, Dr. Frederick Kuegele (see Kuegele Excursus). The latter had first-hand knowledge of the Henkel family and the Tennessee Synod, which he no doubt shared with Eckhardt.

In his historical essay to the 16th Convention of the English District of the Evangelical Lutheran Synod of Missouri, Ohio, and Other States, held at Concordia Teachers College, River Forest, Illinois, in 1936, the Third president of the English Missouri Synod, the venerable Dr. A.W. Meyer, spoke of *"Our English District in Its Early Developments"*:

> We must hark back to Father Paul Henkel; when speaking of our early developments, he can hardly be ignored... He preached his first sermon, in German, and being requested right then and there to preach a sermon in English, he complied. A readiness to speak on any given subject extemporaneously was looked for also in the Ozarks of Missouri... Paul Henkel was for his time and day an important author and publisher. Most influential were his catechism and hymn-books, publications issued in both English and German... These books and others were issued by the Henkel Press established at New Market, VA, in 1806....

Pastor, missionary, author, and publisher, Paul Henkel's end came on November 27th, 1825. A writer says, "As one stands by his grave in the shadow of Emmanuel Lutheran Church in New Market, VA, and reads the epitaph there inscribed, he feels that here is a tribute well deserved: 'His zeal for the promulgation of the Gospel of Christ Jesus was exemplary and his labors many and difficult. He is now with Christ, and no evil can befall him.'"[17]

Just before the outbreak of the American Civil War (1861-1865), many of the Tennessee Synod's congregations became part of what was called the Holston Synod (Evangelical Lutheran Holston Synod). That synod eventually joined the General Council of the Evangelical Lutheran Church in North America in 1874, but then withdrew in 1884 to help form the United Synod of the Evangelical Lutheran Church of the South.[18] In the 19th century, it was very common for synods to come and go, change their affiliations or alliances, and for Lutheran pastors and congregations to do the same. This was often the result of the increasing laxity or stricter adherence to the confessional stances of Evangelical Lutherans in North America. It may be noted in passing that the Tennessee Synod actually helped found Lenoir-Rhyne University in Hickory, North Carolina.

The United Synod of the South, General Council, and General Synod in 1917 agreed to merge. This merger was culminated in 1918 in what was known as the United Lutheran Church in America (ULCA). The previous confessional strength of the General Council, which had broken off from the old General Synod in 1866, dissipated with the passage of years and the "Americanization" of many of the older Lutheran church bodies in North America. By 1920, the Tennessee Synod was down to 40 ministers for its congregations when it merged with the United Synod of the South and eventually the ULCA. Its once strong confessional positions had eroded away.

What distinguished the Tennessee Synod of the early and mid-19th century was its confessionalism and its stance on slavery. Concerning the former, The *Christian Cyclopedia* notes:

> The Synod's ministers were labeled "Henkelites" and lambasted by their opponents. "Henkelites" is a reference to the fact that Paul Henkel and his sons were synod leaders and printer of all synod materials, so the Henkel name was well known. They had a strict standard of Lutheran orthodoxy... In a tribute to their confessional character, Dr. C.F.W. Walther in *Der Lutheraner* of January, 1849 stated "...this Synod [Tennessee] belongs to the small number of those who are determined not only to be called Lutherans, but also to be and to remain Lutherans." But unity was never established with the Lutheran Church—Missouri Synod (LCMS) due to geographic and linguistic separation, the Civil War, and the Tennessee Synod's drift toward union with the less strict North Carolina Synod in the 1880s. However, the Tennessee Synod's English (Evangelical) Lutheran Conference of Missouri applied for admission to the LCMS as a district in 1887, but was advised by Walther to instead form a separate English-language synod. The resulting English Evangelical Lutheran Synod of Missouri and Other States eventually merged into the LCMS as its English District in 1911.[19]

Concerning its stance on slavery, Dr. Socrates Henkel notes the following concerning a favorable examination of a candidate for the Holy

Ministry, a Mr. Conrad Keicher, who (at the Third Session of the Tennessee Synod in October, 1822) asked this question:

> "Is slavery to be considered an evil?" In reply, the Synod unanimously resolved, that it is to be regarded as a great evil in our land, and it desires the government, if it be possible, to devise some kind of way by which this evil can be removed. (The) Synod also advised every minister to admonish every master to treat his slaves properly, and to exercise his Christian duties toward them. This probably was the first move in that direction in the South.[20]

Nevertheless, the Tennessee Synod in its various locations in a number of states, was largely part of the South. Later it would stand with the Army of the Confederate States of America in the matters of military chaplaincy.

Returning to the issue of language, when did the Henkels and the Tennessee Synod in particular make the language switch from German to English? How did they navigate that language change? In a May 1946 *Concordia Theological Monthly* article entitled *"The Missouri Synod and English Work,"* A later historian barely noted in passing that the Tennessee Synod had "…gone through its transition from German to English and had preserved its conservative confessional character."[21]

But how did this happen? This is an important question because the family and the synods they helped to found the English Evangelical Lutheran Conference of Missouri and Other States in 1888 (later "Synod" in 1891), were committed to evangelizing in the *lingua franca* of America: English. This would get at the historic DNA of the English District. According to Dr. Socrates Henkel's *History of the Evangelical Lutheran Tennessee Synod*, the issues which the Henkels and other faithful Lutherans were addressing were largely over theology and not language. It seems there was an almost unspoken assumption that the building of the Evangelical Lutheran Church in America must be in English.

Following the death of Rev. Henry Muhlenberg in October 1787, the Pennsylvania Ministerium abandoned and disparaged his stronger confessional position that embraced the Unaltered Augsburg Confession and the Confessional writings of the Evangelical Lutheran Church in the *Book of Concord* in favor of mixing Reformed and Lutheran doctrine, hymnody, and worship.[22] The Henkels and other faithful English-speaking

Lutheran pioneers, including Rev. Storch of North Carolina and Rev. Paul Henkel, were scandalized by the revivalism and religious fanaticism sweeping the United States in the early 1800s and the mixing of Lutheran and Reformed doctrine.[23] They attentively examined (in English) the doctrines of the Episcopal, Methodist, Presbyterian, and Baptist church bodies in America and found them wanting. They were alarmed by the unionistic tendencies and the "indefinite, unsettled, lax, disintegrated, and dilapidated conditions" that resulted in the May 1820 rupture in the North Carolina Synod.

When Rev. David Henkel was slandered and came under attack in the North Carolina Synod for "false doctrine" for defending historic Lutheran Confessional positions from the *Book of Concord* in both Latin and German, the split was ensured and the Evangelical Lutheran Tennessee Synod was born. "The final rupture was a suitable opportunity."[24] David Henkel, Paul Henkel's son, became the lightning rod for the formation of the Tennessee Synod when he was denied ordination because of his strong confessional stance.

These incidents leading to the Tennessee Synod's formation demonstrate that the language of Lutheran orthodoxy (whether German or English) was not the issue. English was the language of America. The defensive of the historic Lutheran faith could be marshalled from the *Book of Concord*, period. David Henkel himself proved to be very strong in both German and English, as well as Latin, Greek, Hebrew, and theology, even as a candidate for the ministry in the North Carolina Synod. He proved to be the champion needed to move from the rupture in that synod to the newly-formed one, the Tennessee Synod being born on July 17, 1820 at Solomon's Church, Cove Creek, Green County, Tennessee. However, the organization was "under the name and title of the Evangelical German Lutheran Tennessee Conference or Synod," with transactions and written proceedings to be done in the German language.[25]

The next paragraph in the Tennessee Synod's *History*, footnoted with an asterisk (*) is significant:

> The reason why we desire an entire German Conference is, because we have learned from experience, that a conference, in which both languages, the German and the English, are used, the one or the other side will be dissatisfied. If the German is used, the English will

understand little, and often nothing in regard to the matter; and if the English is employed, many of the Germans will not understand more than half of what is said, and hence know not how to act relative to the most weighty matters. Besides, at the present time, we find very few entirely English preachers who accept the doctrines of our Church, or desire to preach them.[26]

However, after a notation in the *History* concerning why German was still used in 1827, Dr. Socrates Henkel simply states: "At a later date the English language was used" for transactions of the Synod.[27] The Synod, not bound in its title to the geographic confines of the state of Tennessee, was only interested in safeguarding historic Lutheran doctrine. Note, though, that early on in its history, through its Henkel Press in New Market, VA, Luther's *Small Catechism* was being published in German and English. By the 1850s, materials started to come out in English, translated from the German, beginning with the *Book of Concord*, followed by Hymns and Prayers, several of Luther's writings and Church Postil(s), and sermons on the Epistles for the Church Year, into "English dress."[28] Dr. Socrates Henkel further adds: "All honor then to the Tennessee Synod for undertaking this work, which has accomplished more in preserving the faith of our fathers in this country than any similar undertaking in the English language."[29]

Decades can often collapse into a seemingly shorter time period when viewed from a vantage point still further decades later. This may have been the case in Dr. Socrates Henkel's assertion that God used the huge 1820 rupture in the North Carolina Synod that brought about the formation of the Tennessee Synod to accomplish "a special purpose for the welfare of the Lutheran Church in America. By means of this division the Symbols of the Lutheran Church were translated into the English language."[30] The early English District "tie-in," alluded to previously, dates back to the fourth Convention of the Tennessee Synod in October 1823. At that time a congregation in Virginia petitioned the Synod for a minister. That congregation was one of the English Missouri Synod's original churches, Keinadt's (Koiner's) Church, Augusta County, Virginia. Decades later, this congregation would be the one served by Rev. Frederick Kuegele, who became the first president of the English Evangelical Lutheran Conference (Synod) of Missouri and Other States. But in 1823, this congregation no longer desired a pastor from the General Synod because they did not regard that Synod as Scriptural and they regarded the Tennessee Synod as "adhering to the Augsburg Confession."[31] The next year, the Tennessee Synod's annual Convention (Fifth Session) was held at Koiner's Church.

Excursus: Koiner's Church

In 1772, four years before the start of the American Revolutionary War, a German Lutheran congregation was organized near South River in northeastern Augusta County, near Crimora, Virginia. Koiner's Church ("Coiner" or "Coyner" or "Keinadt") reflected the heritage of the early German settlers in this region. This congregation was the first Evangelical Lutheran *Gemeinde* (Congregation) in that area of colonial Virginia and the Shenandoah Valley.[32] The Congregation exists today as Bethany-Trinity Evangelical Lutheran Church of Fishersville (Waynesboro), Virginia, making it one of the oldest continuous Lutheran churches in North America.

The initial log building was called Spindle's Meeting House, named for the Rev. Adolph Spindle (or Spindler), who conducted Services there till 1809. The log church was replaced by a brick church in 1834 and by the current building in 1880.

The Church today reflects a form typical among prospering rural congregations in the late 19th Century, including a louvered frame belfry. Enlarged in 1902, the Church retains the pews and interior furnishings from this period. The cemetery contains the tomb of Jacob Barger (1794), one of the most unusual German stones in the Valley. Its elaborately carved designs are reminiscent of *fraktur*,[33] a German font backletter typeface meaning "broken." A number of other early stones feature German inscriptions and other, slightly simpler German designs.

Rev. Frederick G. Kuegele served as pastor of Koiner's Church from April 1879 till his death in 1916. He wrote an obituary that appeared in the *Lutheran Witness* of one of the sons of the congregation, the Rev. Julius Samuel Koiner of the Tennessee Synod, who was received into the English Evangelical Lutheran Synod of Missouri and Other States in 1899. This Koiner was a descendant of Michael Keinadt, who left Germany in 1722 and was the first of the clan to settle in the Valley in 1789. From him are descended an estimated 30,000 Americans living all across the United States today.[34]

Excursus: A Pilgrim Song, Psalm 84—God, Our Shield

Psalm 84 is a beautiful song in the Psalter. Over the decades, this hymn from God's Holy Word, has been quoted by English District bards, pastors and other learned ones, in the context of worship of the Almighty. Psalm 84 reveals much about the eternal Being who is Author of Creation, Author of our Redemption, and Author of our Sanctification, and about the pilgrim Israelite expressing his desire for the House of the Lord.

In the language of love poetry, the psalmist expresses the pilgrim's deep yearning for "home." But the Psalm is far more than a pilgrim's longing for return to the earthly city of Jerusalem and the altar of the Lord in the Temple. It is a song of God's love for His people, His presence and grace, a *"sun and shield"* (vs. 11) and One who *"bestows favor and honor."*[35] This should be remembered as one reflects on this saga of the history and pilgrimage of English-speaking Lutherans who formed the old English Evangelical Lutheran Conference, later Synod, and what would become the English District-LCMS. Psalm 84 has for over a century received prominence in the worship life of the English District, and all to the glory of God (*Soli Deo Gloria*), often noted in the writings of the early founders of the English Synod and District.

This great God of Israel, as stated in Psalm 84, is the eternal Trinity, Father, Son, and Holy Spirit, one God who acted in love and mercy for His creatures, lost humanity, lost in the tragedy of sin (Genesis 3). God is the Shield of His people down through the millennia from the dawn of Creation, past the Fall, through His chosen Israel, whether in their nation-states of Israel and Judah (Judea) or in exile and returning, and especially in Christ Jesus, the eternal Son of God and Savior of the world.[36] Psalm

84 does not specifically speak to the coming Messiah, but as with all of the Old Testament, there is the pointing to God and the fulfillment of His promises, and the Promise is after all another name for the Gospel. God ever remains the Rock and Fortress, the winged Guardian (Jonah 2) and Protector of His people through all ages.

These thoughts are necessary as we see the grace of God in Jesus Christ and the power of His Holy Spirit through the Divine Word, reaching the lost for Jesus Christ. And that is what the English Missouri Synod and English District-LCMS have been about. In its very history and origins, in its pilgrim wanderings, in its plantings and intentional sharing of Christ crucified, risen, and ascended, the English District has been about mission. There is a uniqueness in her historic DNA. In the name of Christ and by the power of His Spirit, the Synod and District have sought to reach the lost for the Lord Jesus Christ, that is, to spread the Word of God, reach out with the saving Gospel, plant congregations, schools, and ministries across North America, and to be a microcosm of The Lutheran Church—Missouri Synod as a servant and missionary vanguard. One might also call her a "garden of the Lord." But that would never have happened had not a merciful God shielded His people on their earthly pilgrimage as part of the *Una Sancta Eccelsia*, the one holy, catholic, and apostolic church.

CHAPTER 3
The Beginnings of the English Missouri Synod

Part One

THROUGHOUT HER HISTORY, the English Missouri Synod and the English District-LCMS have had a variety of slogans or motto expressions. One of them that continued into the 1980s was *"The Faith of the Fathers in the Language of the Children."* Perhaps that slogan began as an English-speaking confession flowing from a comment by Dr. Socrates Henkel in his History of Evangelical Lutheran Tennessee Synod, as noted in the previous chapter. In defending the Tennessee Synod, he mentioned the faith of the fathers in the language of America: English. That Christian faith, grounded in Holy Scripture and the Confessional writing of the Evangelical Lutheran Church, was anchored for early American Lutherans in the German language. That faith was worth defending, but it needed to be articulated in the English language, which even immigrants from a wide variety of European and other countries were having to quickly learn.

The Tennessee Synod was pushing gradually westward into Missouri, and it was only natural that these pioneers would bump up against a decidedly-confessional Evangelical Lutheran group that had come to America in 1839. The German Missouri Synod took a few years to come into existence in April 1847. The forming Convention was held at First St. Paul Evangelical Lutheran Church and School in Chicago. Conferences in Fort Wayne, Cleveland, and St. Louis had preceded it. The churches and pastors that formed the fledgling *Die Deutsche Evangelisch-Lutherische Synode von Missouri, Ohio, und andern Staaten* (The German Evangelical Lutheran Synod of Missouri, Ohio, and Other States) were a mixed group with varying German roots. The largest number were pastors from Franconian Bavaria, sent over by Rev. Wilhelm Loehe of Neuendettelsau. The guiding light in that formation of the German Missouri Synod was a relatively-young Rev. C.F.W. Walther of the Saxon immigrants from Perry County and St. Louis, Missouri. The Franconians and Saxons, later joined by some immigrant Prussian pastors and congregations, formed the

German Missouri Synod, with its two small but growing seminaries in Fort Wayne and St. Louis.

Dr. Walther had been with the Saxon Lutherans who sailed on five boats from the port of Bremenhaven, Germany, to New Orleans in 1839. One boat was apparently lost at sea. After the deposing of their organizer, leader, and bishop, Rev. Martin Stephan, for reasons of alleged sexual and financial misconduct, the groups in Perry County and St. Louis, Missouri, accepted the leadership of Walther. He and the Saxon immigrants founded a college which later became Concordia Seminary, St. Louis. In addition to being the head pastor of the Trinity Evangelical Lutheran Church & School and the *Gemeinde* (congregation) of four parishes in St. Louis, Walther edited *Der Lutheraner*, a leading magazine of the day that reached confessional Lutherans across the country.

What began as 14 congregations and 11 pastors soon became the confessional Lutheran powerhouse synod in the Midwest. It grew rapidly, while conducting worship and teaching and culturally being German. The Constitution of the German Missouri Synod at that time stated that the language of worship, catechesis, schools, and conferences would "forever" be German. Of course, that changed. There were other German-language confessional synods that were established, namely the Buffalo (1845) and Iowa (1854) synods, though the relationship with the Tennessee Synod's confessional Lutherans was with the German Missouri Synod.[37]

So what about those English-speaking confessional Lutherans from the Tennessee Synod? Confessional admiration and loose, scattered, fraternal ties between the Tennessee Synod and German Evangelical Lutheran Synod of Missouri, Ohio, and Other States were slowly developing between 1848 and the 1850s. As early as January 1849 in *Der Lutheraner*, Dr. Walther expressed pleasure in the Tennessee Synod's desire to be and remain Lutheran.[38] The Tennessee Synod was not limited to just the state of Tennessee; it was expanding westward and into other areas of the South. In addition, representatives of the German Missouri Synod and the Tennessee Synod had representatives at each other's conventions in the early and mid-1850s. The American Civil War (1861-1865) and its early aftermath interrupted what appeared to be a healthy, growing relationship.

By the early 1870s, the German Missouri Synod was flourishing. In addition, with the growth of the German Missouri Synod into several states and into four districts (Western, Eastern, Northern, and Central) in 1854,[39] and having waded through the Civil War as a German-speaking church body, somewhat insulated from the division of the nation, the Synod now had formed a larger federation. This was the Evangelical Lutheran Synodical Conference of North America and included the Missouri Synod, the Wisconsin Synod, the Norwegian Synod, the Joint Ohio Synod, and other confessionally-conservative Evangelical Lutheran church bodies, formed in 1872. Now in the summer of 1872, a meeting had been set up with laity and pastors of the Tennessee Synod in Missouri and the top leadership in the Synodical Conference.

Tennessee Synod Pastors, Revs. Polycarp Henkel and Jonathan Moser, were serving widely-scattered English-speaking confessional Lutherans in Missouri who "…gathered into small congregations and built little log 'church houses,' as they called their places of worship." One such place was Zion Evangelical Lutheran Church in Gravelton, Missouri, well south of St. Louis in the foothills of the Ozarks and 40 miles west of

Meeting House, Gravelton, Mo.
(Drawing)

Perry County, Missouri. As early as 1817, English Lutheran work had begun at Gravelton, though the congregation was not officially organized until 1857. Contact was made by the group in Gravelton with Dr. Walther in St. Louis. The guiding hand of Almighty God in shielding the Tennessee Synod and generations of the Henkel family was clear.

It is fitting that this chapter in the English District's saga include this citation concerning the Tennessee Synod's Rev. Polycarp Henkel, grandson of the Rev. Paul Henkel:

Obituary of Rev. Polycarp C. Henkel, D.D. – On the 20th of August, 1820, was born the oldest son of Rev. David and Catharine Henkel, in Lincoln County, North Carolina. That son was the Rev. Polycarp C. Henkel, D.D., who is descendent of a long line of distinguished Lutheran ministers. He inherited very great physical and mental powers from both parents... He died at his last residence in Conover, North Carolina, on the 26th of September, 1889... at the age of 69, 1 month, and 6 days, and was buried at St. Peter's Church, Catawba County, North Carolina, September 28th, 1889.

Dr. P.C. Henkel was an extraordinary man, and unique in his character. He had been so long and so favorably known in this country... Intellectually, he was a powerful man. He was an original thinker and a fine logician. He would clinch every argument, and in debate and controversy was a formidable antagonist... His word was as sacred to him as a most solemn oath. In his manners he was humble and unassuming... Integrity was also a salient point of his character. He was rigidly honest and truthful.

As a minister, he was a power. His style of preaching was expository, plain, and forceful. He entered the ministry of the Evangelical Lutheran Church of the Tennessee Synod, except a few years, while in the State of Missouri, where he led in the organization of the English District of the Missouri Synod. He labored exceedingly hard in the vineyard of the Lord. At one time he had pastoral charge of fifteen congregations. He did an immense amount of missionary work, traveling thousands of miles, in cold and heat, and rain and storm, in obedience to the call of the Master to this work. He never shirked from duty... and [was] ready to speak the word of encouragement to the weak, the word of comfort to the sorrowing, the word of life to those seeking a knowledge of the way of life...

His chief text-books were the Bible and the Confession of the [Evangelical] Lutheran Church. On Dogmatic Theology he was an acknowledged authority... He labored hard and made great sacrifices to establish our school, Concordia College, for the Tennessee Synod, in which the Word of God should be recognized as a factor in education, and in which the Bible and Luther's Catechism should be taught daily. His influence is felt far beyond the limits of his own Synod, even throughout the whole Southern Church. He was in the midst of his earnest labors, both writing and preaching, to raise the [Evangelical] Lutheran Church of the South to a higher plain of doctrine and practice, when the Master called him to his reward. Thus ended his work. A good and great man has fallen.

Returning to the event of 1872 at Zion, Gravelton, a meeting and free conference were arranged for August 16-20, 1872, at the invitation of Pastors Polycarp Henkel and Jonathan Moser of the Tennessee Synod. It was held at the latter's house. The German Missouri Synod was represented by Dr. C.F.W. Walther, Pastor E.S. Kleppisch and, from the Norwegian Synod (part of the Synodical Conference), Professor F.A. Schmidt. H.P. Eckhardt notes that "in addition to Pastors Henkel and Moser and six lay members there was present Pastor Andrew Rader of Webster County, with three lay delegates, from the Holston Synod [connected with the Tennessee Synod] ... At the memorable conference in Gravelton of German Missourians with those English of the Tennessee and Holston Synods, Dr. Walther was the leading and guiding spirit." Walther delivered 16 theses with "a view of ascertaining, as well as giving expression to, our perfect unity in the faith." These theses were each accompanied by a "Testimony of the Church" (usually a quotation from the Book of Concord) and "Remarks." The Theses and lengthier testimonies and remarks are available to the serious historian in the *Proceedings* of a Free English Lutheran Conference Held in the Town of Gravelton, Wayne Co., MO, August 17-20, A.D. 1872.[40]

Walther's 16 Theses

The theses are as follows (and appearing today in the English District-LCMS archives):

Thesis 1: **A.** The written Word of God is the only rule and standard of faith and life. **B.** The written Word of God is the only source of Christian knowledge. **C.** The Word of God is always to be understood literally; not always, indeed, properly; but figuratively only for cogent reasons. **D.** The Word of God is its own interpreter. It is not to be interpreted by reason, tradition, or new revelations.

Thesis 2: Man by nature has no free will in spiritual matters, and hence he is not able to co-operate towards his conversion.

Thesis 3: By virtue of its personal union with the Godhead divine properties are really communicated to the human nature of Christ.

Thesis 4: Christ has perfectly and completely reconciled the whole world unto God.

Thesis 5: A. By the means of grace alone, to wit, the Word and the Sacraments, the merit and benefits of Christ are really communicated to men. **B.** The Gospel is not a mere announcement of the grace of Christ, but it is also at the same time an offer of the same to all who hear, and a communication of it to all who believe. **C.** Private absolution is the Gospel directed to individual persons and an offer and donation of the remission of sins on the part of God. **D.** Absolution demands faith; and faith alone receives what is offered and given by it; neither absolution, nor any other means of grace, operates *ex opera operato*.

Thesis 6: A. Faith alone justifies and saves. This is the main article of the whole Christian religion. **B.** Faith, if it is true faith, renews a man's heart, mind, disposition and all faculties, purifies the heart and is active in charity and good works.

Thesis 7: Good works are only such as are commanded by God, provided they are done in faith.

Thesis 8: A. Baptism effects regeneration and imparts everlasting salvation to them that receive the same in faith. **B.** By sins against conscience the grace of Baptism is lost. **C.** Baptism stands immovable on the point of God, even when man falls; by repentance, therefore, he may and shall return to the same.

Thesis 9: In the Holy Supper the true body and blood of Christ are truly present, are distributed under the bread and wine, and eaten and drank both by worthy and unworthy communicants; by the former for the remission of sins, by the latter unto judgment.

Thesis 10: A. It is a part of Christian liberty to be freed from the Jewish ceremonial and political laws. **B.** By virtue of this Christian liberty a believer in the time of the New Testament is no more bound to the observance of a Sabbath.

Thesis 11: A. The Church, in the proper sense of the term, is the invisible totality of all true believers in Christ. **B.** The characteristic marks of the Church are pure doctrine and unadulterated sacraments. **C.** Ecclesiastical communion is to be cherished only with those who agree in all articles of faith.

Thesis 12: A. It is the duty of the Church to maintain church-discipline and, consequently, to excommunicate obstinate errorists or sinners. **B.** Applicants to communion must be examined ere they are admitted. **C.** Ignorant people are not to be admitted to the sacrament.

Thesis 13: The power of the keys is not an exclusive privilege of ordained ministers, but a power of the whole believing Church that possesses the same originally and immediately.

Thesis 14: A. Ministers do not form a peculiar holy priestly order in opposition to laymen. **B.** The pastoral office is nothing but an office, instituted of God, of ministering unto the Church. **C.** To call preachers is a right of the congregation to whom they are to minister. Ordination is only a confirmation of this call and an apostolic ecclesiastical institution.

Thesis 15: The doctrine according to which a glorification of the Church in a millennial reign is to be expected, is a contradiction to several articles of the Christian faith and is consequently to be rejected.

Thesis 16: The Romish pope is the Antichrist, as prophesied in the Holy Scriptures.

Walther's theses had to be translated into English. This was done by Pastors Moser and Henkel, who would likely have known German since the Tennessee Synod and the Henkel family were originally rooted in both the German and English tongues.

The theses were each read, discussed, and individually adopted, apparently unanimously. A 12-article draft Constitution of the English Evangelical Lutheran Conference of Missouri, based on the adoption of these theses and approved following the closing of the morning session of the Free Conference on August 20, was in harmony with the doctrinal stance of the German Evangelical Lutheran Synod of Missouri, Ohio, and Other States. The questions that were raised at the outset of the Free Conference were the issues that had the German Missouri Synod wary of the English Missouri Conference, namely:

1. What can we (the German Missouri Synod) do for our scattered English Lutherans in the West, especially in regard to procuring faithful ministers for them?
2. The propriety or impropriety of forming some kind of an organization among the English Lutherans of the West [west of the Mississippi River]
3. The establishment of parochial schools.

These were answered with the following:

1. The adoption of Walther's 16 theses.

43

2. The training of Lutheran pastors at the German Missouri Synod's seminaries in St. Louis and Fort Wayne, and the preparatory school, the Lutheran College of the West, also known as Saint John's College, Winfield, Kansas, a college of what became the English Evangelical Lutheran Synod of Missouri and Other States.

3. Parochial schools were established by English Synod and later English District congregations with a view that having such schools provided mission opportunity for reaching English-speaking people.

Dr. C.F.W. Walther then reported on the Free Conference at Gravelton, MO, in his publication *Der Lutheraner*. He stated: "May it please God to lay His further gracious blessing on this small but blessed beginning of organized care for scattered children of our Church in the West who speak the English language! May everyone who loves our Zion assist in requesting this from the Father of Mercy, in the name of Jesus! Amen."[41]

Excursus: Zion, Gravelton, Missouri

Since 1931, Zion Evangelical Lutheran Church of Gravelton has been a member of the Missouri District (previously called the Western District of the [German] Missouri Synod). It sits in the "holler" (hollow, a valley)

in the Ozark foothills on a gravel road ten miles east of Missouri Route 67 and 100 miles southwest of St. Louis, almost frozen in time.[42] It continues as of 2020 to have an 8:00 a.m. Divine Service, faithfully served by the pastor of Trinity Evangelical Lutheran Church, Fredericktown, MO, the larger congregation. Zion has had indoor plumbing since 1988; however, the women's outhouse still stands, unused, behind the church building. It has a wonderful cemetery worthy of careful investigation, directly across the road from the church. Indoor and outdoor plaques given by the English District in 1972 reveal that without a Zion-Gravelton, the LCMS may have lingered even longer in its slow change from the German language to English. In leaving the English District in 1931, no doubt the enculturation process of German-speaking Lutherans in the Missouri Synod and other factors had its effect on whether such congregations might then consider affiliating with the geographic districts of Synod.

Those who served as pastors of Zion Church, as noted in the Concordia Historical Institute Quarterly of January, 1948, were the following:

   1817 – Rev. Christian Moretz
   1828 – Rev. Ephraim Conrad
   1851 – Rev. Jonathan R. Moser
   1869 – Rev. Polycarp Henkel
   1877 – Rev. L.M. Wagner
   1890 – Rev. Oscar Kaiser
   1891 – Rev. L.M. Wagner
   1902 – Rev. S.S. Keisler
   1905-1907 – During these years the Congregation was served by seminarians
       and pastors from the St. Louis area, including Richard Jesse, Alfred
       Doerffler, Louis Buchheimer, M.F. Kretzmann, and A. Bonnet, with the
       Rev. Dr. M.S. Sommer serving as Vacancy Pastor
   1907 – Rev. Henry Kowert
   1912 – Rev. D.H. Schoof
   1927 – Rev. Omar Rau
   1930 – Rev. C. Hafner
   1931 – Rev. Oliver Faszholz
   1932 – Rev. E.C. Boxdorfer
   1933 – Rev. T.C. Predoehl*
   1944 – Rev. H.G. Roschke[43]

   *Rev. Theodore (Ted) Predoehl, a retired, longtime English District-LCMS
   pastor in Green Valley, AZ, and LCMS missionary to Japan, is the son of
   the Rev. T.C. Predoehl.

CHAPTER 4
The Beginnings of the English Missouri Synod

Part Two

IN AN ERA of horse and buggy, trains, and telegraph, but before electric lighting, cars, telephone, airplanes, TV, and certainly before the internet and social media, things moved a lot slower than life a century and a half later. Nevertheless, Rev. A.W. Meyer noted: "Our people were devoted and Biblical. Each family had a Bible, some had the New Market [Henkel Press] *Book of Concord*; and they would read these. They would select Biblical names for their children."[44]

The fledgling English Evangelical Lutheran Conference of Missouri would develop slowly, locating other confessional English-speaking Evangelical Lutheran congregations and pastors from Virginia and Maryland to Tennessee and Missouri and places in between. At first, it was just a Missouri Conference and it met annually. There were no minutes of the next three Conferences in 1873, 1874, and 1875, but those of 1876 (held at St. Paul Evangelical Lutheran Church, Webster County, Missouri), 1877 (held at Hindsville, Arkansas), and 1878 (held at Zion Evangelical Lutheran Church, Caster, Bollinger County, Missouri) recorded with regret that the German Missouri Synod Lutheran brethren were not present and had "...failed for the last three sessions to favor us with any aid or at least one counselor."[45]

In his 1946 Historical Sketch of the English District, author President Emeritus Eckhardt noted that at the 8th Conference meeting held in 1879, again at St. Paul's, Webster County, Missouri, the German Missouri Synod was represented by Seminary Professor M. Guenther and Pastor C.L. Janzow. Both were members of the Mission Board of the Western District of the German Missouri Synod.[46] This is significant because the early German Missouri Synod had mission outreach in its origins, beginning with the Franconians in Michigan, who sought to bring the saving Gospel to the Chippewa Native Americans, and later with a Board for Colored Missions attempting to reach African-Americans in the late 1870s in Mobile, Alabama.[47] At the 1879 meeting of the English

Evangelical Lutheran Conference of Missouri, petition was made to the Missouri Synod's Western District to send a representative to future meetings.

Though the movement was slow in growing, the Conference took heart from the 1885 words of the English Mission Committee of the Western District: "May the Lord prosper His Word among the brethren of the English tongue to the glory of His name and grant unto us cheerfulness for this work."[48] The Conference could also rejoice in the calling of a candidate for the Holy Ministry in 1885. Candidate A.W. Meyer became pastor of an English Missouri Conference congregation, Emmanuel Evangelical Lutheran Church of Webster County, Missouri, located in the Ozarks in southwestern Missouri, just east of

In his autobiography, *My Life,* Rev. Dr. William Dallmann notes some juicy points. Pastor Janzow was so severely ridiculed by some fellow German Missouri Synod brethren for doing work in English that he temporarily resigned as representative to the English-speaking brethren. It took the intercession of no less than the German Missouri Synod's president, Dr. C.F.W. Walther, for Janzow to continue (endnote 44, – pg. 37 in *My Life*). Walther was strongly in favor of doing work in English, even in St. Louis. Walther was ahead of his time in the Missouri Synod!

Springfield. The next year, another Seminary graduate, William Dallmann, was called to St. Paul's Congregation in that same Missouri County. Dallmann would later become president (1899-1901) of the English Evangelical Lutheran Synod of Missouri and Other States after the English Evangelical Lutheran Conference of Missouri and Other States made the name change in 1891. Both men did fine outreach work, with the Conference now growing into Arkansas and Kansas.

At the 13th meeting of the English Missouri Conference in 1886 at St. James Evangelical Lutheran Church, in Barton County, Missouri, a very significant catalyzing event leading to the formation of the English District happened. The Conference appointed a committee, consisting of Pastors

A.W. Meyer, Irenaeus Rader, and William Dallmann, to submit a plan to the German Missouri Synod for the *"Conference to join the German Synod as a separate English District."* Eckhardt intentionally italicized these words in his "Sketch."[49] Dallmann indicated that he wrote this petition.[50] And what did *Die Deutsche Evangelish-Lutherische Synode von Missouri, Ohio, und andern Staaten* do at its 1887 Delegate Synod Convention in Fort Wayne, Indiana? It declined the petition.

This was symptomatic of a larger issue, an acculturation process. The German Missouri Synod, clinging to German language, culture, and education, was not willing to go that route. However, the German Synod did advise the Conference to form "their [its] own Lutheran Synod of English tongue"[51] and to affiliate with the Evangelical Lutheran Synodical Conference of North America. The German Missouri Synod was the leader in this confessionally-orthodox Lutheran federation, begun in 1872. The English Missouri Conference took the German Missouri Synod's advice and joined the Synodical Conference. It is noteworthy that, at the 1887 Synodical Conference of the German Missouri Synod, then 40 years in existence and in the year of Dr. Walther's death, a Board for English Missions was established.[52] In short, the English Lutheran Conference was helping to push the envelope for English to be embraced as a language for mission work by the German Missouri Synod, even as the latter still clung to German as the language of worship, culture, and education in schools, colleges, and seminaries.

Excursus: The Rev. Dr. Frederic(k) Gottlob Kuegele (April 16, 1846—April 1, 1916)

In the 1800s and early 1900s, it was very common for people noted in books, journals, or magazine articles to be known only by their first or first two initials and their last name. In the case of Pastor Kuegele, he was not only simply acknowledged as F. Kuegele, his most common picture was one of him seated on a bench by himself, wearing a bowtie and a simple chapeau, common for that day.

Kuegele was born in Columbiana, Columbiana County, Ohio, and died in Waynesboro, Augusta County, Virginia. In between the dash marks of life, he served as first president of the English Evangelical Lutheran Conference (Synod) of Missouri and Other States. He held that office longer than anyone else (1888-1899). Fluent in both English and German, he knew well the Henkel and Koiner (Coiner) families by virtue of his near 37-year pastorate at Koiner's Church, Crimora, Virginia (1879-1916). In other words, the "and other states" did matter in that small but growing English-speaking church body that was none the less aligned with the German Missouri Synod.

Pastor Kuegele was an 1870 graduate of the German Missouri Synod's Concordia Seminary, St. Louis. He first served as a pastor in Omaha, Nebraska, and then at Trinity in Cumberland, Maryland. Then he accepted a call in 1879 to Koiner's Church, a congregation of the Evangelical Lutheran Joint Synod of Ohio and Other States (usually known as the "Joint Ohio Synod"), which was in pulpit and altar fellowship with the German Missouri Synod in the federation known as the Evangelical Lutheran Synodical Conference of North America. But Kuegele and Koiner's Church severed ties with the Joint Ohio Synod during the Predestinarian Controversy. Kuegele helped form the Evangelical Lutheran Concordia Synod of Pennsylvania and Other States in 1882, which disbanded in 1886. He and the congregation were independent until 1888, when he and Koiner's Church joined the English Evangelical Lutheran Conference of Missouri and Other States and he became its president.

Dr. Kuegele, who later became a vice president of the German Missouri Synod while serving as an English District pastor, was a pioneer in English work. Kuegele wrote two smaller books, *Book of Devotion* and *Your Confirmation Vow*. He was known, though, for his significant work, *Country Sermons*, which were very popular as a guide for German-speaking confessional Lutheran pastors having to learn English. *Country Sermons* was printed in Baltimore, but tragically the plate of the entire stock of books was destroyed in a fire at the Lang Printery. This was a personal loss to the author and to the English Missouri Synod, at the time, which benefited from the sale of his books.[53] Kuegele had first-hand knowledge of the Henkel family and the Tennessee Synod, which he no doubt shared with Dr. Eckhardt, prior to his (Kuegele's) death in 1916.

His grave marker in Trinity Lutheran Church Cemetery, Crimora, VA, contains in English the words of Romans 14:8:

> For whether we live, we live unto the Lord. And whether we die, we die unto the Lord. Whether we live therefore, or die, we are the Lord's.

From Barton County, Missouri, the scene now shifted to St. Louis for the English Missouri Lutheran Conference. At its 15th meeting, held at Bethlehem (German) Evangelical Lutheran Church, St. Louis, October 19-23, 1888, this fledgling group formally became a separate independent Evangelical Lutheran church body, variously known as the General Evangelical English Lutheran Conference of Missouri and Other States.[54] Synodical Conference English-speaking pastors and delegates were invited to the next (1889) Conference held at Bethlehem Church. Even seminarians at Concordia Seminary, St. Louis, were invited to come and observe. Rev. F. Kuegele from Koiner's Evangelical Lutheran Congregation, Augusta County, Virginia, was among those present. He was the preacher for the opening service at Bethlehem Church. At that Conference, a Constitution of the new Conference was adopted.[55] Gratitude was expressed for the late Dr. C.F.W. Walther, a man sympathetic to the cause of English-speaking confessional Lutherans, who had died in the Lord on May 7, 1887. In his book, *Doctor Carl Ferdinand Wilhelm Walther*, Rev. D.H. Steffens, Pastor of Martini Evangelical Lutheran Church in Baltimore, stated concerning Walther: "Plainly, it was his conviction that our fathers' faith was to be preached in our children's tongue."[56] Walther was a man ahead of his time!

Along with Pastor Kuegele, another pastor who was beginning to emerge as a leader in the new Synod was the Rev. William Dallmann (1862-1952). Born and baptized in Pomerania in Prussian Germany, he was confirmed by Rev. Anton Wagner in Chicago, who urged him to serve the Lord as a pastor. After studying at Concordia College in Fort Wayne, he graduated in 1886 at age 23 from Concordia Seminary, St. Louis. Dallmann briefly served the mission-planting cause in Missouri and then was installed at the German Missouri Synod's Martini German

Evangelical Lutheran Church of Baltimore to found the first confessional Lutheran English-speaking congregation in 1888, English Emmanuel, and then in 1892, Jackson Square Ev. Lutheran Church, later renamed Our Saviour,[57] in distinction from the alien General Synod's English-speaking congregation. President Schwan of the German Missouri Synod underscored the importance of successful English work in Baltimore.[58]

In many respects, those who signed the Constitution of the General Evangelical Lutheran Conference of Missouri and Others States are as significant as those pastors and congregations who formed the German Missouri Synod in Chicago in April 1847. These pioneers of "English Missouri" represented a seismic shift in confessional Lutheranism in the Midwest. For now English would become the new *lingua franca* and the dominant language of the (German) Evangelical Lutheran Synod of Missouri, Ohio and Other States in the two decades before the U.S. entry into World War II. The signees of the original constitution were:

Rev. William Dallmann, Emmanuel Congregation, Baltimore, MD
Rev. A.W. Meyer, Emmanuel Congregation, Webster County, MO
Rev. C.F.W. Meyer, St. Paul Congregation, Marshfield, Webster Co., MO
Rev. Frederick Kuegele, Koiner's Church, Augusta County, VA
Rev. L.M. Wagner, Zion Evangelical Lutheran Church, Gravelton, MO
Rev. R.L. Goodman, St. James Congregation, Barton County, MO, and St.
    Peter Evangelical Lutheran Congregation, Cherokee County, KS
Rev. A. Sloan Bartholomew, Salem Congregation, Springdale, AR

And, as advisory members:

Rev. H.S. Knabenschuh
Rev. C. Spannuth
Rev. F. Kroger
Rev. Th. Huegli
Rev. Andrew Rader, Pastor Emeritus, Webster County, MO
Rev. J.E. Rader, parochial school teacher.[59]

At least five states were represented, with many more to come in the 23 years leading up to 1911 and the formation of the English District of the German Missouri Synod. At its 1888 Convention, the new "Synod," still called a Conference, did not have a hymnal, Sunday school literature, official order for the Divine Service, parish register of ministerial acts, seminary or official paper. However, the English Missouri Conference did at this 1888 Convention join the confessional Lutheran federation known as the Evangelical Lutheran Synodical Conference of North America.

The Lutheran Witness

By God's grace, in a short period of time many needs were supplied. *The Lutheran Witness*, edited and published in Zanesville, Ohio, was given to the English Missouri Conference (Synod) in 1889. The Rev. C.A. (Carl Adolph) Frank had served nine years from its inception as editor, and continued on another two years after the *Witness* came under the ownership of the English Missouri Synod.[60] His successor, Rev. William Dallmann noted: "In the 1891 Convention, Pastor Frank, the noble founder and editor of the *Witness*, resigned, and I was doomed to the editorial chair. I made a new heading for the paper…in order to show the unity of the spirit. At the masthead I flew the motto: *'Our Fathers' Faith, Our Children's Language.'*"[61]

The *Witness* had been and continued to be an advocate for solid confessional Lutheran doctrine, especially during the Predestinarian Controversy (1870s and into the 1930s).

Excursus: *The Lutheran Witness* Today

Today *The Lutheran Witness* is the main lay-oriented magazine of The Lutheran Church-Missouri Synod. It was originally published on May 21, 1882, by the Cleveland District Conference. The English Missouri Synod assumed command of publication in 1888, when it was being edited and published in Zanesville, OH, by Rev. C.A. Frank (1846-1922), the Witness' Founder. Pastor Frank was a member of the Central District of *Die Deutsche Evangelish-Lutherische Synode von Missouri, Ohio, und andern Staaten*. (The Central District at that time consisted of what is today the Ohio and Indiana Districts of the LCMS.) He offered *The Lutheran Witness* to the English Evangelical Lutheran Conference (Synod), which immediately accepted his offer. The periodical became the official organ of the Conference (Synod). As the English Missouri Synod was becoming a part of the German Missouri Synod in 1911, *The Lutheran Witness* was received and utilized by the Synod (LCMS), no longer as an

English District publication but as the German Missouri Synod's official English magazine.

At first, in the German Missouri Synod, the English District had the key role in *The Lutheran Witness*. Hence, its early editors were from the English District. By 1945, the English District relinquished any direct involvement or control over *The Lutheran Witness*. The journal is still published monthly and is a proud legacy of the English Missouri Synod and English District-LCMS.

The Common Service

At that same 1889 Convention of the English Evangelical Lutheran Conference of Missouri and Other States, Professor August Crull (1845-1923) of the German Missouri Synod's Concordia College at Fort Wayne, Indiana, offered an English Lutheran hymnal manuscript. Crull put a tremendous amount of effort into the hymnal. It was received with gratitude by the Convention and prepared for usage by Pastors Dallmann and Bartholomew by the addition of an Order of Service that came to be known as "the Common Service."[62] Incidentally, Professor Crull translated several beloved German Lutheran hymns into English, including *"What Is the World to Me?," "Jesus, I Will Ponder Now," "Abide, O Dearest Jesus, "God Loved the World So That He Gave," "Oh, How Great Is Your Compassion,"* and *"Draw Us to Thee."*[63]

The Common Service is affectionately known as "old page 15," from the 1941 *The Lutheran Hymnal*, (TLH) and since 2006 has been utilized as the Divine Service Setting Three (Page 184) in the *Lutheran Service Book* (LSB). The roots of the Common Service go back to Rev. Henry Melchior Muhlenberg, who had in mind a "common Service" for all Lutheran congregations in America. Various Lutheran bodies and pastors used different worship orders for over 100 years before the work of a joint committee of the Evangelical Lutheran General Synod in the United States (General Synod, 1820), the General Council of the Evangelical Lutheran Church in America (General Council, 1867), and the United Synod of the Evangelical Lutheran Church in the South (United Synod of the South, 1863) produced the accepted "Common Service" liturgy in 1888.[64] However, not all pastors and congregations, especially in the General Synod (The Evangelical Lutheran General Synod in the United States), uniformly adopted and used this liturgy. The English Missouri Synod gladly received this liturgy, and by 1906 had a musical accompaniment edition to go with it. Interestingly, *Common Service Music*, as the liturgical book was called, provided for the pastor to chant the liturgy.

Today the Common Service is the most widely-used liturgy in The Lutheran Church—Missouri Synod, in spite of the fact that the *Lutheran Service Book* offers five different liturgical settings, and many congregations use praise/contemporary liturgies. Common Service books for use in Evangelical Lutheran congregations was a parallel development which Rev. Dr. Luther Dotterer Reed of the ULCA details in his 1947 celebrated tome, *The Lutheran Liturgy*.

The 1889 Convention of the English Missouri Conference came to receive and utilize a beloved liturgy, the Common Service, which had major impact on the German Missouri Synod as it slowly moved in the late 19th century and early 20th century to the use of English, eventually replacing German as the language of worship. It was a gift to the German Missouri Synod from the English Missouri Synod of liturgy and hymns that became the *Evangelical Lutheran Hymn-Book* (ELHB), to which Dr. Jon Vieker gives careful detail:

> A year later [1912, following the union on May 15, 1911], the union of English Missouri with German Missouri was blessed with the birth of a new, English-language hymnal, the *Evangelical Lutheran Hymn-Book (ELHB 1912)*. This new hymnal, with tunes, was a completely revised and expanded edition of the *Evangelical Lutheran Hymn Book (ELHB 1889)*, which had been presented and adopted nearly a quarter century earlier at the very first convention of the English Synod [Conference]. As such, *ELHB* 1912 became the first English-language hymnal of the Missouri Synod and clearly pointed this future in a twentieth-century, English-speaking America.[65]

It should also be noted that the English Evangelical Lutheran Synod of Missouri and Other States produced a children's hymnal called *Sunday School Hymnal*. It came out in 1901 by the American Lutheran Publication Board in Pittsburgh, PA, and published by the German Missouri Synod's Concordia Publishing House in St. Louis. The movement to English in the German Synod targeted the young, who were already a generation or two into acculturating to life in North America and the use of the English language. Noteworthy is this humorous fact: The English District-LCMS congregation in Oakmont, PA, the English Evangelical Lutheran Church of Our Redeemer, continued to use the old, maroon *Sunday School Hymnal* for its Sunday School and Bible Class joint opening devotions into the early 1980s.

Name Change and Further Developments

Up to 1889, the English Missouri Lutherans were still called a "Conference." But at its next (second) convention in 1891, held at Grace Evangelical Lutheran Church, St. Louis, the name "Conference" was changed to "Synod." At this convention, 11 congregations were present, representing churches in seven states (Virginia, Missouri, Minnesota, Maryland, Arkansas, Kansas, and Pennsylvania). 14 pastors and one teacher represented an additional four states (Illinois, West Virginia, Louisiana, and New York). The mantel of editorship of *The Lutheran Witness* was given to Rev. William Dallmann, and the place of publication was switched from Zanesville, Ohio, to Baltimore, Maryland, where Dallmann served as pastor of Emmanuel English Evangelical Lutheran Church. Under Dallmann's leadership, Emmanuel Congregation continued to grow rapidly; he also helped organize other congregations. Dallmann needed relief, so in 1895 the editorship was transferred to the Faculty of Concordia College, Conover, North Carolina.[66]

Between 1891 and 1893, the English Evangelical Lutheran Synod published a new hymnbook and other Church literature. Publication boards in Baltimore and Pittsburgh were busy with *The Lutheran Witness*, Sunday school publications, and tracts. One of these was *The Lutheran Guide*, a Sunday School newspaper founded and edited by Rev. A.W. Meyer, who became the English Missouri Synod's third president. Eventually, the newspaper was gifted to the German Missouri Synod.[67] The Word of the Lord continued to spread in the English tongue.

The third Convention of the English Missouri Synod was held in 1893 at the German St. John Evangelical Lutheran Church in Chicago, pastored by Rev. H. Succop. The "mother church" of the English District-LCMS in Chicago (Christ English Evangelical Lutheran Church and School, 1891) had just recently been organized, with Rev. A.S. Bartholomew serving as pastor. That church did not yet have a house of worship and was not able to host the Convention. But St. John's Church offered to host the

Convention at its house of worship. The membership of the English Evangelical Lutheran Synod of Missouri and Other States had increased by 14 pastors and eight churches. There were 19 congregations, representing ten states and the District of Columbia. The Synod adopted the newly founded *The Lutheran Guide* as its Sunday School paper.

The desire of some German Missouri Synod congregational members to transfer to newly organized English Missouri Synod congregations caused some controversy and bitterness between congregations. English Synod President Kuegele delivered a doctrinal paper at the 1893 Convention on "Parish Rights" which was read and discussed, setting forth scriptural principles of the rights of congregations and individual church members. It was agreed that this was a matter of individual conscience, but it revealed some tensions with acculturation and acceptance of language change, not unlike today.[68] It should be noted that this Third Convention of the English Missouri Synod now found the young Synod in possession of two colleges (see the next chapter) in North Carolina and Kansas. Both would eventually become part of the German Missouri Synod's growing number of synodical colleges, universities, and seminaries.

Excursus: The Rev. Dr. William Dallmann (December 22, 1862—February 2, 1952)

Much more needs to be added about the life of Dr. Charles Frederick William Dallmann, the German-born gifted leader who served as the second president of the English Evangelical Lutheran Synod of Missouri and Other States. He succeeded respected Rev. F. Kuegele, serving as president, 1899-1901. Dallmann's highly significant role is summarized in his 1952 obituary, written by Dr. Martin Walker, appearing in *The Lutheran Witness*, of which Dallmann once was editor:

> When we view the transition of the Missouri Synod from the German to the English, we readily recognize that many other men made their contribution toward keeping Synod in the channels of the Scriptures and

the Lutheran Confessions. However, it was William Dallmann whom the Lord of the Church evidently called to the place of leadership. In his staunch adherence to the Sacred Scriptures and the Lutheran Confessions, and in his heroic stand for the truth as it is in Christ, Dr. Dallmann proved himself a worthy disciple of both Luther and Walther [as a seminarian, Dallmann likely had heard Walther's evening lectures on Law and Gospel distinction]. It is my well-considered opinion that next to God we owe it to William Dallmann more than to any other man that we have in The Lutheran Church—Missouri Synod an English Lutheranism that is as scripturally sound, as confessionally loyal, as pure and virile as it is today. His motto throughout his ministry was *"The faith of the fathers in the language of the children."*[69]

Dr. Dallmann wrote an article for *The English District Bulletin* of July 1947, which reveals his humor and recollections. In *"A Look Backward"* to the English Missouri Synod Convention of 1897, Dallmann noted his dear friend, college mate, and successor as Synod President, Dr. A.W. Meyer, affectionately called "Cannibal," because he came from New Zealand.[70] It should also be noted that Dallmann served as a vice president of the Evangelical Lutheran Synod of Missouri, Ohio, and Other States (1926-1932). In his autobiography, *My Life*, Dallmann during his Milwaukee years (1905ff.), quoted a German Missouri Synod pastor who said: "I have no use for English Lutheranism… Because you cannot preach Lutheranism in English." Another said, "If the Americans love God and His Word so much, let them learn German."[71] Humorously pithy comments! The 468-hymn 1901 English-language *Sunday School Hymnal*, a gift of the English Missouri Synod and largely Dallmann's work as that Hymnal's Committee Chair, *"sought to sing the faith of the fathers in the song of the children."*[72]

Chapter 5
The Colleges of the English Evangelical Lutheran Synod of Missouri and Other States

"OH, TO BE a Johnnie!" 1893 marked another milestone for the English Missouri Synod. At its Convention in Chicago, the Synod received two colleges, Concordia College in North Carolina and St. John's College in Kansas. Alumni of St. John's were, and still are, called "Johnnies." Though both colleges are no longer in existence, they were thriving when the English Missouri Synod became the English District of *Die Deutsche Evangelish-Lutherische Synode von Missouri, Ohio, und andern Staaten* in 1911 and transfered ownership of the colleges. Their closures were necessitated by a destructive fire during the Great Depression (Concordia College, 1933) as well as changes in North American higher education and financial reasons (St. John's College, 1986). But what rich histories both schools have!

Concordia College, Conover, North Carolina

Concordia College started in 1877 as a high school of the Tennessee Synod. The first building erected was in 1878, an administration building. It was chartered as Concordia College in 1881 by act of the post-Civil War Legislature of North Carolina.

Presidents of Concordia College, Conover, in the North Carolina hilly Piedmont area near Hickory, NC, were:

Tennessee Synod:
Rev. Dr. Polycarp Cyprian Henkel – 1881-1885
Rev. J.C. Moser – 1885-1888
Dr. R.A. Yoder – 1888-1891
Vacant – 1891-1892

English Synod, and then Missouri Synod:
Rev. Dr. William Herman Theodore Dau – 1892-1899
Rev. George A. Romoser – 1899-1911
Revs. C.A. Weis & A. Kaentschel (Acting Presidents) – 1911-1913
Dr. Henry Bernard Hemmeter – 1913-1917
Rev. Oswel W. Kreinheder – 1917-1928

Dr. C.O. Smith (Acting President) – 1928-1930
Rev. Dr. Henry Bernard Hemmeter – 1930-1935.[73]

Located in heavily Lutheran Catawba County, NC, Concordia College was from its inception "devoutly Lutheran." When the Tennessee Synod withdrew its care of the College as a private institution, its Board of Trustees went first to the German Missouri Synod's Board for English Missions. That board was in contact with the English Missouri Synod, which dispatched Rev. Kuegele from Koiner's Church in Augusta County, Virginia, and Rev. Dallmann from Emmanuel Church in Baltimore, Maryland, to inspect the College. Then, at the 1893 English Missouri Synod Convention, Concordia College's Board of Trustees formally offered the school to the English Synod, which it accepted.

Concordia College peaked in enrollment in 1887 with 112 students. Its next highest enrollment was in 1899 with 100 students, all male. The students, many of whom did not know German well, were trained there in the German tongue before entering Concordia Seminary, St. Louis, for the Holy Ministry. In short, Concordia College became the center for mission work and expansion in the Southeastern part of the United States. On May 15, 1911, the English Missouri Synod became part of the German Missouri Synod as the English District, and the college and property of Concordia College, Conover, North Carolina, was given to the (German) Missouri Synod. In 1919, the English District-LCMS Convention was hosted by Concordia College and Concordia Evangelical Lutheran Church, Conover, NC. At this Convention, one of the resolutions suggested the creation of a new "Southern District" [probably meaning a Southeastern District of the LCMS, which did occur in 1939].[74] By the time of the College's closure, enrollment had fallen to 25. When the Administration Building burned down on April 15, 1933, during a windy storm, the Cleveland Convention of the LCMS (then Evangelical Lutheran Synod of Missouri, Ohio, and Other States) elected to disband the College, since there was at that time an abundance of pastors coming from the Synod's seminaries in St. Louis and Springfield, Illinois.[75]

Excursus: Early 20th Century Lesser Known Servants of the Lord

Rev. W.H.T. Dau (1864-1944), following his Concordia presidency and a pastorate in Hammond, IN, became a professor at Concordia Seminary, St. Louis (1905-1926). Dr. Dau then became the first president of Valparaiso University under the independent Lutheran University Association (but linked closely with the LCMS). He served as president from 1926 to 1929. Dau was followed by Rev. O.C. (Oscar Carl) Kreinheder (1877-1946) at "Valpo" (1930-1939). Dr. Kreinheder had been simultaneously Concordia Conover's president and president of the English District-LCMS (1918-1927). His wife, Hannah, was a Coyner. Rev. Henry (H. B.) Hemmeter (1860-1948), who served as Conover's president twice (1913-1917 and 1930-1935) later became president of Concordia Theological Seminary, Springfield, IL (1936-1945). It was Dr. Hemmeter's dream for the English District-LCMS to start a new synodical district (the Southeastern District-LCMS), and in 1933 it began to materialize. That year, in Convention "…the English District granted permission to its congregations in the Carolinas to petition Synod for authority to organize a new district in the Southeast, in order to exploit the missionary opportunities in this rapidly developing section of the country."[76]

Other names worth noting: Rev. George August Romoser (1870-1936), who served as president of Concordia College, Conover, NC (1899-1911) and was part of the 1911 English Synod "Roll Call," later served as president of Concordia Collegiate Institute (College), Bronxville, NY (1918-1936). Rev. J. Frederic Wenchel, pastor at Christ Evangelical Lutheran Church, Washington, D.C., was Synod's public relations representative at the U.S. Capitol. Many English Missouri Synod men served prominently in the General (German) Synod of Missouri in the early 20th century.[77]

Previous page: Concordia College, Conover, North Carolina, circa 1893. The building on the left was the Boys' Dormitory. The building on the right was the Administration Building and where instruction took place. *Above*: Administration Building after the 1935 fire.

St. John's College, Winfield, Kansas

At the same 1893 Convention of the English Evangelical Lutheran Synod of Missouri and Other States at which Concordia College was received, another college in a far different area of the United States was accepted by the English Synod Convention. Was there a common denominator? Yes.

A German-born layman, Mr. John Peter Baden (1851-1900) of Winfield, Kansas, owner of five successful businesses, wanted to found an English-speaking Lutheran college. He shared this with his pastor, Rev. A.W. Meyer, a missionary pastor who also edited *The Lutheran Guide* and served as president of the English Missouri Synod, 1901-1905. Mission work had been done in Cherokee County in extreme southeastern Kansas and continued further west in Winfield, south of Wichita. Baden put up $50,000 in February 1893. A Board of Incorporators was formed and a Charter drawn up. On April 10, 1893, ground was broken for the new college, and the Synod was presented and received this "princely offer" for an English-speaking Lutheran college. What remarkable faith and zeal on the part of all in response to Mr. Baden's gift, and with what incredible speed! Candidate Henry John Stoeppelwerth of Concordia Seminary, St. Louis, was elected the first professor of St. John's College.[78]

The presidents who were chosen and served as president of St. John's College from its inception to its closing by action of the LCMS in Convention in 1986 were:

English Missouri Synod
Rev. Henry Sieck – 1893-1895
English & German Missouri Synods
Rev. Dr. A.W. Meyer – 1895-1928
Ev. Luth. Synod of Missouri, Ohio... (LCMS)
Rev. Dr. Alfred Rehwinkel – 1928-1936
Rev. Dr. Carl S. Mundinger – 1936-1958
Rev. Reuben C. Beisel – 1959-1972
Rev. Dr. Michael Stelmachowicz – 1973-1978
Teacher, Mr. Gordon Beckler – 1979-1983
Dr. Erich Helge – 1985-1986.[79]

It should be noted that Mr. Baden in 1899 unsuccessfully tried to persuade the English Missouri Synod to move its publication business from Pittsburgh to Winfield.[80] When the College began under the English Missouri Synod, it was the first and only school in the "Missouri" orbit to be co-educational. There were separate Boys' and Girls' dormitories. It was also in the center of the German Missouri Synod's southwestern territory.

In 1908 the college was offered by the English Missouri Synod to the German Missouri Synod. This culminated in the 1911 merger of the English Evangelical Lutheran Synod of Missouri and Other States into the German Missouri Synod.

St. John's College went from a two-year school to a four-year accredited college in the early 1980s. While it grew and thrived, it did suffer a period of enrollment decline and financial instability, which was rectified at the outset of veteran Lutheran educator Dr. Erich Helge's administration.[81] Despite strong opposition by some within the Synod, the 1986 LCMS Convention voted to close St. John's College, once a gift along with many gifts to the Synod from the old English Missouri Synod. The Kansas District of the LCMS recognized that it had indeed lost a prize. The City of Winfield, Kansas, purchased the campus and renamed it Baden Square (a Community Center).

PART TWO

INTEGRATION INTO THE LUTHERAN CHURCH—MISSOURI SYNOD

CHAPTER 6
The Union with the German Missouri Synod

ANY RECORD OF a fourth 1895 Convention of the English Evangelical Lutheran Synod of Missouri and Other States appears to be lost to history. Perhaps there was nothing memorable from it. However, as Dr. H.P. Eckhardt writes: "The fifth convention, held in Emmanuel Church, Baltimore, Rev. Wm. Dallmann, pastor, in 1897, was a memorable one, particularly with regard to progress in publication matters."[82] Not only was an English-language Sunday school hymnal authorized with a musical edition, a new and revised congregational hymnal of the old German hymnal was also authorized. A distinguished committee of four pastors and two laymen was elected, headed by Rev. Dallmann. This hymnal took a great deal of time to prepare. By 1911, with the union of the English and German Missouri Synods, the project was assigned to the Missouri Synod's Concordia Publishing House. Publication finally took place in 1912. The hymnal committee was aided by Dr. Charles Heimroth of Pittsburgh, an outstanding musician and organist.[83]

At the same convention in 1897, the English Evangelical Lutheran Synod of Missouri and Other States resolved to complete an *Agenda,* a Book of Rites and Liturgy as a handbook for pastoral care. The English Synod, anticipating union with the German Missouri Synod, intended this Agenda in the English language to be used by pastors of both synods.[84] Though this volume was not completed at the time of the May 1911 union, its contents were incorporated into the 1927 *Agenda* of the (German) Evangelical Lutheran Synod of Missouri, Ohio, and Other States.

The English Missouri Synod's Convention of 1897 "was noteworthy also for another reason. With the one thought of seeking the good of the church at large, the young and rapidly expanding English Synod deemed it advisable again to consider a closer union with the German Synod."[85]

The German Synod, officially and through such far-seeing men as Walther, Janzow, Guenther, Graebner, and Crull, gave the young English Synod encouragement and support. But there was strong opposition to the establishment of English congregations in many places where German churches were located. This opposition often took the form of official protests and necessitated repeated peace-disturbing intersynodical investigations.[86]

In the late 1890s, *Die Deutsche Evangelisch-Lutherische Synode von Missouri, Ohio, und andern Staaten* was still seeking to preserve German language, culture, and parochial schools. Many pastors in the German Missouri Synod saw the use of English as a threat to preservation of pure doctrine and practice: "The language battle was waged with greatest vigor at the parochial school level. With genuine reluctance, congregations permitted the use of English in instruction."[87] Nevertheless the 1897 English Missouri Synod's Convention still requested that it be allowed to become an English District of the German Synod.

A vote was taken at the 1899 Convention of the English Evangelical Lutheran Synod of Missouri and Other States, held at St. Mark's English Evangelical Lutheran Church, Detroit, Rev. D.H. Steffens serving as pastor. The vote at the Convention was 16 to 8 in favor of requesting union with the German Missouri Synod.[88] Opposition to union within the English Synod by a third of the voting delegates is notable. Again, though, the German Missouri Synod did not respond.

Six years later in 1905, at the Eighth Convention of the English Missouri Synod, held at Grace Evangelical Lutheran Church in St. Louis where Dr. Martin S. Sommer served as pastor, the Convention received a reply from the German Missouri Synod. A joint committee of the two synods received cordial greetings from the German Synod. The German Synod still insisted on its constitution requiring the use of the German language for the meetings of the General Synod, but it would entertain ways to receive into its membership the English-speaking congregations, pastors, and teachers of the English Synod. Both synods were seeking ways to remove barriers and be accommodating without requiring the disbanding of the English Synod and amalgamation of its congregations into the districts of the German Synod. The District also wanted assurance that St. John's College, English-speaking and co-educational, would be received with full financial support of the German Synod.[89]

The English Missouri Synod adopted the report of the joint committee, chaired by Pastor Dallmann, with Rev. H.P. Eckhardt serving as secretary. The report was signed by the representatives of both synods. Another attempt at union had been made. This effort, though, was not lost. Like a good wine in aging, it took time for the union to occur. Meanwhile, the people of the German Missouri Synod were, generation by generation, being assimilated into the American culture, including the use of English as the *lingua franca*.

Eckhardt reported that at the 11th Convention of the English Missouri Synod four years later in 1909, held at the church where he served as pastor, Grace Evangelical Lutheran Church in Cleveland, the following resolutions were adopted calling for a still closer union with the German Missouri Synod:

1. English publications be turned over to the German Synod, but with such publications having a majority of members of the English Synod and that the Editor be from the English Missouri Synod;

2. *The Lutheran Witness* be made the official English publication of the whole (German and English) Synod, with its Editor from and chosen by the English District of the Synod [note the use of "English District"];

3. When the whole Synod would meet, the English language be allowed for usage and with at least a synopsis of the Minutes being read and printed in English;

4. The Mission Board of the "English District" be permitted to start new missions wherever it deemed necessary while respecting the rights of parishes (church membership) and exercising Christian love;

5. Congregations that purely used and spoke English in the whole Synod become part of the English District, however allowing for congregations with special reasons to make their own choices concerning district membership;

6. Concordia College, Conover, North Carolina, be transferred to the General (German) Missouri Synod [St. John's, Winfield, Kansas, having already been transferred]; and

7. The English District be given the right to meet in convention as often as it would choose.[90]

This was approved by the English Missouri Synod in the 1909 Convention (noted later).

Coupled with these were added resolves as to whether congregations of the English Missouri Synod favor organic union and whether that be by an English District within the German Missouri Synod or amalgamation (disbanding the English Synod and having its congregations become members of the geographic districts of the German Synod).[91] The matter of amalgamation was troubling for some within the English Missouri Synod. Among them was Rev. Arthur Theobald Bonnet (1874-1917), who was ordained in Zanesville, Ohio in 1898 and served English Synod and English District churches (Redeemer Evangelical Lutheran Church, Tonawanda, New York; a mission congregation in South Sodus, New York; and Grace Evangelical Lutheran Church, Strasburg, Illinois), dying at age 42 during the 1917 Influenza Epidemic, while serving faithfully in the line of pastoral duty.[92] Rev. Eugene Nissen, in a self-published book of family history, *The Bonnets from Strasburg*, writes:

> In 1910, Arthur T. Bonnet and other pastors of the Southwestern Conference of the English Synod met in Gravelton, Missouri, to discuss membership in the German Evangelical Lutheran Synod of Missouri, Ohio, and Other States... Arthur T. Bonnet strongly opposed any organic merger, setting forth his reasons in a 1910 issue of *"The Lutheran Witness"*:

> There is no need of such a union as is proposed, because we are an independent synod; and if activities, growth, and success in reaching the unchurched are a proof of anything, they tell us that our independence has been no drawback, but a distinctive, positive blessing for the Lutheran Church. We have demonstrated that it is possible to have our fathers' faith in our children's language. Therefore it is wise to let well enough alone. Meddle not with those given to change...

> A possible reason for a closer synodical union would be that we could do more and better work than by remaining independent. This must first be proven...

> It may also be urged that closer union would work for a reduction in expenses for our Synod [the English Missouri Synod] ... The members of our Synod are fully able to meet all their obligations...

> Finally, let us be more independent and educate our own boys for our own ministry. It is a poor showing of independence to let others do for us what we are fully about to do ourselves [i.e., sending English Missouri Synod's young men, in view of the Synod's ownership of two colleges, Concordia College, Conover,

North Carolina, and St. John's College, Winfield, Kansas, to the German Missouri Synod's Concordia Seminary]. God has surely blessed us with men wise enough, and with means sufficient, to give our boys the necessary theological training. If we cannot for the present maintain a theoretical school, then let it be a practical seminary! But it should be our own. Let us use what we have and go ahead as an independent synod.

Bonnet's view did not prevail, and in May of 1911 the English Synod of Missouri voted to join the German Missouri Synod as a non-geographical synodical district... Pastor Bonnet exchanged his deep loyalty to The English Synod for membership in the LCMS. Instead of being known as one of the founders of the non-geographical English District of the Missouri Synod, he might better be known as one of the reluctant founders of the LCMS non-geographic English District.[93]

The Climactic Convention of May 1911

The question of how these two Synods would relate to each other finally culminated in the historic union of the English Evangelical Lutheran Synod of Missouri and Others States and *Die Deutsche Evangelisch-Lutherische Synode von Missouri, Ohio, und andern Staaten*. The English Missouri Synod's convention was May 10-16, 1911, at Evangelical Lutheran Church of Our Redeemer in St. Louis, Rev. Louis B. Buchheimer, pastor. The German Missouri Synod's convention was less than a mile away, also May 1911, at Holy Cross Evangelical Lutheran Church in St. Louis.

However, prior to the conferences and to the "union," many significant "...changes had occurred that altered the German Missouri Synod over the twenty-four-year period between 1887 and 1911... Not the least of these changes was that the original (German Missouri Synod) pastors, who were all born in Germany, would gradually yield leadership to a new generation of pastors who spoke German but were born in the United States and Canada and had begun speaking English. These 1.5 and second generation pastors and their flocks began to think of the United States and Canada as their new home. This was part of the acculturation process of Germans assimilating into an American culture, which has always been more of a 'tossed salad' than a 'melting pot.'"[94] [These important insights were provided by Dr. Cameron Mackenzie at the May 2011 English District Professional Church Workers Conference.]

The "Wedding Day," as some termed it, was May 15. However, there was some "back history." On May 9, the day preceding the May 10 start of the last (12th) Convention of the English Evangelical Lutheran Synod of Missouri and Other States, and with Anheuser-Busch and German beer gardens doing a "land office business,"[95] an English Missouri Synod preliminary committee met to shape the union plans. The preliminary committee's work was based on a still earlier meeting of a joint committee of English and German Missouri Synod men, including Revs. Eckhardt, Dallmann, and Romoser, in Washington, D.C. That "joint committee" had worked on property appraisals and "…planning the prerequisites and proprieties for union with a synod 36 times its size."[96] Their work was based on the seven-point agreement approved at the 1909 English Missouri Synod Convention. The vote on the "Cleveland Articles of Union" at that 1909 Convention was as follows:

> 30 voted "Yes" for District union
> 3½ voted "Yes" for amalgamation
> 11½ voted "no"
> 8 non-voting.[97]

Those on the preliminary committee who met on May 9, 1911, were Revs. Eckhardt, Dallmann, Romoser, and Buchheimer, as well as other pastors and laity. The English Missouri Synod's preliminary committee revealed from the previous convention what was then reported to the 1911 English Missouri Convention. There is no explanation given for the "half" votes, which could occur when a pastoral delegate and a lay delegate were from the same congregation and voted differently. But perhaps no explanation is necessary. Simply put, the English Missouri Synod rejected the idea of amalgamation in decided favor of union with the German Missouri Synod as a distinct English District. And, there were those who feared that the German Missouri Synod might in time try to do away with a distinct, non-geographic English District!

Rev. Dr. H.P. Eckhardt, the fourth and last president of the English Missouri Synod and first president of the English District of the German Missouri Synod, gives extensive detail as to the events of that historic week in his beloved book, *The English District: A Historical Sketch*. Here are the highlights, with this author's inserts:

> The (vast) majority of the congregations [of the English Missouri Synod] had voted in favor of joining as a District. The die was cast. And this decision was at once communicated to the German Synod in session at the nearby Holy Cross Church. [An editorial note is here necessary: The German Missouri Synod, while hoping that eventual amalgamation of congregations into geographic districts might occur, resolved to accept the proposed conditions of the English Missouri Synod that it be a non-geographic District.]

> The union between the two synods was formally consummated on Monday, May 15. The English Synod marched in a body to Holy Cross Church, where the German Synod was in session, and was received at the door by a special committee, which escorted them to seats of honor in the front of the church. I quote from the minutes: "The words spoken on that occasion will never be forgotten by those who were fortunate to be present on that memorable afternoon. The Spirit of God moved us deeply. We all felt the importance of what was transpiring."

> Said President Eckhardt: "Mr. President [Rev. Dr. Johann Friedrich Pfotenhauer, 1859-1939, president of the German Missouri Synod in 1911], I have the honor and pleasure officially to announce the final decision of our Synod as being favorable to District union. And we have come here in a body to ratify in this general meeting the common resolutions of both sides."

> "Such has been the spirit that has manifested itself in our deliberations and yours that we are convinced it was none other than the Holy Spirit of God who ruled and led both bodies... It is significant that this union is being consummated in the city of St. Louis, Mo. For it was in this place that our fathers wrote the early chapters of your venerable German Synod's history. It is in this city, twenty-three years ago, that our English Synod was organized and its opening chapter written. It is this same place that this new chapter is now being written, telling of the union of the two Missouri bodies. May our God in heaven close this chapter with an approving Amen! And we add to it the old motto of

Missouri: *'Soli Deo Gloria!'* [The last two sentences of Dr. Eckhardt's speech have often been quoted. Eckhardt was then followed by lengthy and salient words of Rev. Dr. Frederic Kuegele, the first president of the English Missouri Synod (1888-1899), referring to English Missouri as "our American Lutheran Zion." Kuegele also called the English District in his speech as "The English *Mission* (*emphasis added*) District of the German Evangelical Lutheran Synod of Missouri," and, as an older, veteran pastor, greeted that day of union with great joy.]

The venerable president of the German Synod, the Rev. F. Pfotenhauer, then spoke the following words in German: "This day is a day of great joy for the English and German Missouri Synods, not in this respect that we today for the first time greet each other and sit together as brethren. We have always been brethren, children of one Church. But in this respect is this day a day of great joy, that from today on we would walk together, hand in hand, the way which we regard as most advantageous for the work of our dear Church in this glorious land which is our and our children's earthly fatherland. Now, let us give all glory to Him to whom alone it is due and unite in the singing of the *Te Deum*." ...Thus the long prayed and hoped for union of the two bodies had become an actuality.[98]

Eckhardt's *The English District: A Historical Sketch* contains an English Synod Roll Call in 1911 "at the time of District." History aficionados can consult his volume for a list of the names of pastors (in alphabetical order), congregations, and number of members, and teachers, professors, and lay delegates.[99] One may note pastors serving two or more congregations, whether in North Carolina, Virginia, Missouri, Minnesota, or Oklahoma. Over 70 churches were in the 1911 roll call, representing 17,147 members. Dr. Eckhardt acknowledged a discrepancy in terms of the synodical tabulations in the Statistical Yearbook for 1911, which listed for the English District 64 pastors (serving congregations), 83 congregations, 16,311 communicant members, and 64 Sunday schools with an enrollment of 10,133 students.[100]

Pastors counted among this roll call and their places of service in 1911 included the following:

Arthur T. Bonnet (Strasburg, IL)
William Dallmann (Milwaukee, WI)
John Adam Detzer (Cleveland, OH)
Henry P. Eckhardt (Jersey City, NJ),
George C. Franke (New Orleans, LA),
John H.C. Fritz (Brooklyn, NY),
J.R. Graebner, O.C. Kreinheder (St. Paul, MN),
O.W. Kreinheder (Lancaster, PA),
Frederic Kuegele (Koiner's, Crimora, VA),
A.C. Meyer (Springdale, AR),
H. Prange (Minneapolis, MN),
F.C.G. Schumm (New York City, NY),
Martin Sommer (St. Louis, MO),
Martin Walker (Buffalo, NY)
J. Franklin Yount (Akron, OH).[101]

From this group, later in the history of the English District, the Revs.
J.A. Detzer, O.C. Kreinheder, M. Sommer, and M. Walker would each
serve as president of the English District, and Rev. J. F. Yount would serve
a 50-year pastorate at Concordia Evangelical Lutheran Church in Akron,
OH. The largest of these churches in terms of baptized and communicant
members were:

First English, New Orleans, with 2,350 and 1,950
Grace, Cleveland, with 1,053 and 612
Grace, St. Louis, with 1,700 and 1,363
Redeemer, Buffalo, with 800 and 450.

Many of the oldest congregations of the English Missouri Synod in
time either transferred to a geographic district, were part of the formation
of the Southeastern District, disbanded, merged with other congregations,
or left the LCMS in the 1970s. The current ten remaining English District
congregations of the old English Missouri Synod are also in that list. They
are usually noted in each District Convention *Workbook* of the English
District-LCMS and are the following:

	Date Founded	Entered English Synod
St. Mark, Sheboygan, WI	1890	1911
Christ English, Chicago, IL	1891	1895

Calvary, Buffalo, *now Amherst*, NY	1891	1893
Redeemer, Fort Wayne, IN	1892	1893
Redeemer, North Tonawanda, NY	1897	1899
Calvary, Harrisburg, *now Mechanicsburg*, PA	1899	1899
Redeemer, Oakmont, PA	1900	1907
Mt. Calvary, Lancaster, *now Lititz*, PA	1904	1907
Concordia. Akron, OH	1904	1907
Grace, Elyria, OH	1907	1909.[102]

Following the "union," the English Missouri Synod held one more day of meeting to adopt a resolution that the English Synod was now the English District of the German Evangelical Lutheran Synod of Missouri, Ohio, and Other States, thus writing a "...*finis* to the history of the English Synod of Missouri as a separate and independent body."[103] But a *finis* was not a *tetelestai* ("it is finished"), as later wags would quip in regard to the English District. A new beginning of blessed work of renewed energy would define the English District in the century to come.[104]

"The English Lutheran Synod of Missouri was neither the product of human machinations nor the fruit of wise or unwise church policy. It was the general course of events in the Church that brought this Synod into existence. In its history is traced the hand of the Chief Shepherd and Bishop of His Church on earth who sees the future even as the past and who, as the wise Masterbuilder, makes provision for the good of the Church in advance of the future."

> —The Rev. Dr. Frederic Kuegele, first president, English Missouri Synod (1899) [105]

"...The grave mistake of 1887 was now happily rectified."

> —The Rev. Dr. William Dallmann, second president, English Missouri Synod (written in his 1922 article in Ebenezer.) [106]

The last convention of the English Synod, assembled in the Church of Our Redeemer, St. Louis, MO., May 10-16, 1911

Our Redeemer, St. Louis, MO.

Holy Cross, St. Louis, MO.

Excursus: The Rev. Dr. H.P. (Henry Philip) Eckhardt (January 31, 1866—May 11, 1949)

President Henry (sometimes called Harry) P. Eckhardt served as the veritable English District "George Washington," a consummate leader and churchman. He bridged the "union" of the English Evangelical Lutheran Synod of Missouri and Other States with *Die Deutsche Evangelisch-Lutherische Synode von Missouri, Ohio, und andern Staaten.*

Eckhardt served as president of the English Missouri Synod and English District president, 1905-1912, even while continuing to serve as a parish pastor. His picture, along with those of the other twenty presidents and Bishop/Presidents of the English Synod and District, is in the hallway that connects the bishop's study with the main entrance of the English District office in Farmington, Michigan. It is significant that President Eckhardt's picture appears only once. However, it was placed as the very last of the top four pictures of the men who served as president and were true "bishops" of the old English Missouri Synod: Drs. Kuegele, Dallmann, Meyer, and Eckhardt. Eckhardt was highly revered in the English District-LCMS. A skilled writer, he was also a wise leader who spoke kindly of others, even those who took different positions than he.

Eckhardt was born in Reisterstown, Baltimore County, Maryland and graduated from Concordia Seminary, St. Louis, in 1889. Though American-born, he was fluent in both German and English. He served as pastor of Grace and Redeemer Evangelical Lutheran Churches in Cleveland, Ohio (1889-1909). His other pastorates included Grace, Jersey City, New Jersey (1909-1911), and St. Andrew's, Pittsburgh, Pennsylvania (1911-1942). Each of these churches was part of the "Roll Call" of English Missouri Synod congregations in 1911. Eckhardt served as the last (fourth) president of the English Missouri Synod (1905-1911) and as the first president of the English District of the German Missouri

Synod (1911-1912) and as fourth vice president of the Missouri Synod (1917-1926). He served as president of the American Lutheran Publication Board (ALPB) when it was based in Pittsburgh.

Dr. Eckhardt became an authority in the history of the English Missouri Synod and of the Henkel family. He authored several tracts and two books, *Confirmation Booklet* and the one most frequently cited, *The English District: A Historical Sketch*. While serving as senior pastor at St. Andrew Evangelical Lutheran Church in the Shadyside neighborhood, the "mother English District church" in Pittsburgh, Eckhardt ordained and installed his former vicar (1938-1939), Rev. George W. Bornemann, as pastor *locum tenens* at Redeemer, Oakmont, Pennsylvania in May 1941. Dr. Bornemann eventually became English District president/bishop in 1976.

CHAPTER 7
A Period of Rapid Growth and Change (1911—1941)

ONE MAY WONDER what it was like in the week following the union of the English Missouri Synod and the German Missouri Synod brethren who were present in St. Louis as the English District of the German Evangelical Lutheran Synod of Missouri, Ohio, and Other States was born on May 15, 1911. A historical milestone had been reached, but what lay ahead was not altogether certain. Now there was a non-geographical district in the Missouri Synod helping the church body through a language and cultural transition. Dr. Martin W. Mueller, author of an English District 75th Anniversary publication called *"Amazing Comeback,"* adds these reflective words of perspective:

> Basically the Lutherans of German descent saw their mission as ministering to German Lutherans in their communities and preserving sound biblical and confessional Lutheranism...

> Lutherans of the English Synod – also bent on preserving genuine Lutheranism – were committed to sharing the Gospel with English-speaking children, youth, and adults.

> English Lutherans had a "passion for souls," as missionizing was described by Rev. Dr. John Fritz... When the English Lutherans...became a district of what is now The Lutheran Church—Missouri Synod, they brought with them a zeal to proclaim the faith of the fathers in the language of the children plus a readiness and eagerness to become, as St. Paul puts it in 1 Corinthians 9:22, "all things to all men so that by all possible means I might save some."

> After the English Lutherans were officially accepted as a district, their President, Rev. H.P. Eckhardt, declared that the Holy Spirit had "ruled and led both bodies." "We are contending," he added, "for the same sound Lutheranism for which he (Dr. Walther) unflinchingly stood."

> Not long after May 15, 1911, when World War I erupted, resulting in intense hatred for everything German in many communities of the nation [the United States, and Canada] and

forcing the German [Missouri] Lutheran Synod to rearrange its language and cultural priorities, it became clear that the Lord of the Church had paved the way for a major transition through the English District. Its labors and struggles in the Lord were not in vain.[107]

Pastor Mueller's summary captures well what became a huge paradigm shift of language and culture and yet preservation of doctrine and practice in the wider church body, the (German) Evangelical-Lutheran Synod of Missouri, Ohio, and Other States and in the new English District. Shortly before the entrance of the United States of American into the First World War in late 1917, the Missouri Synod dropped the word "German" from its title and changed the title from German to English. Yet there were obvious tensions within the church body. The Missouri Synod continued to use German. Indeed, many congregations continued to use German up to, during, and a few following World War II (1939-1945; United States entry in December 1941). However, many congregations began adapting, offering Divine Services in German and English.

Dr. Eckhardt's volume contains an Appendix about languages used by LCMS congregations in worship services, compiled by the Rev. R. Jesse, an English District pastor. Pastor Jesse's data, in selective years, is interesting:

Languages Used In Services

Year	Percent of English used in English District	Percent of English used in Synod
1919	100%	38%
1920	100%	40%
1924	99%	49%
1925	99%	52%
1930	99%	58%
1931	99%	59%
1932	99%	61%
1938	99%	69%
1939	99%	71%
1940	99%	72%
1941	99%	75%
1942	99%	82%[108]

With the rapid change in language during the continued acculturation process in the Missouri Synod, there was an increasing number of congregations, baptized and communicant membership, and Sunday schools. The English District was a prime vanguard in the Missouri Synod during this thirty-year period of growth and Christian outreach. However, tensions did exist, particularly in some of the largest cities in the United States and from the large Western District of the Evangelical Lutheran Synod of Missouri, Ohio, and Other States. The Western District in the early 1920's had congregations in Missouri, Tennessee, Kentucky, and Arkansas. It had spawned new districts prior to 1923: Illinois (1875); Iowa (1879); Nebraska (1882); Southern (1882); California-Oregon (1887); and Kansas (1888).

In 1923, the Western District submitted a resolution from its president and circuit visitors calling for the dissolution of the English District and for the congregations to be amalgamated into the various geographic districts where those congregations existed.

The following excerpt from *The English District: A Historical Sketch*, notes as follows:

> Synod resolved: "Since all Districts of Synod are becoming more and more English in their work, we do not deem it wise to reject said memorial outright, but believe this proposal should come from the English District and therefore ask it kindly to discuss the matter.[109]

This notation is important. In the several decades that followed, questions arose in the LCMS regarding whether the English District should continue or be amalgamated. But the Synod's 1923 resolution indicated that the desire or need to dissolve the English District should come at the prompting and will of the English District. Times and circumstances may dictate otherwise. But for the moment in 1923 and 1924, this matter took a turn away from amalgamation as the following states:

> Acting upon this request, the English District in 1924 appointed a committee to consider amalgamation. Upon its recommendation the District at its convention in 1925 adopted the following resolution: "After mature and serious study of the

question of a dissolution of our District and amalgamation of our congregations with other Districts of the General Body (of the Missouri Synod), we beg leave respectfully to reply that we cannot find in the premises a warrant for a proposal on our part for amalgamation." (Reported to General Body in 1926.)[110]

This same thing occurred again in 1932 and 1933 at the General Synod Convention and the subsequent English District Convention with the same results.[111] The English District wanted to and continued to maintain its unique identity as a district in Synod that was still in the vanguard of mission-planting and outreach. Coupled with the English District's approved resolution was a warning that some congregations would leave the larger Synod and form an independent church body if congregational amalgamation and English District dissolution were forced upon the District. Supporting the English District's separate existence as a district within Synod was Dr. Theodore Graebner, Professor at Concordia Seminary, St. Louis. He noted that the English District was still leading the way in a somewhat inward-bred Missouri Synod in terms of "missionary policy" and an example for the rest of the Synod.[112]

While the above discussion may seem a matter of historical curiosity, the English District understood itself as a unique blend of pastors and congregations from across North America with a strong missional zeal (some would say, DNA), an ardent desire to lead the lost to Christ, whether the new immigrant or the isolated city dweller or the religious "seeker." "Listed in the 1919 Convention Proceedings (of the English District) were 96 congregations and 20 preaching stations served by 87 pastors with 27,628 communicants, a 9 percent increase over 1918."[113] Seven of those preaching stations were in West Virginia, Virginia, and North Carolina, intensifying mission starts in the growing southeast of the United States.[114] These numbers do not conform with those of Pastor Jesse listed in Dr. Eckhardt's *The English District: A Historical Sketch*, but they are close. District and Synod numeric accountings often differed slightly, depending on "cut-off" dates and other factors such as listing preaching stations and congregations where a pastor might be a member of the District but the congregation was independent or in the process of transferring to a geographic district.

The latter did indeed happen, where congregations elected to transfer from the new English District to the geographic district of Synod. Hence, using Pastor Jesse's compilations, the English District did see small decreases in the number of congregations in the years 1912 (from 1911) and 1914. However, there then followed a rapid increase in the number of congregations. In 1916, 106 congregations were listed; by 1922 - 129; by 1925 - 149; by 1929 - 163; by 1933 - 182; by 1938 - 185. With the birth of the Southeastern District involving congregations of the English District, there was a dip to 153 congregations in 1939. The number of congregations would rise again to 173 by 1943. The English District was planting preaching stations and new congregations, even while transferring numerous congregations to geographic districts. The District was also moving away from an agrarian culture to an urban culture within the cities teeming with immigrants who wanted to embrace the American dream of a new life in North America. The English District was front and center in embracing these immigrant populations.

There were lingering rivalries in the Evangelical Lutheran Synod of Missouri, Ohio, and Other States and in the constituent synods of the Evangelical Lutheran Synodical Conference of North America. By the 1920s, the Synodical Conference consisted primarily of synods of German ethnic background, with smaller representations of Finnish and Slovak synods aligned with the Missouri Synod. This "rivalry" continued into the 1940s. While the confessional Lutherans were becoming more Americanized, the English District of the Missouri Synod was a bit suspect. Its aggressive evangelistic and mission-planting zeal produced some tensions.

Not all locales felt this tension. Some were more willing to simply witness the expansion of Christ's Kingdom of Grace.[115] But tension was high when areas of urban English-speaking pastors were involved in the planting of new English District churches. These included cities like Lincoln, Nebraska (Redeemer Evangelical Lutheran Church - 1917); Chicago (Bethesda Evangelical Lutheran Church & School - 1920; Ephphatha Evangelical Lutheran Church for the Deaf - 1920; Grace English Evangelical Lutheran Church & School - 1920; St. John the Divine Evangelical Lutheran Church - 1928; and Hope Evangelical Lutheran Church - 1940); Roberts Park Evangelical Lutheran Church [later Savior Divine Lutheran Church], Palos Park, Illinois - 1940); San

Diego (Grace Evangelical Lutheran Church - 1912 and Faith Evangelical Lutheran Church - 1931); San Francisco (Christ Evangelical Lutheran Church - 1912); Milwaukee (Sherman Park Evangelical Lutheran Church - 1923); Los Angeles (Highland Park Evangelical Lutheran Church - 1922 and Eagle Rock Lutheran Church - 1925); and Indianapolis, Indiana (Our Redeemer Evangelical Lutheran Church - 1920). In 1922, the English District even expanded to Missoula, Montana, eventually planting three congregations in that state.

In his book, *My Life*, Rev. William Dallmann anecdotally affirms how transfers and releases from German-speaking Missouri churches were sometimes withheld. Those who wanted a transfer were denied that request, even though they better understood English than German. Dallmann threatened to take them in by profession of faith if their release or transfer was not granted. He noted: "A churchless man wished to join; everything was done to keep him away from English. A brother (pastor) said he would *liefer* (rather) have a General Council man than an English Missourian in his town."[116] This occurred when Dallmann was serving an English District parish in Milwaukee.

Tensions were further exacerbated in the 1930s and1940s in locales such as in Arizona. By the late 1930s, a "love-hate" relationship existed between some Missouri and Wisconsin pastors and congregations, perhaps due to Missouri's willingness in the Synodical Conference to accept the invitation of the United Lutheran Church in America (1918) and the American Lutheran Church (1930) to enter into discussions for closer relationships within North American Lutheranism. That was something abhorrent to the Wisconsin Evangelical Lutheran Synod (WELS) and the Evangelical Lutheran Synod (ELS) within the Evangelical Lutheran Synodical Conference of North America, dominated by the Missouri Synod. Through a comity agreement in the Synodical Conference decades earlier, California mission planting was given to the Missouri Synod and Arizona mission planting was given to the Wisconsin Synod.[117] Nevertheless, the English District of the Missouri Synod began planting new missions in Arizona in the 1940s as Missouri Synod folk moved into that state and were unwilling to be part of Wisconsin Synod congregations in Phoenix and Tucson.

During the era of the 1910s-1940s, the English District had comparatively few Christian day schools (parochial schools). The geographic districts of the Missouri Synod, often with older congregations that had schools and sought to preserve German language, culture, and faith, had far greater numbers of Lutheran schools. Preschools and child care centers would not become an educational endeavor on the part of congregations and districts until the 1970s and onward. Child care centers were sometimes a part of the Christian day schools, but often later they were an independent part of a parochial school or an altogether new ministry of a given congregation.

The most noteworthy movement of congregations out of the English District was a result of the English District's mission work in the Southeastern United States. With congregations located in Washington, D.C., Maryland, Virginia, North Carolina, South Carolina, and the Georgia District initially ceded 32 congregations (38 according to Rev. R. Jesse's appended data, one of which was in Georgia) to form the new Southeastern District in 1939. Some Eastern District congregations also became part of the newly formed district. By the time of Dr. Eckhardt's 1945 book, *The English District: A Historical Sketch*, 82 congregations were released. These included:

3	which were "discontinued" (disbanded)
2	which joined to a German-speaking Lutheran church
1	unaccounted for
1	which returned to the Swedish Augustana Synod, the rest (75) to geographic districts of the (German) Evangelical Lutheran Synod of Missouri, Ohio, and Other States.

These congregations were in the states of Arkansas, California, Georgia, Illinois, Kansas, Massachusetts, Michigan, Minnesota, Mississippi, Missouri, Nebraska, New Jersey, New York, Ohio, Pennsylvania, Wisconsin, Maryland, North Carolina, South Carolina, Virginia, and Washington, D.C. Besides the Southeastern District, which received the largest plurality (38) of those 82 congregations, other receiving districts were the following: Atlantic (10), Western (7), Southern California (4), Kansas (3), Central (2), Eastern (2), Michigan (2), South Wisconsin (2), Northern Illinois (1), Minnesota (1), California & Nevada (1), and Southern (1). This was according to statistics gathered by Pastor

Jesse as of 1944; some of these districts have changed names or been reconfigured.

Churches of note that became part of the geographic districts are listed below with the year released and communicant membership numbers in parentheses:

> Zion, Gravelton, MO (1933 - 129)
> Mount Olive, Milwaukee, WI (1940 - 615)
> Mount Olive, Minneapolis, MN (1945 - 893)
> First, Los Angeles, CA (1936 - 35)
> Culver City, Los Angeles, CA (1930 - 91)
> Highland Park, Los Angeles, CA (1943 - 199) [Highland Park would later rejoin the English District]
> Our Savior, Detroit, MI (1936 - 670);
> Grace, San Diego, CA (1945 - 637);
> Redeemer, St. Louis, MO (1940 - 1,230);
> Christ, Washington, D.C. (1939 - 308)
> Trinity Crimora, Koiner's Church, Waynesboro, VA (1939 - 176)
> Grace, New York City (1934 - 271)
> Trinity, New York City (1939 - 114)
> Emmanuel, Baltimore, MD (1939 - 805), the largest of seven Baltimore churches in the formation of the Southeastern District.

What peculiarly is missing from the list of releases is First English Evangelical Lutheran Church, New Orleans, which was part of the 1911 "English Synod" Roll Call and listed 1,950 members under Pastor G. Franke.[118] The simple answer: While not noted in English District archives, First English of New Orleans had been part of the English Missouri Synod through her long-termed pastor, the Rev. George Christian Franke (1861-1920). The Congregation's 50th Anniversary Booklet states: "…Until 1911, the pastor of First English held membership in the English Missouri Synod. When that became the English District of Synod, First English, through its pastor, became affiliated with the Southern District…"[119] The Congregation later moved from the city to the suburb of Metairie, LA, but in 1911, while still in New Orleans, joined the Southern (geographic) District at the time of the "union" of the English Missouri Synod with the German Missouri Synod. This may have been true with a few other congregations that were part of the English Missouri

Synod and left at the time of the "union" in order to amalgamate, which was an option open to them. But statistics this side of the Kingdom of Glory are and never will be perfect. Some things will remain unexplainable.

The English District experienced remarkable growth in the three decades up to the beginning of American involvement in World War II on the side of the Allies. Along with Canada and the United States, the focus on this external matter captured the will and determination of the people of both nations in a time of war.

Prior to the entrance into World War II and during the Great Depression, the Missouri Synod and the Synodical Conference were grappling with theological issues. These were inter-synodical theses formulated at Chicago, Illinois, after an earlier set of *Chicago Theses* (1913) and a later set called the *Minneapolis Theses* (1925) and again revised in St. Paul, Minnesota, in 1928. These theses were an attempt to resolve within North American Lutheranism issues over predestination and conversion. The latest revision of these theses was presented to the Missouri Synod in convention at Concordia College, River Forest, Illinois, in 1929 and rejected. A Missouri Synod committee and floor committee had first recommended that the *Chicago Theses* not be accepted in the form in which they were presented, and the Synod in Convention rejected these theses. But what came out of these efforts toward doctrinal resolution was a document important to LCMS history: *The Brief Statement.*

The *Brief Statement* came as a result of the rejection of the modified *Chicago Theses* by the Evangelical Lutheran Synod of Missouri, Ohio, and Other States in Convention in 1929. A Committee was appointed to formulate theses concerning the doctrines in controversy and to produce a document that would "...present the doctrines of Scripture and the Lutheran Confessions in the shortest and simplest manner."[120] This Committee was appointed by LCMS President Friedrich Pfotenhauer and included Dr. Franz Pieper, the former president of Concordia Seminary, and Professors F.S. Wenger, E.A. Meyer, L.A. Heerboth, and Theodore Engelder. This committee issued the *Brief Statement of the Doctrinal Position of the Evangelical Lutheran Synod of Missouri, Ohio, and Other States* in 1931, which was approved by the 1932 Synod Convention. The document covered key doctrines of the Christian faith as a basis for seeking unity of doctrine with other Lutheran bodies in North America.

Noteworthy is that none of those named to the "Brief Statement" Committee were from the English District. The members represented the "old guard" of German background in the German Missouri Synod. The Synod was considering possible pulpit and altar fellowship and possible unity with the "old" American Lutheran Church (ALC) of 1930, which was formed by the merger of the Joint Ohio, Iowa, Buffalo, and Texas Synods, largely of German background. At the Convention of 1938, the Missouri Synod actually did accept both the *Brief Statement* and the ALC *Declaration* "...as a basis for future union."[121] Though the ALC did accept the *Brief Statement*, other synods of the Evangelical Lutheran Synodical Conference of North America informed the Missouri Synod that there were still doctrinal concerns. Fellowship between the "old" ALC and the LCMS did not materialize. At issue were attitudes of the ALC toward the lodge, pulpit and altar fellowship with anti-scriptural church bodies, and other forms of unionism. The English District, as a district of the Missouri Synod, held to the same doctrinal positions of the Synod as a whole. But changes were slowly becoming manifest.

Excursus: The English Evangelical Lutheran Church of the Redeemer, St. Albans, Queens, New York (116-01 204th Street, St. Albans, NY)

One example of urban growth was in the New York City Borough of Queens. The English District Mission Board was jumping at opportunities to proclaim the saving Gospel of our Lord Jesus Christ, especially to immigrant populations coming to America's shores. In 1926, the English Evangelical Lutheran Church of the Redeemer was started as a new preaching station before there was a church building by a young pastor, fresh out of Concordia Seminary, St. Louis, and native to Buffalo, Rev. Claudius S. Kulow (1902–1962). He was installed by Rev. Erwin "King" Kurth, of the Evangelical Lutheran Church of Our Saviour in Brooklyn, known as "Covert Street," which began Redeemer as a mission plant (preaching station).[122]

Pastor Kulow powerfully exhibited the missionary character of the English District. He was a calling, house-going pastor and a dynamic preacher. He visited people in their homes, wearing out the soles of his shoes. He invited people in a winsome way to come to church. He faithfully catechized and confirmed adults and young people. Kulow spent his entire ministry in St. Albans (1927-1962), dying in office as a beloved pastor. The house of worship for Redeemer Church was built in 1929, with a small sanctuary for what became a large congregation in the 1940s and 1950s. The LCMS Statistical Yearbook for 1949 listed Redeemer Church as having 1,575 baptized members of which 980 were communicant members. The choir and chancel area was indeed small. Kulow's solution was simply to add more Divine Services on Sundays rather than build a larger structure on the small-sized property.

Redeemer Church was founded by people of German heritage, but already in the 1950s the Addisleigh Park section of St. Albans became the center of a significant demographic shift. A number of notable African Americans bought homes in the community. Among them were Ella Fitzgerald, Lena Horne, Joe Louis, Jackie Robinson, and Roy Campanella. By the 1960s, St. Albans had become a thriving African American community and, under Pastor Kulow, Redeemer became a church serving black and white men, women, and children.

After Kulow's sudden death, Redeemer experienced twin challenges. First, there was a succession of very brief pastorates under both white and black under-shepherds of Christ. Second, unscrupulous real estate practices and fear mongering led to significant "white flight." By 1981, Redeemer had fewer than 35 members worshiping each Sunday and required District support to call a seminary graduate. Rev. Larry Vogel was called as missionary-at-large with the hope that the congregation would survive. Thanks to several deeply committed members who had stayed the course during Redeemer's long decline, and by God's grace, Redeemer Congregation experienced growth under Pastor Vogel's leadership.

During the 1980s, Redeemer added nearly two hundred new members, declined further subsidies from the English District, called Pastor Vogel as pastor, and planted a new but short-lived mission congregation in Far Rockaway in Queens. Like his earliest predecessor, Pastor Claudius Kulow, Pastor Larry Vogel was able to reach into the community and inspire deeper faith and leadership through strong catechesis. He served the congregation until the end of 1990.

During the 1990s, Redeemer again experienced several long vacancies, short pastorates, and financial challenges. In recent years, however, Redeemer has again reached a measure of stability, thanks to the leadership of Rev. Steven Hicks. Pastor Hicks first helped at Redeemer on a part-time basis while an Atlantic District deacon and Lutheran school teacher at Martin Luther Lutheran High School in Queens. After his colloquy into the pastoral office, Pastor Hicks was called by the English Evangelical Lutheran Church of the Redeemer. An example of his deep commitment was his faithful service during the COVID-19 crisis (much of 2020), during which Redeemer lost three members and had numerous others sick and hospitalized with the novel coronavirus. For much of the crisis, New York City was the COVID epicenter within the United States.

One further historical footnote bears mentioning. Pastor Kulow was known as an evangelist and pre-eminent canvasser. However, he was a learned man who read a book per week. He also rescued a number of men who might otherwise have been lost to the Holy Ministry, having gone on a candidate status known as CRM (*candidatus reverendi ministerii*). Kulow had a way of rehabilitating and encouraging them, and giving them a status and place to serve in an assisting pastoral role.[123]

Excursus: Presidents and Bishop/Presidents of the English District, and Notably in the Early to Mid-20th Century

We would be remiss not to review the men who served as presidents or bishops/presidents of the English District, notably in the period from 1911 through the 1950s, and other leaders. Some served very short terms while being full-time pastors or professors. Synodical districts were not administratively top-heavy during those years, but neither were there many of the complications such as extensive call lists, law suits, and substantial ecclesiastical supervision, as well as regional conferences, and church worker health and care issues that began to increase in the 1960s and 1970s.

Presidents serving the English Missouri Synod were Reverend Doctors:

Frederick Kuegele	1888—1899
C.F. William Dallmann	1899—1901
Adolph W. Meyer	1901—1905
Henry P. Eckhardt	1905—1911

Presidents and Bishop/Presidents serving the English District-LCMS:

Henry P. Eckhardt	1911—1912
Martin S. Sommer	1912—1915
J.A. Detzer	1915—1918
O.C. Kreinheder	1918—1927
Guido Schuessler	1927—1936
Paul Lindemann	1936—1938
Martin F. Walker	1938—1945
Herman W. Bartels	1945—1951
Hugo Kleiner	1951—1963
Bertwin L. Frey	1963—1970
John H. Baumgaertner	1970—1974
Harold L. Hecht	1974—1976
Paul G. Barth	April 1976—June 1976*
George W. Bornemann	1976—1984
Donald F. Young	1984—1986
Roger D. Pittelko	1986—1997
David H. Ritt	1997—2006
David P. Stechholz	2006—2015
Jamison J. Hardy	2015—present.

*Dr. Barth was appointed English District president by LCMS President J.A.O. Preus following the Synod president's removal of Dr. Harold Hecht.

Some Missouri Synod leaders in the English District during that 30-year period were less well known, yet they contributed to the life of Christ's Church in unique ways. Dr. Martin Samuel Sommer (1869-1949), was professor of homiletics at Concordia Seminary, St. Louis (1920-1947). He also was a frequent contributor of articles and book reviews in *Concordia Theological Monthly*, served a long tenure as co-editor of *The Lutheran Witness* (1914-1949) and wrote a popular book, *Prayers*.[124] Sommer was the pastor of the largest congregation that stayed with the English District in 1911 at the time of the union of the English Missouri Synod into the German Missouri Synod: Grace Evangelical Lutheran Church in St. Louis, which had 1,363 members.

Above: The English District Office east hallway displays pictures of the Presidents (Bishop/Presidents) of the English Missouri Conference/Synod (1888-1911) and English District-LCMS (1911-present). Below, center section: the top four being English Synod Presidents Kuegele, Dallmann, Meyer, and Eckhardt, and the bottom four being English District Presidents Schuessler, Lindemann, Walker, and Barthels.

Drs. Eckhardt and Kreinheder were noted previously. However, both O.C. Kreinheder and his predecessor as president, J.A. Detzer, had terms that spanned the huge "Spanish Flu" epidemic of 1917-1918. Dr. Guido Schuessler served during that time as English District president, 1927-1936. This was the era of the stock market crash and the Great Depression that financially decimated the United States and many countries throughout the world and when unemployment was at one of its highest points in history.[125] He was greatly disappointed in not being re-elected as District president, something not uncommon during the Great Depression era (1929-1940) as was seen in the defeat of U.S. President Herbert Hoover in 1932 by Franklin D. Roosevelt.[126] Dr. Martin Walker (1877-1967) served as the longtime pastor of Calvary Evangelical Lutheran Church, Buffalo [now Amherst], New York, and was District president (1938-1945) during the entire period of World War II. Canada and the United States experienced the greatest loss of life on foreign soils as military personnel fought for freedom and for the defeat of the totalitarian Axis Powers (Germany, Italy, and Japan), remembering that most members of LCMS congregations had strong German roots. Walker co-authored a timely book, *Greater Love Hath No Man*, fitting during a period of personal and national sacrifice.

Three other names from this period during and between the World Wars also bear mentioning. The first is Rev. Louis Balthaser Buchheimer (1872-1953). He served as professor at the English Missouri Synod's Concordia College, Conover, North Carolina (1893-1896); pastor at various locations, including Redeemer Evangelical Lutheran Church, St. Louis; and vice president of the English District-LCMS (1918-1921). Buchheimer was the author of several sermonic books and other works.

The second is Dr. Paul George William Lindemann (1881-1938), who died in office at age 56 while president of the English District (1936-1938), like a later president, Rev. Donald Young, did in 1986. Lindemann was pastor of the Evangelical Lutheran Church of the Redeemer (1920-1936, St. Paul, Minnesota), having previously served English District congregations in Brooklyn, New York, and Jersey City, New Jersey. He was founder and editor of the magazine, *American Lutheran*, and he authored two books and several tracts.

A third is Rev. E.C. (Ernst Carl) Fackler (1879-1951), pastor of St. Andrew's, the second English District congregation in Detroit, serving from 1910 to 1951. He also served several years as president of the Detroit area LCMS Pastoral Conference and chairman of the board of Evangelical Lutheran Institute for the Deaf. Pastor E.C. Fackler was part of the 1911 English Missouri Synod roll-call on the day of the "union" (May 15) with the German Missouri Synod. Though the mother church of St. Andrew's,

St. Mark's, became much larger (2,150 members by 1919 and had a few distinguished pastors: Revs. J.A. Detzer, C.H. Ruesskamp, and "King" Kurth), St. Andrew's grew under Fackler and his son, Rev. William Fackler (retired and living in Pasadena, California). E.C. Fackler and his congregation served in planting new English District congregations in Detroit. His grandson serves today as a notable Lutheran layman and chairs the board of directors of Glen Eden Lutheran Memorial Park, Livonia, Michigan. E.C. Fackler is buried in the Pastor's Point section of that cemetery.

CHAPTER 8
Symbol of the English District:
The Double-trunked Sycamore Tree

THE FIRST TWO pages of Dr. Henry Philip Eckhardt's book, *The English District: A Historical Sketch*, bear the image of a double-trunked sycamore tree. He then devotes the first page of writing to the symbol or seal of the English District. When it first came into usage, it was "unofficial," as Eckhardt noted. It became the esteemed and recognized symbol of the English District of The Lutheran Church—Missouri Synod. Dr. Eckhardt writes:

When our present Concordia (Theological) Seminary, St. Louis, was erected [in 1925 and dedicated in 1927], the dining halls were dedicated to the history of the Lutheran church. In the south wing, known as Koburg Hall, the ornamental stone and glass, particularly the painted glass medallions, are related to the history of Christianity outside of the United States. In the north dining hall, called Wartburg Hall, the ornamentation in carved stone and window medallions is enlivened with symbolism bearing upon the work of the Lutheran church in the United States. In keeping with the general plan we find that in the long rows of windows on each side each window presents the seal of a District of the Missouri Synod. In the instances of Districts whose seal is not related to their history, the Committee on Emblems and Inscriptions developed an appropriate seal for its purpose. The English District seal, taken from the original drawing, is presented above. As indicated, this is not the official seal of our District, but one developed and used by the Committee on Emblems and Inscriptions.[127]

But why the tree? Dr. Martin Mueller raised that question in his 1986 booklet for the English District's 75th anniversary, and he correctly notes that it was no ordinary tree but a sycamore tree, recalling the biblical story of our Lord Jesus and Zacchaeus, the Jericho tax collector (Luke 19). Zacchaeus wanted to see our Lord, so he climbed up in a sycamore (or sycamore-fig tree), native to both Israel/Palestine and the state of Missouri. While different presidents and bishop/presidents of the English District over the decades have put slightly different spins on explanation of the District's beloved symbol, Mueller's accurate description notes:

> The stout single trunk of the tree represents the common biblical and Lutheran (confessional) origin from which each of the double trunks sprang – the German Lutheran Synod (now the LCMS) and the English Lutheran Synod (now the English District, LCMS).
>
> Among the sprawling roots of the tree are Saxon and Prussian Lutheran immigrants as well as Lutherans from other church bodies in America, such as the Henkels of the Tennessee Synod.[128]

Common Roots - *Die Deutsche Evangelisch-Lutherische Synode von Missouri, Ohio, und andern Staaten* began in April 1847, as a small Midwestern synod of German immigrants with a majority from the Franconian mission-sending of Rev. Wilhelm Loehe in Neuendettelsau and the Saxons of Missouri under the leadership of Dr. C.F.W. Walther. But within the space of twenty years, these early German Missourians were joined by other confessional German-speaking Lutherans in North America, especially those coming out of Prussia and the Buffalo Synod. In other words, the Missouri Synod was not monolithic in its early years. Likewise, the English Missouri Synod, when it began in 1872 as a very small conference of English-speaking confessional Lutherans, had roots in the Tennessee Synod of the Henkels and others, who were quickly aligning with the German Missouri Synod, some pastors of which were educated at the German-speaking Concordia Seminary. It is fascinating to trace the roots of both synods, recognizing that the German Missouri Synod was vastly larger than the small but growing English Evangelical Lutheran Synod of Missouri and Other States.

The common roots indeed were solidly biblical and confessional. Both the English and German Missouri Synods, which Mueller calls the German and English Lutheran synods, held to a *quia* subscription of the Confessional writings of the Evangelical Lutheran Church in the *Book of*

Concord or *Concordia* (1580). Added to this were the writings of Dr. Martin Luther and other reformers and theologians of the era of Lutheran Orthodoxy. Included also were the *Agendae,* Lutheran hymnody, and liturgical heritage of the catholic Church in the Lutheran tradition. The agreement that Walther found with the fledgling Lutheran group of English-speakers at Zion Evangelical Lutheran Church of Gravelton, Missouri, was highly significant. Walther was way ahead of his time in understanding the mission field of North America and the importance of embracing the English tongue. While English was a distraction for many in the German Missouri Synod, it was not for Dr. Walther.

These were the common roots that resulted in a solid confessional trunk, not a trunk of happenstance or generalities. The emergence of two trunks was only natural. Two different languages represented two generally different cultures, but with a common desire to be faithful to what Lutherans believed, taught, confessed, and practiced in the church bodies represented in the English District's symbol. The biblical phrase, *"Man is justified by Faith,"* is the paraphrased Divinely inspired words of the Apostle Paul in Galatians 2:16 (KJV) and 3:11 and especially Romans 3:28. These Scriptural passages accent the central truth of the Gospel, namely, that God declares us (guilty sinners) just or righteous solely as an act of His grace, received through faith in His Son, Jesus Christ, our Savior and Lord. This is the doctrine of justification (Augsburg Confession, Article IV), the central teaching of the Christian faith.[129]

The seal of the English District with its double-trunked sycamore tree has indeed been used on the masthead of District stationery, *The English Channels*, the *Servant to Servant*, and other District publications, as well as various books, including the one edited by former English District Bishop Dr. John Baumgaertner, *A Tree Grows in Missouri.* The seal was especially prominent in *The English Channels*, which was the District's monthly publication, serving for 40 years (1976-2016) as the communications link for the members of English District congregations. The sycamore tree was used on the English District bishop's ring, surrounded by a Latin inscription (1987-2015).[130]

The sycamore is a beautiful tree, often visible from a distance. It thrives along river banks and in low-lying places. A sycamore tree has a trunk diameter ranging from three to eight feet, hence a fitting depiction for the seal of the English District. The leaves on the intertwining branches are huge, symbolic of growth and providing a remarkable canopy of color. In the seal, the intertwining branches and leaves that form the top of sycamore tree are united and often depicted in green, the liturgical color of growth as well as symbolizing the unity of this synodical district and the general synod.

The English District and the Missouri Synod as a whole have borne fruit together, depicted by the canopy of growth in grace, number, and mission. The sycamore tree, though, also represents something that is of the DNA of the District and her predecessor Conference/Synod and is captured in the words of Jesus in the Zacchaeus story in Luke 19:9-10: *"And Jesus said to him, 'Today salvation has come to this house, since he also is a son of Abraham. For the Son of Man came to seek and to save the lost.'"* The English District and her antecedent conference and synod have, for nearly a century and a half, had a missionary spirit of seeking to find the lost for Christ.

At what point did the sycamore tree become the official, District-approved logo or symbol? Nowhere does this appear to be documented, but it came to be accepted after the construction of Concordia Seminary in the St. Louis suburb of Clayton, Missouri, and the inclusion of the seal in a window in Wartburg Hall (circa 1926).

Wags have quipped, especially in gatherings of the LCMS Council of Presidents, that the English District symbol and seal look like the symbolic umbrella of the Travelers Insurance Company. Gentle teasing is fine, but the symbol of the English District carries the weight of history, service, and Christian outreach.

CHAPTER 9
A Unique English District Takes Its Place in the Missouri Synod (1941—1961)

CRACKS WERE BEGINNING to show already in the 1930s in the strong wall of the Evangelical Lutheran Synodical Conference of North America and its largest church body, the Evangelical Lutheran Synod of Missouri, Ohio, and Other States. These cracks were more than just the acculturation process (Americanization) of a largely-German-descent church body, congregations, schools, and pastors. The vast majority of pastors were born in the United States or Canada, and many were no longer using German, though it was still taught and used in courses at the seminaries of the Missouri Synod into the 1930s. Professors were retained who spoke fluently and were able to teach in German. The true cracks were more of a doctrinal nature as it pertained to practice, such as softening on issues like lodge membership, Boy Scouts, chaplaincy ministry in the Armed Forces, and other practices. The latter included participating with other Christian church bodies in theological discussion as opposed to rigidly avoiding any contact with such bodies or Christians of their membership. Formerly, it was not uncommon for an LCMS pastor to move to the other side of the street if a clergyman of another Christian denomination was coming toward him.

The English District, in its zeal to plant congregations and win souls for Christ, took what some would view as a more open approach. Methods of evangelization through *The Lutheran Hour* and the radio ministry of Dr. Walter A. Maier were embraced in the English District. The Synod, as a whole, though, went mildly through these periods in the 1930s (the *Brief Statement*), 1940s (rejection of the Statement of the 44 in 1945), 1950s (Resolution #9 of the San Francisco LCMS Synodical Convention in 1959; later declared "unconstitutional" in 1962), but changed to greater tension in the 1960s and 1970s. This will be examined in Part 3 of this book. Some termed these periods and acts in the LCMS as of "greater rigidity, conformity, and uniformity."[131]

In the two decades that embraced this time of "cracks" in the LCMS, the English District kept cultivating its missional quest to expand the work of Christian outreach. Preaching stations and congregations were being planted. Pastors were reaching new people of various ethnic backgrounds in their neighborhoods and welcoming them into Christ's Church on earth and the English District. The District seemed more concerned about winning souls for Christ than the "cracks" that were emerging within the Missouri Synod, divisions from what was perceived as an overbearing rigidity and "problems of an ingrown legalism and traditionalism."[132]

Statement of the "44"

The District was not immune from the emerging concerns, which the late Dr. Kurt Marquart of Concordia Theological Seminary, Fort Wayne, noted in his book, *Anatomy of an Explosion*. Marquart and his wife, Barbara, held membership at the English District's Redeemer Evangelical Lutheran Church, Fort Wayne, until his death in 2006. Marquart and his mentor, Dr. Hermann Sasse in Australia, saw the up-coming battle in the Missouri Synod. Professor Marquart observed that one of the signers of the "Statement of the 44" in 1945, decrying such ultra-conservatism, was Professor Theodore Graebner, a long-standing professor at Concordia Seminary, St. Louis. Graebner said long ago that "a short-sighted legalism would breed radicalism, liberalism, strife, and division." He was right.[133] Marquart further added:

> Commenting on Missouri's developing crisis already in 1951, Sasse honoured the intention "to repent for the mistakes of the past," but noted that the whole approach of the "44" was purely *ethical,* not *dogmatical.* What was needed was a thorough re-appropriation of the Biblical and Confessional *doctrine* of the church, not merely practical guidelines for this or that situation. Perhaps a kind of biblical isolation of Romans 16:17-18 and of the question of "prayer fellowship" in the "Statement of the 44" was partly to blame for the long and furious but quite hopeless battle which ensued on those issues, and finally resulted in the break-up of the Synodical Conference. The impossible choice seemed to be: either total fellowship with all Lutherans and perhaps beyond, or else no joint prayer with anyone outside the Synodical Conference."[134]

Professor Graebner, Dr. O.P. Kretzmann, the popular president of Valparaiso University, and others of the "44" were seeking closer ties and eventual union of Lutheran church bodies in North America, not skirting doctrine, but re-defining what would constitute altar and pulpit fellowship and attacking the distinction between the "visible church" and the "invisible church." While the "Statement of the 44" in 1945 caused a major flap in the Missouri Synod and Synodical Conference, and while a growing number of pastors sought what some termed the "ecumenical fleshpots," there was a weak conclusion. The "44" withdrew their "Statement" in the interest of peace and harmony in Synod, but did not recant it. Among those who signed the "Statement" were clergy who had ties to the English District—either previously, at the time of signing, or later. These signatories included Dr. Herman W. Bartels (English District president, 1945-1951); Dr. Walter E. Bauer (former pastor at Trinity, Scarsdale, New York, and long-term professor, Concordia Seminary, St. Louis); Rev. William F. Bruening (long-term pastor at Christ Church, Washington, D.C.); Dr. H.B. Hemmeter (president of Concordia College, Conover, North Carolina, and later Concordia Theological Seminary, Springfield, Illinois.); Rev. Karl Kretzmann (later author of the "Mission Affirmations" of 1965); Rev. Erwin "King" Kurth (pastor at Our Savior, Brooklyn, and later Redeemer, Fort Wayne, and author of the popular *Catechetical Helps*); Rev. Fred H. Lindemann (pastor at Holy Trinity, Bronx, New York); and Rev. Herbert Lindemann (long-term pastor of Redeemer, Fort Wayne, and author of the liturgical prayer book, *The Daily Office*).

English District Influence in the Missouri Synod

The English District was having a growing influence on the whole of The Lutheran Church—Missouri Synod in a more "liberal" direction in terms of theology and pastoral practice. Why was this? For one thing, the English District had already been a pacesetter upon entrance into the German Missouri Synod as a district that reached out in the English tongue. The Missouri Synod was slow to embrace English. The acculturation and Americanization process had begun. Gradually pastors who were born in the United States and Canada, even if of German background, accepted English as the language of worship and education.

Second, the English District had moved from being based in the hinterlands (e.g. Zion, Gravelton, Missouri) to fast becoming an urban district. Third, the English District was especially active in the East Coast urban centers in New York, New Jersey, Maryland, and the Carolinas, areas of national political, intellectual, and innovative foment. It was further alleged in the more Midwest and rural-based Missouri Synod that the English District harbored pastors who were soft on lodge issues and open to ecumenical engagement in ministerial conferences of other Christian denominations.

Even as this was occurring, English District congregations and their pastors were active in church planting, eager to reach the lost for Christ. In the early 1940s, it was common for English District parishes to print on signboards, stationery and in public advertising, "The English Evangelical Lutheran Church of…" Clearly, the distancing from things "German" was helpful during both World Wars and in the aftermath of World War II. Even English District pastoral families of German background would use German only as table talk by the parents and not speak German in public or teach it to their children. The emphasis was on being thoroughly American.[135] One congregation, Hope Evangelical Lutheran Church in Chicago, organized in 1917, grew to be the largest congregation in The Lutheran Church—Missouri Synod. Its peak was in 1948 when it had 4,366 baptized members and 3,257 communicant members under Pastor J.A. Leimer.[136] The congregation closed in 2000 but was re-opened as a mission start of the English District in 2001 as New Hope Lutheran Church (Ministries).

In addition to Christian outreach, Lutherans in America, including in the Missouri Synod, were providing aid to post-World War II Europe and since 1939 reaching out to displaced persons from Germany and other countries coming to North American shores. Some of this resulted in cooperation in "externals," such as the Lutheran Refugee Service. This organization was later renamed Lutheran Immigration and Refugee Services (LIRS) in 1967.[137]

Church plants during the two decades of the 1940s and 1950s resulted in many new congregations. Following World War II, especially, there was a stampede to the suburbs, and the English District "…pioneered in advance-site development and putting up first-unit churches."[138] Some of the new congregations had unusual names. Some were short-lived, such as

St. Gregory of Nyssa Evangelical Lutheran Church, Chicago. Others were started but released to geographic districts of Synod, such as Christ Evangelical Lutheran Church in Anderson, Indiana (transferred in 1945); Bethlehem Evangelical Lutheran Church in Boston, Massachusetts (1945); Grand Lake Evangelical Lutheran Church, Oakland, California (1945); and, Grace Evangelical Lutheran Church, San Diego, California (1945). Other congregations started during that period left the Synod and the English District during the 1970s, such as Church of the Savior-Lutheran, Paramus, New Jersey, and Roberts Park Evangelical Lutheran Church (re-named Savior Divine Lutheran Church), Palos Park, Illinois.

During the period in which the Korean War (1950-1953) and the "Cold War" (1947-1991) raged, the English District established a board of directors in 1954 and formally developed four geographic regions within the District. The Eastern Region of the English District consisted of congregations in New York, New Jersey, and eastern Pennsylvania. The Lake Erie Region consisted of congregations in upstate New York (Buffalo), western Pennsylvania (Pittsburgh and Erie), Ohio, Michigan, and the provinces of Ontario and Quebec, Canada. The Midwest Region consisted of congregations in Indiana, Illinois, Wisconsin, Minnesota, and Missouri. The Western Region consisted of congregations in California and Arizona, with those in Montana having been ceded to the new Montana District, formed in 1945. An annual regional conference, to which directors of Christian education and other parish workers were invited to attend, was still largely deemed a "pastoral conference." The District president and some of his staff attended the conferences, usually in the autumn. Scheduling always has been challenging, but not impossible. Those attending found the conferences professional, recreational, worshipful and stimulating.

Before the formal adoption of the English District Board of Directors, the English Missouri Synod and English District had a board of missions. In time, other boards were organized such as parish education and youth ministry, stewardship, evangelism, and social (human care) ministry. Clearly, the mission board was the most influential. Egos among staff executives in the 1940s and 1950s and later often clashed. Rev. O.T. McRee, reflecting back in 1988, noted that Rev. Harry Muhly of Grace Church, Elyria, Ohio, was called as the first executive of the mission board. Muhly moved to Detroit because that was where the mission board was located. All of the District's boards were elected by an area, i.e. missions in Detroit, parish education in Chicago, etc. Rev. Henry Burandt from Redeemer Evangelical Lutheran Church, Cleveland, was the second full-time missions executive, who was followed by Rev. Richard Jesse of Mt. Calvary Church, St. Louis. Pastor McRee was called as Rev. Jesse's assistant, and then succeeded him. The property that became the English District office building on Grand River Avenue in Detroit was purchased in 1955 under Missions Executive O.T. McRee. A study had been made at the time of the decision to build a District office. There was strong "pull" to have the District headquartered in Chicago, but the conclusion was that Detroit was the best location.[139]

Of curious note was that in the *Proceedings* of the 32nd Convention of the English District in 1960 at Concordia College, Milwaukee, an overture (memorial) from the circuit counselors (visitors) was not adopted. That memorial was that $925,000 be the firm figure of the English District's annual contribution to Synod and that the balance of funds received from the congregations be the English District's budget.[140] 1961 marked the 50th anniversary of the English District. Rev. Hugo Kleiner was serving a long tenure as president of the District (1951-1963) and during his terms in office the title "bishop" began to be unofficially used in the English District, perhaps also reflecting a high liturgical stance of many pastors in the District. However, the District was deemed "loyal." *"The English District Story,"* a reprint from the English District supplement in *The Lutheran Witness* in March 1961, included the following:

> The English District is part of the Missouri Synod and has functioned loyally as a District for 50 years. It has been loyal at the pocketbook, manpower, and policy level. It sympathetically and with understanding supported the mother body. It has given the Synod servants who worked in positions of trust in the chaplaincy, student services, institutional missions, charities, public relations, radio, and television phases of the greater work. District men are in India, Korea, West Africa, the Philippines, and until recently in Japan. Eleven are with the military personnel of Synod throughout the world. A half a dozen teach at Synod's schools of higher education, and at least two are in the administrative office at 210 N. Broadway, St. Louis. Are they disloyal to other Districts and to Synod by maintaining their

membership? (The implied answer to the rhetorical question is, of course, "No.") … We must go on, we must endure, with the help of God and in the spirit of our fathers![141]

However, the English District and LCMS were reaching a "turning point." On the occasion of the Golden Anniversary Jubilee in June 1961, the English District met in convention at Concordia Teachers College (later Concordia University-Chicago) at River Forest, Illinois. But just prior to that convention, tribute was paid to the District's past. The following quotes were included at the end of *"The English District Story,"* in the District supplements in *The Lutheran Witness* of March 1961:

STATEMENTS OF EARLY ENGLISH
LUTHERAN LEADERS

"The English Lutheran Synod of Missouri was neither the product of human machinations nor the fruit of wise or unwise church policy. It was the course of events in the church which brought this Synod into existence. In its history is traced the hand of the Chief Shepherd and Bishop of His Church on earth who sees the future even as the past, and who, as the wise Masterbuilder, makes provision for the good of the Church in advance of the future."

FREDERIC KUEGELE (1899)
First President of the English Synod

"May we all continue with ever increasing faithfulness and zeal the great work of spreading God's Word and Luther's doctrine pure in the language of our land."

HARRY P. ECKHARDT (1912)
First President of the English District

"Let us continue faithfully to preach the old, everlasting Gospel of Jesus Christ in all its original truth and purity and honestly and sincerely practice what we teach and confess. The pure Gospel of Christ crucified, and it alone, has always gained the victory until the Lord comes to call His people home to the great festival of eternal peace."

JOHN ADAM DETZER (1918)
Third President of the English District

"The English District does not only take stock of the past, we are assembled primarily to invade the unknown territory of the future. We are to plan and pioneer... Our District has a strategic role to play in God's gracious plan.

HUGO KLEINER (1963)
(Ninth) President/Bishop of the English District[142]

Excursus: 1961 English District Convention and unique *Proceedings*

Rockefeller Memorial Chapel, University of Chicago, Chicago, IL. Site of the English District Golden Jubilee Vespers Service on Wednesday, June 14, 1961. Preacher: English District President Hugo Kleiner, the five District Vice Presidents serving as Officiants.

Every district of The Lutheran Church—Missouri Synod publishes *Proceedings* after the culmination of each year's district convention. It is usually preceded by a Convention *Workbook*. Formerly such *Workbooks*, complete with reports and overtures (memorials) to the district or Synod, and the subsequent *Proceedings* were in the form of printed matter, a booklet of some sort, usually not elegant, just functional. Now such *Workbooks* and *Proceedings* are published online and put on district and Synod websites.

The *Proceedings* of the Golden Anniversary Convention of the English District of The Lutheran Church—Missouri Synod was printed in an elegant booklet, the cover in white with gold lettering. The convention was held on the campus of Concordia Teachers College, River Forest, Illinois, popularly referred to as "RF." The school is still at the same location but is now called Concordia University-Chicago (at River Forest, Illinois).

As a non-geographic district of Synod, the English District uniquely, for many years, held its district conventions at LCMS colleges—mainly at Concordia University-River Forest, but also at Concordia College at Milwaukee [later Concordia University, Mequon, Wisconsin] and Concordia College-Ann Arbor, Michigan [later Concordia University-Ann Arbor]. This worked well for several decades until delegates expressed the desire for hotel accommodations. In recent years, the District held a district convention at Concordia Seminary, St. Louis, for the 100th Anniversary Year of the District, along with a hotel, but it has reverted to holding regular conventions at Concordia University-Ann Arbor, not far from the current District office.

The Golden Anniversary Convention began with an opening Divine Service at Grace Evangelical Lutheran Church, River Forest, Illinois, on the morning of June 13, 1961. The Preacher was LCMS President Dr. John W. Behnken.

The *Proceedings* of the 1961 Golden Anniversary Convention of the English District contained *"The President's Message,"* by President/Bishop Kleiner, entitled *"Come, Holy Ghost, God and Lord,"* based on Luther's Pentecost hymn. He gave a thorough 50-year historical sketch, noting "Time marches on! Fifty years have tramped their God-destined way into the glades of eternity.... The Church's so-called intelligentsia clamors for new light..."[143] Kleiner wrote eloquently of the Word of God still being the Christian Church's "means of preservation and propagation." He also stated that the English District's calling as one of "progressive conservatism" and to have a "keen sense of mission and direction."[144]

In his "Festival Address" entitled *"The Rock and the Pit,"* based on Isaiah 51:1, Kleiner had more to say. He talked of God as the Rock of Ages and that the Golden Jubilee Service was not one to glorify man. Dr. Kleiner concluded:

Brethren, the English District is a unique District with a special mission for unique situations. In recognition of our peculiar position in the Lutheran Church – particularly The Lutheran Church—Missouri Synod – and in gratitude for the blessings of the pastor, and in eager anticipation of the blessings of our Lord and Savior Jesus Christ, I adjure you to lift up your hearts in holy vows. Vow to travel the pathways of the fathers without fear or wavering. Vow to grab opportunity by the forelock, especially in the suburbia of our land. Vow to buckle on the belt of truth. Vow to put on the helmet of salvation. Vow to mark courageously, shod with the seven-fold graces of God's Holy Spirit, into this confused and troubled and trembling and frustrated day which happens to be our day, as did our fathers march and conquer in the day and era which was theirs. So help you God![145]

The "turning point" or harbinger was not in English District President Kleiner's message or his address nor in the 16 untitled resolutions of the "Report of the Floor Committee on the President's Report" which were approved by the District in convention. Half of the resolutions were expressing thanks and celebrating the District's history. Another resolution in its whereases affirmed that the District and Synod presidents both warned of theological liberalism and resolved to reaffirm "our historic doctrine that the Holy Scriptures are the inspired and inerrant Word of God and that the Confessions of the Lutheran Church are the true and correct expositions of the Word of God and that we encourage the pastors, teachers, and congregations of the English District to confirm their preaching, teaching, and practice to the Holy Scriptures."[146] Humorously, a memorial to change the name of the District from "English" to "The Metropolitan District" was rejected and duly noted in EDNA.[147]

However, the "turning point" may well have been the adoption of the "Report of the District Convention Floor Committee No. 19." At its 1960 convention, the English District resolved to ask the Synod to declare the LCMS 1959 San Francisco Convention's approved Resolution 9 "unconstitutional." The 1961 Convention of the English District adopted a resolution "that the 1962 LCMS Convention declare Resolution 9 unconstitutional and that the Synod elect a commission to study the theological and practical problems which are disturbing Synod."[148] The seeds of rejecting the hard edge of Missouri's doctrinal conservatism were being sown.

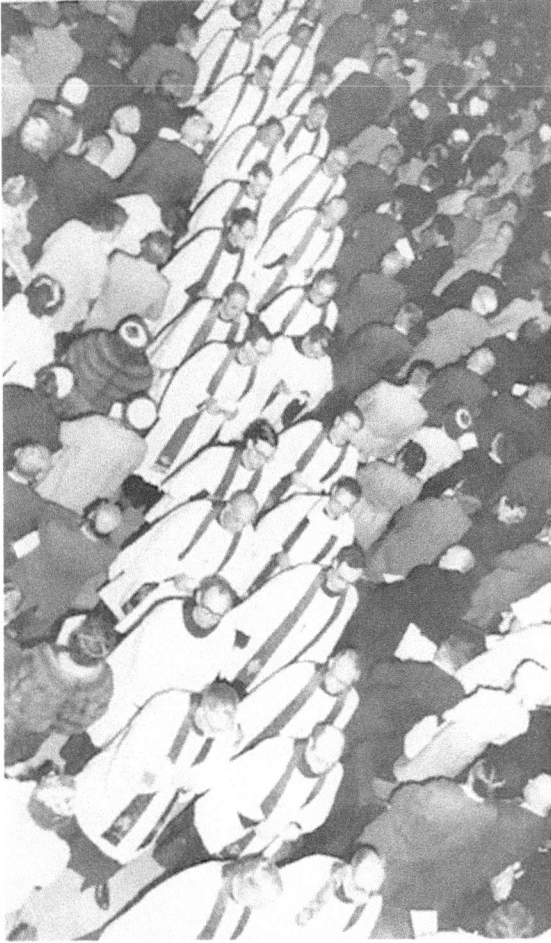

Recessional during the English District Jubilee Vespers Service held at Rockefeller Memorial Chapel at the University of Chicago, June 1961.

PART THREE

CONTROVERSY, RIFT, AND DIVISION IN THE LCMS:
THE SURVIVIAL OF THE ENGLISH DISTRICT AND COMEBACK

CHAPTER 10
Ominous Changes (1961—1969)

The "Turning Point"

RESOLUTION 9 ADOPTED by the 1959 LCMS Convention, held at the Cow Palace in San Francisco, called for a uniform level of harmony and doctrinal fidelity on the part of all Synod pastors, teachers, and professors. Some within the Synod believed that this Resolution took the Synod beyond its requirement of confessional subscription to the Holy Scriptures as the infallible Word of God and a full *quia* subscription to the confessional writing of the Evangelical Lutheran Church in the *Book of Concord*. At issue was the required subscription to the 1932 *Brief Statement* and other synodically approved theses mandated by Resolution 9:

> *Resolved:*
> A.   That Synod further clarify its position by reaffirming that every doctrinal statement of a confessional nature adopted by Synod as a true exposition of the Holy Scriptures is to be regarded as public doctrine (*publica doctrina*) in Synod; and
> B.   That Synod's pastors, teachers, and professors are held to teach and act in harmony with such statements; and
> C.   That those who believe that such statements are not satisfactory in part or in their entirety are not to teach contrary to them, but rather are to present their concern to their brethren in the ministry, particularly in conferences, to the appropriate District officials, and if necessary to the synodical officials.[149]

Others within the Missouri Synod and Synodical Conference felt the encroachment of higher biblical criticism and a movement toward a different view of Holy Scripture. They were fearful of the direction of the Synod.

The storm clouds indeed were gathering during the latter years of the LCMS presidency of Dr. John W. Behnken (1935-1962), with the centers of doctrinal concern being notably Concordia Seminary, St. Louis, and Concordia Senior College, Fort Wayne, established in 1955 as the premier finishing school for men heading to the seminaries. Concordia Teachers College in River Forest, Illinois, and Concordia College, Bronxville, New York, were also showing elements of doctrinal variance in their theological faculties. Valparaiso University, an independent Lutheran university, had close ties with the LCMS. Its formation was largely by LCMS pastors. Its faculty was largely LCMS. The University was under the leadership of the erudite and very popular Dr. O.P. Kretzmann (1943-1968). "Valpo," as it was affectionately called, was also in the forefront of theological change, human relations (the civil rights movement), and ecumenical expansion beyond the LCMS.

Before Resolution 9 was rescinded at the 1962 Cleveland Convention, the English District found herself involved with the resolution at its June 1960 Convention, held at Concordia College in Milwaukee. Dr. Richard Luecke, pastor of The Lutheran Church of the Messiah in Princeton, New Jersey, an English District town-gown ministry to Princeton University, submitted an overture asking for Resolution 9 to be rescinded at the 1962 LCMS Convention. Dr. Roland Wiederaenders, LCMS first vice president, who termed the English District "interesting and unpredictable," appealed to the District to reject the proposed overture. However, the District did adopt the overture as a resolution, calling for the rescinding of Resolution 9 by the Missouri Synod at its 1962 Cleveland Convention. Even Dr. Behnken was unable to prevent the English District, now joined by two other synodical districts – the Atlantic and Southeastern Districts – from requesting Resolution 9 to be rescinded.

The Synod rescinded Resolution 9, doing what it has often done in its history of the last 70 years. The Synod in Convention has often adopted contrary actions or modified or rescinded resolutions. In this case, the 1962 Cleveland Convention of The Lutheran Church—Missouri Synod, led by English District clergy such as Revs. Ernest Eggers, Bertwin Frey, Richard Luecke, Oswald McRee, and John Tietjen, got the Synod to declare Resolution 9 "…unconstitutional on the ground that it 'has the effect of amending the confessional basis of the Constitution of the Synod without following the procedure required by Article XIV of the Constitution.' (see 1962 Proceedings, p. 123)."[150]

This clearly marked a turning point. The LCMS Cleveland Convention backed away from Resolution 9 which stated that pastors, teachers, and professors "are held to teach and act in harmony with" synodically adopted doctrinal statements. It was resolved: "That the Synod beseech all its members by the mercies of God to honor and uphold the doctrinal content of these synodically adopted statements."[151] But the rescission of Resolution 9 was done solely on procedural grounds. The Synod did not equivocate on the need for ecclesiastical supervision in doctrine and practice. Nor did it reject the notion that it would need to speak on doctrinal matters. Synod President Behnken's statement following the rescission of Resolution 9 made that clear:

> Dr. Behnken then asked for the privilege of making a statement. He hoped that the Synod would realize that it had acted here only on a constitutional question and that this action did not indicate that the Synod is not in accord with the Brief Statement, the Statement on Scripture, and the Common Confession. He emphasized that there is a need in our day for statements to make our stand clear on current issues. It may become necessary for the Synod to make definite statements on the central teaching of justification by faith alone, on Law and Gospel, and on other important doctrines.[152]

But the Convention marked a second turning point "in the dealings of Missourians with fellow Christians in general and fellow Lutheran Christians in particular."[153] In the English District history it was previously stated that Dr. C.F.W. Walther, the German Missouri Synod's first president, was a friend, an inspiration, and one who was sympathetic with reaching out with the saving Gospel of Christ Jesus in North America in the English tongue. While some may fault Walther for his democratic polity leanings, he was a giant in his time in seeking unity among North American Lutheran Christians. Yet Walther would in no way abandon, alter, or deviate from orthodox Evangelical Lutheran doctrine, faith, and practice. In that spirit, Synod and the English District, showing ominous signs of possible division, weighed carefully matters of unionism while seeking God-pleasing unity, especially among Lutheran church bodies in America.

A third turning point as a result of the Cleveland Convention had to do with human care and compassionate ministry. While avoiding unionism that would run askew of fidelity to what the LCMS believed, taught, and confessed, there was now a new openness to social ministries in meeting human needs while faithfully proclaiming the Word of God: "While the Cleveland convention acknowledged [that] 'there is a danger to the total program of the church in an overriding preoccupation with political, socio-economic, and cultural questions,' it also declared that 'current questions should be answered in the light of the message of the Cross.'"[154]

The crisis in the life of the LCMS was presented in a positive light by holding in sanctified tension the need for Missouri to be more open toward necessary changes in practice and behavior but "without leaving room for any compromise of the Scriptures and the Lutheran Confessions!"[155] This viewpoint was footnoted by Dr. Carl S. Meyer as coming from none other than the Rev. Martin W. Mueller in an editorial called "Turning Point" in the August 1962 issue of *The Lutheran Witness*. Mueller would later become a pastor in the English District and author of the carefully-nuanced, post-LCMS-split 1986 English District anniversary booklet, *Amazing Comeback*.

In his assessment of the time of crisis within the Synod, LCMS Professor Dr. James C. Burkee termed this decade as "the ecumenical sixties":

> As the LCMS became more modern, its theologians became more theologically modernist and politically liberal. Publicly, this took shape in a new openness of thought and action among professors at Concordia Seminary [not all, but most], who were growing more sympathetic to ecumenism and issues of social justice and action. Privately, students took note of a more dramatic shift. German higher criticism [higher biblical criticism], out of which confessional movements like the Missouri Synod were born in the nineteenth century, was making its way back into the church through its classrooms at Concordia Seminary. At issue in Missouri as in earlier modernist-fundamentalist battles, was the use of methods of historical criticism of the Bible. Increasingly, church scholars were using the tools of modern biblical scholarship, ending matters of biblical authority with question marks where there had been periods. Students and faculty openly challenged Frank Pieper's *Brief Statement* and questioned "inerrancy."[156]

The growing crisis in The Lutheran Church—Missouri Synod could not be underestimated, as has been shown by later historians analyzing the era. Amid the foment of change in the Synod, the English District was gaining significantly in baptized and communicant membership and adding new churches, mostly from new preaching stations and mission plants. Some additions came from congregations transferring from geographic districts into the non-geographic English District. Interestingly, the LCMS changed its nomenclature from "circuit visitors" to "circuit counselors." Not until 2014 did the Synod return to the terminology of "circuit visitor," with its emphasis on visitation, encouragement, and ecclesiastical oversight of congregations, pastors, and other professional church workers. However, the English District notably used the "circuit visitor" nomenclature informally long before 2014.

The growth of the English District from 1950—1969 was amazing. The following table shows the highest points of growth in underlined, bold font.

Year	Congregations	Baptized Membership	Communicant Membership
1950	171	103,477	68,513
1954	180	123,505	78,894
1958	193	142,738	87,655
1960	188	147,711	91,084
1963	200	**155,875**	97,785
1967	208	154,508	**101,971**
1968	**209**	152,601	101,942
1969	207	149,487	100,829

During the 1960s, more pastors were being received into the English District than being transferred to other synodical districts. Among the congregations transferred to the English District or planted in the 1960s were the following: Calvary Evangelical Lutheran Church, St. Louis; St. John Evangelical Lutheran Church & School, Hannibal, Missouri (founded 1860); St. Gregory of Nyssa Evangelical Lutheran Church, a campus ministry at the University of Chicago; Lutheran Church of the Holy Spirit, St. Paul/Oakdale, Minnesota; Grace Evangelical Lutheran Church, Warminster, Pennsylvania; Lutheran Church of the Prince of Peace, Menomonee Falls, Wisconsin; Messiah Lutheran Church, Elmhurst, Illinois; Ramona Lutheran Church, Ramona, California; Grace Evangelical Lutheran Church, South Holland, Illinois; The Lutheran Church of the Holy Comforter, Mt. Vernon, New York; King of Glory Evangelical Lutheran Church, Sylvania, Ohio; Risen Christ Lutheran

Church, Plymouth, Michigan; Prince of Peace Evangelical Lutheran Church, Medina, Ohio; Ascension Lutheran and Holy Trinity Lutheran Churches, Tucson, Arizona.; Christ Memorial Lutheran Church, Montreal, Quebec; Christ the King Lutheran Church, Schaumburg, Illinois; and, St. Mark the Evangelist Lutheran Church, Janesville, Wisconsin. By 1968, the English District claimed to be the fourth largest district in the LCMS with 222 congregations, 292 pastors, and 156,500 members.[157]

Among the congregations that transferred to geographic districts during this period were St. Paul Evangelical Lutheran Church, Clyde, New York (to Eastern District); the District's deaf ministry in St. Louis (to Western District); Cedar Crest Lutheran Church, Cedar Crest (Union Lake), Michigan (to Michigan District); Faith Evangelical Lutheran Church, Fair Oaks, California (to California and Nevada District); the District's once largest congregation, Grace Evangelical Lutheran Church, St. Louis (to Western District); and Mt. Olive Lutheran Church, Pasadena, California (to Southern California District). Several other churches merged together in such cities as Detroit and Pittsburgh.

In 1968, the Rev. Dan R. Ludwig, a District pastor in Ohio and secretary of the English District and member of the board of directors, retired from the District secretary position after several years of service since 1957. It is noteworthy that Pastor Ludwig's son, Dr. Garth Ludwig, served for many years as pastor of Hope Evangelical Lutheran Church, later Upper Saint Clair, Pennsylvania (the same building is now called Peace Lutheran Church, McMurray, Pennsylvania). Pastor Dan Ludwig was also the father of Dr. Mary (née Ludwig) Todd, who later authored the book *Authority Vested*, which challenged the position of the LCMS that, according to Scriptural doctrine, women cannot be ordained into the Holy Ministry.[158]

Events in the LCMS in the 1960s

Regarding the growing crisis in the LCMS and in the English District, four major events were significant in the decade of turmoil:

> 1) Election of Dr. Oliver Harms as LCMS president at the 1962 Cleveland LCMS Convention upon the retirement of Dr. John Behnken

2) Adoption of six Mission Affirmations and the approval of LCMS membership in the new Lutheran Council in the United States of America (LCUSA) at the 1965 Detroit LCMS Convention

3) Replacement of Dr. Harms in the election of Dr. J.A.O. Preus as LCMS president and the declaration of pulpit and altar fellowship with the American Lutheran Church (ALC) at the 1969 Denver LCMS Convention

4) Election of Dr. John Tietjen, American Lutheran Publicity Bureau (ALPB) executive director and English District rostered pastor, as president of Concordia Seminary, St. Louis.

In 1962, Dr. Oliver Harms was elected president of The Lutheran Church—Missouri Synod, succeeding Dr. John Behnken. Harms had been the long-term pastor of Trinity Evangelical Lutheran Church in Houston, Texas. He also served as president of the Texas District, and then as fourth vice president of Synod. Harms was orthodox in his theology, but had an ecumenical and human care ministry bent. Though a disappointment to more liberal and moderate elements in the Synod, Harms, like Behnken before him, was not able to stand up to the *wunderkind* liberal elements of Synod. Drs. Martin E. Marty and Richard John Neuhaus, among others, were formidable opponents. Behnken ended his long service as president of the Synod with parting words to the liberal and moderate folks who were continuing to gain dominance in Concordia Seminary, St. Louis, and other LCMS institutions of higher learning:

> However, a matter which has caused even greater unrest in the Synod is the charge that purity of doctrine is being sacrificed. We must ask in all seriousness whether some are influenced by European neo-orthodoxy, whether the floods of present-day European theology are threatening also our century-old position on the verbally inspired, infallible, inerrant Word of God. If someone is influenced by such modern theology, this demands that proper corrections be made. We know, of course, that the procedure must be both evangelical and firm. This holds true whether it takes place at conferences of pastors and teachers or in the faculties of our colleges and seminaries or among the officials of Districts and the Synod.[159]

Interestingly, Harms was instumental in the appointment of Dr. J.A.O. Preus as president of Concordia Theological Seminary, Springfield, Illinois, the Synod's more "practical" seminary.

Dr. Harms was a kind churchman who viewed things from the eyes and heart of a parish pastor. While he stood up against the lambasts of the Rev. Herman Otten, an uncertified pastor serving an LCMS congregation in New Haven, Missouri, and Otten's weekly paper *Christian News*, Harms was hard-pressed to do a proper theological investigation of the faculty of Concordia Seminary. He deferred to the Synod's new Commission on Theology and Church Relations (CTCR), which was created in 1962. Dr. Burkee appears to have been accurate in stating the following: "Missouri's presidents were consistently baffled by the Concordia [Seminary] faculty. In a dialogue in which theology became a matter of semantics and textual deconstruction [and also the embracing of higher biblical criticism], Harms, like Behnken before him, was poorly armed."[160] One of Harms' loyal allies from the East Coast, the Rev. Ewald Mueller, was among the first to lament the unseating of Dr. Harms as Synod president at the 1969 Denver Convention of the LCMS. Admitting that the LCMS had become increasingly more liberal in its theology at Concordia Seminary, colleges, and among many of the pastors, Dr. Mueller nonetheless felt that Harms could have turned things around in Synod.[161]

Adoption of the Mission Affirmations and approval of LCMS membership in the new Lutheran Council in the United States of America (LCUSA) at the 1965 Detroit LCMS Convention was the second major watershed. A *Report on Mission Self-Study and Survey* was composed by Dr. Martin L. Kretzmann (1906—2000), a missionary to India, theological educator, and brother of the Revs. A.R., O.P., and Justus Kretzmann. The Mission Affirmations were statements based on the report and were entitled as follows:

1. The Church Is God's Mission
2. The Church Is Christ's Mission to the Whole World
3. The Church Is Christ's Mission to the Church
4. The Church Is Christ's Mission to the Whole Society
5. The Church Is Christ's Mission to the Whole Man
6. The Whole Church Is Christ's Mission.[162]

While appreciative of Missionary Martin Kretzmann's concerns of "shallow pettiness and organizationalism" in the life of the Church, Professor Kurt Marquart writes:

> The "Mission Affirmations" include the disastrous proposition: 'That we affirm that the church is Christ's mission to the whole society.' Various qualifying statements, though inadequate, indicate that the proposition was felt to be disturbing. Dr. M.L. Kretzmann's commentary is far from reassuring: 'As the body of Christ in the world, the community of the new creation, the church has a corporate responsibility towards the structures of society.' Despite lip-service in the 'whereases' to Luther's distinction between the two kingdoms – the spiritual and the political – the statements cited effectively wipe out any such distinction.[163]

Marquart then goes on to show that the Mission Affirmations in the next decade contributed to the *Faithful to Our Calling* document of the Concordia Seminary faculty majority and the "Seminex" confession. He summarized the deep concerns that confessional (orthodox), conservative LCMS Lutherans had with the Synod convention-approved Mission Affirmations.

Another major action of the 1965 Detroit LCMS Convention was the adoption of a resolution for the LCMS to join LCUSA. Officially organized in 1966 by delegates of The American Lutheran Church, the Lutheran Church in America, and The Lutheran Church—Missouri Synod, LCUSA's headquarters were in the same building as the American Lutheran Publicity Bureau, 315 Park Avenue, in New York City. The purpose of LCUSA was to coordinate the work of service (human care, social ministry) of the three church bodies, provide for common action together, and develop theological consensus leading toward merger. Yet, as Dr. Samuel Nafzger notes in a concise pamphlet, *"An Introduction to The Lutheran Church—Missouri Synod"*: "Unlike many other [church bodies], the LCMS has never been involved in a major merger."[164] In the Missouri Synod, fears mounted that this was just another step toward weakening of doctrine and practice based on solid confessional Lutheran dogma.

The third major event of the 1960s in the LCMS was the replacement of Dr. Harms by the election of Dr. Jack Preus as LCMS president and the declaration of pulpit and altar fellowship with the American Lutheran Church. The LCMS has had a history of doing contradictory actions, and this was one of them. At the 1969 Synodical Convention, conservative delegates, bolstered by growing lay discontent with the theological direction of Synod, managed to elect their choice to replace Dr. Oliver Harms. That choice was one who had come with his equally theologically-brilliant brother, Dr. Robert Preus, from the "Little Norwegian Synod," the Evangelical Lutheran Synod. Dr. Jack (J.A.O.) Preus (1920-1994) has been wildly caricatured both by his supporters, some of whom later turned on him, and especially by his opponents. His opponents demonized him; his supporters lionized him. But Jack Preus was no academic slouch. An expert of the Lutheran Orthodoxy era, he had both a scholarly as well as a political bent. He showed brilliant scholarship in translating and interpreting the writing of Lutheran theologian Martin Chemnitz (1522-1586). Among Preus' translations of Chemnitz's works into English from the Latin were *The Two Natures in Christ* (1971), *The Lord's Supper* (1979), *Justification: The Chief Article of Christian Doctrine as Expounded in Loci Theologici* (1985), and *Loci theologici* (1989).

Preus came into the LCMS in 1958 as a professor at Concordia Theological Seminary, Springfield, Illinois; by 1962 he became president of that institution. Later, he was elected Synod president and began to reverse the direction of the Missouri Synod away from a liberal trajectory.

At the same 1969 Denver Convention of the LCMS was the declaration of fellowship with The American Lutheran Church, headquartered in Minneapolis, Minnesota. The American Lutheran Church of 1960 represented the merger of the "old ALC" (a 1930 merger of the Joint Ohio, Iowa, Buffalo, and Texas Synods), the National [formerly: Norwegian] Evangelical Lutheran Church (NELC), Lutheran Free Church (LFC), and United Evangelical Lutheran Church (UELC), affectionately known as the "holy Danes." The 1950s and early 1960s were an *"urge to merge"* period within North American Lutheranism. That movement was still going strong, and the LCMS was being drawn into it. Conservatives within the LCMS were furious that pulpit and altar fellowship had been approved with the ALC, a church body that was increasingly less confessional, more social ministry oriented and espousing historical biblical criticism. But as Missouri frequently experienced, two seemingly opposite actions were again taken at a Synod Convention. The turbulence would only increase.

The fourth major event of the '60s was the election of Dr. John Tietjen (1928-2004), an English District rostered pastor, as president of Concordia Seminary, St. Louis in May 1969, just months before the LCMS Convention. He was installed in the Fall. The liberal bloc in the LCMS had still another champion who was front and center of Lutheran ecumenism and the new directions in theology that the majority of the Seminary faculty had embraced. The Rev. Martin Mueller, former editor of *The Lutheran Witness*, wrote: "Some of the corridor talk at the 1969 synodical convention immediately following the 'upset' election of Dr. J.A.O. Preus to the LCMS presidency was quite ominous – perhaps fatal, as it turned out – namely: 'If the 'conservatives' can elect to the Synod presidency the president of the Springfield seminary, the 'moderates' can elect the president of the St. Louis seminary.'"[165]   The storm clouds were quickly gathering.

The 1960s

Church history is not isolated from secular history. The 1960s, often just called the "Sixties," was a highly tumultuous decade. Beginning with the election of a popular president, John F. Kennedy, it was soon clouded with the failed Bay of Pigs invasion of communist Cuba under Fidel Castro and the Cuban missile crisis with the Soviet Union. Kennedy's visit to Berlin and the infamous Berlin Wall marked part of his global popularity in the West. His assassination on November 22, 1963, brought tears to America and a sudden halt for a few days to all activity, except viewing the televised broadcasts of mourning and burial.

The Soviet Union and the United States were involved in both a missile race and space exploration. The Civil Rights Movement led by Dr. Martin Luther King, Jr. climaxed in his assassination in 1968, amid growing turbulence. The Sixties were the era of tremendous unrest with the growing Vietnam War (1959-1975). Major American involvement was from 1963 to 1973. The anti-war movement brought rioting and huge college campus demonstrations. The country was badly divided. Many church leaders across the United States were taking sides or trying to fathom the nature of this unpopular war. Some, including in the English

District, became powerfully vocal, sometimes dividing families. An example of this was the divide between Dr. Armin ("Red") Moellering (pro-war) and his brother, Dr. Ralph Moellering (anti-war), both of whom were once members in the English District. Many pastors became involved in the Civil Rights movement, the more liberal ones often taking up the cause of repressed African-Americans. The country and world were plunging into a counter-cultural revolution of free sex, drugs, and anti-war demonstrations, exemplified in the music, movies, and at Woodstock.

The Sixties were also marked by major race riots across America. Many cities experienced rioting in 1967 and 1968 in response to racial discrimination, poor wages, police brutality, impoverished housing conditions, poor education, and disenfranchisement from the political process. Among those cities torn apart by riots were Detroit; Chicago; Newark, New Jersey; New York City; and Rochester, New York. Many cities suffered the subsequent "white flight" to the suburbs, weakening the cities' tax bases and causing more unrest and violence. English District churches in several cities were affected as they dealt with decreased attendance, membership and financial support. While congregations strived to reach out to their communities, many saw them deteriorate, and some churches were forced to close their doors.

Not all was doom and gloom in the 1960s. In spite of nuclear threats, bomb shelters, and school air raid drills, there was the great event landing a man on the moon in the July 1969 Apollo 11 Mission. Thirty-two African nations gained their independence from European colonial powers, and the United States sent young people to Africa, Latin America, and Asia in the Peace Corps. The cultural era of the Sixties may well have ended with the Watergate scandal in 1972, the American withdrawal from Vietnam in 1973, and the resignation of President Richard M. Nixon in August 1974. But this can clearly be stated: the Sixties had a major influence on Americans, the Church catholic, urban congregations, the English District and Missouri Synod, and even Christians who were beginning to question many truths and the teachings of the Church.

The Close of Dr. Kleiner's Tenure

Dr. Hugo Kleiner's "President's Address" to the 34th Convention of the English District in June 1963, was titled *"And Finally."* The Bishop looked reflectively on his 12 years in office, the longest of any English Synod or District president: "I was enjoined to guide the destiny of our fraternity as long as it pleased the Lord Jesus Christ, the Bishop of the Church... During the past twelve years many far-reaching changes have taken place in the affairs of the world and in the program of the Church, in Synod and in the District."[166] Kleiner urged the District to remain strong in doctrine, the performance of stewardship, in Bible study, and finally to be strong in the Lord and the power of His might.

Reports were given by the five vice presidents, representing the five regions of the District. First vice president at the time was Dr. August Brunn from Pittsburgh, who had succeeded Dr. Eckhardt as pastor of St. Andrew's Church.[167] In addition to numerous reports and overtures of District committees and floor committees, it was reported that the District through its Committee on Scholarships gave financial support (grants) in the amount of $23,197.00 to 82 church work students, including 53 ministerial students (10 to Concordia Seminary students, 25 to Concordia Theological Seminary students, and the rest at synodical colleges), 26 teacher students, and 3 deaconess students.[168]

The Era of Rev. Bertwin Frey as Bishop/President

The 1963 Convention essays were given by Dr. Carl Gross of Michigan State University on the inter-testamental period and Dr. John Tietjen of Teaneck, New Jersey, and the ALPB in New York City, on international ecumenical meetings. The most significant matter of the Convention, though, was the election of a new District president. The Rev. Bertwin Frey, pastor of Messiah Lutheran Church, Fairview Park, Ohio (1957-1963), and a former Eastern District vice president, was elected. Though Frey became a member of the English District in 1957, he was well known as the chairman of the District's "Resolution 9" Committee. With Frey's election, the more liberal wing in the English District had now gained the presidency. The era of four-termed President/Bishop Hugo Kleiner had come to an end.

Frey minced no words in his first written "President's Message" to the 35th Convention of the English District, entitled "God's Will, and Our Convention." He stated: "Woe unto our church if our members are unable to get through to people of our day because we are simply parroting neat little phrases and pat formulas which don't register!"[169] He further added:

> Of course, there are still other reasons for the theological stir in our District and Synod today. Without trying to be iconoclasts or debunkers, a number of our most reverent students of the Word are questioning some of the so-called positions of our Synod that go beyond the Confessions and beyond the Scriptures. The literalistic interpretations of some very picturesque and poetic passages of Scripture that have been generally accepted in our circles but never made normative are being questioned. However, in the months that I have been privileged to observe some of this controversy and discussion as your president, I have not once observed anything but complete obedience to the Scriptures. The only matter that is being questioned is whether or not some of our taken-for-granted positions outside of the Confessions deserve to be taken-for-granted and designated as the only acceptable position in our church.[170]

Frey's 1964 address noted doctrinal discussions as proving a time for theological growth. But his words were not encouraging to the conservative camp within the English District. The Board of Directors was also of the more liberal bent in Synod. An overture from the circuit visitors to change the District's name from the English District to the "General District" was declined. However, it was modified into a resolution to have the District president appoint a committee "to seek a name which appropriately expresses the unique characteristic and image of the District."[171] Approved resolutions encouraged President Frey to focus on doctrinal life of the church where theological controversy could be healthy for the church (Resolution No. 5-1 "Doctrinal Life of the Church") and called for Synod to work toward one new Lutheran hymnal of the Missouri Synod together with other North American Lutheran church bodies.[172] The unstated reality was that church bodies that worship together with the same hymnal often eventually merge together.

With the United States heavily involved in the Vietnam War and anti-war sentiment raging, with civil rights and white racism affecting the nation, and amid calls for greater Lutheran unity, 55 resolutions at the 1968 Convention of the English District reflected events in both church and state. Some were simple resolutions requiring little discussion. But the following resolutions were among those approved:

- to produce printed materials addressing the problem of white racism
- to encourage District congregations to financially support Synod's Board of World Relief
- to provide guidelines that addressed social justice to alter the attitudes of parishioners
- to continue the Synod's understanding of upholding conscientious objection to bear arms and for the government to provide alternate avenues of service,
- to financially support the "Poor People's Campaign" in addressing poverty; and,
- to commend LCMS President Oliver Harms and his colleagues of the LCMS Praesidium in support of steps toward full realization of altar and pulpit fellowship with the ALC (American Lutheran Church).[173]

Declined were resolutions on federal gun control, proposed new circuits, and financial support for the Springfield Seminary's new chapel. It was apparent that the English District's focus was changing to reflect both the ecclesial and secular cultures. Dr. Frey's "President's Address" was entitled, "Don't Just Do Something – Stand There!" It was a call to listen to the Old Testament prophets Isaiah and Amos, to listen to the voices of the ghetto, of students in rebellion, and to "go into God's world as saints alive."[174] The District was also moving toward approval of a full-time District president.

Not withstanding all the commotion, the English District showed some amazing ministry creativity. Under Chaplain Rev. Dave Kreuckeberg (1943-2020), a Race Track Ministry to workers and families in the race track subculture was begun in 1969. While it was to focus on race tracks in Miami and Chicago, it eventually took aim at Arlington International Racecourse and Hawthorne Race Course in Illinois. His emphasis on justice was alongside his ministry to trainers, jockeys, grooms, and others who comprise the race track industry in the Chicago metropolitan area. The Chicago region of the District included Chicago Uptown Ministry, ministering to immigrant Appalachian Caucasians and later to African-Americans in the uptown area. One ministry that closed was Hyde Park Evangelical Lutheran Church (1940-1964), near the University of Chicago. This ministry owned a mansion that would much later be sold to a future president of the United States, Barack Obama.[175]

The era of the Sixties in the Synod climaxed with the election of an English District pastor, Dr. John Tietjen, as president of Concordia Seminary, St. Louis, the election of Concordia Theological Seminary president Dr. Jacob A.O. Preus as president of The Lutheran Church—Missouri Synod, and the 1969 Synodical Convention declaration of pulpit and altar fellowship with the ALC. Tensions in church and state were clearly mounting.

Entrance to the English District office building, 23001 Grand River Ave., Detroit. Pictured are executive staff members, left to right: the Revs. William Woldt, Harold Hecht, and Richard Feucht.

CHAPTER 11
The English District Attempts to Stay United

THE REVOLUTIONARY, COUNTER-CULTURAL changes of the 1960s spilled over into the 1970s. Western, social progressive values continued to grow. A new attitude of individualism caused the Seventies to be labelled the "Me Decade" as reflected in TV series and movies. Communist China, following the death of Chairman Mao Zedong, began opening up to the West, even as the United States was working its way out of the Vietnam War. Violence was increasing in the Middle East, climaxed by the 1979 overthrow of the Shah in Iran and the creation of an anti-American authoritarian Islamic republic. Against this "kingdom of the left" backdrop, the LCMS and English District became increasingly polarized.

The Lutheran Church—Missouri Synod was still growing in membership but was nearing a plateau in attendance. Church attendance in North American Christianity peaked in 1959. The LCMS had released the Brazil and Argentina Districts to become separate Evangelical Lutheran sister church bodies, but it retained its three Canadian districts (Ontario, Manitoba-Saskatchewan, and Alberta-British Columbia). Later, the Canadian districts formed another sister church body, Lutheran Church-Canada (LCC). In 1971, the Synod of Evangelical Lutheran Churches (SELC), previously the Slovak Evangelical Lutheran Church, merged with the LCMS, becoming the SELC District, a sister non-geographic district with the English District. But the broader picture in North America was one of a radicalization of society and culture that did not spare the Church.

How does a District of Synod stay united in its mission of reaching the lost for Jesus Christ when in the thick of controversy? There is the example of Dr. Armin "Red" Moellering (1919-1998), long-time pastor at Grace Evangelical Lutheran Church, Palisades Park, New Jersey (1949-1978) and a prolific author and professor of Exegetical Theology at Concordia Seminary, St. Louis (1978-1990). Moellering was solidly in the "conservative camp" in the LCMS as a member of the Concordia Seminary Fact-Finding Committee, 1970-1971, and the Commission on Theology and Church Relations (CTCR), 1973-1978. Yet he quipped that he could still be friends with his "very liberal" friends in the English District.[176] The English District was a common meeting ground for healthy discussion at circuit winkels, regional pastoral conferences, and professional church worker conferences. District Conventions, though, were often more testy.

1970

Beyond polite pleasantries, the English District continued to become more polarized. While there was sympathy among pastors in the District for the theological and political leanings of the faculty majority at Concordia Seminary, St. Louis, there were also pastors and lay people in the English District who were in harmony with the LCMS in doctrine and confessional stance, though less so in terms of practice.[177] Unlike the typical unillustrated Convention *Proceedings* booklets other than the 1961 Golden Anniversary *Proceedings*, the 1970 District Convention *Proceedings* added many pictures. The booklet-size had given way to larger publications. One immediately sees a full page displaying two pictures and naming Congregational Youth Representatives (38), Circuit Youth Delegates (35), and Youth Counselors (3). As one might expect, some of the youth representatives and delegates were the offspring of some District pastors. They were given voice at the 1970 Convention, which was also the first Convention at which a woman lay delegate spoke from the floor.

District President Bert Frey's convention address was entitled "Toward a Service of Gladness." This would be his last address since he was being succeeded by the Rev. John Baumgaertner of Milwaukee. Frey lauded Synod's decision at the 1969 LCMS Convention to declare pulpit and altar fellowship with the ALC. He went on to add that it would be great if the California and Nevada District's memorial to Synod to declare full fellowship with the Lutheran Church in America (LCA) were adopted by Synod at its 1971 Convention. He further applauded that this 38th Convention of the English District would be the first to hear the voice of women delegates and youth.[178]

The Rev. Dr. Baumgaertner, pastor of Capitol Drive Lutheran Church, Milwaukee, was elected the first full-time District President/Bishop. He would serve in that capacity from Milwaukee and not re-locate to Detroit.

The Rev. Harold Hecht aided as executive secretary at the District office in Detroit. Baumgaertner was elected over several pastors who also stood for election: Revs. George Bornemann, Harold Hecht, Harry Huxhold, and John May. After the elimination of May, Bornemann, and Huxhold on succeeding ballots, Baumgaertner (199) was elected over Hecht (126) on the fourth ballot. The five regional vice presidents elected were then ranked in the following order: (1) Bertwin L. Frey (Lake Erie), (2) George W. Bornemann (Northwest), (3) Harry N. Huxhold (Southwest), (4) Theodore Pelikan (Eastern), and (5) Richard P. Melbohm (Pacific).[179]

The 38th Convention of the English District had as its theme, "What a Great Thing It Is," drawn from Psalm 133 and Psalm 118. President Frey, against the backdrop of the Vietnam War, civil unrest, and growing tension and division in the Missouri Synod, called for a service of gladness. This call was laced with his own strong agenda for Lutheran ecumenism and a "realistic appraisal" that the upcoming LCMS Milwaukee Convention in 1971 would not be favorable toward pulpit and altar fellowship with the LCA.[180]

Among the key floor committee chairmen were the Rev. Ernest Eggers (Nomination for District President); the Rev. Richard Jesse (Mission and Church Extension); Dr. Martin E. Marty (Youth); Mr. J. Harold Roth and the Rev. Reynold Lillie (Synodical Matters); Dr. Richard Stuckmeyer and Dr. Ed Wente (Social Ministry and Contemporary Issues); and Mr. Frederick Schoof and Teacher Edward Weerts (Elections). A record 91 resolutions were brought to the convention floor, many of which were very short and perfunctory in nature. Almost all were adopted or referred to the board of directors. Of special note were the following:

- 8-3 Youth Caucus – adopted a report from the Youth Caucus to be read in all congregations' worship assemblies
- 9-1 Reconsider Full-time Presidency – declined overtures asking for reconsideration of a full-time presidency
- 9-3 Dissolution of the English District – declined a proposal from a District congregation to consider dissolving the District, while asking the president of the District to create a special commission to produce a statement outlining the objectives of the English District and the reason for the District's existence for the 1972 Convention to consider
- 9-4 To Greet the LCA – sending of greetings and good wishes to their Minneapolis Convention, an act customarily done by the Synod as a whole

- 9-13 District Anniversary – this resolution was adopted, though the 1972 Convention would mark the 100th Anniversary of the English Missouri Synod founded in Gravelton, Missouri in 1872 rather than the 1911 establishment of the English District within the Synod
- 10-12 To Memorialize Synod to Reject "An Opinion Regarding Dissenting Groups Within the Synod" – called for the Synod Convention to reject "An Opinion Regarding Dissenting Groups" that had been issued by the Synod Commission on Constitutional Matters
- 10-15 A "Well-Rounded" Theological Education – commended Concordia Seminary, St. Louis, for encouraging voluntary enrollment of her students in courses at the Divinity School of St. Louis University and Eden Theological Seminary, and requesting the LCMS Board of Higher Education to arrange similar programs at other synodical institutions of higher learning
- 10-19 Primacy of the Gospel – asked the Synod Commission on Theology and Church Relations to evaluate a statement on the primacy of the Gospel, including several points:

> 4) that the English District deplore every effort to elevate the Bible above Gospel as the object of faith (or above God, Christ, Holy Spirit) and every effort that would allow the Bible, functioning as Law, to pre-empt the primacy of the Gospel; and
>
> 5) that the English District reject any new yoke of bondage to the law of mere doctrinal conformity that operates out of Law rather than the grace of God, to bind those who have been freed by Christ from every bondage of religion (Galatians 5:1); and
>
> 6) that the English District petition The Lutheran Church-Missouri Synod at its next convention to adopt this statement on the primacy of the Gospel over any doctrine or theory of the Bible and to accept this statement as the Synod's own understanding of what the Bible is chiefly about-that is, the Word of God offering salvation through forgiveness of sins, that all men might have life and hope in Christ by the Spirit.

- 10-20 Fellowship with the LCA – called for the 1971 LCMS Convention to declare pulpit and altar fellowship with the LCA; if that failed to be accomplished, then to allow LCMS congregations and individuals to practice unity with LCA brothers.

- 10-22 To Clarify Intent of "An Agreement" for Merger with SELC – asked for clarification so that congregations of the SELC coming into the LCMS might consider affiliating with the English District
- 11-3 To Let the Gospel Predominate in a Polarized Church and Society – outlined how to have the Gospel direct the Church's activities in the following ways:

> 1) that this convention encourage all members of our Church, in this polarized moment, to deal with each other out of the foundation of the Gospel; and
>
> 2) that we do not fear to resolve conflict but rather understand it as a concomitant to the pursuit of what is good for the people of our Church, nation and world; and
>
> 3) that we rely on the true peace founded on truth and love as exists in Jesus Christ; and
>
> 4) that we resist the temptation to idolize and absolutize our own views and opinions, but be continually prepared to have them corrected, modified, enhanced and deepened by the insights of others; and
>
> 5) that, as we take our stands and fight the necessary battles of our time, we remember Christ and extend to those of opposite opinion the care, freedom and love afforded them by the Gospel.

- 11-7 To Change the Draft Law – called for a repeal of the draft system and to permit conscientious objection to military service in all wars
- 11-11 Theological Study of the Population Problem and a Proposed Amendment to 11-11 – brought the topics of population growth, birth control, and abortion to the Church to determine how it should respond.

It would be interesting if the votes for and against key resolutions were included in the Convention *Proceedings*. This was not the case for decades of English District Conventions in which the simple notation was "adopted" or "defeated." However, the English District was showing itself to be highly activistic and involved in Church and State.

1971

As expected, the Synodical leadership under LCMS President J.A.O. Preus consolidated its strength. The American Lutheran Church at its Convention in 1970 admitted women to their seminaries to seek ordination into the Holy Ministry. This became a touch-point at the 1971 LCMS Convention in Milwaukee. There was a growing fear in the LCMS that the ALC did not have a correct understanding of biblical authority, especially with ordination of women on the horizon. ALC president Dr. Kent Knutson, addressed the 1971 LCMS Convention, asking for acceptance of the differences between the two church bodies. The matter of continued fellowship between the LCMS and ALC was in jeopardy.

Meanwhile, the faculty and president of Concordia Seminary became a target. Synod President Preus had appointed a Fact Finding Committee in 1969 to interview faculty members and report their findings. The Synod was concerned about the use of the "historical-critical method" for biblical interpretation, as embraced by a majority of the faculty. In 1970, a position paper was adopted by some St. Louis area pastors and laity titled "A Call to Openness and Trust." Professor Kurt Marquart, however, later would state the following:

> This document includes a brief list of "items" which "should not divide the Christian fellowship" nor exclude anyone from membership in the Missouri Synod. Among the examples given is not only "the question of factual error in the Bible" but even "the definition of the presence of Christ in the Lord's Supper!"... Yet the December 1972 CTM [*Concordia Theological Monthly*] treated the document as an instance of "loyal opposition" for which there ought to be room in the Synod![181]

However, at the July 1971 LCMS Convention, Synod's doctrinal position on the Lutheran Confessions as true and correct exposition of the Holy Bible was upheld. The conservative, confessional camp of Synod was gaining strength despite "unexpected resistance"[182] by liberals Dr. Bertwin Frey, English District President/Bishop, and Dr. F. Dean Lueking, pastor of Grace Evangelical Lutheran Church, River Forest, Illinois. The LCMS had also reached its peak in terms of congregational membership at 3.1 million (or 2.8 million, with the Brazil and Argentina Districts having become sister confessional Lutheran church bodies).

Was there a balanced, middle ground where most of the LCMS could feel comfortable between scriptural inerrancy and higher biblical criticism? Some LCMS pastors and laity urged Dr. Oswald Hoffmann to run for Synod president. Hoffman had been a young signer of the

"Statement of the 44," a former seminary professor, and later the long-time Speaker of *The Lutheran Hour*. Many felt he could become a healing factor. However, he deemed it best to protect *The Lutheran Hour* and its sponsor, the Lutheran Laymen's League, as the storm clouds continued to gather. Theologians were looking to Dr. Martin Franzmann, also a former Seminary professor, as one who could help find that middle ground. Franzmann chose to stay with the Evangelical Lutheran Church of England and the Westfield House ELCE seminary.

President Preus continued to press his agenda, even while some claimed that Synod's discord was nothing but personalities and politics. While these were factors in the continued hostilities, theological differences lay at the bedrock of the disharmony. Could the English District stay together? Preus issued "A Statement of Scriptural and Confessional Principles," in 1972, actually authored by Dr. Ralph Bohlmann, later president of Concordia Seminary and then president of the LCMS (1981-1992). The document dealt with the inspiration, infallibility, inerrancy, interpretation, and authority of the Holy Scriptures. The majority of the Concordia Seminary faculty found the document revulsive and issued its own document after the Fact-Finding Committee's report, nicknamed the "Blue Book," was released in September 1972. The Faculty's document *Faithful to Our Calling, Faithful to our Lord* was released in January 1973; it embraced Dr. Martin Kretzmann's 1965 Mission Affirmations and spoke of the Church as "Christ's mission to the whole person, the whole Church, the whole society, and the whole world."[183] This was a dangerous position, close to a distorted "social Gospel," which asserts that God in Christ "now promises to free us from any force that enslaves us…"[184]

1972

"The English District's accent is a broad and high one."[185] So stated an attractive brochure produced in 1972 called *"English Accent in the Lutheran Church/Missouri Synod."* The brochure succinctly delivered the history of the District and her antecedents, while also noting that the District was on the cutting edge with "experimental ministries and extraordinary ministers." But the District could not resist the opportunity to declare in the brochure its desire to promote broader ecumenical relationships. It touted its pastors: "This list includes the names of brilliant scholars and able ministers, men who have accepted 'status calls' from the directors of the English District who recognize their Gospel ministry even though it is outside the usual structures of setting."[186] This claim was great, but was the brochure a new set of Icarus' wings in paper form?

The English District met for its 39th Convention, June 23-25, 1972, at Concordia Teachers College, River Forest, which became the ground zero battleground. The Convention theme was "Faithful for All Times." Most of the District was ready to rise to the defense of Dr. John Tietjen and the seminary faculty majority against President J.A.O. Preus. Floor committee chairs and membership were heavily weighted toward those who were opposed to the doctrinal direction of Synod. The large Synodical Matters Floor Committee was co-chaired by the Rev. Dr. Justus P. Kretzmann (pastor, Atonement, Florissant, Missouri) and Mr. Harold J. Meinke (St. James, Grosse Pointe, Michigan).[187] During the 1970s, the District's Commission on Ministerial Health was an important ministry of the District to its professional church workers, an activity that is still continued by the District Ministerial Health Commission.

The commentary part of the President's Report of Dr. Baumgaertner was very short; the longer part was the usual perfunctory reporting of ordinations and installations, transfers and releases in and out of the District. The report of the executive secretary, the Rev. Harold Hecht, was also short, reporting a good relationship of the 12-person staff (four full-time executive staff) with the District president, parishes, and board of directors.[188] Also to be noted are the names of several principals involved with the Synod's ongoing controversy that are listed under "District Advisory Pastors and Professors," including Dr. John Damm (academic dean of Concordia Seminary and later also at Christ Seminary-Seminex) and Dr. John Tietjen.[189]

The report of the Commission on the Ministry of the People of God (COMPOG) in the *Convention Workbook* for the 39th English District Convention stated: "Every Christian is a minister by virtue of his baptism into the Lord Jesus Christ." This was a key phrase from the 1968 resolution authorizing the appointment of that commission: Help us discover how our local congregations can better enable their lay membership to minister in and for the world."[190] The COMPOG report was seven pages, explaining its activities to carry out that principle. Later the Synod would re-think the popular terminology of "everyone a minister" in a biblical understanding of the priesthood of all believers, not to be confused with the office of the Holy (public) Ministry.

The *Convention Workbook* reproduced the full 1971 Synod *Statistical Yearbook* data from English District congregations. The *Workbook* also included all overtures, including those from its more conservative congregations and pastors, such as "Censure Dr. Bertwin Frey," "Sever Connections with LCUSA," "Endorse Scriptural and Confessional Principles," and "Support Dr. Preus." Juxtaposed were overtures calling for "Ordination of Women," "Encourage COMPOG Follow-Through," and several overtures from the Committee on Social Ministry on "Native Americans," "Prison Reform," "Citizens Lobby' for the Hungry," "To Grant Amnesty" (to war objectors who dodged the U.S. military draft), and "To Recognize and Overcome Racial Bigotry." There was even an overture to "Hold Conventions Every Four Years, and Reduce Costs."[191]

The Rev. Dr. Roland Wiederaenders, first vice president of the LCMS, was the synodical representative to the 1972 English District Convention. The essayist was Dr. Herbert J.A. Bouman, a professor at Concordia Seminary, St. Louis, who spoke on "The Ordination of Women and its Implications for Church Fellowship." Besides President John Baumgaertner's address, Dr. John Tietjen, as second essayist, addressed the Convention under the theme, "Faithful for All Times."

These data points help to trace the line of direction occurring in the District, even while the English District was striving to stay united. At the District Convention, as reported in the *Proceedings* for 1972, 80 resolutions were received from the floor committees, most being very brief or of minor importance.[192] A proposed lettuce boycott (Res. 11-15) was defeated. However, four COMPOG resolutions were approved, as were resolutions to memorialize Synod to authorize training and ordaining women to the pastoral office (Res. 11-8). Another resolution (Res. 10-9) expressed the Convention's desire that "the English District request the president of the Synod and the faculty of Concordia Seminary, St. Louis, by mutual agreement, to withdraw both 'A Statement of Scriptural and Confessional Principles' and 'Response of the Faculty, Concordia Seminary, St. Louis, MO.'"[193]

Meanwhile in St. Louis, President Preus gained control of *The Lutheran Witness* and its companion *Reporter* and began what some

139

labelled a "purge" of the LCMS Mission Department and various missionaries. Mission Affirmations author Martin Kretzmann was fired in late 1972. This prompted the moderate 1973 presidential candidate, Dr. William Kohn, executive secretary for World Missions, to resign. In 1974, the LCMS Mission Board fired Rev. James Mayer. "By 1975, Kretzmann, Mayer, and most of the Synod's mission staff were gone."[194]

1973

Prior to the 1973 Synodical Convention at the Rivergate Center in New Orleans, a liberal caucus within the Missouri Synod that included many English District pastors formed a group called Evangelical Lutherans in Mission (ELIM). This was an opposition group to Dr. J.A.O. Preus and the LCMS conservative wing. Its publication was called *Missouri in Perspective.* ELIM developed after the New Orleans Convention, the suspension of Dr. John Tietjen as president of Concordia Seminary, and the "Seminex" walk-out, with lay support coming primarily after the 1975 LCMS Anaheim Convention. Many ELIM pastors and congregations eventually left the LCMS to form the Association of Evangelical Lutheran Churches (AELC) in 1976.

The 1973 Synodical Convention at New Orleans proved to be the watershed, what Synod President Preus called a "doctrinal crossroads."[195] And it was. While Preus felt enormous pressure not just from the liberal "left" wing, he also felt it from the conservative "right" wing, including Herman Otten's weekly tabloid *Christian News*, the Doctrinal Concerns Program (DCP), and Balance Inc., publishers of *Affirm*. The latter helped elect Preus in 1969. Not only was Preus re-elected as Synod president, most of the preferred candidates of the conservative wing for Synod offices were elected, and Ralph Bohlmann's "A Statement of Scriptural and Confessional Principles" was approved by the Convention (Res. 3-01). The Synod Commission on Theology and Church Relations (CTCR) declared the document to be theologically sound. With a majority of the Board of Control of Concordia Seminary now in firm conservative control under its Chair, Rev. E.J. Otto, the Convention adopted Resolution 3-09, declaring the Seminary faculty majority guilty of false doctrine. Debate at the Convention was wild and furious. But after all the shouting, it remained for Dr. Preus and the Board of Control to administer discipline.

1974

That discipline came swiftly in January 1974, with the suspension and eventual firing of Dr. Tietjen as president of Concordia Seminary, St. Louis. It quickly became apparent that the English District's pastors, congregations, and professors (five of whom were faculty at Concordia Seminary) were hopelessly divided.

The English District prepared for its 40th Convention at Concordia Teachers College, River Forest in June 13–16, 1974. Dr. Baumgaertner would not stand for re-election as District president, leaving an open contest among five candidates.

<u>1974 First Ballot Votes for President of the English District</u>

Rev. Paul Barth	60
Rev. Bertwin L. Frey	110
Rev. Harold L. Hecht	96
Rev. Harry Huxhold	30
Rev. Omar Stuenkel	33.[196]

Rev. James Mayer, former Synod Secretary for Missions in Southeast Asia, was the first keynote speaker with an essay on "Our Second Century in Mission."

<u>1974 Second Ballot Votes for President of the English District</u>

Rev. Paul Barth	55
Rev. Bertwin L. Frey	138
Rev. Harold L. Hecht	100
Rev. Omar Stuenkel	22

Barth was the sole remaining conservative candidate following this vote. The third ballot resulted in the following:

Rev. Paul Barth	60
Rev. Bertwin L. Frey	165
Rev. Harold L. Hecht	129.[197]

Synod Vice President Gerhardt Nitz from San Francisco represented Synod President Preus at the Convention. He reviewed the Synod's work in the areas of evangelism and overseas missions and "commended the English District for its specialized ministries, adding: "Synod could learn much from you."[198] He then addressed the new congregations and their pastors joining the Synod and District: Tierrasanta Lutheran Church, San Diego, California; Morning Star Lutheran Church, Lakeside, California; Mount Olive Lutheran Church, Tucson, Arizona; and Messiah Lutheran Church, Forest Lake, Minnesota.

The drama of the election for District president came to an end when the Committee on Elections announced the results of the fourth and final ballot:

Dr. Bertwin Frey	176
Harold L. Hecht	177

Hecht was elected by the slimmest of margins. The motion to make the election unanimous was made, seconded by Dr. Frey, and carried.[199] But the unity of that action by the Convention was fleeting.

The Convention moved on to elect and rank the vice presidents:

1st VP   Rev. George W. Bornemann (Elmhurst, Illinois; Northwest Region)

2nd VP   Rev. Harold N. Huxhold (Indianapolis, Indiana, Southwest Region)

3rd VP   Rev. Theodore Pelikan, (Cleveland, Ohio, Lake Erie Region)

4th VP   Rev. Gordon R. Mackensen (El Cajon, California, Western Region)

5th VP   Rev. Erich Wildgrube (Blue Bell, Pennsylvania, Eastern Region).[200]

This ranking would prove to be significant, as history of the District would reveal. President/Bishop Baumgaertner's address to the Convention expressed his grievances over the direction of the Synod. He announced that he had authorized that the four candidates of "our Seminary in Exile" called to English District congregations be ordained and installed upon receipt of a "Certificate of Eligibility for Ordination and Installation from the Director of Placement of Concordia Seminary in Exile."[201] While expressing the positions of the liberal majority of the English District, Baumgaertner spoke and wrote with a very heavy heart.

Numerous resolutions were adopted, including several that revealed the District's minority theological position within the Synod:

- Supporting the 1965 Mission Affirmations
- Thanks to Rev. James Mayer
- Tribute to President Baumgaertner
- Memorializing Synod to express gratitude for the ministry of Dr. Arthur Carl Piepkorn
- Support of Concordia Seminary-in-Exile (with the names of negative votes recorded)
- Solidarity with John H. Tietjen (with negative and abstention votes recorded)
- Support of ELIM
- Declaring 1973 Synodical resolutions 2-12, 3-01, and 3-09 as unconstitutional (negative votes were recorded), and
- Memorializing Synod to rescind the disciplinary use of and parts of "A Statement" (again, with negative votes recorded). [202]

Two Resolutions bear further notice. Resolution 8-4, which would have required the District president to reside in the Detroit area near the District headquarters, was defeated. Resolution 9-4, which addressed the continued existence of the English District, was adopted, resolving that the English District communicate to the LCMS president, Board of Directors, and Convention that it reaffirms, in accord with the 1911 Agreement, its right to continue as a corporate entity within the Synod. As noted in the last portion of Resolution 9-4, the English District intended to maintain its existing status as a district of Synod, authorizing and directing its board of directors "to undertake whatever actions or procedures that they in good conscience may deem to be required or necessary to protect, preserve and maintain the presently existing status of The English District as a district of Synod."[203]

Like the 1973 LCMS New Orleans Convention, the 1974 English District Convention was gut-wrenching. It was preceded by the usual *Convention Workbook*, but an additional publication was also distributed:

English District Notes & Agenda. This appeared to be random information on different colored pages, including a Supplement to the President's Report. But it also included the minutes that were later produced in the *Proceedings* following the District Convention. The front cover, marked with a hand-drawn Jerusalem or Crusader's Cross, was entitled: "Official District Convention Publication, Authorized and Produced Under the Direction of the President and Secretary of the District."[204] Suffice it to say, this was a highly-charged, politicized, and stressful time amounting to a veritable "civil war" within the English District and The Lutheran Church—Missouri Synod. Efforts to hold the District together were fading.

In 1975, an "English District Centennial Publication" was printed by Agape Publishers, Inc., W. Capitol Dr., Milwaukee: *A Tree Grows In Missouri*. It was claimed that the book had been authorized by the English District, Lutheran Church—Missouri Synod. It begins and concludes with a Whereas and the Resolved (Resolution 9-7 "Stand by brothers and sisters") with these words:

> Whereas, *our District is determined to do all things necessary to maintain our freedom in the Gospel, the brotherly affection, and the bonds of loving acceptance of one another which have marked our fellowship in the past, be it*
>
> Resolved *that we let it be known to all in the Synod that we will stand by our brothers and sisters and our sister congregations when they suffer, and we will continue to offer an open fellowship for pastors, teachers, and congregations in times of distress to strengthen, heal, conserve, and generally support all our brethren for the building up of the Body of Christ.*
>
> Action: Adopted
> From the Convention Proceedings of the English District June 13-16, 1974.

A Tree Grows in Missouri was edited by Dr. Baumgaertner, English District President/Bishop and founding pastor of Capitol Drive Lutheran Church, and produced in time for the 1975 LCMS Anaheim Convention. The authors listed were Revs. John H. Baumgaertner, August F. Brunn, Bertwin L. Frey, Harold L. Hecht, Bernard H. Hemmeter, Harry N. Huxhold, Martin E. Marty, and John H. Tietjen. All but the aged Dr. Brunn were leaders in the liberal cause within the LCMS. The book contains well-written historical facts, but its agenda clearly promoted opinions and theological rationale opposite the direction of Synod following the 1969 Convention and skewed the true District centennial date.[205]

CHAPTER 12
Division

BY THE MIDDLE of the 1970s, suspicion and mistrust were firmly ensconced as part of the English District within The Lutheran Church—Missouri Synod. Friendships dissolved as battle lines became entrenched. What had been a district that helped the German Missouri Synod navigate a language change from German to English and was instrumental in expanding outreach and ministry, especially in urban areas, was now shattered. Sadly, good names were besmirched and anger and rhetoric clouded what was at the basis, namely theological discord over the nature and authority of Holy Scripture.

Seminex (1974—1987)

With the suspension of Concordia Seminary President John Tietjen in January 1974, events unfolded quickly that resulted in a schism in The Lutheran Church—Missouri Synod. A large majority of the seminary students rallied to support Tietjen. On February 19, these seminary students left the Concordia Seminary St. Louis campus in a "walk out" (termed a "moratorium") that made national news. Supported by 45 of the 50 professors, the student "walk out" led to the formation of a new, rival seminary called "Concordia Seminary-in-Exile" or "Seminex," or as it was later named "Christ Seminary-Semiex." ELIM, the network for the liberal wing of the LCMS, quickly threw its support to the students and faculty of Seminex, who met in rented space at St. Louis University and Eden Seminary. Led by many English District pastors, among others, ELIM convened in Chicago with 800 conference delegates, promising moral and financial support for church members who faced pressure due to their opposition to LCMS convention actions. Many 1974 in-coming students to Concordia Seminary now were torn as to where to attend.[206] All of the English District members of the Concordia Seminary faculty who "walked out" and became part of Seminex eventually left the LCMS.

Concordia Seminary, St Louis, with only five faculty remaining—Drs. Martin Scharlemann, Robert Preus, Richard Klann, Lorenz Wunderlich, and John Klotz—continued with the remaining 100-plus students. The

Seminary was aided by professors brought in from Concordia Theological Seminary, its sister school in Springfield, Illinois, and other qualified pastors. Remarkably, the Seminary rebounded in a short number of years. But an issue that quickly arose was whether Seminex graduates could be placed into LCMS congregations. Synod President Preus refused to allow placement of these students. In 1975, eight presidents of the synodical districts were threatened with removal from office because they allowed congregations to ordain Seminex graduates as pastors. Eventually, some Seminex graduates went through a colloquy to serve in the LCMS.[207] In April 1976, four of these District presidents were removed from office, including Dr. Harold Hecht, President/Bishop of the English District. Hecht was replaced by an appointee of the Synod President, Dr. Paul Barth. Barth was a solidly conservative pastor from Nazareth Evangelical Lutheran Church & School, Buffalo, New York. He was a respected and scholarly pastor; however, his ability to serve was minimal due to lack of support from within the English District and the impending English District Convention to be held in June 1976.

District presidents were also removed from office in the Atlantic, Eastern and New England districts. In the wake of the formation of Seminex, and the removal of four district presidents, a movement to leave the Synod ensued between 1975 and 1978 among dissident congregations and church officials, most of them members of ELIM. The largest number of departures came from the English District. 78 congregations with nearly 27,000 communicants left the English District to form the English Synod of the Association of Evangelical Lutheran Churches (AELC) in December of 1976.[208] When the dust settled at the end of 1978, approximately 250 congregations left the LCMS, with approximately 108,000 members and 550 pastors. The AELC had gained far fewer pastors and congregations than initially anticipated by liberal leaders in the English District and ELIM. Many pastors whose congregations were more conservative chose to stay members of the LCMS and continue the fight. The wind was largely out of the sails; the English District would return to more of the traditional, confessionally-conservative positions of the LCMS. If the 1973 New Orleans Convention of Synod had won the so-called "Battle for the Bible" in the LCMS, the 1975 Anaheim Convention sealed the victory.

Not surprisingly, the AELC, with its largest component Synod being the new English Synod, revealed itself to be more theologically, ecumenically, politically, and socially "open" than the LCMS. Though the faculty majority at Concordia Seminary had earlier declined to affirm ordination of women to the pastoral office, shortly after Seminex came into existence, women were certified for holy orders in the pastoral ministry. None could be placed in LCMS congregations, while the men who graduated and wanted to serve as pastors in the LCMS had to complete a colloquy process that had been made more stringent. By October 1977, the AELC ordained its first female clergyperson, Jan Otte Murphy.[209] The AELC would be a catalyst for the eventual "merger" of the AELC, ALC, and LCA, all of them ordaining women, into a new Evangelical Lutheran Church in America (ELCA), with an initial membership of 5.4 million baptized members.

Prior to the 1976 English District Convention, the Missouri Synod held its biennial convention in July 1975 in Anaheim, California. At that Convention, "the conservative majority voted to condemn ELIM as schismatic, and agreed that district presidents who did not follow the procedures of the synod should be removed from office."[210] With that authorization, Preus was able to remove four district presidents from office in the spring of 1976. The 1975 LCMS Convention further consolidated Preus' nearly complete control of the boards, committees, and apparatuses of the Synod. However, the Synod Convention "declined by a voice vote to amalgamate the English District in a year."[211] The District had again avoided dissolution.

The Special Convention of 1975

The English District President/Bishop and board of directors followed up the July 1975 Anaheim Convention with its own "Special Convention." A small workbook was sent out to all delegates to a Special Convention of the English District. President Harold Hecht stated that the workbook materials were for the delegates to study prior to the Special Convention, September 19-21, 1975, at the Northlake Center, Northlake, Illinois, a Chicago suburb. Contained in the workbook were position statements of the English District and board of directors from the 1974 District Convention and actions taken at the 1975 LCMS Anaheim Convention.

The main topic was the future of the English District and how to serve the interests of the Synod.

Among the 1975 LCMS Anaheim Convention issues that were addressed were those of dissolving the English District, and dealing with the District presidents who authorized the ordination and installation of Seminex graduates. The English District was not dissolved, though the failed Resolution 4-02A had directly challenged the understanding that dissolution could happen only if the English District chose to recommend its dissolution and the congregations elected to amalgamate into the other districts. Synod upheld the possibility and likelihood of District presidents being removed from office for authorizing Seminex graduates for ordination and installation who did not go through Synod's colloquy process.

Other actions taken at the Anaheim Convention prompted a resolution for the 1975 English District Special Convention that the District reaffirm its support of President Hecht, urge him to continue to follow his conscience and the directives of the 1974 English District Convention, and that, if he should be removed from office for authorizing such ordinations and installations the District would "not recognize such removal as being valid."[212]

Decades later, some thought this Special Convention never occurred, but it was held.[213] English District pastors and congregational representatives were invited, but some chose not to attend since it was being conducted by the majority liberal wing. However, a number of individuals from the conservative wing did attend and made their opposition known. Years later, Dr. Paul Bacon reported that the Special Convention had a general session, which then broke up into small groups. The central issue was whether the District should remain in the Missouri Synod. When the small groups returned to the plenary or general session, a two-to-one majority felt the District should continue to stay with the LCMS. However, when the "orators," according to Pastor Bacon, took over, the Convention was swayed to begin work toward separating from the Missouri Synod.[214]

The *Proceedings* from the September 1975 Special Convention do not include the names of pastoral and lay delegate attendees, as is normally found. Perhaps this was due to the Convention's special format and purpose as a response to the LCMS Anaheim Convention. Representing the Synod was Dr. Theodore Nickel, LCMS second vice president, from Chicago. Minutes were recorded by the District secretary, the Rev. Robert L. Landeck. Reprinted in the *Proceedings* were the homily for the opening service by the Rev. William H. Kohn; the President's Address by Dr. Harold L. Hecht; presentations to the plenary session by Dr. Leonard O. Roellig and Mrs. Hildegarde Pick, both lay delegates to the 1975 LCMS Anaheim Convention; the Convention essay "A Bible Study on Luther's Concept of Ministry" by Dr. Harry Huxhold, District second vice president; a keynote presentation "Transparent Freedom" by Dr. Martin E. Marty; and, the sermon "Christ Frees – Christ Unites" for the Eucharist Service by the Rev. Henry C. Duwe, where Dr. John Tietjen presided as celebrant.[215]

At the Special Convention, a Position Statement (75-1A) was presented by the steering committee, chaired by the Rev. Victor Brandt. The Position Statement decried "injustice [that] has been done to the faculty and student body of Concordia Seminary-in-Exile," affirmed Hecht's authorization of Seminex graduates' ordinations and installations, supported ELIM, asked the board of directors to deal kindly with pastors and congregations planning to leave the LCMS, and reaffirmed the desire to stay in the LCMS.[216] "The Chair approved a request by the Rev. Paul Barth that the Rev. Herbert Wians read a statement drafted by a committee representing a minority of District members…. The convention agreed to print the minority [statement] with the names of signers attached."[217] While the committee presenting the "Minority Statement" recognized that all would not agree with its position, no malice was intended and that they were all brothers and sisters in Christ. The "Minority Statement" read:

> The English District has served our Lord and our beloved Synod by faith and life for 64 years. We desire to continue our life and service in the English District of The Lutheran Church—Missouri Synod… We therefore believe that we should encourage our brother and our president Harold Hecht to honor our Synod's position by no longer authorizing ordination and installation of Seminex graduates. We also believe that our District board of directors should, at this time, withdraw their "Posture" paper which does not, by its strong statements, promote reconciliation… We respectfully ask our synodical officials to implement Synod's stated desire to determine the theological soundness, or lack of it,

of each member of the Seminex faculty by the appointed interview committee...[218]

The "Minority Statement" was signed by 39 delegates. Among the 12 voting delegate pastors signing the Minority Statement were the Revs. Paul G. Barth, Horace "Chick" W. Garton, Norman T. Laesch, Merlin C. Meyer, John L. Murphy, Edward N. Schulte, W.H. Wetzstein, and Herbert T. Wians. Six advisory delegates and visitors also signed.[219]

The 1975 Special Convention set the stage for the June 1976 Convention of the English District, President Hecht having been removed from office by LCMS President Preus in April. Dr. Paul Barth was serving as president, appointed by LCMS President Preus. Pastor Barth was appointed by Preus only after the latter had twice asked first vice president George Bornemann to assume the acting presidency of the English District.[220] Bornemann declined after careful consultation with the congregation he served as pastor, Redeemer Evangelical Lutheran Church, Elmhurst, Illinois. The 1976 regular English District Convention was again held at Concordia Teachers College, River Forest. The largest concentration of the transcontinental English District congregations at that time were to be found in the six Chicago area circuits, even though the District office was in Detroit. This would be the English District's watershed convention.

Excursus: The Rev. Dr. Martin E. Marty

Whether one agreed with Dr. Martin E. Marty or not, it has to be recognized that he was a formidable figure, a highly influential voice in the English District of The Lutheran Church—Missouri Synod and North American Christianity as a world-class scholar. Marty authored numerous books and thousands of articles, especially on the history of religion in North America.

Dr. Marty graduated from Concordia Seminary, St. Louis, in 1952, having served as a vicar at an English District congregation, Christ Evangelical Lutheran Church, Washington, D.C., in 1950-1951. He earned an STM at Chicago Lutheran Theological Seminary (later, Lutheran School of Theology at Chicago [LSTC] in 1954, and a Ph.D. in 1956 from the University of Chicago. Following two pastorates at Grace Evangelical

Lutheran Church, River Forest, Illinois (assistant pastor), 1952-1954, and as the founding pastor of the English District's Lutheran Church of the Holy Spirit, Elk Grove Village, Illinois, 1958-1963, he became professor of history at the Divinity School of the University of Chicago in 1963, retiring in 1998.

Born in 1928 in Nebraska, Martin E. Marty was married to his wife, Elsa, in 1952. She died in 1981. In 1982, Marty married Harriet Meyer, a musician who had previously served on the faculty at Concordia Teachers College, River Forest, Illinois. For years, Marty was the associate editor of the theological journal, *The Christian Century*, and he was a frequent lecturer and presenter, as well as a celebrated author. Among his works were *A Short History of Christianity* (1959), *Righteous Empire: The Protestant Experience in America* (1970), *Pilgrims in Their Own Land: Five Hundred Years of Religion in America* (1984), a three-volume set, and *Modern American Religion* (1986-1996) which was about the development of American religious life since the late 18th century. He also wrote *When Faiths Collide*, published in 2005, and was the recipient of numerous awards.

Dr. Marty was with Dr. Martin Luther King Jr. in the historic march from Selma to Montgomery, Alabama, in 1965, and involved in the anti-Vietnam War movement. Marty was co-director of the Fundamentalist Project for the American Academy of Arts and Sciences.

Dr. Marty, among others, was removed from the LCMS Roster in 1978, having maintained dual membership in the Association of Evangelical Lutheran Churches and the LCMS, something the LCMS did not permit. He is currently on the roster of the ELCA. His often quoted comment about the English District being among the *"happiest little outfits"* in Christendom was apparently said often in the years prior to 1976. However, in his November 12, 1976 Address to the new English Synod (of the AELC) entitled "A New Song for a New People," Dr. Marty concluded with a criticism of *"dainty singing,"* which was then followed by the robust singing of the late Dr. Martin Franzmann's "Thy Strong Word Did Cleave the Darkness."[221]

Chapter 12

The "Hopelessly Polarized" 1976 Convention of the English District-LCMS

The English District 41st Convention at Concordia Teachers College, River Forest, Illinois, June 17-20, 1976, was utterly gut-wrenching. One lay delegate from San Francisco, whose congregation would leave the LCMS and join the English Synod of the Association of Evangelical Lutheran Churches, was shocked that he saw so many pastors in tears.[222] President Preus was himself present, representing Synod at Convention. Several pastors and congregations were already planning to leave the LCMS and start a new English Synod. Despite having been removed from office by the Synod president, Harold Hecht opened the Convention and served as chairman. A motion to have the Synod-appointed president, Rev. Paul Barth, take the chair was defeated.[223] After some preliminaries and reports, Dr. Paul W.F. Harms gave the Convention essay. The Convention theme was the words of St. Augustine: *"In Necessary Things – Unity, in Doubtful Things – Freedom, In All Things – Love."*

After a bit more Convention business, Dr. Jack Preus addressed the convention on Friday, June 18. His presentation was enhanced by those who accompanied him: Dr. Richard Dickinson, head of the Centennial Black Task Force of Synod; Dr. General Gerhardt Hyatt, a Synod vice president; and, Mr. Carl Muhlenbruch, a member of Synod's Board of Directors. Following his presentation there was a "lively dialogue."[224]

The rest of the Friday afternoon and evening sessions involved dynamic debate over what became combined Resolutions 8-03 and 9-01 "To initiate a process for orderly and peaceful separation" and a substitute motion, "Harmony in Synod," offered by Rev. Milton Nauss. His substitute motion attempted to strike a mediating position, calling for ELIM and Seminex leaders to meet with the Synodical administration for theological discussions, asking to rescind 1973 Resolution 3-09, requesting reinstatement of the suspended District presidents, and encouraging Seminex students to complete the required colloquy programs.[225] The substitute motion failed, while Resolution 8-03 with some adopted amendments was approved "by a very large majority."[226] This revealed the deep polarization of the English District and between the District and the Synod. Dr. Paul Barth as Synod-named "acting President" was accorded the floor, and he "invited delegates to meet with him and others in the interest of continuing membership in the English District."[227]

On Saturday, June 19, 1976, Dr. Harold Hecht convened the Convention and Dr. Paul Harms continued his presentation as essayist. After the adoption of several resolutions from various floor committees, Resolution 8-08, "To provide for an orderly transition" came up but was recommitted to the floor committee. Historians, in writing the "history" years or decades later, often take a sympathetic view of the English District's quandary at that time: how to separate peaceably and honorably. A revised resolution (Res. 8-08A) was brought forth and adopted 296 to 75 after several amendments to revise it were defeated.[228] Because a number of congregations and pastors were leaving the English District to join the new English Synod of the AELC, the further revised and finally approved Resolution 8-08A had four resolves including the following:

- Recognition of property rights of the congregations leaving, including approving "transfers" of pastors and teachers to the new English Synod and charitable dealings by the English District board of directors to those withdrawing
- Expression of "the hope that the Missouri Synod and the English Synod will continue joint ministries" as well as pulpit and altar fellowship
- Until the separation would be complete, to encourage congregations to support present English District ministries, and
- "That the members of the existing English District board of directors who intend to affiliate with the new English Synod, with honor and with concern for the English District, resign their offices and that they be replaced by election at this convention."[229]

Synod President Preus' Address to the Convention, President/Bishop Harold Hecht's Address to the Convention, the lengthy Convention essay by Dr. Paul W. Harms, and Dr. Harvey Stegemoeller's Convention Banquet Address were printed in the Convention *Proceedings*. What should not escape notice from the Convention *Proceedings* were the disbanding of two congregations: Our Redeemer Lutheran Church, Chicago (June 1, 1974) and Good Shepherd Lutheran Church, Maywood, Illinois (June 1, 1976), the latter having been pastored by Rev. Paul Bacon, who would be elected District secretary at the Convention and was installed as pastor of Trinity Evangelical Lutheran Church, New Lenox,

Illinois. Pastor Bacon had a long tenure at this congregation and later served the English District in several capacities as District secretary, circuit visitor, and vice president, including first vice president, and editor of a journal that a decade later came into existence, *The Journal of English District Pastors* (1988-2001), commonly and humorously known as "*JEDP.*"[230]

It was further reported in the Convention *Proceedings* that the constitutions of three churches were approved at the Special Convention of the English District on September 19, 1975: Martin Luther Chapel, the town-gown Lutheran campus ministry for Michigan State University, East Lansing, Michigan; Peace Lutheran Church, Cedar Rapids, Iowa; and New Life in Christ Lutheran Church, Ferguson, Missouri. In addition, 15 congregations were received by transfer from geographic districts, including St. John's, Pembroke, Ontario, the largest congregation in the Ontario District-LCMS, and three congregations in Livonia, Michigan, located near the English District office. These three congregations—Faith, All Saints, and Holy Trinity Evangelical Lutheran Churches—all soon left the LCMS for the new English Synod of the AELC. When Dr. Hecht, having been "fired" by Dr. Jack Preus, was no longer at the English District office on Grand River Avenue in Detroit, the English Synod office for a time was headquartered at Faith Church, Livonia.[231]

Though names of those who made and seconded motions were not recorded in the minutes of English District Conventions, Pastor Bacon was the one who made a motion for a new slate for those who would be staying with the Synod. The motion was tabled and the Nominations Committee was called into session, which then prepared two slates.

That Saturday evening, June 19, 1976, as the Convention *Proceedings* indicate:

> A dramatic procession formed by hundreds of delegates and guests marched to the gymnasium of Grace Lutheran Church, where the Rev. Dr. John Baumgaertner announced that almost all officers of the English District, including President Harold Hecht, and almost all members of the board of directors of the English District, had been named as officers and directors of the new English Synod of the Evangelical Lutheran Church. President Hecht spoke words of acceptance.[232]

The Divine Service on Sunday, June 20, was held at Grace Evangelical Lutheran Church, the church adjacent to the campus of Concordia Teachers College, the Rev. Dr. John Baumgaertner, preaching.[233]

First Vice President George Bornemann chaired the session that included reading of the new slate of nominees and the subsequent election. Those marked with an asterisk (*) were elected:

President:	Paul Barth	68
	George Bornemann	*149
Teacher member, board of directors:		
	Ronald Harman	*194
Lay members, board of directors:		
	Charles Bartells	70
	Edwin Hoeltke	*104 (2 years)
	David Kuhfal	*158 (4 years)
	Fred Marks	72
	Robert Osman	*106 (2 years)
	Herbert Schroeder	33
	Merrill Wyble	*163 (4 years)
	Clarence Kelley	69.[234]

Newly elected President/Bishop Dr. George Washington Bornemann addressed the Convention, stating that he would assure the English District's continuance. The slate for vice presidents was then presented, followed by the election in the afternoon, including that of secretary of the District and pastoral members of the board of directors. Those elected and then ranked by the District as vice presidents were:

1st VP	Rev. Melvin Tassler (Lincoln, Nebraska, Southwest Region)
2nd VP	Rev. Walter Holm (Villa Park, Illinois, Midwest Region)
3rd VP	Rev. Donald Jung (West Bloomfield, Michigan, Lake Erie Region)
4th VP	Rev. Richard Drews (San Diego, California, Western Region)
5th VP	Rev. Theodore Koepke (Cliffside Park, New Jersey, Eastern Region).

The Rev. Paul Bacon (New Lenox, Illinois), unopposed, was elected District secretary. The Rev. Victor Halboth Jr. (Redford Twp., Michigan) and the Rev. William Hughes (Arlington Heights, Illinois) were elected as pastoral members of the board of directors. Even though a motion was made and then tabled to have Dr. Paul Barth, acting president of the District, conduct the Rite of Installation, that rite was actually done by Dr. Harold Hecht. Shortly thereafter, President/Bishop Bornemann called for a meeting of the new board of directors for Friday, June 25 in Chicago and indicated that they would strive to keep the English District-LCMS intact.[235] With that, the 1976 English District Convention was history.

An English District pastor held in very high respect was the Rev. Milton "Mickey" Nauss (1920-2013), the author of the aforementioned substitute motion defeated at the 1976 Convention. Nauss had served as an English District pastor for many decades, including at the campus ministry at Princeton University (Lutheran Church of the Messiah), Pilgrim Evangelical Lutheran Church, St. Louis, and Pilgrim's daughter congregation which Nauss founded, Chapel of the Cross Lutheran Church in north St. Louis County. He served at Chapel of the Cross from its 1965 founding to 1985. Chapel of the Cross also started a daughter congregation in St. Peter, Missouri, of the same name. Under Nauss' dynamic leadership, Chapel of the Cross grew to be one of the largest congregations in Synod at that time with over 3,600 souls. Before the official formation of the AELC, Nauss, as president of the LCMS St. Louis Pastoral Conference, attempted a mediation between Jack Preus and John Tietjen.[236] It was a noble attempt, but the die had been cast for division and separation. Nauss' comments from September 1976 on the behavior of the two parties within the LCMS have been noted by later students of these turbulent times:

> "The Conservatives have been guilty of injustices and lack of integrity. Personally, I believe these charges are justified to a degree. But at the same time, I believe the Moderates are even more guilty of these same things, however, in a more sophisticated fashion." His statement went on to explain that moderates were responsible for inaugurating the controversy by introducing a new method of biblical interpretation.[237]

Dr. Nauss and Chapel of the Cross loyally stayed with the English District and provided strong financial support to the District and Synod in the aftermath of what is often called "the Seminex Era," but in truth was a period of tension, pain, rift, and eventual division.

An Epilogue to this critical period in the English District's history is the November 12–13, 1976, meeting of those who left the Synod and District. This was the First Convention of The English Synod of the Evangelical Lutheran Church, held at the Arlington Park Hilton Hotel, Arlington Heights, a suburb of Chicago. The keynote speaker was Dr. Martin E. Marty. Dr. Harold Hecht also addressed the Convention.[238] Following discussion of the structure, there was an organ recital by Dr. Paul Manz, a lifelong Missouri Synod Lutheran and distinguished musician and composer of numerous organ improvisations, choral works, and other pieces. The Eucharist service had Dr. A.R. Kretzmann of St. Luke Evangelical Lutheran Church & School, Chicago, as celebrant, Manz as Organist, and Dr. Bertwin Frey as preacher. Included in the "Sing A New Song" convention packet was a Covenant of Membership document for membership in the English Synod of the Evangelical Lutheran Church, and a Constitution of new English Synod with a Preamble that briefly presented the history of the original English Missouri Synod and the English District in the LCMS. Of historical value is this part of the Preamble:

> Because of this origin [the English Missouri Synod becoming the English District in the German Missouri Synod], the English District was unique among the districts of the Missouri Synod. However, a controversy within the Missouri Synod in which doctrinal and confessional issues were raised led in 1975 to the adoption of "A Position Statement" by the English District meeting in Special Convention in Northlake, Illinois, wherein it was stated that the English District was prepared to ask its congregations to revert to the status of an independent Synod or seek other institutional affiliation if it became clear that The Lutheran Church—Missouri Synod did not intend to return to its former confessional position and its former Evangelical practice which respects diversity within the unity of the Church. Said Statement of the District further stated that efforts made to discipline the District or its members because of their confessional

stance would be regarded as a breach of the covenant mutually entered into [by] the Synod and the District. It having become clear that such diversities would not be tolerated in the Missouri Synod by the synodical authorities and that such disciplinary actions were to be pursued, this corporation has been formed to continue the mission, ministry, and fellowship of the English District independent from the Missouri Synod.[239]

The English District and The Lutheran Church—Missouri Synod and most of her member congregations, pastors, and other professional rostered church workers would understandably have seen it much differently than what that Preamble portrays. But the Preamble does accurately reflect the pain and suffering of any church body that finally comes to irreconcilable division.

Excursus: Could the Split in the Synod and District Have Been Avoided?

The author of this book asked a younger (but seasoned) pastor whether the rupture in The Lutheran Church—Missouri Synod in 1975-1976 could have been avoided. His response was, "Yes, it could have been avoided." However, he did not care to elaborate.

Was the "split" just "Missouri being Missouri," as some outsiders termed it?[240] The desire for many in the Missouri Synod and especially in the English District was for greater ecumenical inter-Lutheran cooperation, and possibly an eventual merger. The desire for those in the Lutheran Church in America and The American Lutheran Church was for a common hymnal and common worship, closer ties with the LCMS, and for Missouri to join them in working toward a merger in which 95% of North American Lutheranism would be together as one.

This author is not aware of any poll among Lutheran historians, but it is his judgment that the split was inevitable. The events that took place thereafter revealed that those who, painfully so, left the Missouri Synod to start the new AELC regarded Missouri as entrenched in its past. Missouri would not seek closer ties among more "liberal" Lutheran church bodies if it felt that the Bible was being compromised. While things shifted years afterward from the times of the late 1960s and 1970s, it was during those years a "Battle for the Bible." Dr. Milton Nauss, Dr. Vic Halboth Jr., and others, would have frequent phone conversations and meetings together while at District gatherings. But these two pastors, along with Rev. Herbert Wians, represented the largest congregations of the English District. They were not about to leave Synod and the heritage that they held dear. Many would look up to these men. Most laity embraced the desire for a clear affirmation of the Holy Bible as the infallible Word of God, with no JEDPs, two or three Isaiahs, "Q" sources of the Gospels, or higher biblical criticism.

In truth, the laity rose up to reclaim a church body that they felt was being taken away from them, especially by the majority of the faculty at Concordia Seminary and other LCMS institutions. They found their "conservative" champions in J.A.O. and Robert Preus, Karl Barth, and many other pastors in the Synod. What those outside of Missouri could not understand is that the denomination was holding to its doctrinal moorings.

It is true that numerous people were badly hurt by the rupture in the LCMS, though the schism was nowhere as large as had been hoped by those who left. Perhaps, if other leaders had been elected such as Dr. Oswald Hoffmann, the outcome may have been different, but that was not likely. The forces that moved in the late 1960s and early 1970s kept feeding on their own fires. The directions were decidedly different. "The main hope of the AELC was that it could engineer some sort of merger or cooperative arrangement with the LCA and ALC."[241] Ordination of women and other doctrines and positions anathema to Missouri came out quickly as part of the AELC's agenda. Could people have been kinder, more charitable, listening to one another, and seeking to maintain unity of faith, doctrine, and practice? Of course. But history indicated that healing was not possible for the Missouri Synod and one of her "progressive lead" districts, the English District.

CHAPTER 13
The "Amazing Comeback" Era

The Bishop/President Years of
George Bornemann and Donald Jung

FOR STAYING WITH the English District, the Revs. George Bornemann, Victor ("Vic") Halboth, and Milton Nauss, among others, were labelled "Judases." Those who left the English District and the LCMS were also labelled by different people as "Judases." The name-calling and post-split anger and bitterness did not go away overnight. However, the English District was re-grouping and beginning an "amazing comeback." Five days after the 1976 Convention of the English District ended, the new English District board of directors met on Friday, June 25, at the International Motor Inn, Schiller Park, Illinois. Following devotions, President/Bishop Bornemann was elected chairman. All board members and staff were present except one who was excused. The District's finances were in shambles, the high point in congregational giving and contributions to Synod being in 1969. $36,000 was needed monthly for mission subsidies and payroll, with only $38,000—39,000 coming in monthly. Travel by staff had to be curtailed, even though visitation was and still is the lifeblood of this non-geographical district. Faithful District treasurer for 16 years, Mr. Donald Lawrence, was retiring. The Rev. Bill Woldt, who was most unhappy with the direction of the LCMS, nevertheless stayed with the English District

> ### Reflection: "A Judas"
>
> The author, as a "newbie" pastor from Oakmont, Pennsylvania, attending the Lake Erie Fall Regional Pastoral Conference in 1978, witnessed the pain of those whose wounds had not healed. Former District President Bert Frey, now a pastor in the English Synod of the AELC, was invited to "return" and speak, in the presence of President/Bishop George & Helen Bornemann, when the unfortunate labels came out, again. In two years since the 1976 "split," the hostilities and wounds had not yet healed. The "Judas" or betrayer label went both ways, but the pains were considerable. Thanks be to God for His great mercy as His Church received forgiveness in Christ Jesus to overcome the hostilities evident in the wretched labels.

as its Missions executive. Other staff had similar feelings. Nevertheless, their re-appointments were approved through May 31, 1977. Two resolutions were approved to authorize a "Committee on Reorganization of the English District" and to "...encourage the President of our District to postpone authorizing ordinations of Seminex graduates..." for the time being and that the Synod's Colloquy Board be asked to act in good faith to overcome the certification problems.[242]

In its first 64 years, the English District had transferred "some 215" of its congregations to various LCMS geographic districts, including the 38 that were ceded in 1939 to start the "daughter" Southeastern District.[243] But in the much shorter period of 1976—1980, 78 congregations had left for the English Synod of the Association of Evangelical Lutheran Churches. Although 1200 LCMS congregations were expected to leave the Synod, only 250 actually left to start the AELC.[244] Though the Synod's overall losses were significantly smaller than anticipated, the English District endured the greatest loss of any district of the LCMS. While several of these congregations were "big names," many were urban or struggling suburban congregations already in decline due to "white flight," urban sprawl and the attraction of new, vital congregations, and membership losses due to leaving the Missouri Synod. The latter was the case of three Livonia congregations that had transferred from the Michigan District to the English District, then promptly left the LCMS to become part of the English Synod of the AELC. The minority membership from these three congregations banded together to form a new LCMS congregation in the Michigan District, Christ Our Savior Lutheran Church. By 1986, that congregation had built a beautiful, large, new house of worship and became the largest Lutheran congregation in Livonia.

In his book *Anatomy of an Explosion*, English District-rostered professor at Concordia Theological Seminary, Fort Wayne, Kurt Marquart, dealt with the question of "church politics." He asserted that under J.A.O. Preus the surprising thing that happened was "...not that the liberal invasion [of higher critical methodology] was finally repelled, but that it had been tolerated for so long."[245] Marquart also noted that Valparaiso University President Emeritus and Chancellor, the Rev. Dr. O.P. Kretzmann, was not at all sympathetic with the direction of the Missouri Synod under Jack Preus. Yet, Kretzmann would write in an article *"The Sound of a Scream,"* something similar to Milton Nauss' statement from 1976 mentioned in the previous chapter. Through that literary device of "the Scream," Kretzmann in late 1973 essentially charged Concordia Seminary faculty members with being "...evasive, not playing square with the church."[246] But for the English District in late 1976, the "post-mortem" of the LCMS division would have to give way to saving the District and its mission of reaching the lost for Christ.

The leadership and churchmanship of Bishop/President George W. Bornemann (1912-1997) and First Vice President Rev. Mel Tassler (1916-2008) and the board of directors combined well with the pastors and congregations who wanted to move forward. The plunge from 219 to 141 member congregations had created a temporary sag in morale; District finances were in great disarray. "Church Extension Fund withdrawals by departing congregations barred entrance into new fields."[247] The board of directors, recognizing Bornemann's sympathetic pastoral heart and desire for visitation to District congregations and pastors, secured by divine call in 1977 an executive secretary in the person of the Rev. Kenneth Lindsay. He would oversee District missions, stewardship, evangelism, and the Church Extension program, a lot to concentrate in one position.

Lindsay (1921-2002) had served three pastorates in Washington and for 12 years was pastor of Bethany Evangelical Lutheran Church & School, Detroit; his service in the Synod included being a Michigan District circuit visitor. His gifts in administration and public speaking were put to use in several other positions that he held: Director of Development for Bethesda Lutheran Ministries, Watertown, Wisconsin, Director of Public Relations for the LCMS in St. Louis, Executive Director of the Detroit Council of Lutheran Churches, and Editor of *The Detroit Lutheran*. Lindsay was called to the executive secretary position, a post previously held by the Rev. Harold Hecht before he became District president. "Soon after he took office, the District publication, *Lutheran Accent*, and its successor *English Channels*, began reporting signs of an amazing comeback."[248] Lindsay served as executive secretary from 1977 to 1984.

Another "saint" of tremendous help to the English District was Mr. Carl Thomsen, who served for 37 years as the legal counsel for the English District. When Thomsen retired from his law firm, he moved into the English District office "...where he was particularly helpful with Church Extension Fund-related legal matters after the 1976 split."[249] Thomsen was also for 25 years a member of the Mission and Church Extension Board of the English District, a founder of Detroit Lutheran High School, and legal advisor for Glen Eden Lutheran Memorial Park.

The 1978 English District Convention

The 42nd Convention of the English District-LCMS was held June 17-21, 1978, at Concordia College, Milwaukee. A change of venue was called for after holding several consecutive, contentious conventions in the Chicago metropolitan area. The theme of the 1978 Convention was "Jesus Is Lord." Bishop Bornemann, who had relocated to Detroit from Chicago, gave a Christ-centered theological rationale for the choice of that theme, clearly wanting to establish a new tone for the District. It was startling that, as of the May 1978 printing of the *Convention Workbook*, 120 clergy (active, candidate, or emeritus status) and 67 congregations had resigned from the District and Synod between July 1976 and May 1978. In the 1978 Convention *Proceedings* of the English District ten clergy and 12 teachers were noted as having been removed in May or June and especially on June 18, the day of the convention's beginning. They had, however, received notice of the impending action in May 1978 from Bishop Bornemann. Among those removed, having not resigned, were the Rev. Drs. Mark Bangert, John S. Damm, and John Tietjen, all of Seminex, and the Rev. Dr. Martin E. Marty. Those numbers would rise.[250] Many of the pastors on that list had a long lineage in the English District and/or her antecedent, the English Missouri Synod.[251] The number of congregations still considering resignation would also increase.

Appointed by President Bornemann and ratified by the board of directors were the following:

- Rev. Norman E. Laesch (Western Region Vice President)
- Dr. Richard Drews (Board of Directors)
- Dr. Paul Barth (Mission/Church Extension Board)
- Dr. Milton Nauss and Mr. Harry Will (Stewardship/Finance Board)
- Drs. Eldon Weisheit and David Marth and Mr. William Hodgson (Board of Parish Education)

Generally, these appointments reflected a more conservative posture by the District. Three congregations were transferred to LCMS geographic districts.

Prior to the convention, at the February 12-13, 1978 English District Board of Directors meeting in Schiller Park, Illinois, a board resolution reflected a bylaw change in the LCMS Constitution and Bylaws limiting districts to four regions.[252] Since the English District was much smaller than it had been four years earlier, reducing the number of regions and regional vice presidents made much sense.

Moreover, what had begun in the English District was the start of a more-than-30-year tenure of noble service on the Committee on Constitutions and Membership by Dr. Thomas Kraus, pastor of Calvary Evangelical Lutheran Church, Mechanicsburg (formerly Harrisburg), Pennsylvania, and later District vice president, and Dr. Philip Kraft, pastor of Grace Evangelical Lutheran Church, Warminster, Pennsylvania, and later Philadelphia circuit visitor. Their dedication was deeply appreciated within the English District.

At this point in the District's history, it was divided into 16 circuits, each one being an electoral circuit. Later, a number of visitation circuits were added, having to combine per Synod bylaws into a single electoral circuit. The 16 circuit visitors would prove to be strong workmen for the Lord. Bishop Bornemann went so far as to say, "They are the true bishops in the church."[253] Among those serving in that role were Dr. Roger Pittelko as circuit visitor for the Chicago Northwest Circuit and Dr. Frazier Odom as the District's first African-American circuit visitor, for the Chicago Southeast Circuit. Several circuits had two circuit visitors, one at a time, over the course of the biennium.

The report of the board of directors also stated:

> Over the past two years the Board of Directors of the District has undertaken the task of pulling the District together after the English Synod/English District separation that took place at River Forest in 1976. That Convention resolved to make the separation amicable, peaceful, and evangelical… The first resolution of the Board which dealt with synodical matters encouraged President Bornemann to postpone authorizing ordinations of Seminex graduates, meanwhile recognizing the right of congregations to call and ordain whomever they wish. The Colloquy Board of Synod was called upon to act in good faith to overcome the problems of certification for Seminex graduates… At this time, the Board feels that the District is once again on stable ground

167

financially and is looking for opportunities to expand the mission of the English District.[254]

Of note in the 1978 *Convention Workbook* was the first Report of the Committee on Women in the Church, a committee established by Resolution 10-1 of the 1976 Convention. The goals of the committee included (1) enhancing women's roles in the church and (2) making ministries more sensitive to the needs of both women and men, and fostering a better understanding of the changing societal roles of men and women. While calling for more women on District boards and committees, there was no call for ordaining women.[255]

The Synod's representative to the 1978 English District Convention was Dr. Guido Merkens, Pastor of Concordia Lutheran Church, San Antonio, Texas, and Synod's second vice president. Convention essays were given, two each, by Dr. Charles S. Mueller, Sr., president of the Southeastern District, and Dr. Roland Miller, a former missionary to India and expert in Islam. Dr. Oswald Hoffmann, Speaker of *The Lutheran Hour*, was the banquet speaker. The Eucharist Convention Service was held at Sherman Park Evangelical Lutheran Church, which introduced without warning that women would be assisting with the distribution of the Holy Supper. This caused a ruckus.

President/Bishop Bornemann was re-elected by acclamation because none of the other four nominated men chose to allow their names to stand for election. The following were elected as regional vice presidents and eventually ranked:

Rev. Melvin Tassler (Midwest), First Vice President
Rev. Donald Jung (Lake Erie), Second Vice President
Rev. John Sorensen (Arizona-Pacific [Western Region]), Third Vice President
Rev. Thomas Kraus (Eastern), Fourth Vice President.

Of the 41 resolutions that came to the convention floor, one commended Dr. Bornemann for his leadership and deep spiritual commitment (Res. 6-04). Others commended the District's new publication replacing *Lutheran Accent, The English Channels* (Res. 10-02), and affirmed pulpit and altar fellowship with the ALC (Res. 7-03).

All resolutions at this convention were adopted, though following strong debate on some of them. One humorous resolution (Res. 10-03) commended "Pastor Bornemann" for his District pastoral newsletter, the *Monatsblatt*, which was later simply named *"District Newsletter,"* and during the presidency of Dr. David Ritt morphed into the *Sycamorian*. Some concern had been expressed about using the German word, *"Monatsblatt,"* which means "monthly newsletter."[256] Honored at the 1978 District Convention was Mildred Martin as Sunday school teacher of the year; Mildred taught at Redeemer Evangelical Lutheran Church, North Tonawanda, New York, where former District President Hugo Kleiner had served.

The "Comeback" Slowly Continues

The 43rd Convention of the English District was held at Concordia College, Ann Arbor, Michigan, June 16-19, 1980. The *Convention Workbooks* of 1978 and 1980 demonstrated part of the comeback of the District in that congregational giving for Synod missions rose from $285,139 to $305,000. District missions contributions from the congregations in the same period rose from $521,422 to $591,228. The Opening Convention Eucharist was held in the College's Holy Trinity Chapel, complete with a mighty pipe organ and the opening hymn, "Glorious Things of Thee Are Spoken, Zion, City of our God." Dr. Robert Sauer, a former English District pastor and fourth vice president of the LCMS, was preacher, Dr. George Bornemann was officiant, and the Rev. Charles Evanson was celebrant. In praise of Almighty God, it set the stage for a new era in the District.

Convention essayist was Dr. Richard Meyer, president of the Southern District. Dr. George Bornemann's District President's Address followed the convention theme, "The Door Is Still Open – To the World." In it, he noted that the door was open to receiving, transferring, and releasing congregations, but with fairness and good will. He further stated:

> Our District's future is like our past and present. As long as that door is open, and as long as there is the work [that] needs to be done, and as long as there is opportunity to serve, that is how long the District will continue. This is a great District and I'm proud to be its president. The future of the District is contingent not upon

finances or high administration costs. According to fiscal reports in your workbook our administration costs are a mere 12% of the District expenditures... The door is still open and if we want to continue as a District then the posture of being cooperative, supportive, helpful, a servant role to all the Synod, is most desirable.[257]

Continuing his very lengthy President's Address, Dr. Bornemann also addressed several matters including Synod missions, "Forward in Remembrance" (an extraordinary LCMS financial appeal), the status of hymnals, women in the church, and a warning.[258] He stated: "The door is still open for evangelical work in an evangelical manner to promote the evangel of our Lord Jesus Christ by an evangelical church." But his warning was that Synod and District could get so caught up in bylaws, structure, procedures, and mandates, or on the other hand become so loose as to hold nothing together that we abandon an open door of opportunity to evangelize.[259] Bornemann ended with an emphatic statement that the door is not closed but is still open. There was also a lengthy report from Executive Secretary Ken Lindsay. Among the congregations received by transfer into the English District was West Portal Evangelical Lutheran Church & School, San Francisco, California. The Church's school of over 500 K-8 students was the largest school at that time and for the next few decades in the English District.

The banquet speaker was Dr. Jean Garton, the founder of Lutherans for Life and wife of Pastor Horace "Chick" Garton of Martin Luther Chapel, Pennsauken, New Jersey. Her topic was "The Door Is Still Open...On the Family!"[260]

Among the 55 resolutions presented from the floor committees from overtures at the 1980 District Convention, the most significant were the following:

- Tabling a Certification Program (Res. 4-01) that would recognize the validity of the ministries of Seminex graduates serving in Word and Sacrament ministries and to pursue certification through the Council of Presidents and Synod's Colloquy Board
- Adoption of Resolution 4-10 to memorialize the Missouri Synod to re-establish full pulpit and altar fellowship with The American Lutheran Church (ALC)

- Adoption of Resolution 8-06, which paved the way for the Board of Directors of the English District to move the English District into Synod's Lutheran Church Extension Fund (LCEF)

- Adoption of Resolution 7-01, titled "The Ordination of Women to the Pastoral Office," but in the whereases noting "the uniqueness in God's creation of male and female" and that "ordination to the pastoral office of ministry to Word and Sacrament is the charge to tend with episcopal curacy (Acts 20), to serve for the management of God's household (I Timothy 3), and to be stewards of the mysteries of God (I Corinthians 4)," and in the resolve stating: "that the English District memorialize Synod to study further the issue of human sexuality and the partnership of man and woman in home, church, and society, and specifically the issue of the ordination of women to the pastoral office of ministry of Word and Sacrament in Christ's Church."[261]

Resolution 7-01 came out of a special Floor Committee on Women in the Church and overtures calling for the ordination of women to the Holy Ministry. This "hot button" committee was chaired by the Rev. Roger Pittelko; its members included strong proponents for and against women's ordination. The floor committee accepted the erudite doctrinal guidance and leadership of Dr. Kenneth Korby. The floor committee produced an irenic resolution that requested the Synod to study the issue in the light of human sexuality and partnership of women and men in service to God and others, including in the church. The floor committee majority clearly rejected the idea of ordination of women to the pastoral office.[262]

The English District Convention of 1982 included more resignations and transfers of congregations, but also the addition of three new ones. Pilgrim Church in St. Louis and St. Gregory of Nyssa Church in Chicago joined the AELC in December 1981. Two congregations were transferred to the Southern Illinois and Michigan Districts. One congregation was received from the Michigan District. Two new congregations (Alamo Lutheran Church, Alamo, California, later renamed Messiah Lutheran Church of Danville, California, and Faith Lutheran Church, Butler, Pennsylvania) were added as new English District congregations. Among the pastors who resigned from the District and Synod were Dr. John H. Baumgaertner, former District president, and Dr. Martin P. Kretzmann.

The "comeback" was taking its toll on President/Bishop Bornemann, First Vice President Mel Tassler, and others. Both George and Helen

Bornemann had major health challenges in terms of operations and by-passes. This became evident during the 1982 English District Convention held at Concordia College, Milwaukee. That synodical college, incidentally, was in a changed and declining neighborhood. The English District, as a heavily urban district of Synod, did not want to see the College close or flee to the suburbs. Despite that sentiment, Resolution 7-05 "To Oppose the Relocation of Concordia (College), Milwaukee, to a New Location," was defeated after the convention received input from the College president, Dr. John Buuck, and the Milwaukee Circuit.[263] This was not the first and would not be the last time that the English District was a vital voice in synodical colleges, no less the seminaries.

Dr. Joseph Lavalais, Synod's second vice president and highest rank African-American clergyman in the Synod, served as synodical representative for LCMS President Ralph Bohlmann, who had succeeded J.A.O. Preus in 1981. Most of the 74 resolutions were of a minor nature and were approved, including to support 1984 Circuit Convocations as part of the Synod's new triennial meeting cycle and to thank outgoing First Vice President Mel Tassler for his years of faithful service and churchmanship in the English District.

At the 1982 District Convention, Dr. Bornemann was easily re-elected by over 75% on the first ballot, even with three other pastors allowing their names to stand for election. Elected vice presidents were ranked as follows:

> First Vice President, Rev. Donald Jung (Lake Erie Region)
> Second Vice President, Dr. Roger Pittelko (Midwest Region)
> Third Vice President, Dr. Eldon Weisheit (Western Region)
> Fourth Vice President, Rev. Thomas Kraus (Eastern Region).
> Dr. Paul Bacon was re-elected Secretary, uncontested.[264]

A bit of humor: In the daily Convention "EDNA"s was the following:

EDNA... WHO IS SHE?

EDNA – no, that's not the name of President Bornemann's wife. And it is certainly not our own *English Channel*'s Editor Betty Durrenberg's middle name! A convention mystery lady? Wrong again!

It's the name (you guessed it!) of our daily convention news voice. It's called "English District News and Announcements" (EDNA). Actually, we really don't know where the name originally came from...

What we do know is that you'll want to make sure to get your copy every morning when you come into the convention hall. EDNA is truly the "Convention Voice of the English District"...[265]

The Lutheran Church—Missouri Synod in 1965 had moved from a triennial cycle of conventions to a biennial cycle. This meant that District and Synod conventions were held in alternating years. At its 1983 St. Louis Convention, the LCMS returned to a triennial cycle. Following that decision, English District conventions would also be held triennially in the year prior to a Synod convention, starting in 1985.

As the English District continued its "amazing comeback," unbeknownst to the board of directors, the toll on Bishop/President Bornemann was such that he would resign before the completion of his term that was to end in June 1985. Speculation arose as to whether there were staff tensions or whether it was his and his wife Helen's health. In truth, there were both tensions and health concerns.[266] In his letter of resignation to the board of directors (dated September 1983 and effective January 31, 1984), Dr. Bornemann positively stated the following:

Thank you for your service and cooperation in enabling our District do its work so well. The entire District wants to assure you that as you carry on your work in this time of transition until June, 1985, when your terms of office...expire, the parishes and personnel will continue their faithful support. To have completed that same term with you was my hope and prayer, but for personal reasons I chose to retire at this time.[267]

Bornemann had served with distinction, as Secretary Paul Bacon noted in the board of directors report in the 1985 *Convention Workbook.*[268] But his resignation as president was significant, particularly in terms of District administration. A statement in the board of directors report indicates the issues caused by a vacancy in the presidential office: "At the November 1983 meeting, the Board approved the report of the Bylaws task force which stipulated that the president was to be the chief executive officer of the District, responsible for the overall administration of the staff and all board and committee activities."[269]

With Bornemann's resignation, First Vice President Donald Jung became acting District president on February 1, 1984. The 1985 *Convention Workbook* listed Jung as both acting president and first vice president. District Staff Parish Services Counselor, Dr. Delphin "Bud" Schultz, continued in that position, along with Missions Executive the Rev. Dr. Robert Scudieri and District Accountant Lorraine Zimnie. The Rev. Ken Lindsay left the executive secretary position in 1984 in order to become Development Director of Concordia College, Ann Arbor, Michigan.[270]

Excursus: The Rev. Dr. George Washington Bornemann (February 22, 1915—January 23, 1997)

His Christian name was almost prophetic, the same as the first president of the United States. Like many President/Bishops before and after him, Dr. George Washington Bornemann served as a faithful under-shepherd of the Lord Jesus Christ, serving as an English District LWML counselor, circuit visitor, vice president, and finally Bishop/President. Bornemann was born and raised in Pittsburgh, Pennsylvania. He was baptized, attended Lutheran parochial school, and was catechized and confirmed at First St. Paul Evangelical Lutheran Church & School on the city's Southside by the Monongahela River.

George Bornemann attended and graduated from Concordia Collegiate Institute, Bronxville, New York, in 1936; Concordia Seminary, St. Louis, in 1940; and, earned an STM from Lutheran School of Theology at Chicago in 1975. He was awarded an honorary doctorate by his Bronxville alma mater in 1981. Bornemann vicared under sainted Dr. H.P. Eckhardt of storied District fame at St. Andrew Evangelical Lutheran Church, Shadyside, Pittsburgh, where he also served as an assistant pastor, 1940-1941. He married his wife, Helen, of Cabot, Pennsylvania, in 1943, and they raised their four children while he served four congregations: the English Evangelical Lutheran Church of Our Redeemer, Oakmont, Pennsylvania (1941-1947); North Park Evangelical Lutheran Church, Buffalo, New York (1947-1951), the only non-English District congregation that he served; St. John Evangelical Lutheran Church, Toronto, Ontario (1951-1959); and, Redeemer Evangelical Lutheran Church, Elmhurst, Illinois (1959-1976). While at St. John, he founded four congregations, 1952-1954, in greater Toronto: St. Matthew, Scarborough; St. Mark, Mississauga (Port Credit); St. Luke, Willowdale (North York), and St. John Augsburg Polish, Toronto. After his 1984 retirement, George and Helen moved from their small apartment of several years in Southfield, Michigan, near the District office, to Lutheran Haven, Oviedo, Florida. In 1988, Bornemann founded Shepherd of the Coast Lutheran Church, Palm Coast, Florida, an English District congregation.

Dr. Bornemann was not only a decisive leader and a caring, visiting pastor; he was a tireless advocate for the English District. He would occasionally comment about having to "raise the colors" of the English District wherever he visited, a comment that was also told to and repeated later by Bishop Roger Pittelko.

On November 16, 1980, Dr. Bornemann gave the sermon for the dedication of Redeemer Lutheran Church, Oakmont, where he had served 40 years earlier. He had noticed that a brick was visibly missing in the church nave from the 110,000 bricks used in that new church building's construction. The reason for that one missing brick was obvious; it was left open for sound system conduit to later be installed. He told the congregation, "Don't close it up. Leave it exposed as a reminder to you to not be the missing brick in God's house." The congregation did not oblige him, instead filling it in with the speaker. However, the point of his message was taken to heart, as well as something else that Bishop Bornemann observed. There were two double sets of doors into the Narthex. Each door contained 36 small windows. One set of doors thus had 72 little windows, which reminded the good Bishop of Jesus' Sending of the 72. He told the congregation that it should remind each of them to be witnesses for the Lord. By God's grace, Redeemer Church grew in the next decade in both grace and number.[271]

George Bornemann also had a scholarly bent, contributing articles for *Advance, the Concordia Historical Institute Quarterly, Concordia*

Theological Monthly, Concordia Pulpit, and Portals of Prayer.[272] He presented a doctrinal paper to the Council of Presidents in the late 1970s on objective justification by grace at a time when the Synod was in a squabble over that biblical and confessional article of faith. He served on the LCMS CTCR, 1983-1989, and was an LCMS convention essayist in 1985 and 1987. While pastor at Redeemer, Elmhurst, he was an active member of the Rotary Club of Elmhurst, serving for a year as its president.[273] When he retired as head of the English District, his former congregation, Redeemer, Oakmont, Pennsylvania, honored him and Helen. Bornemann preached the sermon on Sunday, February 19, 1984, and the congregation recognized them in the Divine Service and held a dinner reception.[274]

Dr. Bornemann was a member of the Lutheran Academy of Scholarship, American Academy of Religion, the Upper Canada Bible Society, and the Society of Biblical Literature. Though members of St. Luke Evangelical Lutheran Church, the SELC District's largest congregation, in Oviedo, Florida, he maintained his synodical membership in the English District. George died in the Lord in January 1997, his funeral sermon being preached by the Rev. Dennis Lorenz, English District missions executive. Helen received occasional visits from Bishop Stechholz prior to her death on July 18, 2007. The Bornemanns are buried in the St. Luke's Cemetery in Oviedo next to the small, original church building. Dr. Bornemann's legacy was one of a faithful servant who helped hold the District together at its most critical time in its existence and lead an "amazing comeback."[275]

Pastor Donald Jung Assumes the Reins

First Vice President Donald Jung (1926-1987) did not have far to travel to the English District office. He had faithfully served The Lutheran Church of the Shepherd King in nearby West Bloomfield, Michigan, for several years. Jung was regarded as a mild-mannered Christian gentleman who knew well the inner workings of the District. With the Revs. George Bornemann and Ken Lindsay no longer on the scene, Acting President/Bishop Jung began to add new staff and turn the District in the direction of church planting. He was further aided by Mr. Harry Will, well-known owner/director of Will Funeral Homes in the Detroit metropolitan area, who headed a strong District Board of Stewardship and Financial Support. Will helped with District's involvement in Synod's extraordinarily successful fundraiser in the late 1970s, "Forward in Remembrance."

Lengthy reports in the 1985 District *Convention Workbook* were submitted by Parish Services Counselor Dr. Bud Schultz and Missions/Stewardship Counselor Dr. Robert Scudieri, the latter strongly facilitating the planting of new congregations.

After serving as Acting President/Bishop, Jung was elected to that post at the 1985 English District Convention, held June 17-20 at Concordia College, River Forest. In his President's Address, Jung stated, under the convention theme, "Together We Sing To the Lord":

> The basic purpose of our being a district is MISSION, or missions. Eighty-two percent of our District operating budget together supports mission programs through Synod and District. A vital link in this is the Lutheran Church Extension Fund (LCEF). We are going to hear in these days from our new and energetic committee called ADIM [A District in Mission, and the $7.5. million investment goal].[276]

Dr. Jung was elected at 1985 Convention on the first ballot. The three other men who allowed their names to stand for election were the Revs. Roger Pittelko, Richard Drews, and Frazier Odom. The vice presidents elected and ranked were the following:

First Vice President	Dr. Roger D. Pittelko (Midwest Region)
Second Vice President	Rev. Thomas D. Kraus (Eastern Region)
Third Vice President	Rev. Kenneth J. Braun (Lake Erie Region)
Fourth Vice President	Rev. Michael S. Ernst (Western Region)

A highlight of the convention was the program "A District in Mission" presented by the Revs. Gordon Mackensen (First Lutheran, El Cajon, California) and Robert Scudieri (Missions and Stewardship Counselor) and representatives of congregations benefiting from the LCEF loans. Complete with slide presentation, it was the kick-off for District's 75th Anniversary (1986). Also presented was Synod's major 1986 fundraiser "Alive in Christ." Resolutions included were to "Decrease Back Door

Losses" (Res. 5-01) and to memorialize Synod to hold the 1992 Synodical Convention in Pittsburgh (Res. 8-02). Not only did the latter pass, it was approved at the subsequent Synod convention.[277] A resolution (Res. 9-08) was also approved thanking Dr. George Bornemann for his leadership and "untiring efforts...through difficult years and inspiring us to move forward on every frontier for the advancement of the Kingdom."[278]

The District was again growing in number of congregations. By the time of the convention, it was up to 144 congregations from 137 at the prior convention and then up to 155 congregations in 1986. The Rev. Martin Mueller, of *Lutheran Witness* fame, would marry the editor of the *Detroit Lutheran* and the *English Channels*, Betty Durrenberg, and enjoy a "honeymoon cottage." That "cottage" was at the District's new Holy Redeemer Lutheran Church, Sandusky, Michigan, where Mueller would serve as founding pastor. Mueller authored the small but important book, *"Amazing Comeback,"* published in 1986. The upbeat and winsome book was a refreshing statement of a District that had come back from the brink of disaster.[279]

Sadly, but under God's gracious will and plan, President/Bishop Jung would not live to enjoy the English District's 75th Anniversary Year. Jung died of cancer on April 18, 1987. During the time of Jung's illness, Dr. Roger Pittelko as first vice president assumed a "regent" role in early 1986, and then became Acting President/Bishop in May 1986 at request of the board of directors. After Jung officially resigned, Pittelko assumed the presidency on January 1, 1987. Pittelko began his President's Address, recorded in the Convention *Proceedings* of the 1988 English District Convention, with these words: "This report begins with a thanksgiving for the life and ministry of the Rev. Donald Jung, D.D., elected President of the English District in June of 1985. In early 1986 President Jung became ill and continued his fight against cancer. He entered eternal glory on Saturday of Holy Week, 1987 ...(and) now lives with the saints in the joy and bliss of eternal life with Christ the Savior."[280]

Excursus: Grace Church, Redford Township, Michigan

Grace Evangelical Lutheran Church, Redford Township, Michigan, also known as "Grace Redford," is located in an old Detroit western suburb. It has been served in its over-75-year history by three generations of Halboth pastors, the Reverends Victor Halboth, Sr., Dr. Victor Halboth Jr., and the current senior pastor, Timothy Halboth. The Rev. Zach Marklevitz recently served as associate pastor. Grace was one of the largest English District congregations ever, though it endured a huge membership decline as members transferred to far suburban churches following the Detroit race riots of 1967. Yet, it remains the largest English District congregation in the state of Michigan.

What makes Grace Church especially significant in English District history is that during the senior pastorate of Dr. "Vic" Halboth, two English District President/Bishops were back-to-back members of the congregation, Dr. Harold Hecht and Dr. George Bornemann. "Vic" Halboth was pastor to both men at the critical time of the major rupture in the Missouri Synod and English District. Halboth had a challenge in blunting Hecht's influence in Grace Church because Hecht hoped to take it out of the Synod to be the largest and the flagship congregation of the English Synod of the AELC. Halboth was determined not only to keep Grace Church in the English District and Missouri Synod, but also to renounce the theological directions of Seminex and the liberal wing of the LCMS.

Mr. Harry Will and his family transferred their membership from inner city Zion Evangelical Lutheran Church, Detroit, to Grace Church. Will, with his God-pleasing funeral business, was an asset in the congregation's membership. He was involved with the local Lutheran cemetery, Glen Eden Lutheran Memorial Park in Livonia, with Dr. Vic Halboth serving for 26 of his 30 years on the Glen Eden Board of Directors as its chairman.

Although Redford Township is a smaller, changed community in an old neighborhood, Grace is still a vital congregation. During the COVID-19 pandemic, the church conducted gatherings in the large parking lot when it was possible and provided online broadcasting of services. By June 2020, it had reopened, along with most of the congregations in the greater Detroit area.

Pictured at Grace Lutheran Church (left to right): the Rev. John Bush, Bishop Emeritus David P. Stechholz, the Rev. Tim Halboth, and the Rev. Dr. Vic Halboth.

PART FOUR

THE SAGA CONTINUES

CHAPTER 14
A Different Face Emerges for the English District

The Bishop/President Years of Roger Pittelko

THE PERIOD OF English District history from 1987 to 2015 saw a general strengthening of the District during three presidencies or bishoprics of the District. Each of the three English District President/Bishops had different approaches and styles of ministry and leadership, but two common threads were the adoption and implementation of a new governance model. A modified "Carver" model of policy-based governance aided the District in overcoming significant challenges. Other than a few single years of growth, the District was no different from other districts of the LCMS as well as other Christian church bodies in terms of decline in membership and attendance. Yet in the saga of the English District-LCMS, the congregations, their pastors, and other church workers continued to strive to reach the lost for Christ. The English District still continued to be Synod's "expandable district."

District Conventions

During the "Amazing Comeback" Years of the Bornemann Administration and the subsequent presidencies of Donald Jung, Roger Pittelko, David Ritt, and David Stechholz, much attention was given to music and artwork at District Conventions. Rev. Richard "Dick" Patt, a long-time English District pastor in Milwaukee, designed and graced the District with artwork for District convention publications, logos, and banners. In the area of music, Rev. David Stechholz served as Convention organist from 1980 to 2006. For decades, Rev. Robert Burke, long-time English District pastor in Chicago, served as District photographer, and Dr. Lee Settgast, head chaplain in the Los Angeles Prison Ministry and later director of the Los Angeles Nehemiah Project, served as director of public relations at District conventions.

Conventions had normally lasted at least four days. In more recent decades, most districts of Synod had to reduce the length of their conventions due to financial concerns. As of 2012, the English District

Conventions were shortened to two and a half days. The District's geographic expanse required additional travel days for many attendees. To minimize travel expenses, the District would often schedule floor committee and board of directors meetings immediately preceding the Convention or other District conferences and a meeting of the College of Circuit Visitors immediately following those events.

The 1980s

The 1970s were a tumultuous time in North America, an extension of the 1960s. Major national issues were at the forefront of that decade: continued involvement in the Vietnam Conflict; debates over equal rights for women, homosexuals, and minorities; the energy crisis; and, environmental issues. The political sphere was rocked by the Watergate scandal that brought down President Richard Nixon in 1974. The internal strife in the LCMS paralleled this tumult. But toward the end of the 1970s, a remarkable conservative wave began.

Compared to the turbulence of the prior decades, the 1980s were relatively calm. Margaret Thatcher, the British conservative leader, won the first of three parliamentary elections in the United Kingdom; Ronald Reagan was elected president of the United States in 1980. The 1986 Chernobyl Disaster in the Soviet Union brought increased fear of nuclear mishaps. However, hope was seen in the election of a Polish pope in the Roman church, and a friendlier Soviet leadership in Mikhail Gorbachev. The Berlin Wall fell in 1989 as the East German government wilted before a popular uprising, in part spearheaded by Lutherans in Leipzig and elsewhere in the German Democratic Republic. Thus began the closing chapter of the Cold War and a transformation of the world. Fashion of the time included the "big hair" styles, punk rock, and rap music. Sports mania grew. It was a time of contrasts: more conservative and democratic politically and more boldly secular in the general culture. Christianity in North America was affected as church attendance and membership began a steeper drop.

But in the English District...

Dr. Roger D. Pittelko's ascension to District president and bishop happened on January 1, 1987, as he officially took the office from Dr. Donald Jung, who could no longer serve due to illness.

The second three-year cycle of Synod was in effect. The District convention and election of District officers came in the summer of 1988. The 46th convention again met at Concordia College, River Forest, Illinois, June 13-16, 1988. Even as church membership and attendance was sliding across North American Christianity, including in the LCMS, the number of District congregations had increased. In his first District President's Address in the *Convention Workbook* of 1988, Pittelko wrote:

> At the beginning of the triennium in 1985 the English District numbered 151 congregations and preaching stations. At the end of this triennium the District numbers 162 congregations and preaching stations. There has been a 10% growth in communicant membership and a 10% growth in Sunday worship attendance in the District.[281]

Pittelko gave thanks for the excellent work of his two staff counselors, Dr. Delphin Schultz and the Rev. Robert Scudieri, and new addition, the Rev. Victor Willmann. It was a time of transition, not only with the resignation of District President/Bishop Jung, but also the retirement of two other District leaders. Business Administrator Ms. Lorraine Zimnie was replaced by Mrs. Diana Medell; the President's secretary, Mrs. Joanne Chambo was replaced by Mrs. Marlene Geheb. It was humorously observed over the next several years of Dr. Pittelko's long tenure that he and Mrs. Geheb could easily see eye-to-eye, as they were both quite tall! Other staff changes occurred within the District secretarial pool; one to be noted was the beginning of an over 30-year service to the District of Ms. Peggy Gierak (later Oke).

In his report, Dr. Pittelko celebrated the achievement of the $7.5 million ADIM goal of new LCEF investments. He also noted the growth of the Arizona Circuit, which would be divided into two circuits at the convention, and the newly-organized Lutheran Church—Canada (LCC), as well as several new Canadian congregations choosing to stay in the LCMS by transferring into the English District.[282]

In his address to the 1988 District Convention, Pittelko again recalled the late President Jung's dedicated, godly service and great devotion to the Synod and all that the Synod stood for. He then rehearsed the English District's history, the 100th anniversary of the English Evangelical Lutheran Conference of Missouri, and the historic slogan, *"the faith of the fathers in the language of the children."* Bishop Pittelko spent a lot of time regaling the District's importance and the ongoing District need for a life of faithfulness and service.[283]

Convention essayist was Dr. Kenneth Korby, addressing "The Pastoral Office and the Priesthood of All Believers." In three sessions devoted to the topic, Korby gave a stirring presentation, squarely taking aim at the notion of "everyone a minister." He also addressed authority in the Church defending the biblical understanding of fatherhood and directly addressing what has become the feminist and LGBTQ movements. Korby's essay was a very strong defense of the pastoral office.[284] This was a convention of theological heavyweights, including Dr. George Wollenburg, LCMS second vice president and former Montana District president, representing the Synod at the sessions for Dr. Ralph Bohlmann, president of the LCMS.

Pittelko was unopposed as President/Bishop. During the convention, he called President/Bishop Emeritus George Bornemann forward to make a few remarks. This is something routinely done in the English District, with the emphasis on brevity and perhaps wit. Following his greetings, Bornemann was given a button by Bishop Pittelko. The button read, *"It's Hard to be Humble when you are from the English District."* Serving ably behind the scenes as District director of public relations was Dr. Lee Settgast.

1988 Elected Vice Presidents as Ranked by the District

First Vice President	Rev. Kenneth J. Braun (Lake Erie Region)
Second Vice President	Rev. Thomas D. Kraus (Eastern Region)
Third Vice President	Rev. Michael S. Ernst (Western Region)
Fourth Vice President	Rev. Dr. Paul E. Bacon (Midwest Region)

The Rev. David Thiele, pastor of Good Shepherd Evangelical Lutheran Church, Chicago, was elected secretary. The slate of 21 circuit visitors was approved, corresponding to District's increased number of visitation circuits. The elected board of directors had several new faces, including Mrs. Helen Gienapp, former president of the International LWML; the Rev. Richard Drews, pastor of Redeemer Evangelical Lutheran Church, Elmhurst, Illinois; and the Rev. David Stechholz, newly called to Messiah Lutheran Church, Danville, California.[285] Mrs. Diana Medell was serving as District treasurer. For the first time, the list of District officials included the name of President/Bishop Emeritus: Rev. George Bornemann, LLD.

Among the resolutions approved were the following:

- 6-05c "To Encourage Continued Stewardship Growth"
- 4-09c "To Speak Out Against Apartheid"
- 7-01 & 7-02c "To Establish Two Circuits in Arizona" and "To Establish Two Circuits in Canada."

Following the District convention, at the first board of directors meeting of the new 1988-1991 triennium, Dr. Pittelko asked the board to appoint a new committee to study the feasibility of relocating the English District office within the Detroit area.[286] Under Pittelko's leadership, the board of directors moved ahead with a number of new directives:

- Adding a planned giving counselor to the executive staff
- Changing the nomenclature from the terminology of "counselor" to that of "executive assistant to the President" for...various executive positions such as missions, parish services, etc.
- Submitting an overture to the 1991 District Convention to urge congregations to move to weekly celebration of the Lord's Supper
- Setting up a daycare corporation for the purpose of planting new mission congregations
- Approving an Eritrean Mission Initiative with Synod's Board of Missions for sending the Rev. Zerit Johannes to his native Eritrea, following Eritrea's war of independence, as Theological Educator for three years for the Evangelical Lutheran Church of Eritrea, and
- Approving the development of a procedure for the annual awarding of a Doctor of Divinity degree to an English District pastor.

English District
Pastoral Attire

How should a pastor dress? For the past several decades, the "dress code" within the English District is literally all over the map—just like the District itself! During the Seminex era, the more liberal pastors tended to wear clerical collars. That shifted dramatically. By the 1980s, the more conservative clergy began to adopt that traditional clerical garb. Bishop Pittelko almost always wore a clerical collar. However, it was not uncommon to see pastors dress, even for conventions, in suit and tie, business casual, or even shorts and T-shirt. In other words, no dress code exists. The Western Region sported the most exotic combinations at District gatherings, such as full clerical collar with bluejeans and cowboy boots, and clericals of Hawaiian-like color combinations. But since the 1980s it has been more common to see the men of the cloth donning clerical collars.

New District slogan

Also, and perhaps of greatest significance, Bishop Pittelko, with the aid of a Planning Council Committee chaired by Dr. Richard Drews, desired a major thematic change for the English District. The old slogan, *"The Faith of the Fathers in the Language of the Children,"* had served the District unofficially but well. However, something of a new, bold, theologically strong and arresting message was in order. The board of directors on May 16, 1990, adopted a new slogan for the District, *"Worshipping the crucified God and proclaiming new life in Jesus Christ."*[287] This effectively replaced the century-old slogan of the English Missouri Synod and English District until the board of directors would adopt a new slogan after the election of the Rev. David Ritt as president and bishop in 1997. An English District brochure highlighting the slogan was also produced for congregational members.

Excursus: Chapel of St. Robert Barnes

During Dr. Roger Pittelko's tenure, the English District relocated its Detroit office to 33100 Freedom Road in Farmington. Within the new office building, a small room was set aside as a chapel. That chapel was named in honor of the first English Evangelical Lutheran martyr, Dr. Robert Barnes.[288] Though a small room, it was used for daily staff devotions. During Dr. David Ritt's presidency, the chapel was moved into the library/conference room. This larger room was used for daily staff devotions, staff meetings and other

small group meetings, the annual New District Pastors' Conference, and the monthly Detroit Area Lutheran Pastors' Confessional Study Group. A piano was added during Bishop Stechholz's administration.

Robert Barnes has been rightly honored and remembered by the English District as a veritable "patron saint." He was martyred in England on July 30, 1540, at the hands of King Henry VIII. Though once in the king's favor, the Cambridge University scholar Barnes

became a strong supporter of the Lutheran Reformation while studying in Wittenberg in 1528. "There was a bond between Barnes and Luther in the fact that they had both once belonged to the Augustinian Order, and Barnes was to provide the main personal connection between the English and Lutheran Reformers."[289] Barnes had been subjected continually to harassment by churchmen opposed to his biblical stand. He dared all to make known the Gospel throughout England.[290] He became a staunch defender of the true faith, the Lutheran Reformation, and opposition to King Henry's divorces and re-marriages. Eventually things did not fare well for Barnes over against the unscrupulous British monarch. In May 1540, Barnes, along with Thomas Garret, the curate of London, and William Jerome, Vicar of Stepney, were sent to the Tower of London. On July 30, the three preachers were burned at the stake at Smithfield.

Dr. Martin Luther's words about Barnes are affixed to a plaque in the English District's Barnes Worship Center:

> This Doctor [Robert Barnes], I say, we knew very well and it is an especial joy to us to hear, that our good, pious table companion and guest of our home, has been so graciously called upon by God to shed his blood, for His dear Son's sake, and to become a holy martyr...[291]

The 47th Convention of the English District-LCMS was held June 6-9, 1991, at Concordia University, River Forest, Illinois. In the previous year, the synodical college had gained university status due to its continued growth, especially at the graduate school level. However, the gymnasium where the business sessions of the convention took place was not air-conditioned. Temperatures and humidity soared above 90° F; huge fans provided only a minor degree of relief. Delegates greatly enjoyed having the Divine Service in the air-conditioned chapel, along with morning Matins and the Convention Essay; meals were taken in the air-conditioned Koehneke Community Center. The Convention Essayist was the Rev. James McDaniels, who spoke on the topic "We Have Come This Far By Faith." LCMS President Dr. Ralph Bohlmann spoke on behalf of the Synod. He and Bishop Pittelko had both grown up in Oklahoma as sons of pastors. Humorously, as children, one wanted to be an LCMS pastor; the other wanted to become president of the Synod!

In his Address to the Convention, Pittelko explained the theologically-loaded new English District motto, *"Worshipping the Crucified God and Proclaiming New Life in Jesus Christ."* The slogan adopted by the board of directors in the spring of 1990 tied *"A District in Mission"* to the words of this new slogan. In the 1991 *Convention Workbook*, he had given earlier explanation of the change in mottos. It should be noted that the English District had other mottos since the 1970s, only to be quickly forgotten with the passage of time.[292] Would this new motto meet the same fate? In short, the answer would be "yes." Each of the next three Bishop/Presidents put their own new stamp by way of new mottos, replacing what had come before. Each age of the church and even minor passages of time result in new mottos, slogans, accents, approaches, and ideas, fulfilling Tennyson's poetic observation: "The old order changeth, yielding place to new."

The President's Address, coupled with Dr. McDaniels' essay highlighting black ministry in the Missouri Synod, made this statement:

> In the past the city has been our [the English District's] strength. When the larger Synod was rural, we were urban, serving the city. Now because of changes in the cities of North America, because of population shifts, many cities are in trouble, and our congregations also. But where, we ask, are the majority of the people? Why in the cities! And it is because people are in the cities

that our congregations need to be in the cities. It is because we are a District in Mission, a District that worships the crucified God and proclaims new life in Jesus Christ that we need to be in the cities. Only we Christians can give what people so desperately need.[293]

The English District Board of Directors had not yet made the decision to move the District office out of Detroit, even as that city was on a rapid descent that would not end until late 2010, and even then it would still be decreasing in population. In the 1988-1991 triennium, one of the four churches that dissolved was Covenant Evangelical Lutheran Church, leaving only three of what pre-split had been ten English District congregations in Detroit, a city that would go from 1,880,000 residents in 1950 to 650,000 by 2020. Detroit's decline and the loss of congregations in the city provide context to the District's decision to relocate the English District office near but out of the city of Detroit.

At the 1991 convention, Pittelko stood for re-election unopposed; he was elected by a rising vote of acclamation. However, there would be changes in the vice presidents.

1991 Elected Vice Presidents as Ranked by the District

First Vice President	Rev. Kenneth J. Braun (Lake Erie Region)
Second Vice President	Rev. Michael S. Ernst (Western Region)
Third Vice President	Rev. Dr. Martin E. Lundi (Eastern Region)
Fourth Vice President	Rev. John W. Stieve (Midwest Region).[294]

During the 1991-1994 triennium, the roster of vice presidents would change due to two resignations and one call out of the region. As with all conventions, there was the honoring of jubilarians, the hearing of staff and other reports and official greetings, the approval of the slate of circuit visitors, and the passage of resolutions. 394 pastoral and lay delegates, advisors, and guests were present.

Excursus: English District Humor—The Writings of the Rev. Dr. Herman Noodix

The famed University of Chicago professor and American Church historian, Dr. Martin E. Marty, was once a member of the English District of The Lutheran Church—Missouri Synod. He left the Synod during the LCMS "Civil War" of the 1970s. Prior to his exodus, Marty on occasion would quip that he belonged "…to a diocese or district that is *'one of the happiest little outfits in all Christendom.'*"[295] It was not happy, however, during that period of painful separation in the Missouri Synod. Years later, though, Marty was one of a lineup of luminaries who wrote endorsements of *The Epistles of Herman Noodix*, compiled and edited by one English District Pastor, Dr. Frederic "Fritz" W. Baue.

Among the listings of attendees at English District conventions in the 1980s and 1990s, one name would not be seen, Rev. Herman Noodix. Despite his absence from all District conventions and conferences, a curious epistle would frequently be delivered from this alleged member of the English District.

Dr. Baue testifies about this mystery man of the cloth: "For those of you who are not yet fully initiated into the mysteries of the Missouri Synod, the Reverend Doctor Herman Noodix, whose very name reeks of theology, is a Lutheran clergyman with whom I have long carried on an, shall we say, irregular correspondence."[296] This "irregular correspondence" was in the form of a letter, usually submitted as an official excuse from attending the conference, sent to the Rev. Dr. Frederic Baue, Herman's sole friend in the English District. Dr. Baue and his wife Jean, both fine musicians, were the authors respectively of the text and the music of what became a popular catechetical hymn in our Synod, *"What Is This Bread"* (LSB 629), in preparation for reception of the Holy Supper. But in conferences and conventions, it was Fritz who would read to the audience what Noodix had written.

In truth, the character Herman Noodix and his epistles sprang from Fritz's mind; at least, that is what the evidence leads us to say. Dr. Baue, himself a solid confessional Evangelical Lutheran pastor, had Herman Noodix spare no one of his disdain for church politics, including those who served in so-called high offices. Baue finally collected the writings in a volume called *"The Epistles of Herman Noodix*. Most, but not all, District clergy found the excuse letters or campaign platforms for president of Synod or District to be hilarious. Occasionally, the reading of same caused flack among the more sensitive brethren, but rarely among those who were frequently the butt of Herman's ire and pen.

The following is a sample of Herman's letters, which was shared during the 1991 District Convention's "Pastors' Colloquium" on June 7, 1991, with Synod President Bohlmann in attendance:

Herman's Second Presidential Platform: "Cut Out the Dead Wood"

Dear Fritz,

…..Greetings to you and all the brothers at the English District Convention in Chicago. I hate to do this, but once again I must beg an excused absence. I made it to O'Hare just fine. But I must have gotten on the wrong college van. Somehow I ended up at Moody Bible Institute….

…..On to my concerns. Next year is our synodical convention. And, egged on by my growing constituency, it is my solemn duty to once again announce my candidacy for the office of President of The Lutheran Church—Missouri Synod. In these troubled and uncertain times, we need to take draconian measures. We are facing five crises in our denomination: insubordination in the ranks, lack of money, top-heavy administration, the Church Growth movement, and backdoor losses. Accordingly, my campaign slogan will be: CUT OUT THE DEAD WOOD.

…..Why, you ask? Because we need to put some teeth into the Gospel. We need to crack down on the backsliders. Evangelically of course. My platform includes the following planks:

STREAMLINE ADMINISTRATION. As president, my first act would be to fire all presidents of synodical districts, colleges, seminaries, and other institutions. Excepting myself, of course. The resulting lawsuits would create an adjudication gridlock so severe that I would have to appoint acting presidents across the board. They would be so frightened of me that they'd all toe the line.

TRIM THE BUDGET. The financial crisis that bedevils us year after year can be easily solved by selling the Purple Palace [the LCMS International Center]. Let all those bureaucrats go out and find real jobs. Just get me a cellular phone and I can work out of my car. That way I can also handle the Church Growth problem…

DOWNSIZE. …Why should we let our deadbeats slink out the back door a few at a time the way they've been doing? What I say is, kick'em all out at once. Chop the membership by thirty per cent in one fell swoop and get it over with…. Then the rest will think twice before visiting the local megachurch…. Well, that's all for now. See you at the next conference.

Your pal, HERMAN NOODIX[297]

Get a copy of Herman Noodix' *Epistles* and enjoy the edgy humor.

Excursus: JEDP—Journal of English District Pastors
An Unofficial Journal of Theological Opinion and Scholarship

To the theologically knowledgeable and confessionally orthodox, the four letters JEDP cause concern because these letters posited what was a newer "documentary hypothesis" (theory) by Julius Wellhausen (1878). This documentary hypothesis was that the Pentateuch was authored not by Moses but by various writers with a flair beginning with the Solomonic period. This theory was that the Pentateuch was a compilation of four originally independent documents: the Jahwist (J), Elohist (E), Deuteronomist (D), and Priestly (P) sources. So when Dr. Paul D. Bacon and Rev. Allen C. Hoger began to publish a new periodical called the *"Journal of English District Pastors,"* abbreviated *JEDP*, it caused a bit of a stir. However, some confessionally-conservative pastors relished the free opportunity to write articles for the journal.

Bacon, as the chief editor, was totally on board for this venture. He felt that there should be an opportunity for English District pastors to express themselves in writing, and a number did just that in the years that *JEDP* functioned. *JEDP* began in November 1988 during the time of Bishop/President Roger Pittelko who said, *"try it."* It ended in September 2001, shortly after that year's Synod convention. Dr. Bacon granted a lot of latitude to those wishing to write. Among the authors and contributing editors, not all were pastors or members of the English District. *JEDP* had numerous authors besides Bacon and Hoger; contributing editors or frequent authors included Larry Vogel, Frederic Baue, David Stechholz, David Stein, Dean Pittelko, David Thiele, Larry Schneekloth, Lee Maxwell, Peter Mealwitz, Richard Drews, George Bornemann, Charles Hogg, Martin Bangert, Charles Evanson, Robert Scudieri, Walter W. Stuenkel "Prexy", Paul Stodtke, George Wollenburg, Gert Stoffregen, and even Herman Noodix.

Among the titles of essays were "Blameless Pastor or 'Were You Ever Caught?'" (Bornemann); "John 6 and the Eucharist" (C.R. Hogg, Jr.); "Herman on Growth" (Herman Noodix); "Why Are We Not Growing?"

(Stechholz and Vogel, 2nd & 4th VPs, "the even as opposed to the odd vice presidents"); "What Is the Future of the English District?" (Drews); "Roll Over, Wellhausen" (Hoger); "White Smoke" (D. Stein); "The Life of the (Small) Church" (Schneekloth); "Best Convention Ever?" (Vogel). A 2001 Synod Convention issue was published with articles by Bacon, Stein, Stechholz, Herman Noodix, and Paul Stodtke. But after that Convention, no one felt like writing any more. Dr. Bacon was to be commended in initiating and sustaining this noble opportunity called *JEDP*.[298]

In the 1991 Convention, resolutions adopted included:

- 91-3-05: "To Encourage the Eritrean Ministry" – This encouraged the District to take a lead on Eritrean ministries, including having District congregations establish, develop, and support Eritrean missions in their context.
- 91-4-03: "To Ratify Manual of Policy and Operations for the Mission Endowment Fund" – Later on this would simply become the District's Endowment Fund, which the Board could then designate for various causes in the area of missions. This lengthy resolution also established an Endowment Fund Board of Managers.
- 91-4-04: "To Initiate Study of a Corporation for Day Care" – This initiated a feasibility study to create a corporation for opening day care centers as a mission outreach strategy.
- 91-4-06: "To Encourage Participation in Children in Mission Church Extension Savings Stamp Program"
- 91-5-11: "To Further Serious Study and Understanding of the AIDS Epidemic and to Make a Christian Response" – The late 1980s and 1990s marked a time of international concern over the growing AIDS-HIV epidemic
- 91-6-02: "To Urge Weekly Communion" – This strongly encouraged weekly celebration of the Lord's Supper in District congregations and set the stage for a similar resolution later approved by a Synod Convention.

Several adopted resolutions had to do with promoting various stewardship, social ministry, and Christian education endeavors within the District.

The 1990s

The 1990s was a decade of relative peace and prosperity. The fall of Communism in Europe and the dissolution of the Soviet Union into Russia and other independent countries loosely called the "Commonwealth of Independent States" (Russian Union) marked the seeming end of the Cold War. But it was also a time of radical changes in communication, business, and entertainment, with the growing New Age movement and international, national, and even local sports becoming dominant cultural phenomena. Worship of God on Sundays was considered just one of many options so that Christian congregations were "competing" against all kinds of athletic and artistic practices, rehearsals, games, and sports clinics on the Christian Sabbath. Parents became increasingly less concerned about "teaching the faith of the fathers in the language of the children." This exacerbated the rapid decline of Sunday schools and a resolve for the Christian church in North America to find new ways of catechizing and teaching the faith.

United States President Bill Clinton spoke of the new world of internet communications and the doors of opportunity that would open. The 90s were considered by most to be a good decade that saw prosperity and a booming economy that translated into a "luxury fever" of vastly increased consumer spending on gambling, premium cigars, alcoholic beverages, and gourmet coffees. Unemployment was at the lowest level in more than two decades. But for the church in North America, including the LCMS, decline in membership and attendance was coupled with a decline in the size of the nuclear family. However, the English District did not experience as steep of a decline. This was partly due to the addition of some new congregations. Another factor was the rapid growth of the District's two largest mega-churches, Hales Corners Evangelical Lutheran Church & School, Hales Corners, Wisconsin, and Christ Church Lutheran and School, Phoenix, Arizona.

As noted previously, during the 1991-1994 triennium, three of the four District vice presidents either resigned or took a call out of their region. This was most unusual. Dr. Paul Bacon replaced Midwest Regional Vice President John Stieve, who accepted the call to the Lutheran Church of the Risen Savior, Green Valley, Arizona. Rev. David Kruse replaced Western Regional Vice President Michael Ernst, who accepted the call to be senior pastor of Hales Corners Lutheran, Hales Corners, Wisconsin. Lake Erie Vice President Kenneth Braun resigned but was not replaced, since his resignation came so late in the triennium, just prior to the 1994 District Convention. While the District was striving to again reach 200 member congregations, Dr. Robert Scudieri accepted a call to the LCMS as associate executive secretary for North American Missions, leaving the position of District missions executive vacant. Likewise, Planned Giving Counselor Ron Chewning accepted a supervisory position in Synod's Planned Giving Department. Both men had served ably in their District positions, leaving significant holes in the District leadership team.

Bishop Pittelko's report in the *Convention Workbook* for the 48th Convention of the English District-LCMS summarized the District's work in the previous triennium.[299] He noted that the theme was built on the District's mission statement of almost five years, *"Worshiping the Crucified God and Proclaiming New Life in Jesus Christ."* One of the convention highlights was the English District pledging $50,000 to 60,000 above its annual giving to Synod for sending a theological educator to Eritrea. This had been approved by the Mission Board, the Board of Directors, and the annual Professional Church Workers Conference. The Revs. David Thiele, Martin Lundi, and the Rev. Zerit Johannes produced materials that were sent to congregations to garner support. Pittelko highlighted changes in the District in the triennium, but rejoiced in the stability of the College of Circuit Visitors, where 22 of 23 were still in place. In addition to the usual giving of "thanks" to various individuals and boards and committees, the Bishop/President also mentioned the financial struggles, not unique to the English District or the Missouri Synod, but raised the important question of the District's identity. He added:

> Congregations of the English District have an independent spirit. Some see that as a negative. We have made it a positive as congregations have seen and seized local initiative. Many times that local initiative has flourished by itself as new missions and ministries were established. Many times the English District has been able to provide resources to assist the mission work of the local congregation. Through it all, the English District has been and continues to be a Mission District.[300]

The convention was held June 9-12, 1994 at Concordia University, River Forest, Illinois. Pittelko's Convention Address began with a historical perspective as reflected in movies that mark the changing culture. The 1940s reflected on World War II. The 1960s into the 1970s were obsessed with sex, especially illicit sex. The 1980s fixated on violence. His point in reflecting on movies and one in particular, "My Life," was to show society and culture's deep longing for spiritual peace. If that diagnosis was proper, the District's Christian mission and message of life and salvation in Jesus Christ is the needed upbeat message for the world.

The convention's theme was "Every Congregation a Mission." The Convention was structured as a "Mission Convention." At the beginning of the convention, Rev. Zerit Johannes was installed as Theological Educator, a missionary to his own homeland of Eritrea. The essayist was Dr. Glenn O'Shoney, the executive director of world missions for the LCMS. His message was that "Every Christian (is) a missionary!" and "The real business is the business of missions."[301]

LCMS President Dr. Alvin Berry spoke on behalf of the Synod. His message focused on the banner over the podium, the Synod's five-point theme: "Be In The Word, Care For One Another, Tell The Good News, Remain Faithful, Live In Peace." As at previous conventions at Concordia University, River Forest, Dr. Eugene Krentz, the school's president, brought warm greetings to the English District. Years later, in his retirement, Krentz would serve as a seasonal assisting pastor at the southernmost English District congregation, Faith Evangelical Lutheran Church, Naples, Florida.

Once again, Dr. Pittelko was re-elected Bishop/President by acclamation. The following were elected and ranked to serve alongside him as vice presidents of the English District:

First Vice President	Rev. David A. Dressel (Lake Erie Region)
Second Vice President	Rev. David P. Stechholz (Western Region)
Third Vice President	Rev. Paul E. Bacon (Midwest Region)
Fourth Vice President	Rev. Larry Vogel (Eastern Region).[302]

Rev. David Thiele was re-elected as District secretary.

Between sessions in the various dormitory rooms or off-campus, the favored English District beverages still, over the course of decades, seemed to be Scotch and Rusty Nails. The latter beverage was always complements of board of directors' members George Alles and Armin

Bruer, loyal subjects of the Queen from Windsor and Mississauga, Ontario, respectively. Among the approved resolutions were these:

- 2-05-94: "Continuation of Synodical Commission on Worship"
- 2-06-94: "To Consider Staff Reductions"
- 3-04-94: "To Encourage Congregations to Present and Deal with Child Abuse"
- 3-05-94: "To Encourage Health and Human Care Ministries."[303]

Compared to the District conventions held in the 1960s and 1970s, the 1994 Convention spent much less time debating and adopting resolutions. The resolutions that were adopted reflected less strife within the District and Synod.

1994—1997

Following the 1994 District Convention, the board of directors established policies affecting the District president. The board affirmed the use of the term "Bishop" as an alternate term to President of the English District, especially in interchurch relations. It also decided that when a new President/Bishop was elected at the District convention, he would be installed at that convention but would not assume the office until three months after the election. The District policy was that compensation for the new President/Bishop and retirement compensation for the outgoing President/Bishop would go into effect at that time. An installation service would be held on the Sunday following the newly elected president's assumption of office.[304] These policies made sense for the English District because of its non-geographic, coast-to-coast nature.

Another matter addressed at the September 1994 board of directors meeting was the appointment of a new committee to study staff reductions, carrying out the terms of Resolution 2-06-94. At this point, it was assumed that, with declining contributions from the congregations, it would be necessary to make staff reductions, thus calling into question the District's Bylaws requiring certain boards. This seemingly innocuous committee became the catalyst for a major change in the structure of the District in the following triennium. Newly-elected Western Regional Vice President, Rev. David Stechholz, was appointed chair of the committee, with other board members Ron Kasten, George Alles, and Larry Herforth, serving on the committee. This group would hold numerous meetings over the next triennium with Bishop Pittelko, who would eventually see the need for a major overhaul of the District and the Bylaws.

With the rapid urban decay of Detroit, the city's financial woes and declining ability to provide police protection, the loss of two Detroit congregations (Holy Spirit and Good Shepherd), and continued "white flight," the safety of the English District staff at the 23001 Grand River Avenue office was in jeopardy.[305] The presence of a shoddy hotel across the small side street, insufficient police protection, and multiple break-ins at the building convinced the District leadership that immediate action was necessary, though a move had been on the drawing board for a couple years. With the closure of New Mt. Olive in 1997, the District was facing the possibility of having no congregations in the city of Detroit. The transfer of Zion Evangelical-Lutheran Church of Detroit from the Michigan District to the English District approved by the board of directors in January 1995 prevented that from happening.

One of the first acts of the new board of directors was via a "tele-conference call meeting" on October 13, 1994, approving the sale of the English District office building at 23001 Grand River Avenue and the relocation of the office to a new location at 33100 Freedom Road, Farmington, Michigan, about five miles to the northwest of the old office.

The board approved the purchase of a building from the Michigan Osteopathic Association in Farmington. The building, which was on the market, had been spotted by Dr. Pittelko's wife, Beverly, only days earlier. It was determined that the building more than adequately met the needs of the English District and

The English District Office (1995–Present), 33100 Freedom Road, Farmington, Michigan.

was in a much safer area for the District staff and their cars. Only one member questioned the decision to move the District office to the suburbs.

The old office building was appraised at $127,000, but the likely sale price in rapidly deteriorating Detroit was anticipated to be considerably less.[306] District Treasurer and Business Administrator Beth Kavasch explained how purchasing the new District office building would be funded by the English District Canada Corporation (CCEF). The loan would be converted to American funds loaned to the District and repaid later. This difficult international transaction worked. In short, the Canadian contingent of the District came through! The teleconference vote was ratified at the next regular meeting of the English District Board of Directors, January 15-16, 1995, in St. Louis.[307] The English District made the move to the new property and building in the Detroit suburbs in 1995. Equally noteworthy, and as previously mentioned, this was the same meeting in which the English District received the transfer of Zion Evangelical-Lutheran Church of Detroit from the Michigan District. Once again, the English District had a congregation in the city of Detroit.

Another major event of the triennium was work done by the Committee of Staffing. This was not a hiring/firing committee, but rather a committee challenged to balance the District's financial resources with its needs. The outcome of that committee's extensive work would be adoption of a policy-based governance model with only one elected board of directors. All program boards would be eliminated, but not their functions. The board approved this plan of action in April 1996. A single board of directors was seen as cost-efficient, as the District would eliminate expenses of program boards, meetings, flight arrangements, etc. But the lingering concern was whether something significant would be lost in this reorganization. Adoption of a modified "Carver Model" of policy-based governance required major changes to the Bylaws of the District; those changes would be presented to the 1997 English District Convention for approval.

During the 1994-1997 triennium, the number of English District schools continued to grow, especially preschools and childcare facilities. The English District had not historically emphasized the need for parochial schools the way the Missouri Synod had, especially in the Synod's earlier decades of preserving German language, culture, and orthodox Lutheran beliefs. However, the English District was becoming a pacesetter with several large Christian day schools including Hales Corners Lutheran Church & School, Hales Corners, Wisconsin; Christ Church Lutheran &

School, Phoenix, Arizona; and West Portal Evangelical Lutheran Church & School, San Francisco, California. Through the school ministry efforts of Erv Henkelmann, the District began a yearly recognition of two educators, one a synodically-rostered minister of religion: commissioned church worker and the other a lay congregational educator (often a veteran Sunday school teacher) through two *Lumen Christi Awards*. These awards have continued in recognition of the faithfulness and excellence of our District educators.

Also during the 1994-1997 period, the English District continued funding and followed with great interest the work of the Rev. Zerit Johannes in Eritrea. This provided a model for other districts of Synod, as well as a great opportunity for English District congregations to stand behind Pastor and Mrs. Johannes. The District made a $150,000 three-year commitment. The Rev. David Thiele, District secretary, ably served as chair of the Eritrean Support Committee.

During this triennium, the board of directors became increasingly concerned with the advance site purchases that had been made through the Lutheran Church Extension Fund (LCEF) for planting new congregations. The advance sites held an estimated market value of $3,609,000, but were accruing interest during the holding period. Most of these properties which were not performing in terms of a mission plant would cost the District dearly. While the District was advancing with Open Arms childcare centers, it was declining in financial stability—a problem that the next administration would have to address.

During the triennium, a vision statement for the District was adopted:

> The English District glorifies God through the proclamation of the Gospel in congregations and special ministries to bring people to faith in Jesus Christ. In the ministries of the District, the Word of God and the Sacraments are used for the discipling, worship, nurture, and formation and human care of God's people.[308]

Whenever new congregations are received into membership of the Synod and District, their governing documents and application for membership both need to be approved by the board of directors. Curiously, an application for membership that did not materialize was that of St. Timothy Evangelical Lutheran Church in Sunderland, England. It was feared that the Evangelical Lutheran Church of England (ELCE) might fail. If that were the case, ELCE congregations, which are in pulpit and altar fellowship with the LCMS, might consider coming into the English District, whose "patron saint" was the first Lutheran martyr, Dr. Robert Barnes. Thankfully, the ELCE was able to right its situation, and the Sunderland congregation remained in the ELCE.

The triennium witnessed the transfer of churches to geographic districts: Faith, San Diego (to the Pacific Southwest District); Our Savior, Niagara Falls, Ontario (to The Lutheran Church-Canada); and Shepherd's Gate, Shelby Township, Michigan (to the Michigan District). The period was also marked by the closing, disbanding, or dissolving of several churches: Ebenezer, Milwaukee, Wisconsin; Good Shepherd, Pine, Arizona; Mt. Calvary, Chicago; Our Savior, Cincinnati, Ohio; Pilgrim, Sagamore Beach, Massachusetts; and Redeemer, Cleveland, Ohio.

Those losses were more than offset by several gains. New missions were added to the roster of the District: Celebration, Jacksonville, Florida; Crown of Life, Mt. Laurel, New Jersey; Epiphany, Dorr, Michigan; Faith, Chesapeake, Virginia; Mt. Ephraim, Chicago; New Life Chinese Lutheran, San Francisco; Our Savior's, St. George, Utah; and Praise, Fort Wayne, Indiana. Two congregations were received from other districts: Peace, New Berlin, Wisconsin (from the South Wisconsin District) and Zion, Detroit (from the Michigan District). In addition, several new preschools were established.[309] One of the District's "triumphs" at the 1995 Synod Convention was the passage of a resolution that was initiated by the English District encouraging LCMS congregations to move to weekly Holy Communion.

Excursus: Doctor of Divinity

In the 1990s, the English District began a unique practice of awarding an honorary Doctor of Divinity degree, as was the case with some judicatories in Europe and Great Britain. This practice involved much creativity on the part of Bishop Pittelko, who convinced the board of directors that honoring a select long-term English District pastor for extraordinary service in the church would be most fitting. The College of Circuit Visitors would receive nominations and choose the recipient. Though neither an academic degree nor an academically-generated award, the Doctor of Divinity was conferred either at a District convention or at the Professional Church Workers Conference. This usually took place during the Divine Service at the conference and was always met with applause. The honoree and his wife were publicly recognized and often overwhelmed with tears of joy. Past English Missouri Synod and English District presidents were also accorded the degree, though some had earned or honorary doctorates.

The annual awarding of the Doctor of Divinity was discontinued in 2017. The 28 pastors who received the honorary degree are listed below:

1994   Rev. Edgar H. Behrens* and Rev. Gordon R. Mackensen (tie)
1995   Rev. John C. Streit
1996   Rev. Melvin J. Tassler
1997   Rev. Garry D. McClure
1998   Rev. David H. Ritt
1999   Rev. Thomas D. Kraus
2000   Rev. Erich H. Wildgrube
2001   Rev. John W. Fey*
2002   Rev. Victor F. Halboth, Jr.
2003   Rev. Dr. Dusan Toth
2004   Rev. Dr. Martin W. Bangert
2005   Rev. Philip H. Kraft
2006   Rev. Dr. Merlin D. Rehm and Rev. Arnold W. Frank (tie)
2007   Rev. John Wm. Stieve
2008   Rev. David P. Stechholz
2009   Rev. Ronald R. Farah
2010   Rev. David A. Dressel
2011   Rev. Larry M. Vogel
2012   Rev. Dr. Ihno A. Janssen, Jr. and Rev. Michael S. Ernst (tie)
2013   Rev. Robert L. Fitzpatrick
2014   Rev. Joseph P. Fabry and Rev. Dr. Roger D. Pittelko (tie)
2015   Rev. Roger C. Ellis
2016   Rev. Jerome H. Groth and Rev. R. Wayne Morton (tie)
   * deceased, award posthumously

1997 English District Convention

The theme for the 49th Convention of the English District-LCMS, June 12-15, 1997, at Concordia University, River Forest, was *"Jesus Christ the Same, Yesterday, Today, and Forever,"* based on Hebrews 13:8. This would be the fifth of seven consecutive conventions at "CURF," as the school was affectionately known. The District was still under the motto and banner: *A District in Mission – Worshipping the Crucified God and Proclaiming New Life in Jesus Christ.* 1997 was the 150th Anniversary Year of The Lutheran Church—Missouri Synod (1847) and the 125th Anniversary of the English Evangelical Lutheran Conference (1872), which became the English Evangelical Lutheran Conference of Missouri and Other States in 1888 and then the English Evangelical Lutheran Synod of Missouri and Other States in 1891 and finally the English District of *Die Deutsche Evangelisch-Lutherische Synode von Missouri, Ohio, und andern Staaten* in 1911. Bishop Pittelko was ready to rehearse this history at the final convention over which he would preside.

Pittelko's written report to the District began with the anniversaries and the giving of thanks to the Lord. He then reflected on the past three years, expressing thanks to the District praesidium, board of directors, and to the Committee on Staffing and Structure. He proceeded to disclose the staff changes in the District. Pittelko highlighted the deaths of Ervin Henkelmann, executive secretary to the president: parish services, and Dr. George Bornemann, Bishop Emeritus. Henkelmann was tragically killed in a pedestrian accident in San Diego in January 21, 1997. Two days later in Florida, the Lord called Bornemann home to heaven. These two deaths were particularly hard on Pittelko, the Praesidium and board of directors, and many pastors and others in the District. Both men were commemorated in the Convention Memorial Service on June 15.

Pittelko reflected on the new English District office, the District's congregational and pastoral membership in Canada, mission expansion, which had slowed but not stopped in the past three years, and the structure of the English District. He noted the following regarding the Staffing and Structure Committee: "We discovered that from the second convention of the English Synod in 1891 until 1952, the English District had only one standing board. As the United States became more complex in governmental structure, the Synod followed, followed closely by the English District."[310] The new proposed structure would both streamline the District structure and allow executives flexibility to carry out ministry initiatives through Ministry Action Teams (MATs) in the circuits and regions. Pittelko admitted that he had not initially believed that such change was needed, but that he became convinced of its benefits. He also talked in fatherly fashion about the decline in contributions and the need to better emphasize the obligations that congregations have to support the District's programs of planting new congregations and helping existing congregations in need. He highlighted the Eritrean Initiative with the Rev. Zerit Johannes, the Ministerial Health Commission, and the English District as a "city" district. Looking to the future, Dr. Pittelko said it was no longer his to call after leading the District for nearly 12 years. It was a time for new leadership: "For two millennia the Lord has guided His Church. He has not left us without His Spirit."[311]

The highlights of the 1997 convention were the election of a new President/Bishop, adoption of the District restructuring proposal, and the remembrance of those who entered eternal glory, especially Erv Henkelmann and Bishop Bornemann. Bishop Pittelko's address to the convention on June 13 was brief, expressing his hope that the delegates would approve the restructuring proposal. He included one final thank you to the District. Dr. David T. Stein, pastor of Holy Spirit Church, Elk Grove Village, Illinois, and former professor at Concordia University, River Forest, offered a three-part Convention Essay on Lutheran higher education. The Synod representative was LCMS Second Vice President, Dr. Robert King.

Four men allowed their names to stand in the election of president: the Revs. Paul Bacon of New Lenox, Illinois; David Ritt of Villa Park, Illinois; Robert Scudieri, of St. Louis; and Thomas Spahn of Lititz, Pennsylvania. This slate of four nominees included one from the Eastern Region, while the other three were from the Midwest, two from Chicagoland. On the first ballot, Scudieri received the most votes (93) but not a majority of the total votes cast (259). The second ballot produced a similar result; Scudieri received 101 of the 254 total votes. A third ballot was held after Bacon withdrew his name; 257 votes were cast, of which Scudieri once again received the most (109), though not the necessary majority. On the fourth ballot, Ritt emerged as the new leader, outgaining Scudieri in votes 109 to 101; Spahn's receipt of 45 votes prevented anyone from being elected. The fifth ballot would prove to be decisive. With the three candidates remaining on the ballot, Ritt garnered 130 of the 251 votes cast, finally achieving the necessary majority. The election to replace Bishop Pittelko stood in contrast to his previous re-elections by acclamation; the five-ballot contest was a most unusual election.

The Rev. David Thiele was elected secretary. The Rev. David Stechholz, Chair of the District Staffing and Structuring Committee was unseated by one vote as vice president in the Western Region.[312] Stechholz was then nominated from the floor and elected as an at-large clergy member of the board of directors. A slate of 23 circuit visitors was also ratified by the convention.

<u>1997 Elected Vice Presidents as Ranked by the District</u>

First Vice President	Rev. David Dressel (Lake Erie Region)
Second Vice President	Rev. Dr. Paul Bacon (Midwest Region)
Third Vice President	Rev. Thomas Kraus (Eastern Region)
Fourth Vice President	Rev. Arnold Frank (Western Region).[313]

After experiencing multiple-ballot elections using paper ballots, the election committee proposed a resolution that the board of directors explore the feasibility of using electronic voting procedures. The convention delegates unanimously adopted this resolution. Use of electronic voting was employed at the 2000 District Convention and has been used ever since.

The most significant resolution adopted at the 1997 District Convention was Resolution 97-1-01 ("To Establish a Single Board of Directors"), which passed on the second full day of the convention, June 13. The challenge for delegates over the last two days of the Convention was approving each of the necessary bylaw changes to implement the restructuring proposal. Delegates rose to meet that challenge, showing amazing patience in accomplishing the task. Resolution 97-3-02A ("To Give First Priority to Starting and Building New Congregations") was heavily debated by delegates and ultimately defeated. The resolution's defeat was not the result of giving higher priority for English District urban mission work but the financial aspect of the proposal that called for 20 percent of the District's congregational receipts to be used for starting and maintaining new congregations in North America.[314]

President/Bishop-Elect David Ritt spoke words of encouragement to the convention. He described the English District-LCMS as a planting district and stated:

> "The seed is in us. It is up to us to plant and cultivate it. God will do the rest as He always does through Word and Sacrament ministry." President/Bishop-Elect committed himself to be a symbol of unity for the people of the District, that missions will always be a priority, and to focus on the Lutheran family.[315]

On June 14, Dr. Roger and Beverly Pittelko were honored with a plaque, a proclamation from the District, a congratulatory letter from LCMS President Barry, and other gifts. The next day Bishop-Elect Ritt proposed a resolution to confer upon the Rev. Dr. Roger D. Pittelko the title President/Bishop Emeritus of the English District, which was passed with a standing ovation. The closing Divine Service included installation of the newly elected officers and remembrance of church workers in the District who had been recently called to glory. Dr. Pittelko was honored by the Synod, as he was elected fourth vice president at the 1998 Synod Convention. His service to the church also included teaching pastoral theology to future pastors studying at Concordia Theological Seminary, Fort Wayne.

A huge page in the District's history had turned, though not that quickly. A board of directors teleconference meeting was held in the summer following the 1997 District convention. This meeting, chaired by Bishop Pittelko, dealt with two property matters: a property purchase for the new Christ Lutheran Church in Lake Mills, Wisconsin, and a loan for new Bishop Ritt to purchase a home in Livonia, Michigan. Part-time Missions Executive Dr. Richard Drews had resigned; his former duties were handled by Rev. Robert Kavasch until a new mission executive would be chosen.

In 2002 a festschrift was produced in honor of Bishop Pittelko. *Shepherd the Church: Essays in Pastoral Theology Honoring Bishop Roger D. Pittelko* featured a series of articles by a number of English District pastors and professorial friends. It was a fitting tribute to a man who had given so much to Christ's Church on earth. He was also later awarded the English District's honorary Doctor of Divinity in 2014. The English District may be a small niche in North American Christendom, but Dr. Roger Pittelko was a significant and influential part of her rich heritage and history.[316] The Lord of the Church called Bishop Emeritus Pittelko home to heaven on November 12, 2020.

Excursus: Nomenclature Matters

Throughout her history, the English District has discovered that nomenclature matters. Ecclesiastical terminology has changed over the centuries, but Christ's Church is well-served by paying attention to terms that were used in the past, especially those with biblical roots.

Bishop

The English District started using the term "bishop" informally as early as the years of President Hugo Kleiner. It was generally understood to refer to the office of the District president. The term's use was out of respect for the office. From its biblical roots, "bishop" (*episcopus*) means "overseer," one who leads the flock of God's people. In its earliest biblical usage, it referred to the parish pastor. In the progression of the first four centuries of Christianity, it came to mean the "overseer" of the churches and *presbyteros*, the elders or pastors of a geographic area. Hence, the Bishop of Ephesus might have ecclesiastical oversight over a number of congregations and their pastors. This was for the good order of the Church. The Lord God is a God of order. [317]

The English Evangelical Lutheran Synod of Missouri and Other States (1872-1911) and her antecedents had a confessional boldness that honored Scripture as infallible and the only rule and norm of faith and doctrine and the Confessional writings of the Evangelical Lutheran Church as a faithful witness to the veracity of Holy Writ, just like the German Missouri Synod. However, the English Missouri Synod also had a unique bent toward reaching the lost for Christ in the *lingua franca* of the United States and Canada, English. Perhaps because of her different orientation from the German Missouri Synod, which some might call "progressive," the English District did not feel bound by some terminology that the German Missouri Synod had adopted.

During the tenure of President Hugh Kleiner (1951-1963) the biblical term of "bishop" began to be used informally. It was in stronger use during the time of President/Bishop George Bornemann (1976-1984). Finally during the tenure of Bishop/President Roger Pittelko, the term was accepted as official, namely the one who has oversight.[318] It was understood that things hierarchical do not always mean tyranny or oppression, something for which the United States over the course of its history has a huge and understandable aversion. The District's Canadian congregations and pastors long had been very comfortable addressing their District president "Bishop." Hierarchy in the church implies leadership and authority. In the English District, one man is elected to serve as both bishop (ecclesiastical oversight and leadership) and president (administrative and the chief executive officer). During the time of Bishop Bornemann, it became apparent that the District president had to be both bishop and the CEO. During the tenure of Bishop Stechholz, use of the Bishop's cope and crosier became common at District conferences, conventions, and congregational and school visits.

But isn't the term "bishop" too catholic, meaning Roman Catholic or Eastern Orthodox or Anglican? With its solid scriptural roots, the term "bishop" is preferred in the English District over the term "president," which has long been used by the United States government and the business world, as well as secular organizations. Does not the Church have a vocabulary that is its own?

From the time of Bishop Pittelko on, it has been customary in the English District and in a few other districts of the Missouri Synod to honor their District president with the spoken and written title of "Bishop."

The English District has been a pioneer in the use of the term "Bishop." Will this grow in the Missouri Synod? One determining factor in the resistance of the LCMS to use of the term "bishop" may have come from the history of the Synod that, prior to its formation, saw the deposing of Bishop Martin Stephan among the Missouri Saxon immigrants. Perhaps even more influential was the aversion of the American culture to hierarchy. Even the term "President," which Walther adopted for the German Missouri Synod as a populist leadership term, has had multiple understandings in its usage since the adoption of the U.S. Constitution. But the Church catholic is not bound by changing whims of society and culture; she has a unique nomenclature rooted in the Scriptures and ecclesiastical history.

The English District also continued use of the term "circuit visitors," even while using the official terminology of the Missouri Synod that has gone from "visitors" to "counselors" (counsellors in Canada) and back to "visitors." Many a District board of directors meeting over a span of decades included disagreement over use of the "circuit visitors." The

LCMS, influenced by the populist movement in the 1950s, adopted the term "circuit counselor," giving the name of this office a more psychological connotation rather than the previous term "circuit visitor," definitive of one who visits the circuit pastors and congregations in an ecclesiastical role as an extension of the office of the Bishop/President. Will the English District be able to persuade the LCMS to use the term "bishop" for her District presidents (and then as a council of bishops) and with the synodical president being in truth the "presiding bishop" or "archbishop"? Time and wisdom will reveal the future. The point, though, should be clearly made: nomenclature matters.

Symbols of the Office of Bishop

The Ring

The oldest symbol of the office is the ring. From a very early time in Christendom, clergy wore a ring. In the Roman Empire, a ring was worn by slaves to mark them and to denote their master. Likewise, the clergy were to be slaves (bondservants) of the Lord, as St. Paul notes in Romans 6:22. By the 7th century A.D., the bishops of the church wore a ring with the seal of their church or district, diocese, synod, or see. The ring worn by Bishops Pittelko, Ritt, and Stechholz bears the seal of the English District, the double-trunked sycamore tree. Surrounding it in Latin are the words: *"Seal of the Bishop and President, English Diocese (District), Lutheran Church."* The sycamore tree represents the "union" of the English Evangelical Lutheran Synod of Missouri and Others States and the German Evangelical Lutheran Synod of Missouri, Ohio, and Other States in 1911.

The Crosier

The crosier originated as a simple walking stick. This was a personal symbol, which did not designate jurisdiction over a church or district, diocese, synod, or see. In time, the walking stick was given the ornamentation of the shepherd's crook or staff, symbolizing the pastor's care for the flock of Christ. Today the crosier is understood to symbolize episcopal jurisdiction over a church, district or diocese, or synod. It has been used routinely in the English District at ordinations, installations, and

District conventions and conferences. For our partner Evangelical Lutheran church bodies in Africa, especially, the crosier is an important feature and symbol of authority. The crook of the crosier is turned outward toward the people over whom the bishop has jurisdiction in a given place. If brought to a location where the bishop does not have jurisdiction—a practice that is not customary—the crook is turned inward toward the bishop.

The Pectoral Cross

At various times in the long history of Christendom, clergy have worn neck crosses or crucifixes. The crucifix has historically been preferred in the English District. It is customary in The Lutheran Church—Missouri Synod today that most pastors, who are "overseers" (Acts 20:28) of congregations, wear a pectoral cross. It is larger than crosses worn by others assisting, such as acolytes, deacons or elders, or what laymen might have. The emphasis in the pastoral office is on serving (John 13:13-17). For a period of time, some LCMS presidents have given the district presidents (bishops) a pectoral cross in the shape of the Synod logo. Since that logo is not actually a cross because the arms do not intersect, English District bishops have received the gift, while choosing to wear their own crucifixes. Current Synod President Matthew Harrison wears a very large pectoral crucifix. A crucifix is always a reminder of God's redeeming love in Jesus Christ, the sinless Lamb of God who sacrificed Himself on the tree of the cross for the salvation of the human race.

While the wearing of a pectoral cross is a relatively recent custom in our Synod, it is fitting as the local pastor of a congregation wears the best known symbol of the Christian faith, the cross of our Lord Jesus Christ. The District president or bishop wears the same symbol, reminding him and others of Christ's ultimate sacrifice for us.

Purple, Violet, or Scarlet Clerical Shirt and Bishop's Mitre

Though not completely unique to the English District within the Synod, our bishops often wear a purple, violet, or scarlet clerical shirt, especially when they are performing their official oversight duties. This has been a custom since the mid-1970s. A bishop's mitre is a tall pointed hat that is worn by our Lutheran bishop friends in Africa, Europe, and elsewhere. It is rarely used in Canada and the United States among Lutherans, partly because it seems "too catholic" for many of our people. Nevertheless, it is a historic vestment piece which may be worn for part of the Mass.

Bishop's Chair or Cathedra

The English District may have a bishop, but it has no cathedral. Due the District's historic ties to Detroit, some may argue that Zion Evangelical-Lutheran Church, the only Detroit city congregation in the English District, might serve that role. The congregation sets aside the cathedra or bishop's chair for the bishop or his representative (a bishop emeritus) at the church's St. Michael Liturgical Conference and at the Maundy Thursday Mass of the blessing of the anointing oils. But no cathedral has ever been designated, which accords with the Synod's congregational polity.

The English District does have a "chair." It is a fine, transportable chair with the District logo on it in red and gold. It is located in the Bishop/President's study at the English District office in Farmington (suburban Detroit), not far from the old District office building in Detroit. Historically in Christianity, the bishop was the pastor of the most important church of the diocese, district, or see of a given geographic area and had his seat (sedelium) at that church. Since the English District is non-geographic, it is not practical to take the chair all over North America, so it sits in the District office.[319]

CHAPTER 15
Structural Transition, New Growth, and a Centennial

The Years of Bishops/Presidents
David H. Ritt and David P. Stechholz

The Rev. Dr. David Ritt, Bishop/President, 1997—2006

FOR MUCH OF the English District's history, the president served as chairman of the board of directors. The new policy-based governance model implemented by the 1997 convention mandated that neither the president/bishop nor the secretary would be permitted to serve as chair of the board of directors. At the board's first meeting under this new model in September 1997, First Vice President Rev. David Dressel served as the acting chair. All board members underwent a helpful but lengthy orientation process on "The Carver Model of Board Governance." After President/Bishop Ritt shared some initial thoughts on his vision for the English District, Mr. Ron Kasten and Mr. Joel Rittmueller were elected chairman and vice chairman respectively.

The English District Board of Directors and new president were entering a world of change. Policies and procedures, including terminology such as "executive limitations," became part of their vocabulary. At its September 1997 meeting, the board adopted its initial board of director's policies. A new world, indeed![320] At its November 1997 meeting, the board adopted 11 end statements, most of which optimistically called for growth in the District's and congregational life.[321]

In January 1998, the board adopted a new mission statement and reaffirmed its 11 end statements. The new mission statement for what became the nine years of Bishop Ritt's administration of the English District was three short statements:

Partners in Christ, Working Together, Equipping to Gather.[322]

This era under a new president and new structure included the need for the board to evaluate the District's financial status. The board learned that the District ranked 26th out of the 35 LCMS Districts in synodical pledge amounts. That pledge was equal to only 11% of total revenue and 17% of pledged revenue. In addition, the English District had the grave matter of dealing with its advance site losses. Thankfully, a special LCEF Advance Site Committee chaired by Ms. Jean Franz was created to develop a plan, culminating in a Letter of Understanding, which was ultimately adopted and signed by the District president in August 1998.[323] The board was also apprised of front door and back door losses in membership from the District, reflecting what was also happening in Synod and across North American Christianity.

Several aspects of the ecclesiastical landscape of the LCMS were changing in all districts, including the English District. The number of vacant congregations increased. Fewer students were graduating from the LCMS seminaries. Congregational call processes lengthened, while some congregations began to enter "non-calling status." At board meetings, Bishop Ritt would frequently give notice of 20 to 25 congregational vacancies within the District. Another part of the landscape was the new Pastoral Leadership Institute (PLI), established in 1999. This ministry was intended to mentor younger pastors who showed leadership potential. From 1999 through the second decade of the 21st Century, several District pastors and their wives participated in this program. English District pastors, Drs. Mike Ernst and Scott Rische, were among the leaders of PLI.

Another new ministry was The Center for Asian-American Missions and Evangelization (CAME), a mission effort under its executive director, Dr. Jotham S. Johann, the son of an English District Korean pastor in Queens, New York. Triennial National LCMS Youth Gatherings (NYGs), with heavy English District congregational participation, became a larger part of the picture. Later in the Ritt years, School Ministries Executive Tim Ewell would greatly cultivate English District participation in the national youth gatherings or in the smaller Higher Things regional conferences, the latter having appeal to liturgical congregations and their youth.

Much more time at board meetings was dedicated to analyzing data, especially of District finances, crafting and implementing end statements, and assessing other challenges and priorities. But the biggest challenge was the matter of debt reduction payments to LCEF for advance site land purchases.

Though business, financial, and legal matters were receiving great attention by the District leadership, a new spiritual addition to the English District culture was a daily prayer list for the entire year. This was started under Bishop Ritt and continued during the tenures of Bishops Stechholz and Hardy, with the former having added names of congregations, pastors, retired church workers, names of Synod officials, board of directors, committees, and schools, and liturgical days of note. Many English District pastors and congregations regularly remember each other in daily prayer to the Lord. Birthday cards continue to be sent out by English District bishops to pastors on their birthdays.

The financial status of the District led Bishop Ritt and his staff to initiate a new program: Missions Alive – Help Raise the Anchor of Debt. This campaign had the goal to raise $500,000 by November 1999, an amount to be matched 50 cents to the dollar by LCEF. Partners in Christ Convocations held around the District helped member congregations grow in support of this fundraising endeavor. By May 2000, Treasurer Beth (nee Kavasch) Miles reported that $443,121.90 had been received from District congregations through the Missions Alive program. The District had paid $546,784.18 toward the advance site loss debt; a balance of $628,861.13 remained as the debt. There was a way to go, but the District was making significant progress.[324]

A feature of the new Carver model of policy-based governance was an annual review of the work of the president of the District. This review did not evaluate the ecclesiastical oversight role—the "Bishop aspect"—of the office but the administrative, chief executive aspects. For several years, this was a rather uncomfortable process, involving both a Presidential Review Committee and a Salary Review Committee. It was part of a more bureaucratic age in the church, generating review criteria, monitoring executive performance, as well as reviewing the board and its work.[325] Thankfully, the diligence of President Ritt and his staff and the steady hand of Board Chairman Ron Kasten helped to alleviate some of the stress in adapting to the new policy-based governance.

During this period, an idea gaining support within the Synod was a potential realignment of the Synod's 35 districts into 100-150 districts of approximately 60 congregations each.[326] This concept was not favored by either the board or the vast majority of English District pastors, as it would jeopardize the future of the District. Some other districts were not enthused by the idea either. However, the possible synodical district realignment loomed in the back of the minds of English District leaders.

Y2K or Anno Domini 2000

The end of the 20th Century was fraught with emotions from fear and trepidation to great hope for humanity and endless speculation about the future. Many people who had no hope in Christ feared 2000 would be the end of the world. On December 31, 1999, there was a lot of speculation regarding whether the new millennium was to begin on January 1, 2000 or whether it would need to wait until January 1, 2001. For a while there existed a computer programming problem variously known as the Y2K Problem, the Millennium bug, and the Y2K glitch. Nuclear warheads did not suddenly go off. The world did not end. For believers in Christ, it was *Anno Domini* "the Year of our Lord" 2000. The English District and the LCMS marched through this calendar change without trepidation. Believers in Christ Jesus could sing "Auld Lang Syne" and "Our God, Our Help in Ages Past, Our Hope for Years to Come" with confidence in Him who is the Alpha and the Omega, the one eternal God of all ages.

Bishop Ritt and his staff chose a theme for the 50th Convention of the English District: "Go and Tell Until the Trumpet Sounds." The convention was held June 15-20, 2000 at Concordia University, River Forest, Illinois. The artwork was again designed and executed by Rev. Richard Patt, weaving together the themes of "Partners in Christ," "Alive in Mission," and the convention theme. Bishop Ritt's report reflected on the growth of the English District over the course of 50 conventions. He focused on the new administrative structure of the District, the matter of advance site losses and the District's Missions Alive campaign to raise the anchor of debt.[327]

How far that anchor of debt had been raised became clear during Ritt's address to the convention delegates. He noted that the LCEF debt of the District began with the staggering sum of $1,715,000. By June 1, 2000, that amount had decreased to $312,602.14, largely resulting from the work of Jean Franz's committee in partnership with LCEF and the generous contribution of congregations to the Missions Alive campaign.[328]

The convention essayist was the District's own Dr. David R. Schmitt, professor of homiletics at Concordia Seminary, St. Louis. He focused on evangelism as the presence of God, far more than a program, and that it is the mission of God. "Evangelism is God at work through His people bringing His Word to the world." Schmitt concluded: "Don't forget, we have God and He is in mission. Yes, there will be struggle – but 'Go and Tell until the Trumpets Sound!'"[329]

The convention theme proved to be a memorable one. However, the restructuring took its toll. Some District leaders felt that it had robbed the District of its joy. They would choose to translate their mission efforts and zeal elsewhere.

At this convention, Dr. Paul Bacon withdrew his name from the presidential slate and asked the convention to re-elect Bishop Ritt by acclamation. This suggestion met the approval of the gathered delegates.

2000 Elected Vice Presidents as Ranked by the District

First Vice President	Dr. Paul Bacon (Midwest Region)
Second Vice President	Rev. David Dressel (Lake Erie Region)
Third Vice President	Rev. Larry Vogel (Eastern Region)
Fourth Vice President	Rev. Arnold Frank (Western Region)

The Rev. David Stechholz returned to the Praesidium as the elected District secretary. The new board of directors would also include Treasurer Beth Miles; George Alles as CCEF advisory member; Pastors Ronald Farah and John Stieve; commissioned teachers Donna Hay and Kathy Slupik; lay-persons from each region, Linda Domanski, Armin Bruer, Jean Franz, and Joel Rittmueller; and two laypersons as at-large members, Sue Elsholz and Ralph Thiel.

Stemming from concern that potential restructuring of synodical districts might lead to the disbanding of the English District, the convention adopted Resolution 00-2-01: "To Affirm Right of English District to Determine Its Own Status." This restated the District's understanding that its fate should be determined, at least partly, by its will to exist as a district of The Lutheran Church—Missouri Synod. Nine other resolutions were adopted, several of which addressed topics that were facing the Synod at the time:

- Res. 00-2-02 "To Encourage the Training of a Commissioned Diaconate"

- Res. 00-2-03 "In Support of 'For the Sake of the Church'"
- Res. 00-4-02 "To Express Support for Lutheran-Roman Catholic Ecumenical Efforts"
- Res. 00-4-03 "To Express Support for LCMS Reaction to the Joint Declaration on the Doctrine of Justification"
- Res. 00-4-04 "To Request Clarification of Synod's Stance on Women in the Church"
- Res. C-00-01 "To Call for The LCMS in Convention to Reject the Fellowship Document, 'The Lutheran Understanding of Fellowship'"

The First Decade of the 21st Century

The new millennium's first decade witnessed several impactful events and concerns, but none was more significant to world history than 9/11. On September 11, 2001, Al-Qaeda terrorists highjacked four planes, crashing two of them into the two World Trade Center buildings in New York City, one into the Pentagon in Washington, D.C., while the fourth plane, thought to be targeting either the White House or Capitol Building, was forced down near Shanksville, Pennsylvania. The United States was brought to its knees in abject horror. Nearly 3,000 people were killed at "Ground Zero," and it would take more than a decade before the new 1776-foot high One World Trade Center, the tallest building in the Western Hemisphere, was erected on the site of the 9/11 destruction in lower Manhattan.

The 9/11 attack led to the American invasion of Afghanistan in October 2001 and triggered a war with Iraq, starting in 2003, involving a coalition led by the United States. This war brought down the regime of Saddam Hussein, who allegedly supported terrorism against the United States, Israel, and other countries. He was eventually captured and executed. It would also lead to the killing of the mastermind of the 9/11 terrorist attack, Osama bin Laden, in Abbottabad, Pakistan in May 2011.

Though the 9/11 attacks stand out in this decade, there were other events in a time of relative peace among major world powers, which left the United States as the sole superpower. The Fourth Industrial Revolution, as it's been termed, began in the early 21st century and included genetic engineering and huge advances in the telecommunications industry. Members of the Christian underground church in China were arrested. There was increased concern over global climate change. The world population had soared to seven billion. The election of a German pope, Benedict XVI, after the death of John Paul II, moved the Roman Catholic Church in a more traditionalist, conservative direction.

The Lutheran Church—Missouri Synod and English District were adversely affected for several years following the 9/11 attacks and the public prayer event held at Yankee Stadium on September 23, 2001, which involved Atlantic District President Dr. David Benke. After being temporarily suspended from his duties, Benke was effectively pardoned and restored to his office. The result of this incident and process once again polarized the Synod, though not to the same extent as the Seminex era. Most of the so-called "salt water districts" of the Synod were supportive of Benke, while many districts based in the Midwest were disgruntled with his prayer and civil participation in the Yankee Stadium event.

The 2009 decision of the Evangelical Lutheran Church in America (ELCA) to allow same-sex marriages among its clergy resulted in a split in that church body, more than ever estranged from the LCMS. A large, organizationally flat confederation of congregations called Lutheran Congregations in Mission for Christ (LCMC) had previously emerged with the ELCA. Following the ELCA's landmark decision; over 420 congregations with a membership of 142,000 broke from the ELCA and formed a new body, the North American Lutheran Church (NALC). Just prior to its forming, the bishop of the English District and other LCMS district presidents reached out to some of the congregations and pastors with sympathetic ears.[330] While these pastors expressed gratitude to the LCMS, they were more intent on starting a new church body. The NALC is more theologically conservative than the ELCA and is opposed to homosexual marriage, yet it ordains women clergy and maintains broader ecumenical ties in world Lutheranism than the LCMS. Fraternal talks have occurred between the NALC and the Missouri Synod, but these have not led to the NALC wholly adopting the theological positions of the LCMS.

Pastors in the LCMS and English District were increasingly concerned with declining church membership and attendance in public worship and Bible study as well as decreasing offerings. Faithful pastors, Lutheran school teachers, deaconesses, and other professional church workers, along with the lay leadership in congregations, grasped at what might work to "bring them in." Some adopted church growth principles and language.

Others felt clergy trained through the Pastoral Leadership Institute (PLI) might be the answer. In the English District, a more conservative, confessionally oriented clergy became more influential through *Gottesdienst* and other liturgical and confessional publications or online blogs.

However, the common denominator in the English District still was its mission focus on reaching the lost for Christ. This was expressed not just in English District board meetings and in the *English Channels* and *JEDP*, but also in Bishop Ritt's monthly or semi-monthly *Bishop-to-Bishop* online newsletters to ordained and commissioned church workers within the District. Following Ritt's tenure, Bishop David Stechholz renamed the online newsletter "Servant to Servant," which was sent to pastors, other professional church workers, and lay leaders in the District and congregations.

Noticeable in the early years of the 21st century was the planting of new ethnic ministries within the English District, especially through immigrant pastors aligning with District congregations. Outreach was beginning in Vietnamese (Martin Luther Chapel, Pennsauken, New Jersey); Sudanese and other immigrant African languages and cultures (Christ Lutheran, Lansing, Michigan); Mandarin and Cantonese Chinese (through and at West Portal and New Life Chinese churches, San Francisco); Nuer-speaking Sudanese, Eritrean, and other African immigrant ministries in Canada (Gethsemane, Windsor, St. John's Toronto, St. Luke, North York, and St. Mark, Mississauga, Ontario); Telugu Indian ministry (Bethesda, Chicago); immigrant Liberian ministry (Bethany, Ewing/Trenton, New Jersey); and continued African-American Deaf Ministry (Ephphatha Evangelical Lutheran Church of the Deaf, Chicago). Not all of these efforts would blossom and continue into strong, healthy ministries or new congregations, but the mission endeavor was being made. This multi-ethnic outreach was bold in a district named "English."

Another area of District mission work were the campus ministries serving students and college communities. Campus ministries within the English District were located at Princeton University (Messiah, Princeton, New Jersey); Slippery Rock University (All Saints Church, Slippery Rock, Pennsylvania); Michigan State University (Martin Luther Chapel, East Lansing, Michigan); University of Arizona (at first a pan-Lutheran ministry and later an English District ministry among the Arizona South Circuit congregations, Tucson, Arizona); and at San Francisco State University (West Portal and New Life Chinese, San Francisco, California). Some of these were unique peer group ministries; others focused on international students. All of them had special Bible studies and fellowship opportunities. The English District's strength in campus ministry was a model for the Synod. The English District also adopted an LCMS Recognized Service Organization (RSO), the Lutheran Campus Ministry Association (LCMA).

During this time, the District board of directors requested the president/bishop and his staff to present a five-year plan for ministry, including a vision description of ministry, anticipated funding levels year by year, annual objectives, and measures to be reported annually.[331] An increasing amount of board time was spent on policy, process, and procedure, which are part and parcel of policy-based governance. Following the 2000 District Convention, Rev. John Stieve was elected by the board as board chair and Mr. Joel Rittmueller as vice chair. In a board brainstorming session, the question came up, "Is money driving the mission of the English District?"[332] It was agreed that Christ's dominical commands and our Lutheran confessional theology should be driving the mission. But the money problem persisted.

A major board concern that absorbed considerable time between 2000 and 2001 involved the closure of what had once been the largest congregation in the English District, Hope Evangelical Lutheran Church, located at 64th and Washtenaw Avenue, Chicago. Rather than selling the property, the decision was made to call Rev. Paul Anderson as Missionary-at-large, charged to take over the building, develop New Hope Lutheran Church, and restore the school. This plan initially seemed successful, but in later years no reports were given on the status of the church and school. The board had nearly come to the decision to close the mission effort, but it elected to give it another chance, selling it to New Hope Lutheran Ministries for $1, while retaining a reversionary clause. At one point, a fifth of the District's mission budget was subsidizing that one mission effort, which seemed to be a risky mission venture. Direction was given to New Hope to work on a cooperative arrangement with Luther High School South, Chicago, which was heading toward its own closure. The board of directors toured New Hope Lutheran Ministries during its August 12-13,

2002 meeting in Chicago.[333] The ministry continued on its own after District subsidy was terminated.

Missions Executive Rev. Robert Fitzpatrick transitioned back to the Parish ministry, accepting a call to Redeemer Church, Elmhurst, Illinois. No longer were staff members necessarily present at board of directors meetings, as in the past. They attended at the pleasure of the District bishop/president in his CEO role as president. However, both Bishop David Ritt and his successor, Bishop David Stechholz, usually preferred to have their executive staff members present. This was often beneficial to the president when board members wanted to receive information from the staff but less than beneficial whenever the president and a staff member had conflicting viewpoints. The Carver Model did not necessarily fix the problems when such conflicts arose. Each bishop/president handled these matters differently and lived with the results. However, finances were more frequently dictating staffing arrangements.

The 51st Convention of the English District was again held at Concordia University, River Forest, Illinois, June 19-22, 2003, under the theme *"One Gospel – Many People – Share the Joy."* Though a different organist was initially used as an excellent "ringer," the old organist, the Rev. Stechholz, still played at this gathering, though his time of providing that service was drawing to a close. The 2003 Convention was preceded by a theological convocation, as called for by the LCMS President, Dr. Gerald Kieschnick. Synod had mandated such convocations for all the districts. For a non-geographic district, this was best handled by attaching the convocation to the district convention at which both pastors and laity would be assembled. A timely presentation was given by Dr. David L. Adams of Concordia Seminary, St. Louis, revising a paper that he had originally prepared as a presentation to the LCMS Council of Presidents and faculties of the two LCMS seminaries in March 2002. The topic was *"The Church in the Public Square in a Pluralist Society."* (That presentation had been generated by the actions of Atlantic District Bishop/President Benke in the "Yankee Stadium incident" and the aftermath.) A four-part series of questions were addressed:

- How do individual believers relate to persons of other faiths (and persons of no faith) in the public square in a pluralistic society?

- How does the church corporately address public policy issues in the public square in a pluralistic society?
- How does the church relate to other churches and faith communities in the public square in a pluralistic society?
- How does the church relate to American Civil Religion in the public square?[334]

The fourth part under question #4 carried with it a series of theses well worth noting:

- American Civil Religion is the state religion of the United States of America.
- American Civil Religion is now irreducibly polytheistic.
- American Civil Religious events bridge the gap between worship and civic events.
- American Civil Religious events are themselves a spectrum of activities.
- Both the mission of the Church and the obligation to work for the welfare of our neighbor requires the Church to be engaged with the broader society.
- The limits and form (of the) Church's engagement with the world are shaped by the mission imperative and the necessity of faithfulness to the teachings of the Word of God.
- To the extent that a Civic Religious Event is an event involving Christians of different confessions, participation in the event must be governed by the same principles that govern our interaction with other Christian church bodies.
- To the extent that a Civic Religious Event is an event involving participants from non-Christian faith groups, participation in the event must be shaped by the requirements of the First Commandment.
- To the extent that a Civic Religious Event is primarily civil in nature, participation in the event must be shaped by an appreciation of the tension between the interests of the Church and the state.
- Sometimes it is necessary to restrict our own freedom as Christians for the sake of others, and at the same time to forgive those who err, and to do both for the sake of the unity of the Church and the mission of the Gospel.[335]

Following these ten theses was an essay written by Dr. Herbert C. Mueller, Jr., president of the Southern Illinois District, "How We Deal with Diversities and Differences in Our Midst," which he had also presented to the March 2002 meeting of the Council of Presidents and seminary faculties.[336] Dr. Edgar Keinath served as moderator for the table discussions and plenary sessions of the District Theological Convocation. Pastor Keinath, a fellow with Peace in the Parish Ministries, shared the ground rules for table discussions, facilitated this excellent convocation, and made observations, commending Bishop Ritt for his unwavering loyalty to the English District. Rev. Keinath found this leadership "so refreshing to work with." [337] It proved to be a great Convocation.

At the 51st Convention, the essayist was the ever-popular speaker, Dr. Reed Lessing, assistant professor of exegetical theology at Concordia Seminary, St. Louis. (Lessing would later serve an English District parish, St. Michael Evangelical Lutheran Church & School, Fort Wayne, Indiana.) A renowned expert on the book of Jonah, Lessing delivered an essay entitled "A Journey with Jonah: Conviction – One Gospel, Destination – Many People, Determination – Share the Joy. "[338] The two-part essay with a strong Christological emphasis –"One greater than Jonah"– was also well received. Lessing concluded with a call for bold Christian witness and outreach and evangelization of all nations.

District bylaws limited officeholders to three consecutive terms in office. Under that limit and without any opposition, Bishop Ritt was unanimously approved for a third and final term by motion from the floor. A video report of the Synod was given by the Rev. Dr. William Weinrich, fifth vice president of the LCMS, representing President Gerald Kieschnick. Elected and ranked as vice presidents were:

First Vice President	Rev. Larry Vogel (Eastern Region)
Second Vice President	Rev. Roger Ellis (Lake Erie Region)
Third Vice President	Rev. Arnold Frank
Fourth Vice President	Dr. Martin W. Bangert.[339]

Two individuals received honors for their service to the District: Lay member Ralph Thiel for 31 years of service on the board of directors or mission board, serving under seven president/bishops, and the Rev. Paul Bacon for 27 consecutive years of service as circuit visitor, vice president, District secretary, and board of directors member. The Rev. David Stechholz was re-elected District secretary, and the slate of 24 circuit visitors was approved with two circuit visitor positions to be appointed. Jean Franz and Ralph Thiel, among others, were re-elected to the board.

Convention delegates adopted 14 resolutions, including Resolution 03-2-1. "To Increase the Percentage of Mission Funding," which called for the District to dedicate more budget funds to the Synod and for planting new English District missions.[340] Several adopted resolutions reflected the multi-ethnic ministries found in the District:

- Res. 03-2-2 "Outreach among Hindu Backgrounded People"
- Res. 03-2-3 "In Support of EIIT [Ethnic Immigrant Institute of Theology]"
- Res. 03-4-05 "To Encourage DELTO [Distance Education Leading To Ordination] and TEE [Theological Education by Extension]".

The lingering effects of the Benke Yankee Stadium incident and conflict in the Synod also led to three resolutions adopted by the convention:

- Res. 03-4-04 "To Encourage Fellowship with Respect"
- Res. 03-4-11 "Dispute Resolution Process"
- Res. 03-4-12 "Romans 16:17 in the Constitution of The Lutheran Church—Missouri Synod"

During the Pittelko, Ritt, and Stechholz administrations, the secretary of the District was asked to formally write to the president and secretary of the Synod to ask for exceptions to be granted in terms of electoral circuits at upcoming synodical conventions. The Synod president finally makes that determination. For the English District, exception requests were a significant concern. Some of the District's electoral circuits (often a combination of two or even three visitation circuits) did not have either the minimum number of congregations (7) or the minimum number of communicant members (1500) but had one or the other. Usually the president of the Synod would grant an exception, but the English District, due to its non-geographic nature, often had the highest number of exception requests among synodical districts. Increasingly, with the passage of years and pressures placed upon them, Synod presidents were found granting fewer exceptions per convention.

By April 2003, the English District discontinued financial support for the Eritrean mission work, since Pastor Zerit Johannes was concluding his work in Eritrea in June 2003. It should be noted that Pastor Johannes and his wife Rahel presented the English District with a processional cross made out of bullet casings. At its meeting just prior to the District convention, the board approved Bishop Ritt's proposal for a deployed missions staff (regional assistants to the president/bishop and a missions coordinator, Dr. Ron Farah).[341] Bishop Ritt's final three years as leader of the District would emphasize implementation of a new mission model for the English District.

2003—2006

With Treasurer Beth Miles and her husband moving to Las Vegas, Nevada, the board expressed its thanks to her on behalf of the District for years of faithful service. Miles had repeatedly sounded the alarm about the District's impending considerable financial difficulty due to declining revenue, barring an increase in congregational giving and applied stewardship. She was replaced by Mr. Daniel Miller as District treasurer and executive assistant to the president/bishop for business and finance. The Rev. John Stieve, board chair, continued his exemplary job of helping the board of directors learn, appreciate, and fully implement the Carver policy-based governance model.

The use of Regional Assistants to the President (RAPs) for missions was a bold move. Though an excellent experiment in priming the pump for greater District mission activity, it would not be continued by Bishop Ritt's successor. RAPs were full-time pastors. Their work would have to be done without sacrificing their full-time parish ministry responsibilities. It would involve travel to congregations and pastoral conferences, but not to board of directors meetings. The goal was to help ignite the planting of new, local mission starts. Despite that set goal, only one of the RAPs really made a strong effort to accomplish that, while the board gave considerable time to reviewing "mission metrics." Much more significant to the District was the board-generated adoption of the "Pray, Proclaim, Provide" (PPP) initiative.

The board of directors, with full knowledge of the District's finances, felt it important to get around the District despite the consequent increased travel and lodging costs. At least one board meeting would be held annually at a "mission" site. The January 27-28, 2004 meeting was held in Phoenix, Arizona. The board was graciously hosted by Christ Church-Lutheran, Phoenix, which at the time was the District's second largest congregation and site of an excellent parochial school. Phoenix was also the location for the District's sole high school, Valley Lutheran High School; Christ Church-Lutheran was the high school's biggest support in finances, number of students, and faculty. The board enjoyed the tour, fellowship, and the opportunity to see VLHS's proposed major new facility. Tim Ewell, executive assistant to the president/bishop: parish services, was rendering exemplary service to the schools and teachers and youth of the District, including Lutheran Education Association (LEA) and CONFEDEX conferences (Lutheran educators conferences), LCMS National Youth Gatherings, and National Lutheran School Accreditation (NLSA) through the District's NLSA team.

The Lord in His infinite wisdom called Jean Franz of Chicago, a valuable member of the English District Board of Directors and Good Shepherd Lutheran Church, Chicago, out of this life before the May 2004 board meeting. At that meeting, the nomenclature of using the term "bishop" interchangeably with "district president" was again affirmed. After that meeting, the PPP Initiative was ready to move forward, complete with a video for showing in each District congregation. The Rev. Larry Vogel, English District first vice president, was chair of the Pray, Proclaim, Provide Initiative Task Force. A glossy brochure was unveiled. The *Minutes* recorded: "The goal of the initiative is to raise the consciousness and sense of ownership and involvement by the people and congregations of the English District in the overall mission of the District."[342]

With problems at the building of the English District office, part of the August 9-10, 2004 board meeting was held at that facility. This afforded a wonderful opportunity to get away from meeting at a hotel and to interact with both the support staff and the District executive staff. The board of directors engaged in some creative thinking, reviewing the six adopted triennium end statements and core values, but tabling concerns for a re-modeling of the office building.[343]

The board of directors held its August 8-10, 2005 meeting where First Vice President Larry Vogel served as Pastor, Martin Luther Chapel and School, Pennsauken, New Jersey. This congregation is in a suburb, next to the city of Camden, New Jersey, across the Delaware River from Philadelphia, Pennsylvania. At that meeting, a request was made for a new mission that was being planted, Epic Lutheran Church, in suburban Detroit. The request was for a $89,000 five-year loan to buy "a church in a box," a so-called portable church. The board co-signed this loan.[344]

As the District and board of directors prepared for the 2006 District Convention, not only were annual budgets prepared and finalized, but the District joined with the Synod and the other 34 districts to provide relief and support following Hurricane Katrina. The 174-mile-per-hour hurricane devastated New Orleans and several of the states surrounding Louisiana in August 2005. The storm's impact was calculated at 1,883 dead and $125 billion in damages. The District allocated $75,000 to the relief effort from funds coming from District congregations. By January 2006, an amazing $107,000 U.S. and $25,000 Canadian had been received as donations for the hurricane disaster relief. Some English District congregations were involved in New Orleans "Camp Restore" clean-up and re-build efforts. Among them were members of Peace Lutheran Church, Windsor, Ontario, led by their pastor, the Rev. (Chaplain) Greg Lutz.

At the time, the District's finances were helped by the sale of properties from the closure of congregations in Milwaukee, Wisconsin, and Rochester Hills, Michigan. By the end of 2005, 116 of the 165 congregations and preaching stations of the English District had been visited by board members, District staff, or other volunteers as part of the "Pray, Proclaim, Provide" initiative. While the initiative did not generate the funds hoped for to advance the planting of new missions, it did cultivate a greater appreciation of the ministry and mission and work of the English District in attempting to reach the lost of North America for Jesus Christ.

One huge challenge to the District was its campus ministry at the University of Arizona. The Lutheran Campus Ministry was a joint LCMS–

ELCA ministry. As such, it conflicted with the LCMS bylaws. Even more importantly, the pro-homosexual agenda of the ELCA campus pastor was an affront to the LCMS biblical stance and to members of the Arizona South Circuit and the English District. The resignation of the LCMS LCM Board member and English District Pastor, the Rev. Ian Pacey, raised the situation to a crisis that would be finally resolved at the beginning of the administration of Bishop Stechholz.

The English District's 20.188% ownership stake of the University of Arizona Campus Christian Center (CCC) building gave the needed leverage. In January 2006, the District board of directors resolved to "...take the necessary steps to dissolve the Lutheran Campus Ministry as it is currently constituted." The board further decided that the District would continue its involvement in the CCC as an owner, establishing its own campus ministry presence at that building without compromising the doctrinal position of the LCMS.[345] Later in 2006, Pastor Pacey became the new campus pastor for a new and highly successful LCMS campus ministry at the CCC of the University of Arizona.

The 52nd Convention of the English District-LCMS was held at the Hyatt Regency Hotel in the Chicago suburb of Schaumburg, Illinois, June 22-24, 2006. Acquiescing to the desires of many District pastors that they be in their own pulpits on the Lord's Day, Sunday, the Board decided to conclude the convention on Saturday morning.

The theme of the convention was "Hearts Ablaze – Sharing the Savior's Love." Since the Rev. David Stechholz was serving as District secretary and was one of the two candidates for president/bishop, the Rev. David Rutter, Pastor of St. Paul Evangelical Lutheran Church & Preschool, St. Claire Shores, Michigan, an accomplished organist, stepped in to lead the convention in the first of several 10-minute hymn sings. Representing the Synod was President Gerald Kieschnick and Synod First Vice President Dr. William Diekelman, who had previously served as Oklahoma District President. Dr. Jeffrey T. Schrank, executive pastor of Christ Church-Lutheran, Phoenix, gave a stirring homily during the opening convention service. (Seven years later, he would lead the second largest congregation in the English District into the Pacific Southwest District, claiming that its interactions were almost exclusively with the Pacific Southwest District and Phoenix area congregations and pastors.)

Bishop Ritt's report began with a review of the English District as of 2006:

> To give you an idea you an idea of the scope of our non-geographic district, there are 300 clergy on the roster, 200 commissioned ministers [teachers, deaconesses, DCEs, and other rostered church workers], 150 non-commissioned workers, over 150 preschool teachers, 67 schools with 6,000 students, and 17 different languages spoken within the district. There are 70,000 members in the English District, comprised of four regions... The amazing thing about our regional non-geographic district is that it works! Our district is very much like the disciples on the road to Emmaus, walking together and pinning their hopes and eternal destination on a God who came to each in the form of flesh, died on a cross, rose from the dead, and now lives and reigns one God, forevermore.[346]

He then proceeded in his report to discuss in five sections what *"Hearts Ablaze"* meant.

The first business item in the June 22 session was the joyous reception of the newest English District congregation, St. John Evangelical Lutheran Church, Germanicus (Golden Lake), Ontario. Following that, Bishop/President Ritt gave his presidential address. He applied the mission slogan of his tenure, "Partners in Christ, Working Together, Equipping to Gather" to the *"Hearts Ablaze"* convention theme. An avid golfer, Dr. Ritt used a golf motif to declare "It's Moving Day," and he called upon the assembly to keep the man who would be elected the next bishop/president in their frequent prayers to the Lord. He made this memorable comment:

> A District should never be defined by its president/bishop, only led and spiritually modeled by him. Rather, a district should be defined by its people, the membership that sits in the pews on Sunday mornings, the clergy who are called to serve, not to be served, and the faculties of its schools who continue to "shine like stars in the night" in our District and Synod.[347]

Seven men had received nominations for president/bishop of the English District. Five declined, leaving two candidates: the Rev. John Stieve and the Rev. David Stechholz, both pastors of congregations in the Western Region. Having all the candidates solely from the Western

Region was a first for the District. Both also allowed their names to stand for three different elected positions. Whomever would be elected District bishop/president would withdraw his name from other elections. This willingness to serve even if not elected president had occurred throughout the English District's history among leaders in the District.

Both candidates were well qualified, with long tenures of service in the English District. Both men were very close friends. Both had late fathers who had served as pastors, including decades earlier in human care ministry in New York City.[348] Perhaps the most obvious, humorous difference between the two was their ardent New York baseball allegiances: the Rev. Stieve being tied to the Yankees' pinstripes and the Rev. Stechholz donning the Mets' orange and blue.

But the convention would have to choose one of these two men as Bishop Ritt's successor. Following the casting of votes, the Rev. Wayne Morton, the election committee chairman, announced the results:

> 103 for the Rev. John Stieve, representing 50%
> 105 for the Rev. David Stechholz, representing 50% of the vote. [349]

The Rev. David P. Stechholz was declared the new president/bishop of the English District-LCMS.

Nine years earlier, the 1997 Convention had witnessed the drama of a five-ballot election for District President. The 2006 Convention witnessed a one-ballot election decided by the nearly slimmest of margins. Not since 1972 had there been such a close vote in electing the president or bishop/president of the English District. After "hearts ablaze" for the Lord stopped beating so hard as a result of the close election, the new Bishop/President-elect Stechholz and his wife, Janet, were introduced to the convention. Immediately after that, a motion to bestow the title of "President/Bishop Emeritus" upon Dr. David Ritt, receiving a standing ovation of approval.

The official report of the Synod was given by LCMS Vice President Diekelman and a video by the LCMS President, Dr. Gerald Kieschnick, was shown. Then followed the election and ranking of the vice presidents:

First Vice President	Rev. John Stieve (Western Region)
Second Vice President	Rev. Larry Vogel (Eastern Region)

Third Vice President   Rev. Roger Ellis (Lake Erie Region)
Fourth Vice President   Dr. Martin W. Bangert (Midwest Region)[350]

At the Convention Divine Service on the evening of June 22, the homilist was LCMS First Vice President Diekelman, who also installed the president/bishop and the regional vice presidents.

After a question and answer time with LCMS First Vice President Diekelman, Dr. Andrew Bartelt, professor of exegetical theology at Concordia Seminary, St. Louis, as Convention Essayist, addressed a study of 1 Peter 2:8-9. His presentation on "The People of God in Christ's Mission" was excellent and very well received. Other elections were held, with Rev. Robert Fitzpatrick elected District secretary. A full complement of board of directors members and nominations committee were also chosen. The youth presented a devotional skit.

Bishop/President-elect Stechholz gave his address entitled *Jesu Juva* (Jesus Help). He noted that Christianity in North America was suffering but not dead, drawing on the Lord's words, *"I will build My Church and the gates of hell shall not prevail against it"* (Matthew 16:18). Stechholz thanked various people, including Bishop Ritt for a job well done and the seven men who had been nominated for president/bishop, especially his dear friend the Rev. John Stieve. He also asked the delegates to take the mission of the English District and the convention's many positive aspects home to their congregations.[351]

"Hearts Ablaze" presentations were made during the convention. One of the highlights of the convention was the remarks given by the Rev. Dr. David Tswaedi, bishop of the Lutheran Church of Southern Africa, a partner church body with the LCMS. Bishop Tswaedi spoke about a new AIDS/HIV Southern African initiative and invited the English District to help. District leader the Rev. Dr. Arnie Frank noted that a team had gone over to South Africa from Christ Church-Lutheran, Phoenix, and would be going again.[352]

The convention adopted several resolutions. The most significant and far-reaching for the District's future was Resolution 06-3-05: "To Establish the English District Endowment Fund." This established a new endowment fund for the District with a newly constituted Board of Managers.[353] Bishop-elect Stechholz had the opportunity to play the organ at one of the later Convention hymn-sings. Outgoing Bishop Ritt served as homilist at the closing Divine Service and installed the new District secretary and board of directors.

Excursus: Fall Regional Pastoral Conferences

To keep their clergy spiritually, intellectually, and physically sharp, the boards of directors of synodical districts provide for pastoral and other professional church worker conferences. In small geographic districts, this might be a district-wide event. In large districts, there might be two or more regional conferences. The regional arrangement is used by the English District, though it did not have regular regional conferences until the 1960s. There were initially five regions, called "conferences." Following the Seminex-era division in 1976, the English District realigned to four regions and four vice presidents in compliance with Synod bylaws.

The fall regional conferences have been for many pastors the highlight of their year in the District. These gatherings usually are held over the course of three days. A formal dinner or two may be held. But the more important aspects of the regional conferences are the marvelous camaraderie, daily worship, Divine Service, and free time on the second day for rest or recreation.

Regional conferences provide time for reports from the bishop and other District staff and a professional presentation by a speaker selected by the Regional Conference Planning Committee, often a seminary professor. During his tenure, Bishop Stechholz introduced the option for pastors to meet privately with him for spiritual uplift, advice, confession and absolution, encouragement, or to express concerns.

Each region has its own "personality," though that can change with the passage of years and the personalities of leading pastors.

The Eastern Region has most frequently held its fall conferences at the Port-O-Call Hotel in Ocean City, New Jersey—affectionately called the "Pink Flamingo" by attendees—and their conference Divine Service often at a nearby SELC District congregation. The enjoyable boardwalk made this place a hit with the brothers and their wives, those who could attend. The conference would occasionally be held at other locales, including Lancaster, Pennsylvania in Amish country or Niagara Falls, New York (hosted by one of the Buffalo circuit congregations). In the 1960s and 1970s, this conference sometimes met as a quad-conference with the

Atlantic, New Jersey, and New England Districts, with each district having its own breakout time, but this practice has faded away. A story from the 1980s was of a young pastor who wanted to go to a casino in nearby Atlantic City and try his hand at gambling. The accompanying brothers allowed him $20 and took his wallet to alleviate any further temptation. At first, he had a few good "wins," but he caught the bug, and soon lost all of the $20. The older brothers consoled him as they walked the Atlantic City Boardwalk. He was cured!

The Lake Erie Region used to have its fall conferences at Atwood Lake Lodge in eastern Ohio. This was quite a distance for the pastors who came from Michigan and Ontario. It was a splendid place, but over time it became too expensive. The conference voted to move to a Methodist retreat center near Sandusky, Ohio, but after a few years of going "dry," the conference moved to a Holiday Inn Express nearby, staying at that location for several years. In recent years, the conference has been held at other sites, including Epiphany Church, Dorr, in western Michigan. This conference is unique—at the first dinner night at a local restaurant, the large gathering of pastors lustily sings "O Canada" and then the "National Anthem of the United States" or some other American song.

The Midwest Region had its fall conference for many years at St. Mary's Seminary and Retreat Center, a Roman Catholic campus of elegance and beauty, just north of Chicago. Other sites included Concordia Seminary, St. Louis, and churches of the Milwaukee area. The latter included boat rides on the Milwaukee River. This region included the broad St. Louis Circuit, which extends from Vine Grove, Kentucky, near Fort Knox, through St. Louis and Hannibal, Missouri, to Lee's Summit, a suburb of Kansas City, and on to Redeemer Church, Lincoln, Nebraska. Sometimes this region would also hold a Circuit Winkel during the conference, which was helpful to the St. Louis Circuit.

The Western Region has historically been the most relaxed. Fall conferences rotate between five cities: San Diego, Los Angeles, San Francisco, Tucson, and Phoenix. However, Phoenix has held a couple of conferences at Shepherd of the Hills, Payson, Arizona, or at Peace in the Valley, Benson, Arizona. This region had the luxury of meeting in a hotel whether at Fisherman's Wharf in San Francisco, down the road at the Assilomar Retreat Center on Monterey Bay, at a lovely Roman Catholic retreat center in Malibu, at Mission Bay in San Diego, or at a Roman

Catholic retreat center at Picture Rocks in Tucson. No matter which venue was chosen, regional pastors could hold their conference Divine Services at a nearby English District congregation. In 1989, the pastors voted 18-6 to have their Western Regional Fall Conference in Las Vegas instead of Los Angeles because there were easy plane flights and better hotel rates in the casinos. But "Sin City" was all around, so at the end of the conference the brothers unanimously voted to never return to Las Vegas again! One unfortunate story tells of a brother who led devotions at the Malibu retreat center and challenged tenets of the faith by referring to the Lord as "Mother God." He was challenged by a couple pastors and reprimanded by the District president/bishop. After years of continued romancing with the ELCA and adopting several doctrinal aberrations, the pastor was removed along with his congregation from membership in the LCMS.[354]

The Rev. Dr. David Stechholz, Bishop/President, 2006—2015

Elected bishop/president by a scant two votes was the Rev. David Stechholz, Pastor of West Portal Evangelical Lutheran Church and School, San Francisco, a congregation of the Western Region of the English District. The two previous bishop/presidents, Drs. Pittelko and Ritt, had come from congregations in the Chicago area in the Midwest Region. Electing a president from the Western Region marked a new milestone in the English District's history.

Pastor Stechholz's acceptance speech to the District in convention was titled *Jesu Juva,* the Latin for *"Jesus, Help,"* a phrase that Johann Sebastian Bach used at the beginning of several of his musical works. For Stechholz, this divine help was needed as he relocated to Michigan to take up his duties. Like Drs. Pittelko and Ritt before him, he and his family chose to live in Livonia, Michigan, near the District office in Farmington. Stechholz had hoped that he might still be able to serve West Portal Lutheran as an assistant pastor, but the congregational leaders assured him that the geographic distance made such hopes unfeasible. Nevertheless, he and his wife kept their membership at West Portal during his nine-year tenure rather than transferring membership to a congregation near the District office.

As is often the case, District presidents are "on the road" most Sundays, visiting congregations and schools across the District. Bishop

Stechholz found it best to structure visitation with options. A typical English District episcopal visit might include a Saturday afternoon visit with the pastor in his study, dinner with the pastor and his wife or with the church council and/or elders, preaching and addressing the congregation in the Divine Service(s) and leading a Bible class or presentation, with a congregational luncheon following worship. In some cases, visitations might include another evening dinner with the pastor or a group of pastors. Monday morning would often include a circuit meeting, a visit to the parish school, and then a return to Detroit via airplane or car. Most English District bishops found the travel schedule challenging. Anything less than a five-hour road trip was considered a short trip in the English District and so the car was used. On occasion, the bishop's wife would accompany him on a weekend visit. In Stechholz's case, a West Coast visitation or a trip to Florida or Georgia would occupy several days with a series of visits in multiple congregations, pastors, schools, and circuit conferences.

2006—2009

"Igniting Christ's Church in Mission" became the new slogan of the English District, replacing the two previous administrations' slogans and harkening back to the District's original motto of "The Faith of the Fathers in the Language of the Children." Tying in with the Synod's new "Ablaze!" campaign, the new motto was meant to help congregations, schools, and individuals of the English District fulfill the biblical mandate of making disciples of all nations.

From the outset of his service as bishop/president, Stechholz desired to see the English District exist in the Synod as a "servant district,"—a servant both to the congregations and schools of the district and to the other districts and the Synod. The District sought to help in situations and circumstances where other districts could not carry out their goals and needed help. Within the Synod, the District would promote the mutual faith and doctrine, one in purpose and in organization. Despite the English District's effort to serve, other district presidents frequently questioned the need for the non-geographic SELC and English Districts.

As in each new triennium, new core values and end statements, appointments, budgets, and salaries were approved. The board of directors agreed to support the Synod's "Fan into Flame" initiative.[355] Though not

without successes, the first triennium of Stechholz's tenure was marked
by several challenges:

- Decreased congregational contributions to the District, leading to several
  immediate staff changes and having to strive for a balanced budget with
  less staffing.
- Helping struggling congregations, particularly those in Detroit,
  Cleveland, Buffalo, Milwaukee, and Philadelphia/Camden, five of the
  ten poorest cities in the United States.
- A lawsuit by St. John's, Toronto against the District in 2007, eventually
  resulting in a legal settlement and the peaceful departure of that historic
  Toronto congregation from the English District.
- Requesting the resignation of the pastor of Zion Evangelical-Lutheran
  Church, Detroit, on Reformation Sunday, October 29, 2006, who took
  members of the congregation with him into the Antiochian Orthodox
  Church.
- A Detroit-area congregation posting highly controversial advertising to
  gain worshippers, achieving notoriety and bad publicity for the English
  District.
- Increasing mental, emotional, and spiritual health concerns among
  pastors, teachers, and other church work professionals.

The Lord God graciously guided the District through these challenges.
Pastoral encouragement, new ideas, some of which worked and others
didn't, and new energy came to bear. The board of directors also had a
number of new members. The board continued to adapt to the policy-based
governance model. Missions Executive Rev. David Thiele provided new
thoughts in mission direction, especially for reaching individuals in
Generation-X and millennials, and starting a new but short-lived missions
newsletter called *"Moving in Mission,"* which was edited by Mr. Bob
Fischer of Fairlawn Lutheran Church, Fairlawn, Ohio.

A new "peace" with Lutheran Church-Canada was nurtured. In 2008,
the English District bishop was invited to address the LCC Convention in
Windsor, Ontario. For several decades, congregations of the English
District in Ontario were viewed as being too liberal in theology and
Communion practice. The LCC president, Dr. Robert Bugbee, told Bishop
Stechholz, that this opportunity to make a cordial greeting would not have
occurred even a few years earlier. Two major factors played into this "new
peace." First, the Rev. Steven Alles, the new senior pastor of St. John

Evangelical Lutheran Church, Pembroke, and son of English District board member George Alles, met with the Ontario pastors in the greater Ottawa area. He demonstrated a strong stance on the sanctity of human life; the area LCC congregations and St. John's became united in upholding the biblical teachings concerning human life, both at its inception and at life's end. Second, the need for joint mission outreach in the Greater Toronto Area (GTA) was realized by both LCC and LCMS Canadian congregations and pastors. The English District Board of Directors held its August 12-13, 2008 meeting in the GTA, hosted by the Lutheran Church of St. Luke, North York, Ontario. The board visited a number of churches and ministries in the GTA.[356]

By 2009, the English District numbered 158 congregations, seven new mission starts, two human care ministries, and 66 school ministries. At the start of his term, Bishop Stechholz eliminated the part-time deployed mission team in favor of a traditional approach of having an executive assistant to the bishop/president for missions, a role filled by the Rev. David Thiele. Mr. Dale Lewis, English District LCEF vice president, was helpful in securing large loans for congregations such as West Portal, San Francisco, to replace its Sunset Campus building; Angelica, Allen Park, Michigan, for roof repairs; and Hales Corners, Hales Corners, Wisconsin, for building a new campus with church and school buildings. These two executives were joined on the executive staff by Mrs. Sally Naglich, business administrator and District treasurer, Mr. Tim Ewell, parish services executive, and later Theresa Fairow, LCMS Foundation Planned Giving counselor. Support staff continued to give invaluable assistance at the District office. Growth of ethnic missions meant that the District was now worshipping the Triune God and teaching the Christian faith in over 20 different languages and dialects. In 2007, the District witnessed a gain in communicant members after enduring decades of generally downward losses. Though the increase of communicant members from 2006 to 2007 only totaled 239 individuals, this was the second largest increase that year, behind only the Texas District.[357]

The 53rd Convention of the English District was graciously hosted by Hales Corners Lutheran Church & School, Hales Corners, Wisconsin, June 18-20, 2009. While delegates billeted at a nearby hotel, all of the convention was held at the largest church in the Synod. The LCMS had embarked on a major outreach and fundraising endeavor called "Ablaze!"

and "Fan into Flame." Though conservative members of the Synod, including in the English District, were opposed to various aspects of this endeavor, the District leadership and Hales Corners Lutheran Church were supportive, provided that the Christocentric heart of "Ablaze!" remained Christ and not human efforts to grow His Church. Hales Corners even had hosted a fundraiser at a church member's antique car showroom, with the Rev. Dr. Gerald Kieschnick, president of the LCMS, on hand along with the Rev. Mike Ernst, executive pastor of Hales Corners.[358]

Stechholz reminded the District of its past history and the blessings of Almighty God:

> Where we want to be is…"home" with our Lord Jesus in Paradise.
> … The Church has eschatological eyes. We look for Christ's return and for us, His Bride, to be taken into the eternal city, there to *"celebrate the marriage feast of the Lamb in His kingdom which has no end"* (LSB Divine Service, Setting 4, page 212) …
> In the meantime…we want, by the power and grace of Almighty God through His means of grace, His holy Word and Sacraments, to walk with Jesus, nurture the family of God, and to reach out to those outside the ship of Christ's Church and bring them to Christ and into His family.[359]

Bishop Stechholz repeated the new mission statement of the District:

> Congregations and schools of the English District, in worshipping the Lord God, are: *Serving* in our communities, *Connecting* with the unchurched and dechurched, *Growing* in faith and numbers, and *Reproducing* by planting new churches.

The mission statement emphasized transformation in the Church worked by God's unfettered Word. The Divine Word always accomplishes its saving purpose, transforms hearts, and spreads the saving Gospel.

Stechholz also shared a model that he had developed, "The Church's Life, Mission, and Ministry," based on the autobiography of Rev. Berthold von Schenk called *Lively Stone.* Von Schenk was pastor of Our Saviour Evangelical Lutheran Church & School in the Bronx, a high liturgy congregation that melded strong worship, a weekly Eucharist, and Christian service and evangelization.[360] The District was grateful for

Pastor von Schenk's concepts that became a model used by the English District. Stechholz's model fell into disuse by his choice when the Synod president and his staff developed a similar model called "Witness, Mercy, Life Together" in 2010.

The model focuses on the Lord Jesus Christ, the Head, Lord, and Bridegroom of His Bride, the one holy, catholic, and apostolic Church. The three points of the Church's life, mission, and ministry around Him who is the Word of God, made flesh, are Worship, Witness, and Mercy Ministry or Human Care (Service). The Greek New Testament words are included.

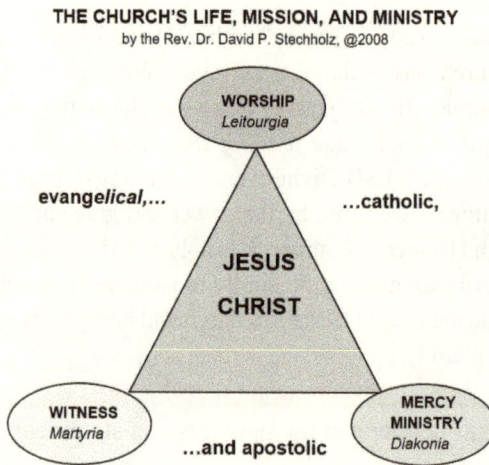

THE CHURCH'S LIFE, MISSION, AND MINISTRY
by the Rev. Dr. David P. Stechholz, @2008

WORSHIP
Leitourgia

evangel*ical*,...   ...catholic,

JESUS

CHRIST

WITNESS   MERCY
Martyria   MINISTRY
                    ...and apostolic   *Diakonia*

Representing the Synod at the 2009 English District Convention was LCMS 5th Vice President Dr. David Buegler (former Ohio District president). From his long-term service in Cleveland, Buegler had a warm and close relationship with English District pastors. The convention essayist was the Rev. Daniel Gilbert, president/bishop of the Northern Illinois District. Gilbert had vicared at Hales Corners Lutheran Church, which was hosting the convention. The convention theme was *"Let the Children Come to Me,"* fitting in a setting with a very large school ministry and for a district.

Dr. Buegler promoted the Synod's "Ablaze!" movement begun by the LCMS in partnership with sister Lutheran church bodies worldwide to reach the lost for Jesus Christ. Approved at the 2004 Synodical Convention in St. Louis, "Ablaze!" and the "Fan into Flame" initiative were to help fund 2,000 new mission starts, 2,000 congregational revitalizations, and reach 100 million people by the 500th anniversary of the Reformation in 2017. Though "Ablaze!" fell well short of those lofty goals, it was one of two major efforts of the Kieschnick administration of the Synod, the other being a total restructuring of the Synod.

Dr. Dan Gilbert's theological essay was *"Let the Little Children Come to Me: The Mission of God."* The full essay is in the Convention Proceedings, but his excellent presentation was interrupted by an air conditioning unit failure on the roof of the church! Due to the automatic fire department call triggered by this failure, the building had to be temporarily evacuated. Gilbert addressed several false doctrines pertaining to missions. He also raised a helpful question: "What's your Areopagus?" alluding to St. Paul on Mars Hill in Athens (Acts 17) and the notion of missions being incarnational and personal.[361]

Stechholz's re-election was unopposed, so he was granted another term of service by acclamation.

<u>2009 Elected Vice Presidents as Ranked by the District</u>

First Vice President	Rev. Roger Ellis (Lake Erie Region)
Second Vice President	Rev. Wayne Morton (Western Region)
Third Vice President	Dr. Martin Bangert (Midwest Region)
Fourth Vice President	Rev. Jamison Hardy (Eastern Region).

Those elections brought about and foreshadowed significant leadership changes within the District. Previous First Vice President Dr. Larry Vogel, had accepted a call to serve as the associate executive director of the Synod CTCR in St. Louis, leaving the Eastern Region, though he stayed a member of the English District and a close friend to Bishop Stechholz. Dr. John Stieve was not re-elected as Western Region vice president; he was later elected as a pastoral member of the board of directors. Stieve also served ably as chair of the English District Structure Task Force.

As with all convention workbooks, detailed reports were given by the executive staff, regional vice presidents, various committees, and circuit visitors.[362] Among the circuit visitor reports was the account by Cleveland East-Akron Circuit Visitor Robert "Bob" Tauscher. Pastor Tauscher was serving a three-year term as circuit visitor in Akron, having twice faithfully served as a circuit visitor in both the New York-New Jersey and Philadelphia Circuits.

Bishop Stechholz and the regional vice presidents were installed by LCMS Vice President Buegler at the Divine Service at the Chapel of Christ Triumphant at Concordia University, Mequon, WI.[363] For many of the delegates, this was their first time on the campus of the largest school of the Concordia University System. An outdoor barbecue and tours were provided on campus. Except for a some veteran pastors in the District, few recalled the "old days" when English District conventions were occasionally held at the former Concordia College, Milwaukee campus.

Unlike the packed business agenda at previous conventions, the 2009 Convention considered only two resolutions. Resolution 09-3-01 "Against the Dissolution of the English District of the LCMS" was overwhelmingly adopted, hopefully laying to rest in the Synod any rumors of dissolving the English District! The delegates defeated Resolution 09-3-02 "To Decline the BRTFSSG Proposals and to Provide for Congregational Study." This concerned the LCMS Blue Ribbon Task Force on Synodical Structure and Governance (BRTFSSG) proposals for a major restructuring of the Synod.[364]

A highlight of the convention for the delegates and guests was touring Hales Corners' House of Worship, office & meeting facilities, the school and community center as well as the old campus and Steeple View Retirement Center. This District convention emphasized and demonstrated hands-on mission and ministry rather than the passage of numerous resolutions. Most everyone was deeply grateful to Hales Corners Congregation, pastors and staff, and the 30+ children who sang for this huge hosting of the 53rd Convention of the English District.

2009—2012: The English District's Centennial Triennium

By 2009 and 2010, the District had several task forces, teams, focus groups, committees, networks, and commissions in addition to the board of directors. These included:

- the Praesidium,
- the College of Circuit Visitors
- the Ministerial Health Commission
- the District Constitutions and Membership Committee

- Pastoral Ministry Formation Task Force
- Campus Ministry Focus Group
- Fall Regional Pastoral (and Other Church Workers) Conference Program Committees
- a District Missions Task Force, which eventually became in 2012 a Mission Council, able to meet by conference call or online
- Coaching Teams and four Revitalization/Transformation Learning Communities
- School NLSA Accreditation Task Force
- District Youth Committee and District Children's and Family Ministry Task Force
- Regional managers and an English District Endowment Fund Board of Directors
- Network of Parish Nurses; Detroit volunteers from local congregations for District mailings
- a new District Emergency Preparation, Disaster, and Response Task Force
- a new but short-lived District Missions Quarterly Newsletter
- a new Evangelization "Ablaze!" Team.

Later in the second triennium, a District 100th Anniversary Committee and still later in the third triennium of the bishop, a District Life Ministry coordinator and committee were added. The District was adding Mission Action Teams, part of the District's modified Carver model of leadership and governance.

January board meetings were consistently being held via Internet teleconferencing, saving both time and travel expenses. Dr. David Dressel was re-elected by the board of directors as its chair; Dr. John Stieve became the Vice Chair. Even while frequently debating over funding of the mission of the District at the November 8-10, 2010 meeting at the Crowne Plaza/St. Louis Airport in Bridgeton, Missouri, board members rejoiced in a $40,000 grant from Angel Tear Ministries of Concordia Lutheran Ministries, Cabot, Pennsylvania, through the work of Rev. Dr. Jamison Hardy. Also, board member Judy Anderson from Chicago presented New Hope Lutheran Ministries' continued efforts to work with the former Luther South High School to restart the high school and develop a vast Martin Luther Square ministry.[365] It was a tremendous effort, but the endeavor did not succeed. The board meeting also included a tour of the LCMS International Center and a visit with LCMS President Matthew Harrison and LCMS First Vice President Herb Mueller.

During the 2009-2012 triennium, pastors in greater Philadelphia, first under Rev. Tom Engler and later under Rev. Robert Kieselowsky, nurtured what came to be Philadelphia Lutheran Ministries (PLM). Continued stewardship education was fostered, especially through materials and books produced by Ron and Phyllis Chewning. A District Millennials Church Workers Gathering was held in San Diego in January 2012. Also during the triennium, three District parochial schools were named as "exemplary schools" in the Synod through the National Lutheran Schools Accreditation (NLSA).

But what was one of the most noteworthy events during the 2009-2012 triennium of the District was the 2010 Synodical Convention in July 2010 in hot, humid Houston. The Synod's Blue Ribbon Task Force on Synod Structure and Governance presented a major overhaul of the LCMS. Most of its proposals were approved by the Synod in convention. But the convention delegates later provided an ironic twist. The restructuring of the Synod that LCMS President Kieschnick had worked hard to develop was adopted, but then he was voted out of office and made President Emeritus. Elected in his place was the Rev. Matthew Harrison, executive director of LCMS World Relief and Human Care, who had made a major presentation on Mercy and Human Care Ministry at the 2008 English District Professional Church Workers Conference. Harrison had not favored the restructuring measures, but now he had to implement them as the Synod convention mandated. Once again, the LCMS had shown its unique propensity at a Synod convention for doing "opposites" in the same convention.

President Harrison and his new team and synodical Praesidium worked diligently to implement the decisions of the convention and the restructuring. The new Synod theme, interestingly, became "Witness, Mercy, Life Together." Does that sound familiar? There was no attempt, after the BRTFSSG had carefully considered it, to restructure the districts of Synod. The English District's sails would continue to fly.

Preparations for the 100ᵗʰ Anniversary of the District

Seven people comprised the 100ᵗʰ Anniversary Committee of the English District, which met 21 times with the bishop over the course of two years. None were face-to-face meetings, expect for a gathering of three committee members in Philadelphia during an episcopal visit in that vicinity. These dedicated people were Mrs. Eva Fronk (serving vacancy principalships in her native Philadelphia at Martin Luther Christian School in Pennsauken, New Jersey, and West Portal Lutheran School, San Francisco); Mr. John Krueger (Risen Savior, Green Valley, Arizona), Rev. Tim Halboth (Grace, Redford Township, Michigan), Mr. Ernie Seaman (West Portal, San Francisco, California), Dr. Robert Scudieri (retired, Grace, Naples, Florida), Mr. Neil Sanders (Prince of Peace, Menomonee Falls, Wisconsin), and Mrs. Pat Gilde (Martin Luther Chapel, Pennsauken, New Jersey, and Chair of the Anniversary Cookbook sub-committee).

This Committee produced or was involved with the following:

- A District Centennial kick-off at the May 2001 Professional Church Workers Conference, complete with professional presentations, gifts, and displays, including Dr. Cameron Mackenzie's presentation on the English District's origins
- The May 15, 2011 Divine Services (hosted in the St. Louis area District birthplace by Chapel of the Cross Lutheran, St. Peters, Missouri, and a 100ᵗʰ Anniversary Commemorative "Walk" in St. Louis, with the assistance of Chapel of the Cross, St. Louis North County, and the Missouri District's Holy Cross Congregation, St. Louis
- A District 100ᵗʰ Anniversary PowerPoint presentation
- Several articles in the *English Channels* and *Servant to Servant* and other communiques, as well as one in the *Concordia Historical Institute Quarterly,*
- An Anniversary (366 days) Prayer List
- Centennial Year coasters, mugs, and binoculars (complements of LCEF), lapel pins and letter seals (underwritten by donors)
- Lists of over 100 ideas for local church and school Anniversary Year mission projects like "Soles for Souls" and including anniversary and birthday cakes and cookies
- A 100ᵗʰ Anniversary hymn by the Rev. Robert & Sandy Voelker of Gethsemane, Windsor, Ontario
- 100ᵗʰ Anniversary cakes and cookies in various congregations

- A District logo and Anniversary Scripture theme verse from I Corinthians 15:58
- 100th Anniversary concerts
- A District Office display with historical memorabilia, later converted in a District Archival Museum
- *The Great Potluck Across the English District*, a District 100th Anniversary cookbook.[366] The cookbook was a huge success, with special thanks to its Sub-Committee: Pat Gilde, Chairperson, and Mrs. Ruth Mayer of Ascension, Tucson, Arizona, and Mrs. Shelby Kampert of Trinity, Villa Park, Illinois.[367]
- In addition, a 100th Anniversary banner - with the traditional District logo of the sycamore tree - was created by Mrs. Kay Ardner of Calvary, Mechanicsburg, PA. The 100 leaves on the tree represented the 100 years of the District's existence.

"Faith Driven – Future Focused": The 53rd (100th Anniversary Commemoration) Convention of the English District-LCMS, St. Louis, Missouri, June 27-29, 2012

With Synod's restructuring, the English District had perhaps a new role. In his District *Convention Workbook* report, Bishop Stechholz highlighted the 100th anniversary theme verse, *"Always abounding in the work of the Lord…"* (1 Corinthians 15:58), under the District slogan of *"Igniting Christ's Church in Mission"* and the 100th Anniversary theme, *"Faith Driven – Future Focused."* He wrote as follows:

> The English District has a unique missional role as a "servant" district, a catalyst in and microcosm of Synod and in partnership with our other synodical districts. I believe that if the Synod did not have an English District, it would have to invent one. In the Old Testament, God's chosen people of Israel had "cities of refuge." In a similar way, the English District of the LCMS is a "safety net" in Synod, provided this special role is not misused to harbor either false doctrine and practice as a "lone ranger"/ "I'm

out of sight" mindset. There are, however, circumstances in which a congregation and/or pastor in the LCMS in Canada or the United States finds it more beneficial to be in the English District rather than in the geographic district. Conversely, we in the English District ceded congregations to the geographic districts. It works both ways. The English District, though, has a pioneering spirit of mission planting and collaboration that uniquely benefits the whole of the LCMS...

If, however, the English District believes that it is no longer viable and useful to the Synod as a unique, mission-pioneering and "servant" district, then we have an obligation to fold our tents. I do not believe this is the case. But then we must practice what we preach in terms of mission planting and helpfulness and collaboration wherever we are located....[368]

The centennial anniversary of the English District's formation was May 15, 2011. That date began a year-long anniversary, culminating in the 53rd Convention of the English District-LCMS at the end of the anniversary year. Concluding the celebration at a District convention in 2012 was due to the Synod's three-year meeting cycle: circuit convocation year, district convention year, and Synod convention year. While the circuit convocations proved in the English District to be more of a "year off," the District and Synod convention years were filled with all the preparation, anticipation, fellowship, churchly activity, and joy that marked the particular year, and this one especially.

The 2012 convention was remarkably positive. The joy of celebrating 100 years of the Lord's blessings upon the English District was evidenced in the group picture taken just prior to the Convention Jubilee Divine Service at which Synod President Dr. Matthew Harrison preached and Bishop Stechholz served as celebrant, assisted by the four vice presidents and other District pastors.

The English District convention attendees enjoyed a German *Oktoberfest* with beer, bratwurst, and sauerkraut on the Seminary's Quad and took tours of the seminary grounds and buildings, even seeing the Seminary Library Rare Book Room. Special greetings and a prayer were offered by Seminary Professor Dr. Tim Saleska on behalf of Concordia Seminary President Dr. Dale Meyer. Greetings were also given by Bishop Emeritus Dr. David Ritt. Bishop Emeritus Pittelko was unable to attend.

Many delegates enjoyed seeing one of the Synod's two seminary campuses for the first time.

Pictured above: Bishop Stechholz and his wife Janet (left) and Bishop Emeritus David Ritt and his wife Carol (right) are flanked and backed by convention delegates, guests, and Divine Service attendees in front of the Chapel of Sts. Timothy & Titus on the campus of Concordia Seminary, St. Louis. In typical English District fashion, some were outside of the picture, others were hiding behind the bushes, and some chose to be anonymous. However, the old District practice from the 1910s and 1920s of having a group picture was re-instituted in the English District.

Business sessions took place at the Sheraton Westport Lakeside Chalet in St. Louis, Missouri. On the second day of the convention, LCMS President Harrison presented the first part of his report. The second part was given later in the convention by LCMS First Vice President Herbert Mueller, Jr. "Herbie," as he was affectionately known to some, had begun his ministry at an English District congregation in Chicago in 1981. Following the president's report, the English District's Doctor of Divinity degree was awarded to the Rev. Michael Ernst, former District vice president and emeritus pastor of Hales Corners Lutheran Church. A second recipient was Dr. Ihno Janssen, who at one time served as a counselor in the 1950s in the English District office in Detroit before serving as pastor of West Portal Evangelical Lutheran Church and School in San Francisco from 1959–1982. Janssen was unable to attend the convention due to lost eye sight. His friend and successor at West Portal, Bishop Stechholz, flew to the West Coast in August to present the award to Dr. Janssen, who was residing in the foothills of the Sierra Nevada Mountains in Sonora, California.

Four candidates allowed their names to stand for election as president of the English District: the Rev. Jamison Hardy (District vice president from McMurray, Pennsylvania), the Rev. Rob Rogers (District vice president from Villa Park, Illinois), the Rev. Dr. David Stechholz (the current District president), and the Rev. David Thiele (District mission executive and LCEF District vice president). Stechholz received 68% of the votes on the first ballot and was re-elected as bishop and president of the English District.

2012 Elected Vice Presidents as Ranked by the District

First Vice President	Rev. Wayne Morton (Western Region)
Second Vice President	Rev. Nathaniel Schwartz (Midwest Region)
Third Vice President	Rev. Jamison Hardy (Eastern Region)
Fourth Vice President	Rev. Derek Mathers (Lake Erie Region).[369]

Rev. Robert Fitzpatrick was re-elected as District secretary. The makeup of the board of directors underwent a massive change, as four lay members were elected to their first term on the board. Two church worker members of the board were also elected to their first term: the Rev. Ben Eder and Mrs. Gail Holzer. Pastor Eder was a veteran pastor in the District from Kenmore, New York. Mrs. Holzer was a highly recognized principal of Redeemer Lutheran School, Oakmont/Penn Hills, Pennsylvania. The slate of circuit visitors was approved without any changes made by the convention delegates.

One of the outstanding highlights of the Centennial Anniversary Convention was the convention essay given by Dr. William W. Schumacher, professor of historical theology at Concordia Seminary, St. Louis, and a former LCMS missionary to Botswana in southern Africa. *"Why Us? Remembering to Understand"* was his essay title. He reflected on the roots of the English District, briefly citing Dr. Carl S. Meyer of Concordia Seminary, a Synod historian *par excellence* in the 1960s, who died in 1972 before he could write a definitive history of the Synod. Schumacher warned against using history as propaganda, instead urging the convention to trust God for the future. He noted: "We remember to understand."[370] After sharing the English District's roots and German Missouri's reluctance to incorporate the English Synod as an "English Mission District," he explained the matter of amalgamation and its detractors and when the Missouri Synod was finally willing to see an English District as a "special arrangement." Schumacher added:

> For these proponents of amalgamation, past and present, the line between "us" and "them" still persists and constitutes a threat to the unity of the Church, as they understand it. And perhaps for those who still resist such amalgamation, the line between "us" and "them" is also important in other ways to their identity and their mission.[371]

After exploring the "missional openness" of the English (Missouri) Synod, Professor Schumacher stated that "…the English District arose as an action, not a reaction," further stating:

> The existence of the English District is a reminder that the frontiers of mission are never simply – or even primarily – geographical boundaries. The borders which must be crossed with the Gospel are not simply between "here" and "there" but between "us" and "them."[372]

Schumacher raised two hard questions for the road ahead for the English District:

- Why do you serve?
- To whom are you [as a District] accountable?: Noting that "missionary fervor without biblical, confessional clarity and accuracy in the message is just sociology and PR, and the mission of communicating the good news of Jesus Christ so that people can believe and live instead of dying – that is what doctrine is for.[373]

The District was blessed to have a scholar who had served as a missionary raise questions that it must continually address.

On the evening of June 27, a Lutheran Malaria Initiative (LMI) hospitality gathering was held. The English District, under the leadership of DCE Rod Lane of Redeemer Lutheran Church, Lincoln, Nebraska, played a major role in the LCMS in support of the LMI. LMI in Synod was under the directorship of Martha Mitkos. Both Lane and Mitkos addressed the convention delegates. The English District version of the LMI at the convention was called "Under the Net."

Another highlight of the centennial convention was a Thursday, June 28 tour of the LCMS International Center and Concordia Historical Institute Museum at the International Center (IC) in suburban Kirkwood, Missouri. The closing hymn and prayer were at the IC Chapel. The next morning at the convention hotel, Dr. Larry Vogel led a theological convocation under the theme *"Being Lutheran in the 21st Century – Does It Really Matter?"* The lively convocation was then followed by a 100th anniversary celebration luncheon and the address by the bishop/president. As is customary at English District conventions, the Canada Corporation meeting and the circuit caucuses to elect delegates for the next Synod convention were both held at the end of that convention business day.

Dr. Herb Mueller, LCMS first vice president, preached at the closing Memorial Divine Service, installing the newly elected District officials. The District also took a special 100th anniversary offering.

The convention approved eight of nine resolutions presented. Two of those resolutions addressed matters of human life: "To Commend the Roman Catholic Church for its Stance on Religious Freedoms and Defense of the Rights of the Unborn" (Res. 12-01-02), and "To Encourage Prompt Response of the CTCR to the 2010 Synodical Convention Resolution on Cremation" (Res. 12-01-01). The English District was a leader in Synod in wanting the matter of cremation thoroughly addressed theologically. A third resolution "To Improve Circuit Forum Election Processes for Nominating Circuit Counselors" (Res. 12-03-01) introduced a proposed Synod bylaw change to permit use of teleconferencing for elections at Circuit Forums; this idea would later be adopted at by the Synod.

During the centennial convention, delegates, guests, and their families had the opportunity to visit Concordia Seminary, the International Center, Concordia Publishing House, the "old" Seminary, and historic Holy Cross Evangelical Lutheran Church, historic Trinity Evangelical Lutheran Church in the Soulard district in St. Louis, Concordia Cemetery in St.

Louis, as well as the St. Louis Arch and the Jefferson National Expansion memorial. For many, it was a convention like no other.

2012—2015

Financial support for both the Synod and District from congregations continued to decline. Some properties were sold, including the "Ablaze!" Center at the former Berea Church site in Riverview, Missouri. It was also necessary to make staffing changes. The Rev. David Thiele became full-time English/SELC District LCEF vice president. The part-time mission executive position was replaced with a bishop-appointed mission council. Following the departures of Mrs. Theresa Fairow and Mr. Tim Ewell, Mrs. Gail Holzer became part-time deployed parish services (school ministry) executive, vacating her seat on the board of directors. The ten full-time executive and secretarial staff at the beginning of Bishop Stechholz's tenure in 2006 decreased by 2015 to four full-time and four part-time staff. However, the District was living within its means and still contributing at least $200,000 annually to the Synod; as overall District receipts decreased, the percentage of congregational offerings forwarded to the Synod was actually increasing.

The August 2014 English District Board of Directors meeting was held at Concordia Theological Seminary, Fort Wayne. A new 4th vice president was appointed; the Rev. Rob Rogers replaced the Rev. Nathaniel Schwartz who had accepted a call out of the District. One of the values in having an annual board meeting at a different locale from where English District congregations or new missions are located was exemplified for new board member Richard Hesselroth of West Portal Church, San Francisco. Hesselroth had never been to a synodical institution. Because the board met at the Fort Wayne Seminary, Hesselroth and others saw Synod in action in a new way. This motivated him and his wife, Terry, to include visiting Synod schools in their travels. Hesselroth's faithful work in West Portal Church as president has continued for several years.

The board meeting in Fort Wayne though had another joyous event. The board was informed by the Lutheran Church Extension Fund of a refund to the District of approximately $805,000 in settling costs for advanced site losses in the 1990s.[374] The long-term debt anchor had finally been lifted from the District! This was a huge morale and financial boost and a boon to the English District Endowment Fund to help with future mission work.

The board chose to meet again closer to District congregations and new missions and ministries, having the November 2014 board of directors meeting at Lutheran Church of the Risen Savior, Green Valley, Arizona, and visiting the campus ministry at the University of Arizona. The board also adopted new parameters for mission funding.[375]

The phenomenon of declining revenue across middle judicatories in North American church bodies (districts, synods, presbyteries, or dioceses) was largely due to Americans contributing less percentage-wise and dollar-wise to the work of Christ's Church. While the LCMS continued to see contributions go up due to direct giving to specific Synod work, actual unrestricted dollars coming from congregations through districts to the Synod was eroding. Staff cuts and downsizing of services by districts and Synod became common. Often the Missouri Synod IC would try to delegate certain responsibilities to the synodical districts and *vice versa,* even though general good will and cooperation existed. With the election of LCMS President Matthew Harrison and a restructured Synod, the LCMS moved in a more confessionally conservative direction with strong theological application of doctrine to practice. At the same time, Harrison's Koinonia Project offered hope for resolving some of the brotherly disagreements within the Synod over practice, particularly in matters of congregational communion admission policies, declining cooperation with the theologically aberrant ELCA, and mission work at home and abroad. The English District had also moved into the mainstream of Synod's historic confessional positions, and many newer pastors brought this confessional solidness to bear, while still embracing the English District's unique zeal for reaching the lost for Christ.

The newly elected board of directors of the English District had many new members, but they chose the experienced Dr. John Stieve as chair. Mr. Paul Lagemann, one of the new members of the board, was elected vice chair. Within the first half of the triennium, four of the board members resigned and had to be replaced. In addition to District staff changes and board changes, the English District's second largest congregation, Christ Church-Lutheran and School, Phoenix, and its partner Valley Lutheran High School, Phoenix, requested and received transfer to the Pacific Southwest District. Some of the largest giving congregations also cut back on their contributions to District and Synod, resulting in further need for changes. Through all these vicissitudes in the English District, the spirit of mission adventure, reaching the lost for Christ, evangelization, missions, and outreach still marked the vision of the District, as it was about "Igniting Christ's Church in Mission."

The theme for the 2012-2015 Triennium was "Christian Faith Expressed in Courageous Action." Following the 2013 Synod Convention and the passage of a resolution supporting visitation at all levels - synod, district, and circuit - the president of the Synod or one of his vice president representatives would make a triennial visit to each District, meeting with its president, board of directors, and college of circuit visitors. Visits to the English District were done by Synod Vice Presidents Daniel Preus and John Wohlrabe in 2012 and Synod First Vice President Dr. Herb Mueller in 2015.

The biggest joys and blessings in the triennium—some several years in the making—were the Dominican Republic Lutheran Mission partnership, saving Concordia-Ann Arbor, visitation, worker care, robust congregational and school ministries, vibrant campus ministries, the establishment of Lifeline, new congregations, and the District LWML.

Excursus: The English District LWML (Lutheran Women's Missionary League)

The Lutheran Women's Missionary League, formed in 1942, is the official women's auxiliary organization of The Lutheran Church—Missouri Synod. In the LWML, there are 40 districts, each divided into various zones. There are also individual congregational LWML units. Some LWML units at English District congregations have chosen to affiliate with the geographic or synodical LWML district. That makes the English District LWML smaller than most LWML districts. But size does not always determine strength, especially in the LWML!

There currently are seven English District LWML zones: Arizona, Greater Chicago, Greater Milwaukee, Western Michigan, Greater Detroit, Pittsburgh, and Philadelphia. Several LWML units in English District congregations that are somewhat geographically isolated belong to the English District LWML without belonging to a zone.

The LWML is all about missions and service, and sometimes goes by the name, "Lutheran Women in Mission." Since its formation, LWML has contributed $100 million in national and international grants—money raised by LWML members, their families, and their congregations. These gifts have come through their mite box contributions (inspired by the widow's mite mentioned in Luke 21:1-4), bequests, and Legacy Circle gifts, all dedicated to spreading the saving Gospel of our Lord. The LWML also engages younger women and ladies of different ethnicities (Heart to Heart Sisters). LWML conventions keep business to a minimum and focus on missions and fellowship. The uniqueness of the English District LWML, like the District itself, is that conventions span the whole country. This results in a unique fellowship of sisters in Christ not bound geographically.

Some English District women have served on the National LWML Board of Directors or chaired important committees. Among those who have recently served in those capacities are Sylvia Johnson (Hales Corners/Milwaukee, Wisconsin), Marilyn McClure (Tucson, Arizona), and International LWML President Helen Gienapp of Michigan (1979-1983, d. 2013), who also served on the English District Board of Directors (1988-1995).

English District LWML women were the great minds on the English District's 100th Anniversary Committee who developed the District anniversary cookbook, *The Great Potluck From Across the English District,* published in 2011, "a collection of recipes from the churches of the English District-LCMS."[376] The cookbook was a smashing – correction – delicious success!

Dominican Republic Lutheran Mission Partnership

Beginning in 2012, Bishop Stechholz began exploring the possibility of District service in the Dominican Republic. This came to fruition in 2013 and was strongly promoted in the English District by the Mission Council.[377] The English District is a managing partner of the Dominican Republic Lutheran Mission (DRLM). The District provides prayer and financial support, leadership, encouragement, and visitation to our DRLM team missionaries. This gives the District international partnership in mission within the context of the LCMS. The lead missionary in the

Dominican Republic is the Rev. Theodore Krey, who along with his family are from Ontario, Canada, but members of Zion Evangelical-Lutheran Church of Detroit.
Pastor Krey is a rostered member of the English District and serves as the LCMS Latin American and Caribbean regional mission director. The District's previous mission efforts in South Africa were not for naught; the close relationship with Bishop David Tswaedi

Pictured is a mission group to the Dominican Republic which included Deaconess Cheryl Naumann, Vice Presidents Jamison Hardy and Nat Schwartz, and Bishop Stechholz, all members of the District Board of Directors.

and the Lutheran Church of Southern Africa continued, though not in the nature of a District-wide project.

Serving as a managing partner of the DRLM gave the English District a stake in the direction of missions in the Dominican Republic and in other areas of Latin America through the *Foro* (Forum) held in the Dominican Republic. After the board of directors approved the District's involvement, strong congregational support, over and above annual pledges and contributions, came especially from three of the District's highest contributing congregations: Redeemer Lutheran Church & Preschool, Lincoln, Nebraska; Lutheran Church of the Risen Savior, Green Valley, Arizona; and, West Portal Evangelical Lutheran Church & School, San Francisco.

Many other congregations in the District also lent their financial support over and above their annual contributions. Bishop Stechholz brought other English District leaders with him to the semi-annual Foro meetings in the DR, and they added their support.

Bishop Hardy, who succeeded Stechholz in 2015, continued strong support of the DRLM partnership, providing financial support and service through mission servant trips and links with missionaries.

Saving Concordia, Ann Arbor

Concordia University, Ann Arbor, Michigan, was in serious trouble. It faced declining enrollment, severe financial woes, and leadership problems over the course of several decades. The university reached a point of crisis. In 2007, CUAA President Dr. Thomas Ahlersmeyer made a strategic move that was greatly successful. He secured the CUAA Board of Regents' blessing to add three additional District presidents to the board as "Advisory Regents." In addition to the Rev. David Maier, Michigan District president, the district presidents of the Ohio, Indiana, and English Districts were added. All four districts pledged and supplied financial support. The English District provided the first gift of $250,000 to help rescue one of the Synod's "jewels," as the colleges were often called. This financial infusion was providentially given when it appeared that the school might have to close unless it received financial support. The support came from the four districts that largely comprised CUAA's region and the strong financial, missional, and administrative support from Concordia University Wisconsin.

After the amalgamation of the two schools into one Concordia University with one president (Dr. Patrick Ferry) and one board of regents, decades of decline began to be reversed. Enrollment at Ann Arbor moved from a low in 2008 of just over 500 students to nearly 1200 by 2018. Morale on campus and new vision immeasurably improved when these became new realities:

- Parking lot and sidewalk replacements and enhancements
- Two $3,000,000 refurbishing and upgrades to the existing Science building and the Kreft Center for the Arts building
- Improved dormitories

- A football team and stadium and a marching band
- Additional team sports
- The Thunder Sports Complex
- A School of Nursing and new North Building on a separate campus.

All these were added over the course of less than a decade. CUAA's annual Boars' Head Festival weekend was enhanced as more donors came forward. The English District's role may seem small in the larger historical picture of the school, but it was absolutely pivotal in helping Concordia University-Ann Arbor survive and then thrive.

Visitation

The English District continues to be a district of visitation at all levels. As most of our bishop/presidents have affirmed over the decades, "visitation is the lifeblood of the English District." Congregations and schools are visited by circuit visitors. Volunteer leaders made visits during the "Pray, Proclaim, Provide" initiative. Bishops spend many weekends traveling to preach, lead Bible Class, and meet with congregations, pastors, parish leaders, as well as attending circuit conferences. This provides the example for pastors and teachers to faithfully visit their parishioners in their homes, hospitals, nursing homes, and retirement facilities. By doing this visitation, some English District congregations – notably Christ Lutheran Church, Lansing, Michigan; West Portal, San Francisco; St. Luke's, North York (Toronto); and, St. Mark's, Mississauga, Ontario–became highly multi-ethnic congregations, all for the purpose of strengthening the people of God in Christ.

Worker Care

Pastors and other professional church workers are not without personal weaknesses, deficiencies, addictions, and behavior issues. For decades, the District has been blessed with an excellent Ministerial Health Commission (MHC). The commission met quarterly, either face-to-face or by web conference, providing mental and emotional health guidance for workers in need through the bishop president, vice presidents, circuit visitors, senior pastors and principals. The needs of pastors' wives and families were also given consideration. District bishop/presidents authorized MHC volunteers, all health care trained professionals, to minister to pastors and other church workers and spouses without fear of recrimination, balancing confidentiality with assistance to the bishop. This service was publicized within the English District.

Congregational and School Ministries

With 80-85% of Christian congregations in North America in serious decline, the English District gave thanks to God for her congregations, some small and fragile but exhibiting robust ministries. Most District congregations have healthy Word and Sacrament ministries. They show vitality and vibrancy by the power of God's Word, good pastoral and lay leadership, unity in mission and ministry, and an outward emphasis on the mission field of the world in their immediate locales. Many congregations in the District view themselves as "mission outposts," seeking to bring the Gospel to the lost and erring and to bring blood-bought souls into Christ's Church. Visitation to congregations often witnessed great hope. Bishops heard amazing stories of dedicated laypeople. One highlight was the dedication of Redeemer Lutheran School in Penn Hills, Pennsylvania, part of the ministry of the English Evangelical Lutheran Church of Our Redeemer, Oakmont, Pennsylvania, but a PreK through 12th grade ministry embraced by SELC, Eastern, and English District congregations of the greater Pittsburgh area.

Vibrant Campus Ministries

During the years of 2006-2015, campus ministry work in the English District expanded, as well as support for all of the colleges and universities of the Concordia University System. Dr. David Dressel, the recognized "dean of campus ministry in the District," served as chair of the English District Campus Ministry Focus Group. A new campus ministry was initiated at the University of Toledo in Ohio. It was common for our District bishop/presidents to make annual visits to several of these campus ministries, such as those at Michigan State University and Martin Luther Chapel, East Lansing, for the annual "sending" of collegians to mission sites in North and South America during that university's Spring break. At the new Toledo campus ministry, engineering students, in addition to regular Bible study, restored a house in a blighted neighborhood. The campus ministry at Slippery Rock, Pennsylvania, and Mrs. Augusta Mennell of All Saints, reported an astounding number of young people who were led to Christ. Each of the campus ministries has its own unique forms of outreach, growth, and service.

Lifeline

The English District is a leader in the Missouri Synod in upholding the sanctity of human life from conception to eternity. Twenty-six English District students, faculty, the bishop, and others were at the 2015 March for Life (January 22) in Washington, D.C., the largest of any district of the Synod. They attended the LCMS Life Conference, where over a third of the almost 400 people were under 25, part of the "New Pro-Life Generation." Other English District people participated in the West Coast March for Life in San Francisco, led by the pastors and members of the two San Francisco congregations. The District's Lifeline Ministry Team was led by the Rev. Michael Brown from Lincoln, Nebraska, until he accepted a call out of the District. The Team made presentations at District conventions and supplied congregations and schools with ideas and strategies for upholding the sanctity of life.

New Congregations

Decades ago, the English District ceded a couple small congregations in the Finger Lakes area of New York to the Eastern District. After an awkward split in an LCMS Eastern District congregation in Syracuse, the English District was able to help a group of African immigrants start a new congregation using a donated downtown church building. Walking a path of diplomacy and fidelity to faith and doctrine, Hope Community Liberian Lutheran Church was established in 2014 after several visits and meetings

Pictured are English District Staff and New District Pastors at the New Church Workers' Conference of the English District, August 2013.

with African Lutheran pastors, often with minimal seminary training, who were willing to work through the Synod's colloquy program. Though the members were financially impoverished, their courage, energetic worship, and love of the Lord was beautifully evident. This kind of story is not uncommon in the English District.[378] In the 2012-2015 triennium, a total of ten new congregations were established in the states of Nevada, Wisconsin, New Jersey, Michigan, Indiana, California, New York, and Kentucky.

2015 Convention of the English District—LCMS

The end of the nine-year tenure of Bishop Stechholz was approaching with the 55th Convention of the English District of The Lutheran Church—Missouri Synod, held at Concordia University, Ann Arbor, June 17-20, 2015. A month earlier, CUAA had graciously awarded Stechholz an honorary Doctor of Divinity.[379] But the focus of the convention would be on the election of a new bishop. Stechholz recommended that the District adopt a four-term limit on service for the bishop/president and other officers after electing his successor. His rationale was that this might attract more younger, but experienced pastors to allow their names to stand for that office.

Three men were nominated as potential successors of Bishop Stechholz: the Rev Ben Eder, pastor of Pilgrim, Kenmore, New York, and member of the board of directors; the Rev. Dr. Jamison Hardy, pastor of Peace, McMurray, Pennsylvania, and vice president of the Eastern Region; and, the Rev. Dr. Robert Roegner, pastor of Peace, O'Fallon, Missouri, and former executive director of LCMS World Missions. The first ballot produced mixed results: 55 votes for Eder, 68 votes for Hardy, and 75 votes for Roegner. On the second ballot, by a 100 to 96 vote, the English District elected the the Rev. Dr. Jamison Hardy as the 21st bishop/president of the English District-LCMS (1911-present) and her antecedent, the English Evangelical Lutheran Synod of Missouri and Other States (1888-1911).[380] A new generation of District leadership had begun.

Bishop Stechholz's written report in the *Convention Workbook* shared eight challenges and realities facing North American Christianity and affecting the LCMS congregations in 2015, even while Christianity is growing in the Global South (Africa, Latin American and the Caribbean) and Global East (China, southeast Asia). He stated these challenges and realities as follows:

- **The rapid secularization of society** (consumerism, materialism, "redefinition" of life, marriage, family, and the home, sports excesses, de-personalization, entitlement, narcissism, dishonesty, etc. [during his tenure, District congregations were victims of ten embezzlements or financial malfeasances, all needing investigation]
- **The rapid rise of Islam and Hinduism** in the Western world and especially Canada and the U.S., including Muslim demands in some areas for Islamic Sharia law
- **The declining birthrate** among Caucasians and African-Americans, and the loss of a generation of Lutherans of child-bearing age from the church resulting in overly aging congregations
- **The growing North American immigrant population** and with it huge outreach opportunities
- **Changes in employment,** a trend of increasing job loss and lack of employment opportunities in an "information society," and a de-personalization in employment
- **In communication, the shift from a "Gutenberg world"** of printed information **to a digital "Google world"** (an unprecedented seismic shift to a world of internet communication)
- **Apathy, lethargy, or "spiritual numbness"** (a tendency to give up or reluctance to step out in faith and action in our congregations), and
- **Moral, morale, and other weaknesses in the Church** (scandals of various kinds, weakness in doctrine and faith, in-fighting and back-biting, bullying, congregational dissension fueled by the Old Evil Foe, power and control issues leading to financial decline and an inward focus, lack of sustainability, and a self-preservation mindset).[381]

However, the bishop juxtaposed these challenges and realities with significant opportunities, encouraging hopefulness because Christ Jesus is the Head and Lord of His Church and the ultimate victory has been secured by Him. He stressed a biblical Theology of the Cross and that as the Bride and Body of Christ, His Church, *"we are more than conquerors through Him who loved us"* (Romans 8:37).

Under the banner of the District's motto, the 2015 English District Convention was blessed not only with President Harrison's presence but also with that of the Rev. Ted Krey, lead missionary in the Dominican Republic and regional director for Latin America and the Caribbean. Krey gave a presentation on *"Theology of Mission and the DRLM."* Dr. Joel Lehenbauer, executive director of the CTCR, was the facilitator for the Theological Convocation on *"The Mission of Christ's Church in an Age of Moral Collapse."* Dr. Heath Curtis, co-director of the LCMS stewardship department in the Office of National Mission, spoke on *"Placing Stewardship within Our Theology and Our Congregations."*

In addition to the election of Bishop/President Hardy, the following were elected and ranked as District vice presidents:

First Vice President	Rev. Ben Eder (Eastern Region)
Second Vice President	Rev. Zerit Yohannes (Lake Erie Region)
Third Vice President	Rev. Todd Arnold (Western Region)
Fourth Vice President	Rev. Robert Rogers (Midwest Region)[382]

This election was notable. The Rev. Wayne Morton, previous first vice president, declined to serve again. Though each of the elected individuals had served in the pastoral ministry for over twenty years, they were all elected to their first term as vice presidents.

The Rev. Luke Zimmerman, who had served on the District constitutions and membership committee and is pastor of Calvary, Mechanicsburg, Pennsylvania, was elected District secretary. The slate of circuit visitors was approved.

All 14 proposed resolutions were approved by the Convention. Six of the resolutions dealt with theology, including those on the theological implications of the practice of cremation (Resolution 1-1A), and reaffirmation of the six-day Creation (Resolution 1-2A). Resolution 1-3B was the most controverted, "To Reaffirm in Practice the Biblical Qualifications for the Office of the Holy Ministry in The Lutheran Church—Missouri Synod," dealing particularly with admission to the seminaries of men who had been divorced. It was approved 79-53.[383] For the English District, the resolution that would have perhaps greatest impact for the District was the approval of Resolution 3-4 by a narrow 78-74 vote. This resolution implemented Bishop Stechholz's recommendation to amend the District Bylaw to permit four consecutive terms in office. Adopted later in the convention, the resolution noted that this bylaw change would be implemented "subsequent to the election of the District President…in 2015."[384]

A kind and warm celebratory outdoor dinner was held under the white canopies of Concordia University-Ann Arbor next to Concordia's signature Earhart Manor. The District bade farewell to Bishop Stechholz and his family from District elected leadership. After he was roasted and toasted and his staff, the Praesidium, circuit visitors, and the board of directors were honored, Dr. Jamison Hardy was welcomed as the new bishop/president. LCMS President Harrison and his banjo were part of the evening's musical gala and celebratory comments.

"Passing the baton of leadership" (noted later in the Statistical section, English Missouri Synod and English District Conventions): The crosier is passed by Bishop Stechholz to newly elected and installed Bishop Hardy at the close of the 2015 English District Convention.

PART FIVE

QUO VADIS

CHAPTER 16
Crossing the Digital and Other Divides

The Bishop/President Years of Jamison Hardy

THIS HISTORICAL CHAPTER is currently still being written. The Rev. Dr. Jamison Hardy was elected bishop and president at the 55th Convention of the English District-LCMS in June 2015. His predecessor, Bishop David Stechholz, had served the maximum of three consecutive three-year terms totaling nine years, as permitted by the District Bylaws in force at the time of the convention.

Hardy's election was significant. For the first time in the District's recent history, a man under the age of 50 was elected to lead the District. The election of a younger bishop was coupled with a Bylaws change that extended the term limit from a maximum of three terms to four terms. The bishop would have to stand for re-election at every convention, but the change in Bylaws allowed the possibility of a bishop/president to serve 12+ years in office. At the time of this writing, Bishop Hardy is in his second term.

Hardy's election marked a new era of leadership. Having grown up using Internet, laptop computers, tablets, smart phones and social media, Hardy was able to navigate communication forms with ease that were confounding to many of his predecessors who were rooted in the "Gutenberg Era" of printed books and periodicals. His familiarity with digital communications allowed Bishop Hardy to continue to serve at Peace Lutheran Church, McMurray, Pennsylvania, as an assistant pastor. At the time of this writing, he serves as an associate pastor alongside Rev. Christopher Thoma at Our Savior Evangelical Lutheran Church & School in Hartland, Michigan. This deployed status was enabled by the service of his administrative assistant, Mrs. Kathryn Stanis.

Unlike his predecessors, Bishop Hardy's service in the District was all under the newer policy-based governance system that had been approved by the English District at its 1997 convention. His familiarity with that system coupled with his doctoral degree in business and finance, something quite uncommon for an ordained pastor, were especially helpful as Hardy began to implement new directions for the District.

One of the first shifts in direction was phasing out the *English Channels*. This had been a monthly publication of the English District since February 1976, but, with declining readership, it had become a bimonthly newsletter before its elimination. During the time of Bishops Ritt and Stechholz, new e-communiques were added alongside the printed "Sycamorian" for church workers. After termination of the *English Channels*, Bishop Hardy revised the e-communique "Servant to Servant" from semi-monthly to weekly online publication. The news update is sent to all District pastors, board of directors and committee members, congregational leaders, and anyone else interested in receiving it.

During the last term of the Stechholz administration, the District's small endowment fund received a major boost by a refund from the Lutheran Church Extension Fund, raising it to nearly $900,000. The LCEF refund came as a result of unused advanced site purchases made by the District in the '80s and '90s that were later sold. An endowment fund board was formed, and given high priority in stewardship. Bishop Hardy emphasized that a strong endowment fund would enable the District to utilize earned interest for expanded mission work. The Lord blessed these efforts, and the District is thankful for the leadership of Dr. John Stieve and initial contributions of his congregation, Risen Savior Lutheran Church, Green Valley, Arizona. The effect of the LCEF refund cannot be understated. Bishop Hardy and the English District Board have developed ways of utilizing the endowment fund for expanding the work of the English District.

In August 2015, the new English District Board of Directors met at Angelica Evangelical Lutheran Church, Allen Park, Michigan. This was the first meeting after the 2015 District Convention. At the initial session, Dr. John Stieve, whose elected service to the District had ended, served as chairman pro tempore to lead the election of a new chair. The board elected the Rev. Wayne Morton to that post. Mr. Paul Lagemann was re-elected as vice chair.

One of the board's first decisions of the triennium was responding to the transfer request made by Chapel of Cross, St. Peter, Missouri, one of the English District's largest congregations. This transfer to the Missouri District was granted.[385]   Bishop Hardy's vision for the triennium was encapsulated in the new slogan, "Love Your Neighbor as Yourself." The Rev. J. Derek Mathers was appointed as mission executive and assistant to the bishop. Other staffing changes occurred, though Mrs. Sally Naglich (business administrator/treasurer) and Mrs. Gail Holzer (part-time school ministry) continued in their executive positions.

Other highlights of the triennium included activities connected to emphases of the District, support for international and domestic missions, and ministry to students at colleges. In 2016, the District entered into a partnership with the Lutheran Church in Hong Kong (LCHK), though that would later discontinue due to a conflict that arose between the LCHK and the LCMS over the sale of an LCMS property in Hong Kong. The English District also received the transfer of First Trinity Evangelical Lutheran Church, Pittsburgh, from the Eastern District in October 2016. Located near the campuses of the University of Pittsburgh, Carnegie Mellon University, and Chatham University, First Trinity serves as the center for LCMS campus ministry in Pittsburgh.

Continuing its emphasis on the importance of being among the congregations of the District, the board of directors held meetings hosted by congregations in the metropolitan areas of Detroit, Philadelphia, San Diego, Chicago, St. Louis, and Milwaukee, as well as in smaller locations in Medina, Ohio, and Palm Coast, Florida.

56th Convention of the English District, 2018

The 2018 English District Convention met June 19-21, 2018. It was again held at Concordia University-Ann Arbor, Michigan, in close proximity to the English District office. When the four LCMS Districts of English, Michigan, Ohio, and Indiana had banded together and provided funds, along with the partnership of Concordia University-Mequon, Wisconsin, there was a vested interest in CUAA. Three of the four districts –Ohio, English, and Michigan—in that order, elected to hold their respective District Conventions at CUAA in consecutive weeks. This resulted in savings for those three districts, since they were able to share the help of CUAA staff and meal-plans, the electronic voting firm, and other services needed to hold conventions.

The Rev. Dr. Jamison J. Hardy was re-elected bishop/president on the first ballot, receiving 156 out of 181 votes cast. The vice presidents elected and ranked by the convention were:

First Vice President	Rev. Jeff Miskus (Lake Erie Region)
Second Vice President	Rev. Ben Eder (Eastern Region)
Third Vice President	Rev. Robert Rogers (Midwest Region)
Fourth Vice President	Rev. Todd Arnold (Western Region).

The Rev. Luke Zimmerman was again elected as District secretary.[386] Dr. Patrick Ferry, president of Concordia University, Ann Arbor, Michigan, and Mequon, Wisconsin, welcomed the convention delegates and guests. He thanked the English District for its support for Concordia-Ann Arbor and the Concordia University System (CUS) colleges and universities, noting that he was a graduate of St. John's College, Winfield, Kansas, a school of the English Missouri Synod that was deeded to the LCMS. That college was closed by the LCMS in 1986. Ferry spoke on the challenges facing higher educational institutions in the 21st century, but noted the "Concordia Promise" special tuition grant assistance initiative, meant to entice Lutheran students to enroll at the Synod's schools.

The convention banner, carrying the convention theme "Love Your Neighbor as Yourself," was designed by Rebecca Kaiser, Bishop Hardy's sister-in-law, and Carol Leu, mother of District Treasurer Sally Naglich and aunt of Board member Terry Leu. At times in the English District, we keep it "in the family"!

The agenda for the 2018 convention included a theological convocation for delegates and guests. Dr. Larry Vogel, associate executive director of the LCMS CTCR, led the convocation entitled "Eat, Pray, Love," which focused on the District's theme of "Love Your Neighbor as Yourself." Synod President Dr. Matthew Harrison was on hand to represent the LCMS.

Each District convention has a special offering. The 2018 collection was designated for a new mission start, Concordia Lutheran Mission, Myerstown, Pennsylvania. Several Synod officials were given opportunity to speak to the assembly. The District's new "1-1-1 Mission Funding Initiative" was shared by the Rev. Tom Engler, pastor of the Lutheran Church of the Prince of Peace, Menomonee Falls, Wisconsin. Unlike previous District initiatives, the "1-1-1" effort is an ongoing opportunity for individual congregational members to support designated mission projects of the English District.

The five new congregations received during the 2015-2018 triennium were recognized: Tree of Life, Inverness, Florida; Apostolic, Moses Lake, Washington; St. Paul, Long Beach, California; First Trinity, Pittsburgh, Pennsylvania; and, Trinity, San Dimas, California. Sadly, one of the District's long-time congregations, St. Michael, Fort Wayne, Indiana, was granted a peaceful transfer to the Indiana District. But the English District understood that ceding a congregation to a geographic district had blessed the Synod as a whole.

The 2018 convention saw an increase from previous conventions in the number of resolutions considered by the delegates. A total of 18 resolutions were adopted, some dealing with internal matters such as amending District Bylaws and other policies. Other resolutions addressed concerns that the District had with current activities of the Synod and the future of funding the church's work:

- Resolution 1-01 ("To Restore Both Biblical Languages to the Education of Future Pastors") and Resolution 1-02 ("To Improve the Specific Ministry Pastor Program") expressed the District's desire to add requirements to the training of ministers.
- Resolution 2-02 ("To Invite and Encourage Congregations of Our English District to Begin and Join in 1-1-1 Mission Funding through Our District") established a new mission funding initiative in the District.
- Resolution 3-01 ("To Move Our Concordia Universities and Seminaries to Independence from Government Funding") was in response to limitations being placed on schools who take Federal grant and student loan monies.
- Resolution 4-01A ("To Support the Well-being of All the Church's Workers and Church Worker Families in the English District") addressed the concern for those who serve the Church.

The new board of directors was elected and the slate of circuit visitors was approved, now up to 24 visitation circuits. The convention closed with a Vespers Service, where LCMS Second Vice President Dr. John Wohlrabe installed Bishop Hardy and other elected District officials.

Excursus: English District Communications

How does a non-geographic judicatory communicate with all its constituents across five time zones? That question has faced the English District since its expansion into Arizona, California, Nevada, and Utah. You may say, the English District is present in only four time zones, more than any district of The Lutheran Church—Missouri Synod except the Northwest District, which crosses the international dateline into east Asia. But the English District as a managing partner of the Dominican Republic Lutheran Mission is represented in the Atlantic, as well as the Eastern, Central, Mountain, and Pacific time zones. If you include missionaries rostered with the English District, that would currently include several more time zones where missionaries on the English District roster are in India and Sri Lanka, Hong Kong, Japan, the Dominican Republic, the Czech Republic, Kenya, and more. One may say, "the sun never sets on the English District," similar to the old British Empire.

So how is communication done besides personal visitation, the "lifeblood of the English District"? In the 21st century, communication happens face-to-face, by telephone, and online, including texting, video teleconferencing, and social media. The English District has had a century of practice, particularly in distributing printed matter. The District and her predecessor English Missouri Synod also held yearly or biennial conferences, while more frequent cluster meetings of pastors beyond regional conferences and circuit winkels was common.

Following are examples of methods of communication used within the English District and her antecedents.

Printed "paper," bulletin, or tabloid for pastors, teachers, and congregational members:
- *The Lutheran Witness* (the original publication of the English Evangelical Lutheran Synod of Missouri, 1882–1899 and since 1911–current)
- *The English District Bulletin* (Supplement in *The Lutheran Witness*, 1947–1975), and separately, 1938–1972
- *English Channels*, 1976–2016
- E-newsletter: called *"Servant to Servant"* (No longer in printed form)

Newsletters, primarily for pastors and other professional Church workers:

- *"Matters"* (sometimes called *"English District Matters"*), July 1974–August 1976
- "Monatsblatt" *(*humorously, "newsletter*"* in German*)*, September 1977–September 1978
- (continued as): *"District Newsletter,"* October 1978–November 1984
- (continued as): *"Cross-Country Connection,"* January 1985–March 1987
- (continued as): *"District Newsletter,"* April 1987–October 2002
- (reformatted and continued as): "Sycamorian," November 2000–November 2009.
- *"Moving in Mission,"* a District missions newsletter, Fall 2009–Summer 2012
- Printed newsletters were then discontinued. The *"Bishop to Bishop"* merged with the *"Servant to Servant,"* and since 2015, the online newletter comes out weekly every Friday at noon, since virtually everyone uses online communication.[387]

During the COVID-19 pandemic, the Rev. Dr. Roger Pittelko was called to the nearer presence of the Lord Jesus. He died in November 2020. In memory of his service to Christ's Church, a new award was established. Bishop Hardy introduced this award at a February 2021 church workers' "online" meeting. The award bears the name of the late Rev. Dr. Roger Pittelko, who served the English District and The Lutheran Church—Missouri Synod in numerous capacities, including as bishop and president (1986-1997). The Roger D. Pittelko *Ille Dilexit Ecclasiam* Award "He Loved the Church" was created to recognize and celebrate pastors who have served God's people well in the English District. Such a recipient would be one who is an ordained pastor who served in the English District, has retired from full-time active parish ministry, and who has exhibited a lifetime of faithfulness to the Lord God and His people in congregations and in the wider field of the English District. This award was presented posthumously to Bishop Pittelko himself and to Rev. Dr. Frank J. Pies, pastor emeritus of Our Savior Evangelical Lutheran Church & School, Hartland, Michigan, at the June 13, 2021 "Thy Strong Word" online Gala of the English District.

CHAPTER 17
Hallmarks of the English District

A DISTRICT OF The Lutheran Church—Missouri Synod should have a healthy regard for its heritage, partnership, and accomplishments under God's grace. The English District is no exception. This chapter should not be regarded as boasting, because the honor for anything accomplished belongs to God alone. *Soli Deo Gloria!* Thanks be to God for graciously allowing the English District to have distinctive characteristics that can be mentioned.

These hallmarks are not in any particular order. Rather, they are significant marks of our heritage that come to the mind of this author who was called to humbly serve 42 years – his entire pastoral ministry – in this little niche of North American Christendom called the English District-LCMS.

One: The Weekly Eucharist, the Holy Supper of our Lord Jesus Christ

One of the greatest blessings in the one holy catholic and apostolic Church, the family of God, is the administration of and reception of the Holy Supper of our Lord's true body and blood, the Holy Communion or Eucharist. No church body, no synod, no district or diocese, and certainly no single congregation has a monopoly on the Lord's Supper. Rather, this Meal of Jesus is for the forgiveness of sins and strengthening of the faith of believers who rightly receive the very body and blood of Jesus Christ, the eternal Son of God, under the consecrated bread and wine.

For several decades, the English District has promoted a weekly celebration of this Most Blessed Sacrament "for Christians to eat and to drink" by her congregations. Along with the proclamation of God's Word in the sermon, reception of the Lord's Supper is the other high point in the Divine Service. Even before the District adopted resolutions encouraging weekly celebrations, the English District strongly encouraged the use of this Means of Grace in our congregations on a regular basis.

Two: A DNA of and Zeal for Missions – Envisioning, Planting, and Calling All God's People to Serve, Led by Faithful, Called and Ordained Pastors and Commissioned Church Workers

Beginning with the Henkels and the Tennessee Synod and the pioneer English-speaking evangelical Lutheran forefathers, the English District-LCMS had a passion for mission work to reach the lost for Christ. They lived out "the faith of the fathers in the language of the children." This unique DNA, if we may call it that, has been a hallmark of our District and her predecessors to the present day.

The English District was a pioneer in identifying, purchasing, and planning "advance sites" for future congregations. While this was a negative point with some, it clearly showed the spirit of the District for planting new missions. While people tend to focus on the "failures," there were some wonderful, God-blessed "successes" along the way.

Two decades into the 21st century, the English District continues to strongly reach out to people of every color, race, language, and ethnicity. Whether building a relationship and giving *Portals of Prayer* to neighbors, restaurant servers, fellow passengers while traveling, or engaging in prayer walks in a neighborhood, some pastors and laity have made such personal witnessing habitual. Some congregations have developed small group Bible studies or human care ministries to which friends in the neighborhood can easily be invited. Other congregations have strengthened or empowered God's people to live out their calling in the priesthood of all believers with the intent of leading others to Jesus. While these are not exclusive to any one district of our Synod, it has been a hallmark of English District folk to build relationships and let the Gospel light of Christ shine into the hearts of those outside the faith.

Churches in the English District sponsor or participate in various public events to further the Christian witness. Our Savior Evangelical Lutheran Church & School, Hartland, Michigan, sponsors conferences on timely church-state issues, regularly welcoming as keynote speakers the likes of Ben Shapiro, Candace Owens, Dennis Prager, Charlie Kirk, Dinesh D'Souza, and numerous other well known political influencers. Several of our Christian day schools, such as Redeemer Lutheran School, Oakmont/Penn Hills, Pennsylvania, have participated in the annual Sanctity of Human Life March in January in Washington, D.C., and other churches have been involved in such peaceful but purposeful marches in other areas of North America. A small congregation, Zion Evangelical-Lutheran Church of Detroit, sponsors the annual St. Michael Liturgical Conference in late September, giving witness to excellence in liturgical worship. The congregations of the Arizona-South Circuit together sponsor a lively campus ministry at the University of Arizona.

The English District also engages in missions outside of the United States and Canada. One of the four regional directors of our Synod's Office of International Mission (OIM) is on the roster of the English District-LCMS. Rev. Ted Krey is the lead missionary in the Dominican Republic and the major force behind the Dominican Republic Lutheran Mission (DRLM) and its *Foro*. He is also OIM regional director for the Latin America and Caribbean Region. English District-rostered missionaries serve in several countries. Besides the Kreys, our missionaries include Dr. Daniel & Joan Jastram (Japan), Rev. Dale & Suzanne Kaster (Czech Republic), Dr. Jonathan & Deaconess Cheryl Naumann (Dominican Republic; Jonathan is also chaplain for all missionaries in Latin America), and Dr. Edward & Monica Naumann (Sri Lanka & India).

Three: Canada and the United States

There is something very special about a district that has active ministry in two different countries. The SELC District also has congregations in Canada and the United States. A few other districts have a congregation in another country. But to have congregations intimately involved in the district and not just a far-flung outpost is unique. It's far more than having two flags on the dais at conventions and conferences.

While the English District pastors and congregations have a Canada Corporation (Canadian Church Extension Fund) for purposes of loans, like our LCMS Lutheran Church Extension Fund in the United States, and while they have their own special fellowship gatherings such as an Advent Vespers and pre-Christmas dinner, they also share their extraordinary Canadian humor with their brethren to the south—with exception of Windsor across the Detroit River from Detroit, which is the one place in the Lower 48 portion of the United States where a traveler actually goes south into Canada. Ties between the Canadian and American members of the District are witnessed in the annual Fall Lake Erie Regional Pastoral Conference with the singing at dinner of both national anthems. But the true bonds are expressed in the beautiful interaction of pastors and other church workers from peaceful, neighboring countries exchanging ideas, concerns, and missional opportunities. Pastors and laity in the English District enjoy and respect this friendship and consider it a blessing of God that they can interact and listen to each other.

The dozen congregations in Canada frequently contribute at a higher percentage in mission giving to District and Synod as well as supplying pastors as leaders in the English District. Currently, the Rev. Jeffrey Miskus, senior pastor of the multiethnic Lutheran Church of St. Mark, Mississauga, Ontario—a large western suburb of Toronto—serves as the District's first vice president. A decade earlier, the Rev. Dr. Roger Ellis, pastor emeritus of Redeemer Evangelical Lutheran Church, Sarnia, Ontario, had also been elected to that post. The Rev. J. Derek Mathers is currently serving as District mission executive. The Rev. Justin Laughridge, senior pastor of Lutheran Church of St. Luke, North York (Toronto), Ontario, serves as mission council chair. The Rev. Robert and Sandy Voelker of Gethsemane Lutheran Church, Windsor, Ontario, have penned lyrics and music to several thematic hymns for English District conventions. Our Canadians have won the admiration of their brethren throughout the English District-LCMS.

Four: A Spirit of Service and Camaraderie, Together and Trans-continentally

Just as there exists a blessed partnership involving two nations represented in one district, so there is something extraordinary witnessed in the English District when pastors from opposite coasts and in between meet together at a professional church workers conference or District convention. There is often an electricity, a dynamic in terms of relationships that cannot be easily put into words.

The common denominator, though, is the passion to serve and reach out with the saving Gospel in word and deed to lead other people, by the power of the Holy Spirit through the Word of God, to Christ Jesus, our Lord. No matter the location of a congregation, school, or mission planter, there is an eagerness to spread the message of God's redeeming love in

Christ. This is found in working together as congregations to support the DRLM and seeing localized mission-planting work. Two recent examples of these are in Pennsylvania. One is the attempt to establish a new LCMS congregation in the largely ELCA territory of Central Pennsylvania by congregations of the Philadelphia Circuit. Concordia Lutheran Mission in Lebanon County was the product of a joint effort by Calvary, Mechanicsburg, and Mount Calvary, Lititz, and their respective pastors, the Rev. Luke Zimmerman and the Rev. Adam Koontz. The mission, sadly, closed during the COVID-19 pandemic. The second example is the planting of a new congregation in an old Pittsburgh neighborhood and the development of another congregation in nearby Clarksburg, West Virginia. The Pittsburgh Circuit congregations and pastors, led by Circuit Visitor Rev. Brian P. Westgate, made this marvelous Pittsburgh plant, Holy Cross in Hazelwood, utilizing the training and help of vicars under the supervision of the Rev. Dr. Doug Spittel from First Trinity, Pittsburgh. They also helped to nurture St John, Clarksburg, West Virginia, into a growing congregation.

This common denominator to faithfully serve is expressed nicely by the Rev. Martin W. Mueller in the concluding words of his *"Amazing Comeback"* book:

> Yet the love of Christ constrains us to do our best and to give our utmost for His mission to the cities [and suburbs and rural areas – ed.] – mindful always that He gave His all for us and for our salvation."[388]

Five: Robert Barnes

The story of our "patron saint," the Rev. Dr. Robert Barnes, was recounted in chapter 14, so those details will not be repeated. It is special, though, to recognize one who was martyred for our Lord Jesus and the truths of God's Word. Barnes upheld the Reformation tenets, even at the cost of his life. Honoring Barnes helped to create a genuine relationship with the Evangelical Lutheran Church of England (ELCE).

The Rev. Dr. Jonathan and Deaconess Cheryl Naumann served in the ELCE for 2 decades and then in the English District and again on the mission field. One son, the Rev. Gordon Naumann, now serves Trinity, Scarsdale, New York, following a pastorate in Wales; another son, Dr.

Edward Naumann, is a missionary in the former British colonies of Sri Lanka and India.

On the English District daily prayer list for July 30, the District gives thanks and praise to God for His faithful servant who was burned at the stake in 1540 in England, never backing down on the teachings of God's holy Word and the Lutheran Confessions that he held dear.

Martin Luther, in whose home Barnes lived while in Wittenberg, noted seven identifying marks of the church as:

- The Holy Word of God
- The Sacrament of Holy Baptism
- The Sacrament of the Altar (the Holy Supper of our Lord)
- Confession and Absolution and the Office of the Keys
- The Holy Ministry (called ministers, the Pastoral office)
- Prayer and Worship, and
- The Holy Cross of suffering and persecution

Barnes knew too well that seventh identifying mark, yet remained faithful to our Lord in death.

Six: Human Care Ministry

The English District historically was ready and willing to go into an area to establish or support a ministry, despite the fact that it would not be a large financial contributor to the District. This was particularly true of inner-city missions and human care efforts such as Uptown Chicago. The congregation was always small, but the compassionate ministry to people of highly diverse ethnic and sociological backgrounds was heartwarming. Sadly, that ministry was discontinued around 2010. Chicagoland was also the home to the unique human care Racetrack Ministry of the Rev. David Krueckeberg. For decades Pastor Dave ministered to the forgotten people in the back track, the stables. They were often poorly paid, but through Pastor Krueckenberg they were cared for spiritually and in any many other ways, even at the risk of his own livelihood when race track owners did not appreciate this care ministry.

Another human care ministry was that of Lutheran Social Services (LSS) of the Southwest, which provided excellent opportunities for "cooperation in externals." Some districts of the Synod shy away from urban ministries and ministry to the poor, drug addicted, homeless, and outcasts. But, such ministries have been a part of the English District since the 1920s. It might be easier to work in suburban ministries and developing towns, the English District still has a heart for service in urban areas, seemingly left behind, a motive captured well in Bishop Hardy's motto of "Love Your Neighbor as Yourself."

Seven: Rehearsing Our History

English District leaders usually relish retelling the English District story, rehearsing names of the past: Kuegele, Dallmann, Eckhardt, Bornemann, Pittelko, and some less known, who gave tireless service in the District and in The Lutheran Church—Missouri Synod. Some have served as Synod vice presidents or on boards, committees, or commissions. Others, like a former English District pastor, the Rev. Steven Voelker, served so faithfully at a small, rural English District congregation in western Michigan, bringing life, joy, and energy back to Holy Trinity Evangelical Lutheran Church of Lakeview, and never seeking glory, recognition, or a leadership role. So many of these leaders were unsung heroes much like Robert Barnes, minus the martyrdom.

Toward the conclusion of his book that told of the English District's place in the history of North American Lutheranism, the venerable Rev. Dr. H.P. Eckhardt wrote on May 1, 1945, from Pittsburgh, Pennsylvania:

> A review of the history of the English Conference, the English Synod, and the English District will clearly show that it pleased God to use these bodies – one and the same – in the cause of upholding and spreading true Lutheranism among English-speaking people of America and also to prepare the way for the transition in the mother Synod from the German language to that of our country. Small though that body was, God used it in a great work. God blessed its labors beyond human expectations. To Him be all glory![389]

CHAPTER 18
A Bright Future?

IS THE FUTURE of the English District and our "mother" Synod bright? Has the passion for seeking and finding the lost for Christ yielded to apathy or secularism, as is found among many who profess to be Christian in North America? If the torch is lifted high for the extension of Christ's Kingdom, where is it burning the brightest? Clearly, this history is still in the making.

The July 2019 LCMS Convention, held for the first time at Tampa, Florida, saw the re-election to a fourth term of Synod President Matthew Harrison by just under 52% of the delegate voters. The Rev. Peter Lange, Kansas District president, was elected to a first term as first vice president. Only two English District people were elected to synodical positions: the Rev. Robert Dargatz to the CTCR and Ms. Susan Elsholz to the LCEF Board. The Rev. Mark Braden was later appointed to the Concordia University System Board, and Bishop Emeritus David Stechholz continued in his six-year term on the Board for International Mission. Bishop Jamison Hardy served as chairman of floor committee 3 on "Mercy" at the convention. No significant shifts in the LCMS occurred, making it a joyful, but quiet convention.

So what is the future of The Lutheran Church-Missouri Synod and her synodical districts? In the past decade (2011–2020), ecclesiastical middle judicatories have been declining in North America. In *The Death of Middle Judicatories*, Dick Hamm stated that, beyond financial support, the so-called "hub and spoke" model is ineffective. Middle judicatories are entities within a larger church. (Different church bodies have their own nomenclature and divisions, such as diocese, district, deanery, or conference; within the LCMS, the terms used are districts and circuits.) Hamm noted that, besides monetary support, what was killing national denominations, churches, and judicatories was "the breakdown of connection between congregations and colleagues; the loss of denominational loyalty; the multiplicity of perspectives in the culture and in church life; the failure to adopt more relevant models of governance; the increase in destructive conflicts in congregations; and the list goes on."[390] However, he suggests the possibility of resurrection of middle judicatories through moving toward a matrix of relationships including resource teams, affinity learning groups, and communications networks. The jury is still out on this and other various notions of church leadership in a post-modern era.

In the LCMS, middle judicatories primarily refer to the current 35 synodical districts. They are of two types. Thirty-three are geographic; two are non-geographic—the English District and the SELC District. The two non-geographic districts number approximately 160 (English) and 50 (SELC) congregations. They also include a few churches in Canada, mostly in Ontario.

Both geographic and non-geographic districts are declining in number of churches, attendance, parish membership, and parochial schools. Nearly all of the 35 LCMS districts have reduced the size of their district staffs and budgets as contributions received from district congregations has decreased. This decrease in contributions has had a domino effect: less "mission money" is forwarded by the districts to the Synod.

What is said about the LCMS is also true in Lutheran Church—Canada (LCC), headquartered in Winnipeg, Manitoba, which was formed in 1988 from the three Canadian districts of the LCMS. The LCC's three districts have recently disbanded and represent areas of the LCC but no longer serve as middle judicatories.

This is also the case of Roman Catholic, Eastern Orthodox, Mainline, and Evangelical dioceses, districts, presbyteries, etc. In short, middle judicatories are declining. This is a painful reality in North America at this juncture in human history. Their demise has been suggested a number of times in studies that transcend church bodies and even non-denominational churches. It should be noted that most so-called "non-denominational churches" are Anabaptist in their theology. Many larger non-denominational churches have daughter congregations that effectively form a church body, whether a flat, loose ecclesiastical organization or a group (e.g. Vineyard churches).

Decades ago, when this author was a novice pastor about ready to lead the November 16, 1980 Dedication of the new House of Worship of the English Evangelical Lutheran Church of Our Redeemer, Oakmont, Pennsylvania, his bishop took him on a little journey. Dr. George Bornemann took young Pastor David Stechholz to a high hill behind downtown Pittsburgh, Pennsylvania. The Ohio River forms at the confluence of the Allegheny and Monongahela Rivers at Point State Park. Two hundred-fifty-plus years prior, the French and later the British had forts at that confluence, Fort Duquesne and Fort Pitt. Bornemann and the young pastor stood on a hill behind run-down Second Saint Paul Evangelical Lutheran Church near downtown Pittsburgh, a church that closed its doors a couple years later. It was down to just a few members.

Bishop Bornemann, pointing, said, "Dave, look over the Monongahela River to the Southside (a neighborhood of Pittsburgh) by the river. What do you see?" I replied, "An old, seemingly abandoned run-down parking lot." "Exactly," he said. "That was the site of historic First Saint Paul Evangelical Lutheran Church and School, where I was baptized, catechized, and confirmed, and where I went to Lutheran parochial school. The church and school closed decades ago, the congregation merged with one of her daughter congregations in the suburbs, and the buildings were eventually torn down. Let that be a reminder to you. Churches, congregations, and pastors come and go, but *the Word of the Lord endures forever.*" Bornemann was a language scholar. I don't remember whether it was then or another time that he quoted these beloved expressions: *Verbum Domini Manet in Aeternum,* Latin for "The Word of the Lord endures forever." and *Gottes Wort und Luthers Lehr, vergeht nun und nimmer mehr*, German for "God's Word and Luther's teaching, endure now and ever more." For me, it was a very memorable moment on a cool but sunny autumn day.[391]

A similar thought is expressed by Rev. Dr. Frank J. Pies, a long-time friend and English District pastor. Pastor Pies had roots in the old National Evangelical Lutheran Church (NELC), a small Finnish Lutheran church body historically aligned with the LCMS. His late father, the Rev. Frank Pies Sr., was a pastor in the NELC. The NELC ceased to exist when it amalgamated into the LCMS in 1962; most of its few congregations were absorbed into the Michigan, North

> A growing shortage of ordained pastors + small, declining congregations + a decline in North American Christianity = ?

Wisconsin, and other LCMS districts. Dr. Pies made this priceless statement to me in reference to Bishop Bornemann's excellent words: "Not only churches and pastors come and go, so also synods and districts." Dr. Pies knew that first hand from his own family history in the NELC.

Over the course of a century and more recent decades, it has been suggested that what happened to the NELC should also happen with the English and SELC Districts. It has been said that these two non-geographic districts should admit that their historical reasons for existing (the use of English and Slovak when the Missouri Synod was German-speaking) no longer apply. Both districts, though, have argued for their continuing as non-geographic districts, and the reasons have changed over the decades.

At present, it seems that all current districts of the Synod will continue, though declining. Numerous congregations are too small to support a pastor, leading them to disband, merge with a sister LCMS congregation, or become dual or triple parishes served by one pastor. Coupled with this is a significant decline in the number of men enrolling at the two LCMS seminaries in Fort Wayne and St. Louis as M.Div. students or in distance-learning programs for Specific Ministry Pastors (SMP). Many smaller congregations are being served by retired pastors or permanent vacancy pastors with little chance of numeric growth.

This situation is not unique to The Lutheran Church-Missouri Synod. It is the case across North America. While many Christians are becoming more stalwart in the faith in the Lord Jesus Christ and their witness to the truth of God's holy Word directing souls to Christ, church attendance, membership, and offerings are in decline. The largest growth in religious demographic categories is among the "Nones" (people expressing no religious affiliation, though some may claim faith in some kind of a divine being or force). The second largest growth is among Muslims. Islamic American families are often of larger size. The "boats from Europe" long ago stopped coming to the shores of North America, but the number of non-Christian immigrant groups has increased. The "traditional" White, Anglo-Saxon, Protestant population of America has seen a significant decline in number of children per family. The nuclear family of father, mother, and children is now the minority among families in our public schools.

Most of our Lutheran parochial schools not only have lower enrollment and struggle to stay in existence, they also experience many of the same problems as public schools relative to families, mores, and social behavior. This is not to cast aspersions on anyone. The Almighty God loves all people. He sent His Son Jesus Christ to redeem all people. But the reality facing synodical districts is part of a vast array of problems and challenges facing Christianity in North America. And this does not even address the secularism that has pervaded our world and North America especially.

COVID-19 Pandemic

Against this backdrop of secularization in North America, a viral outbreak occurred in Wuhan, China, apparently in the latter part of 2019. A city of 11,000,000 people, Wuhan was once three separate cities, one of which was the site of a Chinese Lutheran Seminary developed by the LCMS prior to the Communist takeover of China in 1948 and 1949.[392] Wuhan became of the epicenter of a novel coronavirus: SARS-CoV-2. This virus rapidly spread across the world, primarily through air travel and then further contact with people in various countries. At first, China was the hardest hit with this novel viral disease, known as COVID-19. China and other East Asian countries, including Japan, South Korea, and Vietnam, instituted very strict shelter-in-place (SIP) regulations. The virus spread from Asia to Europe, initially striking Italy, then Spain, while spreading to other European nations. But the worst affected of all countries was the United States, while still later Brazil, Mexico, and other countries became hotspots for COVID-19.

The United States was late in getting into SIP measures of quarantining, social-distancing, mask-wearing, and increased personal and corporate sanitization. During the first wave of COVID-19 flowing over America, hospitals in Washington State, New York City, Detroit, and New Orleans were greatly overwhelmed.

A timeline of incidents from December 2019—May 2020 demonstrates the rapid spread of the COVID-19 plague in America. (Information is accurate as of the time of this writing.)

DEC 31   World Health Organization (WHO) reports mysterious respiratory sickness in people from an unknown source in Wuhan, China

JAN 11   China reports first coronavirus death

JAN 23   SIP "Lock-down" in Wuhan, China

JAN 30   WHO declares global health emergency as virus spreads internationally

289

FEB 5	Cruise ship quarantined off coast of Japan; likewise other cruise ships
FEB 11	Novel coronavirus disease renamed COVID-19 by WHO
FEB 26	First suspected COVID-19 case in the U.S. of local transmission
FEB 29	"Leap Day" first documented COVID-19 death in the U.S. in Washington State; nursing homes and over 65 elderly declared at highest risks
MAR 3	Center for Disease Control (CDC) in U.S. issues guidelines for virus testing; fears of a pandemic spread
MAR 11	WHO declares COVID-19 a pandemic
MAR 13	President Trump declares national emergency in USA
MAR 15	CDC warns against any large gatherings of 50+ people
MAR 17	Coronavirus present in all 50 states; Northern California orders SIP
MAR 19	Italy's death toll surpasses China's reported death toll
MAR 20	New York City declared U.S. epicenter of virus outbreak; dire conditions in NYC hospitals
MAR 26	U.S. leads countries of the world in number of COVID-19 cases
MAR 27	President Trump signs $2 trillion stimulus relief bill to add unemployed, people on fixed incomes, and U.S. business and industries
APR 2	Global COVID-19 cases total 1,000,000
APR 11	U.S. records over 2,000 deaths in one day due to virus
APR 12	Easter Sunday, Festival of the Resurrection of our Lord
APR 18	2,249,717 COVID-19 cases world-wide; 154,271 deaths
APR 30	Gradual re-opening of some states begins with requirements for mask-wearing, social-distancing, and size of groups
MAY 5	Pandemic count continues to rise with slower rate: Worldwide: 3,671,540 cases; 253,218 deaths 1,211,131 recovered

United States: 1,213,855 cases, 69,956, 188,068 recovered

MAY 25 COVID-19 pandemic epicenter no longer the United States

This pandemic has been declared analogous in terms of death and devastation to the Exodus Plagues in Egypt, plagues during the Roman Empire, the Bubonic Plague in Europe in the Reformation and post-Reformation eras, World War II, and epidemics of the 20th Century such as the Spanish Influenza of 1918, and the Ebola, West Nile, AIDS/HIV, Swine Flu and other epidemics.

The nature of the COVID-19 pandemic was its rapid, international spread that was generally indiscriminate of gender or ethnicity. Elderly and poor people, nursing home residents, and health care workers were at a much greater risk of contracting the disease. Since COVID-19 was a novel disease, there was no vaccine to slow or cure the virus; treatments had to be improvised, leading to different results for patients.

Economies in the world were decimated and people were without income and in some cases without food. In the United States, two federal government-sponsored financial relief efforts kept many Americans afloat. Some state governments implemented freezes on rent collection and loan payments.

In the United States, front-line caregivers in hospitals were themselves contracting the deadly virus. By the end of March, the entire country was shut down with many people unemployed and following strict SIP guidelines and later national and state governors' stay-at-home ordinances.

By May 27, 2020, three months into the pandemic in the United States, 100,000 Americans lost their lives to the COVID-19 disease. By July 8, 3,000,000 COVID cases were recorded in the United States. Though the death rate had slowed and states gradually began to re-open in May and June, the novel virus again reared its ugly head. By early July, half of the states that had previously witnessed a turning of the curve now saw increasing case numbers. By mid-July, Texas, Florida, and Arizona experienced huge spikes in the number of cases; some hospitals were again being taxed to their utter limit, especially in places like Houston. Large social gatherings, especially in bars, at beaches, at civil unrest protests, and even in large church gatherings were blamed for the rapid increases.

Granted, more testing was being done in the United States, so naturally more people having been exposed to the coronavirus would be revealed.

The concerns from medical health and disease control experts continued to increase. During the summer of 2020, increasing numbers tested positive to the coronavirus. The rate slowed in late August, only to increase again in the fall. Tragically, the COVID virus was also found to have a higher incidence among Black Americans and those of Hispanic origin.

Amid this pandemic, Christians around the world prayed for deliverance. Christian congregations, including those in the LCMS, were forced to temporarily suspend public worship. Pastors attempted to provide pastoral care and worship opportunities to their congregants. Some emailed liturgies, hymns, and sermons to their parishioners. Others organized online live-streamed worship with only themselves, musicians, and videographers present. Some churches were able to meet for public worship, as long as they met the local governmental limits on attendance, usually set at 10 or 25. As the country gradually "reopened" and churches were able to hold public worship with numerous safety precautions (e.g. masks, social distancing, sanitizing), stories came out in churchly circles. Some told of member deaths because of the coronavirus and the difficulty of ministering to parishioners, particularly to those in nursing homes or other group residences.

Amid this "lock-down" in Canada and the United States, the English District held district-wide Zoom online pastoral meetings. The first one on April 2 had 100 participants, the maximum that could be online at once. The second on April 17 had even more participating, as the online capacity was increased. Bishop Hardy led these meetings, providing information and recommendations, encouragement, and prayer. Bishops Emeriti Ritt and Stechholz were also asked to add remarks, as were members of the District staff and other District leaders. These meetings allowed pastors to ask questions and add comments, discussing how they were dealing with the pandemic in their settings. Continuing into 2021, the almost monthly meetings have been beneficial to attendees. Bishop Hardy and his staff address COVID and other related issues, including financial care for pastors and their families, other church workers, and even congregational members. At the time of the April 17 meeting, 672,293 COVID-19 cases and 33,325 deaths of people with the virus had been recorded in the United

States. Medical experts warned of a possible resurgence of COVID-19 in the autumn of 2020, which then actually did occur. This second wave continued through the holiday seasons of late 2020 and into 2021, even as vaccines rolled out with increased production.

At a circuit winkel of the two Detroit circuits of the English District on April 21, these realities emerged:

1. The worst part of the coronavirus pandemic as it affected pastors and congregations included not being able to gather for public worship and be with the faithful in the Divine Services and Bible classes, and the fear of isolation, distance, and loneliness.
2. The specter of an empty church increased the anxiety of both pastors and congregational members.
3. A question that arose was, "What is the essence of the church?" The fear was expressed that things would not return to the old "norm," and that a new "norm" would have different understandings of the church (ecclesiology), pastoral care, visitation, and acceptance of pastoral leadership.
4. There was, however, a deeper appreciation of episcopal oversight and encouragement. The brothers were deeply appreciative of the local brotherhood of the circuit pastors and were comforted by the leadership and care of their bishops, both LCMS President Harrison and English District Bishop Hardy.
5. There was a fear of coming back to church after several months and finding members not returning. At the same time, there was the hope that the faithful would be eager to return to worship and fellowship.
6. Feelings of exhaustion and being overwhelmed were noted, while trying to minister to congregational and school members via phone, letter, email, and pastors' frustration with not being able to serve their congregations.

The same sentiments and prophecies were issued at similar conferences throughout the English District.

The June/July issue of *The Lutheran Witness* was devoted to addressing the pandemic. Outstanding articles by Synod President Matthew Harrison *"Does God Will Suffering and Affliction?,"* Concordia Theological Seminary President Dr. Lawrence Rast Jr., *"Another Scourge,"* and English District pastor, the Rev. Christopher Thoma *"Executive Orders – Divine Commands: When Does the Church Say, 'Enough'?"* addressed various aspects of Christian faith, the church's response, and "making disciples for life" during this time of international health crisis.[393] One article in particular, *"Gathering Again: It Will Not Be the Same,"* by Dr. Mark A. Wood, director of the LCMS Witness & Outreach Ministry, stated that "God created us to live not in isolation, but in community." In his powerful, poignant lament, Wood rightly issued an indictment:

> Public gatherings became a casualty of our COVID-19 response. Workplace meetings shifted to the web; restaurants closed their dining rooms; retailers created drive-up stations. Drive-up, drive-through, and drive-by combined with virtual presence replaced all types of gatherings, including gathering for worship. And it was not the same.
>
> The casualty of public gatherings especially affected the church. While our culture had inadvertently positioned itself for isolation through a pervasive individualism, the church was caught flat-footed by stay-at-home orders. The church thrives on gathering; it is part of the church's DNA.... Our response to the sudden changes of COVID-19 restrictions looked a lot like the response of the world around us. Worship services were streamed on the internet, congregations held drive-in services and Communion was distributed to communicants in their cars. Online, drive-up, drive-through and drive-by worship replaced gathering in our sanctuaries. And it was not the same. Time will tell what lasting impact the isolation of COVID-19 will have on the church.[394]

Civil Unrest

Amid the COVID-19 pandemic, presidential and national, state, and local elections, demonstrations around the United States called for re-opening over against state governmental decrees. Adding to this already tumultuous time, George Floyd, a 46-year-old unarmed African-American man, was killed in Minneapolis while in police custody on Memorial Day, May 25, 2020. Floyd had been arrested for allegedly purchasing cigarettes at a convenience store with a counterfeit $20 bill. He was handcuffed and held on the ground by several police officers; one of them had his knee on Floyd's neck. Bystanders recorded video of the incident, in which Floyd was heard saying several times, "I can't breathe," while the officers continued to hold him in custody. Floyd died of cardiopulmonary arrest while being detained.

The viral video recording of the officer holding Floyd down resulted in the arrest of that officer and several others. The first officer was fired and charged with 2nd degree murder. But before any indictments could be issued, let alone a trial held, the incident spawned months of nationwide protests and demonstrations. It also led to civil unrest: violence, looting, and fires that raged in all large and even many smaller American cities. The nation seemingly boiled over with anger. In America, curfews were imposed after intense outrage over George Floyd's murder resulted in huge protests over police brutality and targeting minorities, African-Americans and Hispanics in particular. Demonstrations were seen in other nations, supporting those calling for change in the United States.

The Floyd murder was followed by other police-involved shootings of minority suspects. Each incident received widespread coverage on cable news networks and social media. In the summer heat, daily protests and violence were occurring. Some smaller cities such as Livonia, Michigan, witnessed the police department being charged with targeting black people in traffic stops, adding to the unrest, confusion, and hatred that went both ways. Thankfully, the police chief in Livonia disavowed any such targeting, calling it both immoral and unconstitutional.

Meanwhile, the COVID-19 epidemic was again growing in most states. With much of the population unemployed or furloughed because of the virus, many flooded city streets at night. Wearing masks and social-distancing were not always observed during many demonstrations and looting. At the same time, the pandemic again began to spike. As of late October, the upcoming November elections, replete with political ads on TV, in social media, and in peoples' conversations, only added more disharmony. The nation seemed divided, angry, anxious, and confused. Months after Floyd's murder, the demonstrations, and his burial in his hometown of Houston, the COVID-19 epidemic was again worsening in most states.

While "Black Lives Matter" demonstrations and other protests decreased as fall approached, the 2020 elections sparked a new wave of protests and violence. Following the election of Joseph Biden and Kamala Harris as president and vice president in November 2020, a crescendo of demonstrations culminated in a January 6, 2021 riot at the United States

Capitol. The nation was horrified. The violent actions in Washington led to a second impeachment of President Donald Trump in the waning days of his presidency, leaving the nation badly divided politically. While political healing was needed in the United States, the nation faced a harsh month in terms of physical health. January 2021 marked the highest point of infections and deaths in the pandemic, as more Americans were testing positive for COVID and new variants of the virus from overseas were emerging in North America. By the end of that month, there were over 25,300,000 total documented cases of the coronavirus and over 423,500 COVID-related deaths. Increased safety measures were called for by newly-inaugurated President Biden and health care professionals, even as efforts were being made to greatly increase the number of Americans receiving the first of two vaccine injections.

The development and production of the vaccines raised serious issues. LCMS President Matthew Harrison, in a January 21, 2021 letter to Synod congregations, pastors, and other church workers, with an accompanying CTCR sheet, noted that he had received numerous inquiries about the COVID-19 vaccines, even as Synod members were seeking "to maintain their support for the sanctity of life and for religious freedom."[395] Some vaccines in the world related to embryonic stem cell lines from aborted fetuses. While it was reported that the domestic U.S. Pfizer and Moderna COVID vaccines were not developed or produced using such lines, other vaccines did use such cell lines. Harrison stated that the Synod did not have an official position on such vaccines. Yet, he affirmed the Synod's commitment to sanctity of life positions.

Over-arching Reality

Yet, there is an over-arching reality. God's Word endures. God's people of all time take comfort in Christ Jesus and His promises. They do not become paralyzed in fear. Through His prophet Isaiah, the Lord God proclaims:

> "Fear not, for I am with you; be not dismayed, for I am your God;
> I will strengthen you, I will help you, I will uphold you with My
> righteous right hand." (Isaiah 42:10)

If the English District is to be a humble servant-leader in The Lutheran Church—Missouri Synod and an important niche in North American Evangelical Lutheran Christianity, she must take local and global initiative. This is especially true during a time of pestilence, national upheaval, and unrest. The District, her congregations, and her parishioners have an agenda to carry out:

1. Boldly be the church. Advocate for public worship and continue to offer public Word and Sacrament to God's people, even in the face of government mandated SIP orders, while following other health actions and the biblical command to "love your neighbor as yourself."
2. Pastors should make daily contact with church members. Home visits should be offered where possible. Even one phone call, compassionate listening, and prayer with a parishioner per day will be the church ministering to and gathering with her flock.
3. Lay people should be empowered to serve as the priesthood of all believers, offering up daily prayer for fellow church members, community leaders, and neighbors. They are to help meet human care needs, visiting and taking food and supplies to others, where possible.
4. Christian homes should bear a physical emblem of the Christian faith in that home.

Should the LCMS Undergo Another Structural Reconfiguration?

It would be easy to sermonize as people are continuing to find themselves fearful, angry, or bitter. But suffice it to say, the Lord Christ has not abandoned His Church. Christianity, in looking to Christ and being strengthened through God's holy Word and Sacraments, does not despair. Our Lord comforts us: *"In the world you will have tribulation. But take heart; I have overcome the world"* (John 16:33b). However, the continued existence of districts as currently constituted in the LCMS, is open for review. Amid a global pandemic and civil unrest, though, this may seem a small point for the moment.

How will The Lutheran Church—Missouri Synod and the English District and other synodical districts "come back"? Will churches fill up or will the decades-long skid continue? Will North American society grow even more hostile toward Christianity, including Christ-centered, biblical, confessional Evangelical Lutheranism, with the culture, the media, and materialism and hedonism breathing threats, no less intimidation? Could persecution arise in our lands?

Those are the larger and more important questions. Other questions must be addressed. This author is not advocating structural changes to the LCMS, but the reality may be before us. If, by God's grace, the world sees an end to the COVID-19 pandemic and a greater measure of justice that quells civil unrest, the lesser questions can be dealt with.

One possibility in The Lutheran Church—Missouri Synod might be to restructure Synod by eliminating all current districts and going with six or seven larger regions. In an internet age of digital communication and ability to procure information, goods, and services apart from synodical districts especially as demonstrated during the coronavirus pestilence, it is helpful to reflect on the early history of the LCMS when districts were first formed. LCMS congregations, pastors, and other professional church workers might be ably served by the Synod at its International Center, by its publishing arm (Concordia Publishing House), and by the regions, each headed by a regional bishop (vice president) who works under the presiding bishop (Synod president). Currently the Synod has one full-time vice president based in St. Louis and five part-time vice presidents based in each of the regions of the Synod. (While many of our partner ILC church bodies do not use the biblical term "bishop," this is not the main issue.)

A willingness of the LCMS Council of Presidents to take the lead for the good of the Synod and call for the dissolving of all current districts of Synod would establish the circuit visitors as the true overseers of the church. Circuit sizes might be increased to around 20 congregations, allowing the circuit visitor to be a full-time parish pastor, seminary or Concordia University System professor, or retired pastor. His duties would be ecclesiastical, not administrative. He would be charged with ecclesiastical supervision and assisting congregations in the calling process. Bishop Emeritus Roger Pittelko has stressed the necessity of oversight, that is, the maintaining of ecclesiastical oversight in its many facets.[396] This is the heart and center of what current District presidents do.

Information, goods, and services, including needs for Christian day schools, preschools, high schools, as well as congregational outreach, witness, and stewardship, would be supplied by Synod or the regions, each with a regional office. Regions would not be involved in ecclesiastical supervision. The overhead from maintaining 35 district offices and staffs and good and services could be vastly reduced by a few regional offices. Naturally, the official LCMS positions on faith, doctrine and practice would remain. That is our bedrock foundation that must continue solid.

This step toward a major reconfiguration of Synod and her districts would be a difficult one, particularly since our Synod and districts have historically resisted any change of this nature. The reality of bureaucratic growth in Synod and districts and of declining judicatories and their ability to stem the current tides make this a time of faith, courage, and godly resolve. The English District and her antecedents have been a wonderful niche in the history of North American Christianity and in the LCMS. But there comes a time when, for the sake of the pure Christian faith and the spread of saving Gospel, a church body has to take a hard look at what future changes may be needed. The COVID crisis has tested the church's ability to adapt. Critical evaluation is necessary to calculate the cost to faith and doctrine, worship and Communion practice, pastoral care and spiritual care among the people of God in our churches and schools.

The 2010 LCMS Convention enacted what had seemed to be substantial changes to the Synod's structure. But with continual changes in communication, the changes called for by the Blue Ribbon Task Force on Synod Structure and Governance seem now in the space of one decade to have paled in comparison. Yet the Church marches on. The Church Militant, of which the LCMS is a small but significant part, looks steadfastly to Christ Jesus, Savior and Lord. She makes changes over against the backdrop of human history that will help fulfill the Lord's mission which He has assigned to her.

A Corollary

The English District has "worked." It still seems to work as a middle judicatory in the LCMS. It might seem like a non-geographic district should not work since it is much too easy for pastors at a district convention or conference to cluster with those from their region or circuit or in their ministry or worship types and ignore others. However, if District pastors and other professional church workers and congregations can accept the fact that this district is uniquely different and can find blessing and joy in the benefits of being a trans-continental microcosm of the Synod while building relationships with one another, the English District will continue to work and benefit those who serve Christ and His people and to reach the lost for the Savior.

The English District also functions best when it applauds all of the seminaries of the Synod and her sister churches. In its history, the English District has at times shown partiality toward one seminary or the other. In the last four decades, the District has been blessed with pastors who were trained at Concordia Lutheran Theological Seminary, St. Catharines, Ontario; Lutheran seminaries in Adelaide, Australia; Waterloo, Ontario, Canada; Thiensville, Wisconsin; Bratislava, Slovakia; the Ethnic Immigrant Institute of Theology, St. Paul, Minnesota; the Center for Cross-Cultural Ministries, Irvine, California; and Lutheran seminaries in Africa as well as Concordia Seminary, St. Louis, Missouri, and Concordia Theological Seminary, Fort Wayne, Indiana. Pastors have also colloquized from other denominations or completed the Synod's Specific Ministry Pastor programs.

As might be expected for an LCMS district, the majority of English District pastors have come from the Synod's two seminaries in Fort Wayne and St. Louis. The English District functions best when men from these two seminaries work together and the District bishop/presidents work with congregations to call the right man regardless of his alma mater. The District will be healthy by honoring both major seminaries and embracing placements from both schools.

Another part of the corollary has to do with rigid polarizations that convey any unfriendly spirit. This is more out of the realm of theological discourse and has more to do with personality. Does a district have a personality? One pastor attending his first English District convention in 1982 at Milwaukee observed that, even with some theological differences left over from the "Seminex Era," he saw clear signs of a District alive and practicing earnest fellowship and camaraderie. He noted that over the years it has moved away from that to aggressive mentalities that were less friendly, even at times unfriendly.[397] Historians are on thin ice when discussing "preferred futures." Nevertheless, as observers they can warn against trends that can hinder the health of this joyful and loyal group known as the English District of The Lutheran Church—Missouri Synod.

Epilogue

The English District with its unique formation and non-geographical nature has been a helpful leader in the Synod's history in mission expansion and evangelistic outreach, embracing immigrant ethnicities and languages. Also, with strong confessional theology the District has been steadfast in promoting liturgical and musical recovery of our Lutheran heritage. Could the English District also take the lead in helping to restructure the Synod in an age where middle judicatories are shrinking and may no longer be vital to the church in North America?

It is certainly this author's desire to see the English District, all other districts, and The Lutheran Church—Missouri Synod continue and to again grow in number as well as grace. But the realities of decline, especially in the midst of a pandemic and its impending aftermath, may dictate otherwise.

The English District's history has been an epic journey for those of us who have called this little niche our home within The Lutheran Church—Missouri Synod and the family of Christ's Church on earth. It has also been a saga of godly faith and doctrine, practice and fellowship, gathering English District pastors and congregations around God's Means of Grace, His holy Word and Sacraments, and drawing them to discussion, study and service.

Quo vadis? "Lord, You have been our Dwelling Place in all generations... Let Your work be shown to Your servants, and Your glorious power to their children. Let the favor of the Lord our God be upon us, and establish the work of our hands upon us; yes, establish the work of our hands" (Psalm 90:1, 16-17).

Soli Deo Gloria

The Christus Rex was at the former Detroit office and is in the current Farmington office of the English District.

ENGLISH DISTRICT STATISTICS, CONGREGATIONS, AND OTHER INFORMATION

Data from Statistical Yearbooks of
The Lutheran Church—Missouri Synod and (earlier) and
English Ev. Luth. Synod of Missouri and Other States

Bold Italics indicates statistical peaks in individual categories. **Bold underline** text indicates statistical lows in individual categories.

\# Switching from English District data in Dr. Eckhardt's book to LCMS Statistical Yearbooks. The differences as listed in the number of congregations was probably due to the English District including preaching stations, whereas the Missouri Synod's Statistical Yearbooks breaks out preaching stations separately. During the existence of the English District, congregations at their request were transferred to the geographic districts.

† The major decline in the number of English District congregations, pastors, and baptized and communicant membership, 1975-1977, was the result of about one-third of the District's congregations leaving the Missouri Synod in the "Seminex era" division in Synod. Those that left formed a new English Synod of the AELC [Association of Evangelical Lutheran Churches], which eventually became part of the "merger" that formed the ELCA in 1988.)

Year	Pastors	Congs.	Preaching Stations	Baptized Members	Communicant Members	+/- Bapt. (prev. yr.)	+/- Comm. (prev. yr.)
1888	8	17			419		
1889							
1890							
1891	14	13			925		
1892							
1893	16	28			2,084		
1894		34			3,362		+ 1,278
1895							
1896	29	54			3,076		
1897							
1898	28	42			4,000		
1899							
1900							
1901	37	60			4,098		
1902							
1903	50	62			8,300		
1904	51	74			10,380		+ 2,080
1905	53	89			11,604		+ 1,224
1906	55	84			12,547		+ 943
1907	57	85			12,842		+ 295
1908	56	85			14,814		+ 1,972
1909	58	93			15,668		+ 854
1910	60	102			14,742		- 926
1911*		70+			17,147		+ 2,405
	64	83			16,311*		
1912	65	73			17,813		+ 666
1913	71	81			17,982		+ 169
1914	68	78			21,424		+ 3,442
1915	72	81			22,930		+ 1,506
1916	82	106			24,567		+ 1,637
1917	87	110			25,443		+ 876
1918	88	112			27,467		+ 2,024
1919	94	110			28,982		+ 1,515
1920	93	117			30,160		+ 1,178
1921	108	129			32,331		+ 2,171
1922	114	125			34,055		+ 1,724

Year	Pastors	Congs.	Preaching Stations	Baptized Members	Communicant Members	+/- Bapt. (prev. yr.)	+/- Comm. (prev. yr.)
1923	119	130			34,801		+ 746
1924	125	136			36,162		+ 1,361
1925	128	149			38,148		+ 1,986
1926	127	144			39,084		+ 936
1927	136	152			40,733		+ 1,649
1928	141	158			42,691		+ 1,958
1929	146	163			44,252		+ 1,561
1930	151	174			45,615		+ 1,363
1931	158	180			48,025		+ 2,410
1932	160	178			49,476		+ 1,451
1933 #	162	160	8	87,024	51,715		+ 2,239
1934	161	160	8	88,486	52,893	+ 1,462	+ 1,718
1935	164	161	13	91,106	54,400	+ 2,620	+ 1,507
1936	166	164	10	91,562	56,287	+ 456	+ 1,887
1937	164	162	11	92,196	57,604	+ 634	+ 1,317
1938	173	164	9	94,448	59,239	+ 2,252	+ 1,635
1939	148	135**	9	87,160	55,719	- 7,288	- 3,520
1940	156	137	8	86,407	55,188	- 753	- 531
1941	158	157	2	87,606	57,054	+ 1,199	+ 1,866
1942	159	164	5	89,804	59,226	+ 1,998	+ 2,172
1943	167	173	*15*	91,160	61,181	+ 1,356	+ 1,955
1944	165	167	5	93,862	62,655	+ 2,702	+ 1,474
1945	164	163	4	92,575	62,004	- 1,287	- 651
1946	164	170	3	94,449	62,202	+ 1,874	+ 198
1947	179	158	4	98,006	64,451	+ 3.557	+ 2,249
1948	176	161	2	98,977	65,090	+ 971	+ 639
1949	183	170		102,203	66,757	+ 3,226	+ 1,667
1950	186	171	3	103,477	68,513	+ 1,274	+ 1,756
1951	186	170		109,367	70,975	+ 5,890	+ 2,462
1952	188	172		110,116	71,422	+ 749	+ 447
1953	196	174		116,591	74,675	+ 6,475	+ 3,253
1954	196	180		123,505	78,894	*+ 6,915*	*+ 4,219*
1955	199	187		127,497	80,822	+ 3,992	+ 1,928
1956	200	184	1	130,584	81,284	+ 3,087	+ 462
1957	198	192	1	136,260	84,200	+ 5,676	+ 2,916
1958	193	193	1	142,738	87,655	+ 6,478	+ 3,455
1959	206	192		146,207	89,749	+ 3,469	+ 2,094
1960	206	188		147,711	91,084	+ 1,504	+ 1,335
1961	211	192		151,359	94,407	+ 3,648	+ 3,323
1962	208	191		154,117	96,463	+ 2,758	+ 2,056
1963	211	200	1	*155,875*	97,785	+ 1,758	+ 1,322
1964	214	202	2	153,872	98,093	- 2,003	+ 308
1965	222	203		154,972	99,368	+ 1,100	+ 1,275
1966	222	206		155,248	100,835	+ 276	+ 1,467
1967	218	208		154,508	*101,971*	- 740	+ 1,136

Statistics

Year	Pastors	Congs.	Preaching Stations	Baptized Members	Communicant Members	+/- Bapt. (prev. yr.)	+/- Comm. (prev. yr.)
1968	215	*209*		152,601	101,942	- 1,907	- 29
1969	218	207		149,487	100,829	- 3,114	- 1,113
1970	218	206		146,329	101,019	- 3,158	+ 190
1971	216	205		142,646	99,944	- 3,683	- 1,075
1972	213	204	1	137,096	96,883	- 5,550	- 3,061
1973	223	203	1	135,575	97,344	- 1,521	+ 461
1974	*224*	205		130,536	95,418	- 5,039	- 19,26
1975	212	202		127,626	93,766	- 2,910	- 1,632
1976	203	205	4	127,086	94,485	- 540	+ 699
1977 †	131	155	4	86,771	64,487	**- 40,315**	**- 29,998**
1978	123	140	4	77,070	58,334	- 9,701	- 6,153
1979	127	140	4	77,705	59,028	+ 635	+ 694
1980	133	140	4	75,840	57,901	- 1,865	- 1,127
1981	139	135	8	75,095	57,715	- 745	- 186
1982	136	135	2	71,345	55,338	- 3,750	- 2,377
1983	136	136	2	70,715	54,998	- 630	- 340
1984	137	137	3	69,952	54,246	- 763	- 752
1985	152	143	6	69,635	54,111	- 317	- 135
1986	146	144	4	68,486	53,801	- 1,149	- 310
1987	152	145	5	68,545	53,506	+ 59	- 295
1988	155	157	2	68,844	53,708	+ 299	+ 202
1989	156	157	2	68,547	52,916	- 297	- 792
1990	144	161	7	68,309	52,178	- 238	- 738
1991	151	165	*15*	68,687	52,198	+ 378	+ 20
1992	152	166	6	66,276	50,045	- 2,411	- 2,153
1993	149	167	4	65,514	49,729	- 762	- 316
1994	142	166	7	64,755	49,012	- 759	- 717
1995	149	171	5	65,514	49,729	+ 759	+ 717
1996	142	170	5	64,775	49,012	- 739	- 717
1997	146	170	4	65,245	49,534	+ 470	+ 522
1998	146	170	4	64,957	49,425	- 288	- 109
1999	145	171	3	64,334	48,854	- 578	-529
2000	146	170	3	63,929	48,551	- 320	- 235
2001	144	164	2	63,141	48,512	- 788	- 39
2002	150	161	1	61,526	47,656	- 1,615	- 856
2003	150	159	2	61,711	47,908	+ 185	+ 252
2004	148	156	2	61,453	47,319	- 258	- 589
2005	147	155	2	60,832	47,155	- 621	- 164
2006	145	155	2	60,099	47,080	- 733	- 75
2007	148	156	1	58,902	45,556	- 1,197	- 1,524
2008	142	157	3	59,400	46,534	+ 498	+ 978
2009	132	158	3	58,859	46,089	- 541	- 445
2010	146	159	5	57,397	45,137	- 1,074	- 642
2011	147	156	4	57,418	44,888	+ 21	- 249
2012	154	158	2	55,894	43,910	- 1,524	- 978

Year	Pastors	Congs.	Preaching Stations	Baptized Members	Communicant Members	+/- Bapt. (prev. yr.)	+/- Comm. (prev. yr.)
2013	163	157	1	53,861	42,677	- 2,033	- 1,233
2014	165	167	2	53,926	42,564	+ 65	-113
2015	172	159	1	51,010	40,206	- 2,916	- 2,358
2016	159	159	3	48,623	38,509	- 2,387	- 1,697
2017	162	159	1	49,961	36,425	- 1,162	- 2,084
2018	154	159	4	40,949	33,103	- 6,012***	- 3,322
2019	159	160	2	40,131	32,248	- 818	- 855
2020	156	158	2	38.030	30,712	-2,101	-1,536
2021	153	161	2	38,230	30,720	+200	+8

Notes about the Statistics

1. LCMS *Statistical Yearbooks* were discontinued after 1994. Data would henceforth be available and retrieved online from Synod or from *The Lutheran Annual*. Statistics of the year listed are from the data from the preceding year or two preceding years. While statistics do not always match as they should due to varying cut off dates, one can still discern overall trends.

2. The English Missouri Synod did not have a statistical yearbook as such but was rather a compilation. See Dr. Eckhardt's *The English District: A Historical Sketch*, data appendix compiled by the Rev. R. Jesse.

3. No statistics were provided by the English Missouri Synod for 1889, 1890, 1892, 1895, 1897, 1899, 1900, and 1902.

4. Statistical Summary Tables in the LCMS *Statistical Yearbook*s and *Lutheran Annual*s per each District were and are listed by Pastor first, not by Congregations. This was also the case in the English Missouri Synod's compilation.

5. Early German Missouri Synod *Statistical Yearbook*s were in German.

6. 1911 marked the end of the English Evangelical Lutheran Synod of Missouri and Other States and the start of the English District as a synodical district of the German Missouri Synod. The single asterisk reveals what Dr. Eckhardt notes as a discrepancy in the statistics. It may well have been that at this period the two synods had differences in the tabulation of data, for example, including or not including those in preaching stations. Several congregations that had been part of the English Missouri Synod, after the May 15, 1911 union with the German Missouri

Synod, amalgamated into Synod in 1911 and 1912, resulting in a small, temporary decline in number of English District congregations.

7. The English District Office has Yearbooks, 1934-1994.

8. Schools were broken out from the Districts' data in the Yearbooks in later years. Earlier they were included as "Christian Day Schools," long before pre-school/child-daycare centers were started and then included in the Statistical Yearbooks.

9. *Statistical Yearbook*s in the 1930s included data on the percentage (%) of German, English, or mixed language use.

10. *Statistical Yearbook*s of the Missouri Synod go back to 1888.

11. *Statistical Yearbook*s (1934-1949) included a separate number of English District pastors, baptized and communicants, day schools, and property value by State and Province

12. Voting members was also listed per Congregations and Districts (1934-1949).

13. In the 1938 *Statistical Yearbook,* the English District had the highest General Church Extension Loans: $181403.50, more than double the next highest district, $69,216.12.

14. 1939, with two asterisks, notes a significant decline, but that was due to the English District ceding its congregations in Maryland, Washington, D.C., Virginia, North and South Carolina, and Georgia to start the English District's daughter district, the Southeastern District.

15. The number of pastors listed is that of "parish pastors," not including those who are on emeritus status (retired), those serving as professors whether at Synod colleges, universities, seminaries, high schools, foreign missionaries, domestic missionaries, chaplaincies, specialized ministries, or on candidate status. This is by the current definition of "parish pastors."

16. In the 2018 statistics, with three asterisks, the largest congregation in the Missouri Synod and English District, Hales Corners Lutheran Church & School, Hales Corners, WI, cleaned up its membership records, after trying first to win back non-attenders. The result was the Congregation going from 8,596 to 4,500 baptized members. While a huge "loss," it painted a more accurate picture of what is still a mega-church in Synod, and this reflected also in the District's data with a huge "loss" in that year, along with membership decline throughout all of Synod.

17. "Preaching stations" also includes other kinds of ministries that were included in English District data, such as Chicago "Uptown Lutheran Church," which was really a social welfare (human care) ministry.

Number and Location of Known Resolutions at the English Evangelical Lutheran Conference of Missouri, English Evangelical Lutheran Conference/Synod of Missouri and Other States, and English District—LCMS Conventions

One of the most important reasons for Synodical and District Conventions is to act on overtures (memorials) that came from Congregations, official Conferences of the District, and from District Board of Directors and District Boards and Committees.

Resolutions not approved were either defeated, sent back to the floor committee with no further action, or referred to the Board of Directors. Some of the approved resolutions per specific conventions, were an omnibus resolution to respectfully decline one or a number of overtures (memorials) that had been submitted to the District Convention.

English Evangelical Lutheran Conference of Missouri

Conv. Num.	Conv. Year	Convention Location	Res. Pres.	Res. Adopt.	Notes on Convention
1	1872	Zion, Gravelton, MO			Historic August 16-20 Meeting of Dr. C.F.W. Walther, et. al., with English-speaking confessional Evangelical Lutherans led by Prs. Polycarp Henkel and J.R. Moser of Tennessee and Holston Synods. Walther's 16 theses unanimously approved.
2	1873				*No minutes available*
3	1874				*No minutes available*
4	1875				*No minutes available*
5	1876	St Paul, Webster County, MO			Minutes for meetings 5, 6, and 7 record with regret the absence of any German Missouri Synod brethren
6	1877	Hindsville, AR			Notice that most of these "meetings" of the

						"Conference" taking place in the Ozarks or Ozark foothills
7	1878	Zion, Caster, Bollinger County, MO				
8	1879	St Paul, Webster County, MO				German Missouri Synod brethren again present; English Conference asks Western District of German Missouri Synod to send delegate to their meeting.
9						
10						
11						
12	1885	Emmanuel, Webster County, MO				Seminary Candidate A.W. Meyer called.
13	1886	St James, Barton County, MO				Seminary Candidate William Dallmann called. Conference petitions German Missouri Synod to become an English District in the Synod.
14	1887					English Conference advised by Delegate Synod (Convention) of German Missouri Synod to form their own Lutheran synod in the English tongue.

English Evangelical Lutheran Conference/Synod of Missouri and Other States

Conv. Num.	Conv. Year	Convention Location	Res. Pres.	Res. Adopt.	Notes on Convention
1	1888	Bethlehem, St Louis, MO			Began as the 15th annual Meeting (Conference) of the English Ev. Lutheran Conference but then officially became the General Evangelical Lutheran Conference of Missouri and Other States.

					Constitution of Conference adopted. New hymnal with an order of service (Common Service) adopted.
2	1891	Grace, St Louis, MO			Changes name from "Conference" to "Synod" and receives *The Lutheran Witness* as its official magazine
3	1893	St John, Chicago, IL			English Synod receives Concordia College, Conover, NC, and St. John's College, Winfield, KS; Doctrinal discussion of 7 Theses on Parish Rights.
4	1895	Redeemer, Fort Wayne, IN			Doctrinal discussion on 6 Theses of Lutheran Church polity and policy.
5	1897	Emmanuel, Baltimore, MD			Conventions continued the practice of having a Doctrinal Discussion (later replaced by an Essayist)
6	1899	St Mark, Detroit, MI			Vote of 16-8 in favor of "union" with German Missouri Synod. Founding President Kuegele passes the baton of leadership to new President William Dallmann of Baltimore, MD.
7	1901	Calvary, Buffalo, NY			54 pastors, 5 teachers, and 45 congregations now on roll of the English Synod. 5-part, 97-page Essay delivered by Dr. Wm. Dallmann on *"Why Do I Believe the Bible is God's Word?"* President Dallmann passes the baton of

					leadership to new President Prof. A.W. Meyer of St. John's College, Winfield, KS. Report given concerning the Evangelical Lutheran Synodical Conference of North America, of which the English Missouri Synod had become a member
8	1903	St Andrew's, Pittsburgh, PA			Essay on "The Parochial School" by Rev. S. Stoeppelwerth of Winfield, KS. Rev. H.P. Eckhardt continues to Chair the Synod Mission Board. New editions of Hymnbook and Sunday-School Hymnal. Resolution approved of two missionary journals re: work with "Negro Missions" in Synodical Conference
9	1905	Grace, St Louis, MO			President Meyer passes the baton of leadership to new President Rev. H.P. Eckhardt of Cleveland, OH. Many prominent leaders of German Missouri Synod present. New Synod Hymn-book adopted. English Missouri Synod now having regular (regional) conferences, termed "Conference Districts" (Eastern, Southeastern, Central, Northwestern, and Southwestern). Rev. John H.C. Fritz becomes Chair of

					Synod's Mission Board.
10	1907	Mt Olive, Milwaukee, WI			Prof. C.A. Weiss of Concordia College, Conover, NC, gives essay on "Conversion."
11	1909	Grace, Cleveland, OH			Publication Board of Synod continues prominent work of publications under Chairmanship of Rev. W.H. Dale of Pittsburgh, where Synod publications were produced, and serving as President of the ALPB (American Lutheran Publication Board). Rev. George A. Romoser, President, Concordia College, Conover, NC, gives essay on "Church and State." Series of resolutions approved concerning affiliation with the German Missouri Synod. The Pastors' Widows' and Orphans' Fund Committee becomes a Board, complete with Bylaws.
12	1911	Redeemer, St Louis, MO			38-page essay on "The Unity of the Christian Church" given by Rev. Martin S. Sommer, Pastor, Grace Church, St. Louis, MO. May 15, 1911, Articles of "Union" with German Missouri Synod considered one-by-one and adopted. English Synod officially unites ("union consummated" as termed in 1911

					Convention *Proceedings*) with the German Evangelical Lutheran Synod of Missouri, Ohio, and Other States; becomes the English District of the German Missouri Synod. It did meet after the "union."

English District – Missouri Synod

Conv. Num.	Conv. Year	Convention Location	Res. Pres.	Res. Adopt.	Notes on Convention
1	1912	Jackson Square, Baltimore, MD			95 delegates present; 69 congregations represented. District officially incorporated in New York. Essay by Rev. Wm. H. Dale on "Building a Truly Lutheran Church." Baton of leadership passes from Dr. H.P. Eckhardt to new President, Dr. M. Sommer.
2	1915	Redeemer, St Paul, MN			Doctrinal essay by Rev. Martin Walker on "Christian Stewardship." Baton of leadership passes from Dr. Sommer to new President, Dr. J. Adam Detzer.
3	1916	Trinity, Pittsburgh, PA			31-page Doctrinal Essay by Dr. H.B. Hemmeter, President, Concordia College, Conover, NC, on "The Fatherhood of God and the Brotherhood of Man." Noted in a resolution that some Synod (LCMS) brethren did not appreciate English District brethren's high regard of the Sunday School.

4	1918	Redeemer, Chicago, IL			Baton of leadership passed from Dr. J.A. Detzer to new President, Rev. Dr. O.C. Kreinheder. 39-page Doctrinal Essay on "The Millennium" by Rev. F. Kroencke of Cincinnati. Proceedings noted several pastors resigned their pastorates to enter U.S. military chaplaincy in World War I.
5	1919	Concordia, Conover, NC	6	5	45-page Doctrinal essay by Rev. J.R. Graebner of Fort Wayne on "The Lodge."
6	1921	St Mark, Sheboygan, WI	5	4	30-page Historical essay on "Miles Coverdale" by Dr. William Dallmann, now of Milwaukee.
7	1922	Trinity, Oak Park, IL	1	1	No essay noted or recorded in Convention *Proceedings.*
8	1924	Our Savior, Cincinnati, OH	6		157 present: 105 pastors & professors; 52 laity. Number of congregations and pastors growing; new "Pacific Conference" added. No essay noted.
9	1925	Calvary, Buffalo, NY	7	7	Doctrinal essay on "The Relation of a Congregation to Synod" by Rev. E.H. Paar of Harrisburg, PA. Special Committee of Amalgamation respectfully cannot find warrant for amalgamation into the Missouri Synod by dissolving the English District.
10	1927	Redeemer, Chicago, IL	6	6	Baton of leadership passed from Dr. Kreinheder to new

					President, Rev. G. Schuessler. 40-page Doctrinal essay on "Authority in the Church" by Rev. Harry E. Olsen of Milwaukee. Office of District Archivist created. One approved resolution asked Dr. F. Pieper to have his *Dogmatiks* published in English.
11	1928	Lutherland, Pocono Pines, PA	4	4	District was the "guest" of the Eastern Conference (Region). 33-page Doctrinal essay on "The First Christian Church (Acts)" by Dr. W.H.T. Dau, President, Valparaiso University. Mission Board noted year-by-year increase. District now with 3 VPs
12	1930	Concordia, Akron, OH	3	1	Doctrinal essay again Dr. Dau on "The Preparation of the Church For Its World Mission." President Schuessler notes the close relation of the District with Valparaiso (Lutheran) University.
13	1931	Uptown Bethany, Chicago, IL			Doctrinal essay again by Dr. H.B. Hemmeter, President, Concordia College, Conover, NC, on "Modernism in Religion." Committee on Petitions and Resolutions serving as "floor committee" recommended adoption of petitions and resolutions; apparently all adopted.
14	1933	Concordia Teachers Seminary – River Forest, IL	1	1	Doctrinal essay on "The Christian Creeds" by Prof. E.J. Friedrich. English District "Bulletin" began

					publishing with 3 issues in 1932 (mimeographed). Southeastern "District" (Region) of English District petitions to form a new synodical district in the Missouri Synod. District Amalgamation Committee recommends amalgamation into the Synod, no action taken, deemed "premature."
15	1934	Concordia Teachers Seminary – River Forest, IL	1	1	Doctrinal essay on "The Christian Creeds" by Prof. E.J. Friedrich (concluded).
16	1936	Concordia Teachers College – River Forest, IL	2	2	Historical essay on "Our English District in its Early Development," by Rev. Dr. A.W. Meyer, 3rd Pres. of English Missouri Synod (1901–1905). Second essay, on "Spiritual Stewardship" by Rev. Martin Walker, District First VP, Buffalo, NY. Baton of leadership passed from Dr. Schuessler to new President, Rev. Paul Lindemann, Pastor, Redeemer, St. Paul, MN. Rev. Schuessler's keynote of Convention: "All Glory Be to God on High." LCMS President J.W. Behnken present. Board & Committee Reports still prime in adoptions.
17	1937	Concordia Teachers College – River Forest, IL	3	3	Doctrinal essays on "Christian Citizenship" by Dr. Theodore Graebner, Concordia Seminary, St. Louis, and on "The Lord's Supper a Priceless Inheritance" by

					Rev. H.W. Bartels, Cleveland, OH, and on "What Is the Business…of Church in These Religiously Confused and Socially Distraught Times?" by Rev. Theo. H. Schroedel, Minneapolis, MN. Among new mission stations: Redeemer, Sarnia, ON, Canada. *[See also Note A below.]*
18	1939	Concordia Teachers College – River Forest, IL	8		Baton of leadership passed from Rev. P. Lindemann to new President, Rev. Martin Walker of Buffalo, NY. Doctrinal essays on "Ye Shall Be Witnesses unto Me" by Rev. R, Jesse, St. Louis, and on "The Technique of Personal Evangelism" by Rev. Hugo Kleiner, North Tonawanda, NY. English District gets Synod approval and new synodical Southeastern District formed in 1939; 38 congregations and 28 pastors eventually released to new daughter district.
19	1940	Concordia Teachers College – River Forest, IL			Doctrinal essays on "Church Discipline… Matthew 18" by Rev. Bernard H. Hemmeter of Chicago (33 pages), and on "Buchmanism" (Oxford Group Movement) by Prof. Rev. W.G. Schwehn (14 pages), and on "Laymen's Opportunities for Greater Participation in the…Convention" by Mr. J.W. Bosse of

					Indianapolis, IN (5 pages).
20	1942	Concordia Teachers College – River Forest, IL	15	14	Doctrinal essays on "The Christian Assurance of Faith…" by Prof. J.T. Mueller, Concordia Seminary, St. Louis (35 pages), and on "The Value of a Matured and Experienced Ministry" by Rev. A.H.A. Loeber of Detroit (14 pages). Rev. George Bornemann's first English District Convention. 10 new congregations received, including Grace, Redford Twp. MI; Greenfield Park, Milwaukee, WI; Trinity, New Lenox, IL; Markham, Markham, IL; and two in Montana.
21	1943	Concordia Teachers College – River Forest, IL			Large attendance during war time: 149 member congregations, 147 voting pastors, 45 advisory pastors (profs., etc.). 4 independent congregations, 5 preaching stations, 18 teachers, 147 laity. No essay noted or included.
22	1945	Evangelical Lutheran Institute for the Deaf – Detroit, MI	16	16	Doctrinal essay on "Faith" by 2nd VP E.L. Wilson of St. Louis; devotional addresses by Dr. Oscar C. Kreinheder and Rev. H.W. Rosmoser. *[See also Note B below.]*
23	1946	Concordia Teachers College – River Forest, IL			District still has only three Vice Presidents.. Doctrinal essayist by former President, Pr. Roger L. Sommer, on "Sanctification."

					Pastors and Teachers would meet in an evening for separate conferences. Separate pastors conference and two lay conferences in evenings Convention sermon printed for first time. Several overtures on amalgamation for and against.Committee on Amalgamation gave its report: continued existence in view of "promising mission fields."
24	1948	Concordia Teachers College – River Forest, IL	14	12	Essayist: Dr. A.M. Rehwinkel, on "The Christian and the Social Order."
25	1949	Concordia Teachers College – River Forest, IL	12	12	Essayist: Pr. B.A. Maurer on "A Glorious Church." Dr. Sommer reported on English District Supplement included in 26 issues of "Lutheran Witness" since 1948. Archivist W.G. Schwehn's report included in *Convention Proceedings.* Convention upholds Committee on Amalgamation's Report deploring pressure put on English District from certain geographic districts.
26	1951	Concordia Teachers College – River Forest, IL	10	10	Essayist: Pr. A.H.A. Loeber, Detroit, on "Present-Day World Events in the Light of the Doctrine of the Last Times." Baton of leadership passed from Dr. Walker to new President, Rev. Dr. Hugo Kleiner of North Tonawanda, NY.

27	1952	Concordia Teachers College – River Forest, IL	7	7	Essayist: Dr. Arthur Carl Piepkorn, Concordia Seminary, on "What the Symbolical Books of the Lutheran Church Have to Say About Worship and the Sacraments." Rev. L. Granville Leonard, Pastor of Redeemer, Oakmont, PA, appointed by President Kleiner as District representative for the Lutheran Hour.
28	1954	Concordia Teachers College – River Forest, IL	11	11	315 delegates and advisory members; over 500 attendees. Essayist: Dr. Richard R. Caemerer, Concordia Seminary, on "Church and State – The Rule of Christ and the Rule of Men."
29	1955	Concordia Teachers College – River Forest, IL	14	14	Essayist: Dr. Alfred P. Klausler on "Your Christian Vocation" (37 pages).
30	1957	Concordia Teachers College – River Forest, IL	11	10	393 delegates and advisory, the highest number to date. Essayist: Dr. Jaroslav Pelikan on "Luther's Doctrine of the Lord's Supper." Board of Directors' Convention reports now included.
31	1958	Concordia Senior College – Fort Wayne, IN	5	4	First Convention not at River Forest since 1946. Essayist: Rev. Julius W. Acker on "Worshiping at Strange Altars" (later printed as a book). Dr. Oliver Harms, LCMS 4th VP, served as President Behnken's representative. Rev. Dr. August Brunn continues service as VP of District (1957-1970).

						Executive Secretary Rev. O.T. McRee gives special address to Convention. Floor Committee's report of major Bylaw revisions adopted.
32	1960	Concordia College – Milwaukee, WI	16		16	Noteworthy resolutions were adopted at the Convention. Resolution #9 concerning the 'Brief Statement' adopted by Synod at San Francisco 1959 viewed as unconstitutional…" Number of VPs increased from 3 to 5. 433 delegates & advisory in attendance at Convention. Essayist: Dr. Paul M. Bretscher on Faith Tried and Triumphant."
33	1961	Concordia Teachers College – River Forest, IL	22		16	Golden (50th) Anniversary Service held at Rockefeller Chapel, University of Chicago. 470 delegates & advisory in attendance at Convention, plus guests. Rev. Daniel Ludwig, District Secretary (1957-1968), placed a "Convention Digest" into *Proceedings*. LCMS President Dr. John Behnken spoke on the work of the Synod. Three essays given: (1) Dr. Richard Caemmerer on "The Word of God," (2) Prof. Harry Coiner on "Holy Baptism", both of Concordia Seminary, St. Louis, and (3) Dr. W. Wolbrecht, Executive Director of LCMS, on "Holy Communion, A Sacrament of Thanksgiving…"

34	1963	Concordia Teachers College – River Forest, IL	18	12	Dr. Hugo Kleiner retires after 12 years. Rev. Bertwin L. Frey elected new President/Bishop. A printed *"In Memoriam"* in Convention Proceedings of "Mr. Delegate" William Kroeger who attended Conventions from 1907 to 1961 and present in 1911 District "union." Amalgamation Committee alerts E.D. Convention of Synod's new Committee on Realignment of Synodical Districts." Convention Essays: "Between the Testaments: The Silent Years," by Dr. Carl Gross, Michigan State University; and "Helsinki, Rome, Montreal," by Rev. Dr. John Tietjen, Leonia, NJ
35	1964	Concordia Lutheran Junior College – Ann Arbor, MI	68	62	New LCMS President Oliver Harms presents on Synod. Firm commitment to Synod of $1.5 million. Essayists: Rev. Dr. Karl Lutze of Valparaiso University on "The Christian Position in Human Relations," and Dr. Martin Koehnecke, President, CTC, River Forest, IL, on "The Dramatic Dream."
36	1966	Concordia Lutheran Junior College – Ann Arbor, MI	50	47	Rev. Harold Hecht serving as Mission Counselor at District Office; Rev. Bertwin Frey serving a part-time President/Bishop, like predecessors, from Cleveland, OH.

					18 Circuits & Counselors (Visitors). LCMS 1st VP Roland Wiederaenders presented daily on Synod. Dr. Martin Franzmann presented on "The Theological Climate of the Synod," and four laity presented practically on "How We Did It." Convention essay: "Realigning for Mission," by Dr. David S. Schuller
37	1968	Concordia Lutheran College – Ann Arbor, MI	55	48	Convention essay: "Saints Alive," by Mr. Alfred Jordan. Resolution adopted to make District President full-time. Dr. Hecht serving as District Executive Secretary and Rev. Bill Woldt as Mission Counselor.
38	1970	Concordia Lutheran College – Ann Arbor, MI	90	84	Rev. Dr. William Buege serves as LCMS President J.A.O. Preus' representative. Dr. Frey steps down; Rev. Dr. John Baumgaertner of Milwaukee elected over Dr. Hecht in final ballot as President/Bishop. Amalgamation Committee dissolved.
39	1972	Concordia Teachers College – River Forest, IL	81	80	"Lettuce boycott" resolution is defeated. 5 "COMPOG" resolutions adopted.
40	1974	Concordia Teachers College – River Forest, IL	66	61	Numerous approved resolutions supporting Seminex, ELIM, etc., but Convention allowed minority negative votes and names to be recorded.

X	1975	Northlake Center, Northlake, IL	1	1	"Special" Convention of District. Adoption of- Position Statement" (75-1A) in preparation for the likely departure from the LCMS.
41	1976	Concordia Teachers College – River Forest, IL	38	34	The "hopelessly divided" Convention of the English District and "division." Rev. George Bornemann elected President/Bishop, after Dr. Hecht was removed from office by Dr. Preus. Hecht becomes new President of English Synod (AELC) at separate Convention. 3 resolutions withdrawn.
42	1978	Concordia College – Ann Arbor, MI	40	40	Dr. Bornemann re-elected by acclamation.
43	1980	Concordia College – Ann Arbor, MI	55	44	Dr. Bornemann re-elected by acclamation. Dr. Jean Garton, founder of Lutherans for Life and wife of Pr. "Chick" Garton, banquet speaker, on "The Door Is Still Open…On the Family!"
44	1982	Concordia College – Milwaukee, WI	76	72	President/Bishop Bornemann easily elected to new three-year term. 1st VP Tassler retires; Rev. Donald Jung becomes 1st VP. 386 total delegates & advisory.
45	1985	Concordia College – River Forest, IL	60	59	Rev. Donald Jung, having been "acting President" since Bornemann's retirement on 1/31/1984, is elected President/Bishop. Convention illustrated essay by Dr. Ralph Schultz, President, Concordia College, Bronxville, NY, on

					work of J.S. Bach under Convention theme of *"Together We Sing to the LORD."*
46	1988	Concordia College – River Forest, IL	37	35	Upon resignation due to terminal cancer of Dr. Jung, 1st VP Roger Pittelko serves first as "regent," then "acting President/Bishop" as of 1/1/1987; elected DP/Bishop by acclamation at Convention. 38-page Doctrinal essay by Dr. Kenneth Korby on "Pastoral Office and Priesthood of All Believers."
47	1991	Concordia University – River Forest, IL	43	43	Dr. Pittelko elected by acclamation as President/Bishop. LCMS President Dr. Ralph Bohlmann addresses Convention. District now at 22 visitation circuits.
48	1994	Concordia University – River Forest, IL	16	16	Dr. Pittelko again elected by acclamation. LCMS President Dr. Alvin Barry addresses Convention on 5-point theme of LCMS.
49	1997	Concordia University – River Forest, IL	7	6	Bishop Pittelko retires due to term limits. Rev. David Ritt elected President/Bishop on 4th ballot. Convention approves major restructuring of District to policy-based governance and a single Board of Directors.
50	2000	Concordia University – River Forest, IL	18	14	Dr. Ritt elected to second term as President/Bishop. Essay given by Dr. David Schmitt of Concordia Seminary on Evangelism.

					Rev. David Thiele completes years as District Secretary, replaced by elected Rev. David Stechholz
51	2003	Concordia University – River Forest, IL	14	14	Bishop/President Ritt elected by acclamation. District Convention Theological Convocation held. District now at 24 visitation circuits.
52	2006	Hyatt Hotel, Schaumburg, IL	9	8	Baton of leadership extended by term-limited President/Bishop Ritt to Rev. David Stechholz. Rev. David Rutter becomes new convention organist.
53	2009	Hales Corners, Hales Corners, WI	4	2	Numerous District Bylaw changes were handled and approved separately by resolutions.
54	2012	Concordia Seminary & Sheraton Westport Hotel – St Louis, MO	9	8	End of 100th Anniversary Year. Anniversary Service and barbecue held at Concordia Seminary, Clayton (St. Louis), MO. Delegates visit LCMS International Center and other historic sites around St. Louis.
55	2015	Concordia University – Ann Arbor, MI	14	14	District approves a maximum 4 term (12 year) tenure for District Officers. Baton of leadership passes from Bishop Stechholz to newly-elected Rev. Dr. Jamison Hardy, who chooses to remain in Pittsburgh while still full-time Bishop/President. Convention group picture.

						Three districts meeting consecutively at CUAA
56	2018	Concordia University – Ann Arbor, MI	18	18		Dr. Hardy re-elected on first ballot as Bishop/President. Half of District staff now largely deployed. Major Bylaw revisions and amending of Corporate Operations Manual approved

Notes on Convention Chart

A. Committee on Amalgamation, chaired by 1st English District Pres. H.P. Eckhardt, and with Rev. Martin Walker as Secretary, reported to 1937 Convention in reaction to certain overtures of the 1935 Synod Convention that "the time has not yet arrived to propose to our congregations that the English District be dissolved and amalgamated into the territorial Districts of Synod."[398]

B. Overture on Amalgamation proposed by Pilgrim ELC, Chicago, and Bethesda ELC, Chicago calling for dissolution of the English District and amalgamation of congregations into the territorial Districts of Synod. The overture went to the Committee on Amalgamation and the Committee on Petitions and Resolutions. The latter stated that "amalgamation should remain our goal" but that "the (English) District, for the immediate future, should continue its existence."[399]

Lutheran Church—Missouri Synod Conventions

[Including prior names: *Die Deutsches Evangelisch-Lutherische Synod von Missouri, Ohio, und andern Staaten* (1847—1917) and The Evangelical Lutheran Synod of Missouri, Ohio, and Other States (1917—1947).]

Number	Year	Location	Notes
1	1847	Chicago, IL	The German Evangelical Lutheran Synod of Missouri, Ohio, and Other States, meeting at First St. Paul Evangelical Lutheran Church & School, Chicago, is officially organized.
2	1848	St Louis, MO	
3	1849	Fort Wayne, IN	
4	1850	St Louis, MO	
5	1851	Milwaukee, WI	
6	1852	Fort Wayne, IN	

7	1853	Cleveland, OH	
8	1854	St Louis, MO	Congregations of the Missouri Synod are divided into four districts.
9	1857	Fort Wayne, IN	
10	1860	St Louis, MO	
11	1863	Fort Wayne, IN	
12	1864	Fort Wayne, IN	
13	1866	St Louis, MO	
14	1869	Fort Wayne, IN	
15	1872	St Louis, MO	Following Convention, Walther meets with English-speaking confessional Lutherans in Gravelton, MO.
16	1874	Fort Wayne, IN	First Delegate Convention
17	1878	St Louis, MO	
18	1881	Fort Wayne, IN	
19	1884	St Louis, MO	
20	1887	Fort Wayne, IN	
21	1890	Milwaukee, WI	
22	1893	St Louis, MO	
23	1896	Fort Wayne, IN	
24	1899	St Louis, MO	
25	1902	Milwaukee, WI	
26	1905	Detroit, MI	
27	1908	Fort Wayne, IN	
28	1911	St Louis, MO	"Union" of English Missouri Synod with German Missouri Synod; English Synod becomes the English District. Official accord signed.
29	1914	Chicago, IL	
30	1917	Milwaukee, WI	*Die Deutsche Evangelisch-Lutherische Synode von Missouri, Ohio, und andern Staaten* changes its name in the year of the U.S. entry into World War to "Evangelical Lutheran Synod of Missouri, Ohio, and Other States."
31	1920	Detroit, MI	
32	1923	Fort Wayne, IN	
33	1926	St Louis, MO	
34	1929	River Forest, IL	
35	1932	Milwaukee, WI	
36	1935	Cleveland, OH	
37	1938	St Louis, MO	
38	1941	Fort Wayne, IN	
39	1944	Saginaw, MI	
40	1947	Chicago, IL	Synod's 100th Anniversary. Synod changes name to The Lutheran Church—Missouri Synod.
41	1950	Milwaukee, WI	
42	1953	Houston, TX	
43	1956	St Paul, MN	

44	1959	San Francisco, CA	
45	1962	Cleveland, OH	
46	1965	Detroit, MI	Adoption of "Mission Affirmations."
47	1967	New York, NY	
48	1969	Denver, CO	Election of Dr. J.A.O. Preus. Declaration of altar and pulpit fellowship with The American Lutheran Church (ALC).
49	1971	Milwaukee, WI	
50	1973	New Orleans, LA	Concordia Seminary, St. Louis Faculty majority charged with false doctrine, leading to suspension and removal of Dr. John Tietjen as Seminary President, walk-out, and Seminex, and eventual split in Synod.
51	1975	Anaheim, CA	
52	1977	Dallas, TX	
53	1979	St Louis, MO	
54	1981	St Louis, MO	
55	1983	St Louis, MO	
56	1986	Indianapolis, IN	
57	1989	Wichita, KS	
58	1992	Pittsburgh, PA	
59	1995	St Louis, MO	
60	1998	St Louis, MO	
61	2001	St Louis, MO	
62	2004	St Louis, MO	
63	2007	Houston, TX	
64	2010	Houston, TX	
65	2013	St Louis, MO	
66	2016	Milwaukee, WI	
67	2019	Tampa, FL	

Roster of the English District—LCMS
(As of January 1, 2021)

Officers

Rev. Dr. Jamison J. Hardy, Bishop and President
Rev. Jeffrey G. Miskus, First Vice President (Lake Erie Region)
Rev. Ben C. Eder, Second Vice President (Eastern Region)
Rev. Robert A. Rogers, Third Vice President (Midwest Region)
Rev. Todd W. Arnold, Fourth Vice President (Western Region)
Rev. Luke T. Zimmerman, Secretary
Rev. Dr. David P. Stechholz, Bishop Emeritus
Rev. Dr. David H. Ritt, Bishop Emeritus

Circuit Visitors   (Visitation Circuit # and Name)

Rev. Dr. Martin Erhardt   (1, New York-New Jersey)

Rev. Robert Kieselowsky	(2, Philadelphia)
Rev. William Douthwaite	(3, Florida)
Rev. David Miller	(4, Georgia)
Rev. Dwayne Hendricks	(5, Buffalo)
Rev. Brian Westgate	(6, Pittsburgh)
Rev. Gregory Lutz	(7, Canada–East)
Rev. James Leistico	(8, Canada–West)
Rev. James Gau	(9, Cleveland East–Akron)
Rev. Joshua Moldenhauer	(10, ClevelandWest)
Rev. Brad Scott	(11, Detroit–South)
Rev. Daniel Grams	(12, Detroit–North)
Rev. Eric Forss	(13, Western Michigan)
Rev. Chad Trouten	(14, Indiana)
Rev. Anthony Oliphant	(15, Chicago–North)
Rev. James Huenink	(16, Chicago–South)
Rev. Fred Reaman	(17, Milwaukee)
Rev. Ted Laesch	(18, St. Louis)
Rev. Nick Wirtz	(19, Arizona–North)
Rev. Dr. Michael Morehouse	(20, Arizona–South)
Rev. Travis Lauterbach	(21, Nevada–Utah)
Rev. Steve Duescher	(22, San Diego)
Rev. Michael Payne	(23, Los Angeles)
Rev. Curt Binz	(24, San Francisco)

Executive Staff   (Executive & Support Staff, and Appointed are deployed)
Mrs. Gail Holzer, Assistant to the Bishop/President and School Ministry Executive (and Parish Education Committee Chair)
Rev. J. Derek Mathers, Assistant to the Bishop/President and Mission Executive (and Ministerial Health Commission Chair)
Mrs. Sally Naglich, Assistant to the Bishop/President for Business, Finance and Treasurer
Rev. David Thiele, LCEF Vice President (through October 2020), succeeded by Rev. Daniel Lepley, LCEF Vice President (began October 2020)

Support Staff and Appointed Positions
Mrs, Kathy Stanis, Executive Assistant to the Bishop/President (Pittsburgh)
Mr. Ron Grimm, Gift Planning Counselor (Toronto)
Mrs. Peggy Oke, Administrative Assistant to the Business Manager (Farmington, MI)
Mrs. Natalya Hrecznyj, Accounting Assistant (Farmington, MI)

Mrs. Holly Scheer, Communications Director (Cheyenne, WY)

Mr. Jim Bretthauer, Youth Ministry Committee Chair (Medina, OH)

Rev. Mark Braden, Continuing Education Chair (Detroit)

Rev. John Diener, Evangelization Committee Chair (Grand Rapids, MI)

Rev. Dr. David Dressel, Campus Ministry Committee Chair (Lansing, MI)

Rev. Daniel Grams, Constitutions & Membership Committee Chair (Detroit)

Rev. James Hennink, Lifeline Ministry Committee Chair (Chicago)

Rev. Raymond Kirk, District Endowment Fund Chair (Kitchener, ON)

Rev. Justin Laughridge, Mission Council Chair (Toronto)

Rev. Dr. Wayne Morton, Board of Directors, Chair (Shipshewana, IN)

Rev. Michael Scheer, Stewardship Committee Chair (Cleveland)

Rev. Dr. David Stechholz, District Archivist (Detroit)

Mr. Jim Thelen, Canada Corporation (CCEF) Chair (Windsor, ON)

Rev. Brian Westgate, Human Care & Disaster Relief Coordinator (Pittsburgh)

Congregations of the English District by Name
(As of October 1st, 2020)

Abiding Savior, North Royalton, OH

Advent, Zionsville, IN

Agnus Dei, Marshall, MI

All Saints, Slippery Rock, PA

Angelica, Allen Park, MI

Apostolic, Moses Lake, WA

Ascension, Atlanta, GA

Ascension, North Olmsted, OH

Ascension, Tucson, AZ

Ascension of Christ, Beverly Hills, MI

Beautiful Savior, Lees Summit, MO

Bethany, Chicago, IL

Bethany, Ewing, NJ

Bethany, Fort Wayne, IN

Bethesda, Chicago, IL

Blessed Sacrament, Hayden, ID

Borrego, Borrego Springs, CA

Calvary, Amherst, NY

Calvary, Mechanicsburg, PA

Catalina, Tucson, AZ

Celebration, Jacksonville, FL

Chapel of the Cross, Mission Hills, CA

Chapel of the Cross, Saint Louis, MO

Chatham Fields, Chicago, IL

Cho won (Korean), Palisades Park, NJ

Christ, Lake Mills, WI

Christ, Aurora, ON

Christ English, Chicago, IL

Christ Our Redeemer, Allen Park, MI

Christ the King, Grosse Pointe Woods, MI

Christ the Shepherd, Alpharetta, GA

Christus Rex, Rio Rico, AZ

Concordia, Akron, OH

Concordia, Berwyn, IL

Crosspoint, Sahuarita, AZ

Ephphatha Deaf, Chicago, IL

Epic, Shelby Twp., MI

Epiphany, Dorr, MI

Eternal Life, Mesa, AZ

Fairlawn, Fairlawn, OH

Faith, Arlington Heights, IL

Faith, Chesapeake, VA

Faith, Chicago, IL

Faith, Naples, FL

Faith, Overgaard, AZ

Faith, Tucson, AZ

Faith, Watertown, WI

Family of Christ, Phoenix, AZ

First, El Cajon, CA

First Trinity, Pittsburgh, PA

Gethsemane, Windsor, ON

Gloria Dei, Blue Bell, PA

Good Shepherd, Akron, OH

Good Shepherd, Toledo, OH

Grace, Akron, OH

Grace, Elyria, OH

Grace, Mitchell, ON

Grace, Oberlin, OH

Grace, Palisades Park, NJ

Grace, Redford, MI

Grace, Vine Grove, KY

Grace, Warminster, PA

Grace, Wyoming, MI

Grace English, Chicago, IL

Greenfield Park, West Allis, WI

Hales Corners, Hales Corners, WI

Highland Park, Los Angeles, CA

Holy Cross, Cleveland, OH

Holy Cross, (Hazelwood) Pittsburgh, PA

Holy Redeemer, Sandusky, MI

Holy Spirit, Elk Grove Village, IL

Holy Trinity, Albion, PA

Holy Trinity, Lakeview, MI

Holy Trinity, Tucson, AZ

Hope, Bellaire, MI

Hope, Fremont, CA

Hope, Grand Rapids, MI

Hope, Hastings, MN

Hope, Kitchener, ON

Hope Community, Syracuse, NY

Iglesia Cristiana Hispana, Cleveland, OH

Immanuel, Alexandria, VA

Immanuel, Flushing, NY

Immanuel, Howell, MI

Immanuel, Orange, CA

Jacob's Well, Fort Wayne, IN

King of Glory, Sylvania, OH

Living Hope, Racine, WI

Living Water, San Diego CA

Logos, Philadelphia, PA

Markham, Markham, IL

Martin Luther Chapel, East Lansing, MI

Martin Luther Chapel, Pennsauken, NJ

Messiah, Tucson, AZ

Messiah, Danville, CA

Messiah, Elmhurst, IL

Messiah, Forest Lake, MN

Messiah, Parker, AZ

Messiah, Princeton, NJ

Mount Calvary, Lititz, PA

335

Mount Olive, Cleveland Heights, OH

Mount Olive, Tucson, AZ

Nazareth, Buffalo, NY

New Beginnings, West Branch, MI

New Hope, Chicago, IL

New Life Chinese, San Francisco, CA

Our Savior, Hartland, MI

Our Savior's, Saint George, UT

Our Saviour, Valley Stream, NY

Our Saviour's, Chatham, ON

Peace, Fremont, IN

Peace, McMurray, PA

Peace, New Berlin, WI

Peace, O'Fallon, MO

Peace, Palm Desert, CA

Peace, Windsor, ON

Peace in the Valley, Benson, AZ

Pilgrim, Kenmore, NY

Prince of Peace, Stroh, IN

Prince of Peace, Medina, OH

Prince of Peace, Menomonee Falls, WI

Prince of Peace, Mesquite, NV

Redeemer, Elmhurst, IL

Redeemer, Fort Wayne, IN

Redeemer, Lincoln, NE

Redeemer, North Tonawanda, NY

Redeemer, Oakmont, PA

Redeemer, Sarnia, ON

Redeemer, St. Albans, NY

Rehoboth Afaan Oromo, Philadelphia, PA

Resurrection, Shawano, WI

Risen Christ, Plymouth, MI

Risen Savior, Green Valley, AZ

Saint John, Springfield, PA

Saint John the Divine, Chicago, IL

Saint John, Clarksburg, WV

Saint John's, Golden Lake (Germanicus), ON

Saint John's, Hannibal, MO

Saint John's, Pembroke, ON

Saint Luke, North York, ON

Saint Mark the Evangelist, Janesville, WI

Saint Mark, Mississauga, ON

Saint Mark, Sheboygan, WI

Saint Matthew, Toronto, ON

Saint Paul's, Long Beach, CA

Saint Paul's, St. Clair Shores, MI

Saint Thomas, Streetsboro, OH

Shepherd King, West Bloomfield, MI

Shepherd of the Coast, Palm Coast, FL

Shepherd of the Mountains, Pinetop, AZ

Shepherd of the Pines, Payson, AZ

Sherman Oaks, Sherman Oaks, CA

Saint Luke's, La Mesa, CA

Tree of Life, Inverness, FL

Trinity, Erie, PA

Trinity, La Porte, IN

Trinity, New Lenox, IL

Trinity, Ocala, FL

Trinity, San Dimas, CA

Trinity, Scarsdale, NY

Trinity, Villa Park, IL

West Portal, San Francisco, CA

Zion, Detroit, MI

Congregations of the English District by Region

(As of October 1, 2020)

Number (#) indicates the Visitation Circuit of each Congregation

1	New York-New Jersey	13	Central/Western Michigan
2	Philadelphia	14	Indiana
3	Florida	15	Chicago South
4	Georgia	16	Chicago North
5	Buffalo	17	Milwaukee
6	Pittsburgh	18	St. Louis
7	Canada East	19	Arizona North
8	Canada West	20	Arizona South
9	Cleveland East/Akron	21	Nevada/Utah
10	Cleveland West	22	San Diego
11	Detroit South/Toledo	23	Los Angeles
12	Detroit North	24	San Francisco

Eastern Region

All Saints, Slippery Rock, PA (6)

Ascension, Atlanta, GA (4)

Bethany, Ewing, NJ (1)

Calvary, Amherst, NY (5)

Calvary, Mechanicsburg, PA (2)

Celebration, Jacksonville, FL (3)

Cho won (Korean), Palisades Park, NJ (1)

Christ the Shepherd, Alpharetta, GA (4)

Faith, Chesapeake, VA (2)

Faith, Naples, FL (3)

First Trinity, Pittsburgh, PA (6)

Gloria Dei, Blue Bell, PA (2)

Grace, Palisades Park, NJ (1)

Grace, Warminster, PA (2)

Holy Cross, Pittsburgh, PA (6)

Hope Community, Syracuse, NY (5)

Holy Trinity, Albion, PA (5)

Immanuel, Alexandria, VA (2)

Immanuel (Korean), Flushing, Queens, NY (1)

Martin Luther Chapel, Pennsauken, NJ (1)

Logos, Philadelphia, PA (2)

Messiah, Princeton, NJ (1)

Mount Calvary, Lititz, PA (2)

Nazareth, Buffalo, NY (5)

Our Saviour, Valley Stream, NY (1)

Peace, McMurray, PA (6)

Pilgrim, Kenmore, NY (5)

Redeemer, North Tonawanda, NY (5)

Redeemer, Oakmont, PA (6)

Redeemer, St. Albans, Queens, NY (1)

Rehoboth Afaan Oromo, Philadelphia, PA (2)

Saint John, Springfield, PA (2)

Saint John, Clarksburg, WV (6)

Shepherd of the Coast, Palm Coast, FL (3)

Tree of Life, Inverness, FL (3)

Trinity, Erie, PA (5)

Trinity, Ocala, FL (3)

Trinity, Scarsdale, NY (1)

Lake Erie Region

Abiding Savior, North Royalton, OH (9)

Advent, Zionsville, IN (14)

Agnus Dei, Marshall, MI (13)

Angelica, Allen Park, MI (11)

Ascension, North Olmsted, OH (10)

Ascension of Christ, Beverly Hills, MI (12)

Bethany, Fort Wayne, IN (14)

Christ, Aurora, ON (7)

Christ Our Redeemer, Allen Park, MI (11)

Christ the King, Grosse Pointe Woods, MI (11)

Concordia, Akron, OH (9)

Epic, Shelby Twp, MI (12)

Epiphany, Dorr, MI (13)

Fairlawn, Fairlawn, OH (9)

Gethsemane, Windsor, ON (8)

Good Shepherd, Akron, OH (9)

Good Shepherd, Toledo, OH (11)

Grace, Akron, OH (9)

Grace, Elyria, OH (10)

Grace, Mitchell, ON (8)

Grace, Oberlin, OH (10)

Grace, Redford, MI (12)

Grace, Wyoming, MI (13)

Holy Cross, Cleveland, OH (10)

Holy Redeemer, Sandusky, MI (12)

Holy Trinity, Lakeview, MI (13)

Hope, Bellaire, MI (13)

Hope, Grand Rapids, MI (13)

Hope, Kitchener, ON (8)

Iglesia Cristiana Hispana, Cleveland, OH (10)

Immanuel, Howell, MI (13)

Jacob's Well, Fort Wayne, IN (14)

King of Glory, Sylvania, OH (11)

Martin Luther Chapel, East Lansing, MI (13)

Mount Olive, Cleveland Heights, OH (9)

New Beginnings, West Branch, MI (12)

Our Savior, Hartland, MI (13)

Our Saviour's, Chatham, ON (8)

Peace, Fremont, IN (14)

Peace, Windsor, ON (8)

Prince of Peace, Stroh, IN (14)

Prince of Peace, Medina, OH (10)

Redeemer, Fort Wayne, IN (13)

Redeemer, Sarnia, ON (8)

Risen Christ, Plymouth, MI (11)

Saint John's, Golden Lake (Germanicus), ON (7)

Saint John's, Pembroke, ON (7)

Saint Luke, North York, Toronto, ON (7)

Saint Mark, Mississauga, ON (7)

Saint Matthew, Scarborough, Toronto, ON (7)

Saint Paul's, St. Clair Shores, MI (12)

Saint Thomas, Streetsboro, OH (9)

Shepherd King, West Bloomfield, MI (12)

Trinity, La Porte, IN (14)

Zion, Detroit, MI (11)

Midwest Region

Beautiful Savior, Lees Summit, MO (18)

Bethany, Chicago, IL (16)

Bethesda, Chicago, IL (16)

Chapel of the Cross, St. Louis Co. North, MO (18)

338

Chatham Fields, Chicago, IL (15)

Christ, Lake Mills, WI (17)

Christ English, Chicago, IL (16)

Concordia, Berwyn, IL (15)

Ephphatha Deaf, Chicago, IL (15)

Faith, Arlington Heights, IL (16)

Faith, Chicago, IL (15)

Faith, Watertown, WI (17)

Grace, Vine Grove, KY (18)

Grace English, Chicago, IL (16)

Greenfield Park, West Allis, WI (17)

Hales Corners, Hales Corners, WI (17)

Holy Spirit, Elk Grove Village, IL (16)

Hope, Hastings, MN (17)

Living Hope, Racine, WI (17)

Markham, Markham, IL (15)

Messiah, Elmhurst, IL (15)

Messiah, Forest Lake, MN (17)

New Hope, Chicago, IL (15)

Peace, New Berlin, WI (17)

Peace, O'Fallon, MO (18)

Prince of Peace, Menomonee Falls, WI (17)

Redeemer, Elmhurst, IL (16)

Redeemer, Lincoln, NE (18)

Resurrection, Shawano, WI (17)

Saint John the Divine, Chicago, IL (15)

Saint John's, Hannibal, MO (18)

Saint Mark, Sheboygan, WI (17)

Saint Mark the Evangelist, Janesville, WI (17)

Trinity, New Lenox, IL (15)

Trinity, Villa Park, IL (16)

Western Region

Apostolic, Moses Lake, WA (24)

Ascension, Tucson, AZ (20)

Blessed Sacrament, Hayden (Coeur d'Alene), ID (24)

Borrego, Borrego Springs, CA (22)

Catalina, Tucson, AZ (20)

Chapel of the Cross, Mission Hills, CA (23)

Christus Rex, Rio Rico, AZ (20)

Crosspoint, Sahuarita, AZ (20)

Eternal Life, Mesa, AZ (19)

Faith, Overgaard, AZ (19)

Faith, Tucson, AZ (20)

Family of Christ, Phoenix, AZ (19)

First, El Cajon, CA (22)

Highland Park, Los Angeles, CA (23)

Holy Trinity, Tucson, AZ (20)

Hope, Fremont, CA (24)

Immanuel, Orange, CA (23)

Living Water, San Diego CA (22)

Peace, Palm Desert, CA (23)

Messiah, Tucson, AZ (20)

Messiah, Danville, CA (24)

Messiah, Parker, AZ (19)

Mount Olive, Tucson, AZ (20)

New Life Chinese, San Francisco, CA (24)

Our Savior's, Saint George, UT (21)

Peace in the Valley, Benson, AZ (20)

Prince of Peace, Mesquite, NV (21)

Risen Savior, Green Valley, AZ (20)

Saint Paul's, Long Beach, CA (23)

Shepherd of the Mountains, Pinetop, AZ (19)

Shepherd of the Pines, Payson, AZ (19)

Sherman Oaks, Sherman Oaks, CA (23)

Saint Luke's, La Mesa, CA (22)

Trinity, San Dimas, CA (23)

West Portal, San Francisco, CA (24)

The Ordained Clergy Roster of the English District
93 on Emeritus (retired) status with asterisk *
(As of October 1, 2020)

Adams, David
Alles, Stephen C.
Anderson, Jeffrey O.*
Anderson, Paul W.
Andrae, Eric
Andrae, Hans*
Arnold, Todd W.
Aufdenkampe, Charles R.*
Bacon, Paul E.
Baue, Frederic*
Bauernfeind, Peter A.
Beckmann, William C*
Beffrey, Ryan D.
Bell, Larry
Benfey, Matthias
Berkesch, Wayne C.*
Bingue, Jean
Binz, Curtis
Bischoff, Clifford L.*
Boelter, Randy S.
Boudreau, Kenneth
Braden, Mark P.
Braun, Thomas
Bruggeman, Robert
Bumby, Norman A.*
Burch, Don E.*
Burfeind, Peter M.
Burke, Robert F.*
Burmeister, Devin
Carlson, Eric
Claycombe, Howard E.*
Cockran, Kurt
Dargatz, Robert
De La Rosa, Victor Manuel
De Santo, Steven
Diener, John
Dietrich, Joel
Dorr, Paul

Douthwaite, William J.
Drehman, Arthur
Dressel, David A.
Drews, Michael P.*
Drews, Richard D.*
Duescher, Steven
Duy, Douglas
Dwyer, Curtis E.
Ebert, Mark H.
Eder, Ben
Eggold, Paul E.*
Ellis, Roger C.*
Elseroad, Kevin P.
Elsner, James*
Engler, Thomas
Erhardt, Martin
Erickson, John B.*
Ernst, Michael S.*
Esala, Luther P.
Esget, Christopher
Fabry, Joseph P.*
Fedder, Andrew
Fiene, John*
Fitzpatrick, Robert L.*
Forss, Eric C.
Fox, Charles
Frese, Michael
Fuehrer, Nathan
Gai, Philip
Gandy, Amadeus
Gau, James
Gerike, Henry V.*
Gerlach, Fred
Goerss, John M.*
Grady, James
Grams, Daniel
Grieser, Winston
Gruen, Jonathan P.

Gruenwald, Daniel J.
Haberkost, Daniel R.
Haberstock, Paul*
Hahn, Ernest N.*
Halboth, Timothy P.
Hardy, Jamison J.
Hendricks, Dwayne
Henry, Patrick*
Hicks, Steven
Hildebrandt, Bradford
Hoag, Douglas E.
Hoeppner, Seth
Hoke, James*
Holls, Joel
Holzerland, Timothy A.
Huenink, James
Hursh, Terry*
Ingmire, Richard L.*
Jameson, Leon
Jasper, James W.*
Johann, Simon S.
Johnson, Keith L.
Just, Christian
Kade, Timothy
Kaiser, David
Kaster, Dale W.
Katari, Shadrach
Kaufmann, Reinauld
Kerr, J. Wayne
Kieselowsky, Robert
Kimari, Wallace J.
Kinslow, Keith
Kirk, Raymond*
Klein, Richard
Koester, Paul R.*
Kogutkiewicz, Chad
Koontz, Adam
Kramer, Kenneth*
Krause, Paul*
Krey, Theodore
Kunsman, Jeffrey*
Lach, Noble P.*
Laesch, Theodore
Laue, Ronald H.*
Laughridge, Justin

Ledic, Peter
Leistico, James
Lentner, Charles D.*
Leuthaeuser, Larry*
Liefeld, David R.*
Loree, Larry
Lorenz, Jonathan
Luck, Gerald
Lunneberg, Allen*
Lutz, Gregory R.
Maass, Robert W.*
Mackay, Marcus
Maconachy, Samuel*
Mader, Myron G.*
Marklevitz, Zachary
Marsh, Prentice D.
Mathers, J. Derek
Matz, Brett
Maxon, Bradford C.
Mayer, Robert F.*
McCall, Jonathan
McClure, Garry D.*
Mealwitz, Peter E.*
Meier, William E.*
Meilaender, Gilbert*
Mertz, Robert*
Michel, Gregory
Millard, Ronald
Miller, David
Millhorn, Henry O.*
Mills, Peter E.
Mirtschin, Neville*
Miskus, Jeffrey G.
Moldenhauer, Joshua
Molitoris, Joseph*
Morales, Christian G.
Morehouse, Michael
Morton, R. Wayne*
Musolf, Gregory
Naumann, William
Naumann, Edward
Naumann, Gordon
Naumann, Jonathan
Oehlerts, Gary*
Okpisz, Steven

Oliphant, Anthony
Olse, Noel
Park, Jung Hun
Patt, Richard W.*
Payne, Matthew
Petersen, David
Pierson, Mark
Pies, Frank J.*
Pillay, Dereck
Pittelko, Roger D.*
Pourchot, Daniel*
Pratt, Brian
Predoehl, Theodore G.*
Prok, Myron K.*
Radke, Edward F.*
Rand, Neil*
Rankin III, Kenneth C.*
Reaman, Frederic J.
Rendahl, Craig
Repp, Arthur C.*
Retzlaff, Brady
Reuning, Daniel G.*
Rey, Phillip Sang
Ring, Robb
Ritt, David H.*
Robinson, James
Rogers, Robert
Rutter, David
Sabol, Alexander
Sachs, Jonathan
Sanders, Thomas J.*
Saylor, Kevin*
Schaetzle, George*
Scheer, Michael
Schindler, Vernon*
Schmidlin, Paul R.
Schmidt, Justin R.
Schmidt, Karl E.*
Schmidt, Travis
Schmitt, David R.
Schneekloth, Larry G.
Schneider, Ryan
Scholl, Louis N.*
Scholle, Raymond*
Schultz, Gary

Scicluna, Jon D.
Scott, Bradford E.
Seaver, Todd
Seaver, Wade
Seifferlein, Christopher
Simon, Jordan
Simpson, Scott E.
Speaks, Keith
Spittel, Douglas
Stechholz, David P.*
Stein, David T.*
Steinke, Mark*
Stennett, Arthur R.*
Sterling, Aaron D.
Stevens, Robert
Stieve, John W.*
Strohschein, John*
Stuckmeyer, C. David*
Stuenkel, Roger*
Sutterer, Paul*
Sutterer, Steven
Tannahill, David*
Tauscher, Robert W.
Taylor, Michael S.
Teeple, Jeffrey
Thagarajan, Alfred
Thiele, David L.*
Thoma, Christopher I.
Thompson, Adam
Tillinger, Dusan
Timmermann, Norman A.*
Toth, Dusan*
Treglown, Donald E.
Trouten, Chad
Ulm, Joshua
Urlaub, Bradley
Van der Bloemen, Thomas*
Varsogea, Charles
Viets, Mark*
Voelker, Robert E.
Vogel, Guy A.*
Vogel, Larry M.
Warner, Daniel M.
Wedajo, Alemayehu
Weinrich, Charles A.*

Weldon, Robert
Westgate, Brian P.
Williams, Herman J.*
Wirtz, Isaac
Wirtz, Nicholas D.
Witt, James*
Wood, Christian
Wood, Mark

Wright, C.J.
Wyppich, Raymond W.*
Yoder, Roger
York, Ronald
Young, David Mark
Zill, Marcus
Zimmerman, Luke
Zwonitzer, Rodney

* Several emeriti pastors serving as an Assistant to the Pastor, Archdeacon, Minister of Music, or in some capacity in addition to supply-preaching and serving as a Vacancy Pastor.

Bibliography

A Centennial of Grace 1888-1988 First English Lutheran Church. No publisher is listed. The booklet is dated July 17, 1988.

Adams, Bruce W. *"Robert Barnes: Luther's Ambassador to the English"* (pamphlet). Adelaide, Australia: Lutheran Laymen's League "Life at Best", 1986.

---------------------- *"An English Prior and Reformer Speaks to Our Times: Dr. Robert Barnes (1495-1540), The Lutheran.* February 10th, 1986, pg. 40.

Bacon, Paul, ed. *Journal of English District Pastors* (JEDP), An unofficial journal of theological opinion and scholarship. Vol. 1, No. 1—Vol. 13, No. 1. Published at Bethesda Lutheran Church, 6803 N. Campbell Ave., Chicago, IL, 1988-2001.

Baepler, Walter A. *A Century of Grace: A History of the Missouri Synod – 1847-1947.* St. Louis, MO: Concordia Publishing House, 1947.

Baue, Frederic W. *The Epistles of Herman Noodix.* St. Louis: Pergola Press LLC, 2011.

Baue, Frederic W., Fenton, John W., Forss, Eric C., Pies, Frank J., and Pless, John T., , Eds. *Shepherd the Church: Essays in Pastoral Theology Honoring Bishop Roger D. Pittelko.* Fort Wayne, IN: Concordia Theological Seminary Press, 2002.

Behrhorst, Wallace. *St. John's College, 1893-1986.* Winfield, KS: St. John's College Alumni Association, 2007.

Bente, Frederick. *American Lutheranism, Vol. I, Early History of American Lutheranism and The Tennessee Synod.* St. Louis: Concordia Publishing House, 1919.

Bente, Frederick, ed. *Historical Introduction to the Symbolic Books, Concordia Triglotta: The Symbolical Books of the Evangelical Lutheran Church* (Book of Concord). Concordia Publishing House: St. Louis, 1921.

Book Review, online. *"The Amazon Book Review," An Historical Visit to Michael Keinadt's Virginia / Old Coiner Homes and Farm Tours*, by Lewis Coiner (paperback).

Braun, Mark E. *A Tale of Two Synods.* Milwaukee: Northwestern Publishing House, 2003.

Burkee, James C. *Power, Politics, and the Missouri Synod: A Conflict That Changed American Christianity.* Minneapolis: Fortress Press, 2011.

"Christ Frees, Christ Unites," a booklet for a "Special Convention of the English District of The Lutheran Church—Missouri Synod," Chicago, IL. Northlake Center, Northlake, Illinois, September 19-21, 1975.

The Church of Our Savior – Evangelical Lutheran. 75th Anniversary (Diamond Jubilee) Service Folder. Baltimore, MD: 1967.

The Common Service with Music. As adopted by the (English) Evangelical Lutheran Synod of Missouri and Other States. Pittsburgh, PA: American Lutheran Publication Board, 1906.

The Complete History of Capitol Drive Lutheran Church. (A photocopied history pamphlet). Capitol Drive Lutheran Church: Milwaukee, WI, 2013.

Confessional Lutheran Migrations to America, 150th Anniversary. (Published by the Eastern District of The Lutheran Church—Missouri Synod, in observance of the 150th Anniversary of these Migrations of German Lutherans), 1988.

Dallmann, William. *My Life: Personal Recollections of a Lutheran Missionary, Pastor, Churchman, Lecturer, Author.* St. Louis, Concordia Publishing House, 1945.

------------------ *"Robert Barnes: English Lutheran Martyr."* Decatur, Illinois: Repristination Press (originally published by Concordia Publishing House, St. Louis, MO), republished, 1997.

------------------ *"The English Work of the Missouri Synod,"* Concordia Historical Institute Quarterly, Vol. 70, No. 3. St. Louis: Concordia Historical Institute, Fall, 1997. [This article is reprinted with a forward in this CHIQ; it is a reprint of Dallmann's article in the 75th anniversary book, *Ebenezer*, edited by W.H.T. Dau (pp. 422-430).]

Dau, W.H.T., ed.. *Ebenezer:* Reviews of the Work of the Missouri Synod during Three Quarters of a Century. St. Louis: Concordia Publishing House, 1922.

Eberhard, David, ed.. *Histories of the Lutheran Churches in the City of Detroit, Michigan.* Dau Church History Library, Historic Trinity: Detroit, 2000.

Eckhardt, H.P. *The English District: A Historical Sketch.* Published by the English District of the Evangelical Lutheran Synod of Missouri, Ohio, and Other States, 1946.

English District—LCMS

Convention Workbook of the 39th Convention of the English District of The Lutheran Church—Missouri Synod, Assembled at Concordia Teachers College, River Forest, IL, June 23-25, 1972.

Convention Workbook of the 42nd Convention of the English District-LCMS, Concordia College, Milwaukee, WI, 1978.

Convention Workbook of the 44th Convention of the English District-LCMS, Concordia College, River Forest, IL, 1982.

Convention Workbook of the 47th Convention of the English District-LCMS, Concordia College, River Forest, IL, 1991.

Convention Workbook of the 48th Convention of the English District-LCMS, Concordia University, River Forest, IL, 1994.

Convention Workbook of the 49th Convention of the English District-LCMS, Concordia College, River Forest, IL, 1997.

Convention Workbook of the 50th Convention of the English District-LCMS, Concordia College, River Forest, IL, 2000.

Convention Workbook of the 51st Convention of the English District-LCMS, Concordia College, River Forest, IL, 2003.

Convention Workbook of the 52nd Convention of the English District-LCMS, Hyatt Regency Hotel, Schaumburg, IL, 2006.

Convention Workbook of the 53rd Convention of the English District-LCMS, Hales Corners Lutheran Church & School, Hales Corners, WI, 2009.

Convention Workbook of the 54th Convention of the English District of The Lutheran Church—Missouri Synod, Concordia Seminary, St. Louis, and the Sheraton Westport Lakeside Chalet, MO, 2012.

English District—LCMS

Proceedings of the 17th Convention of the English District of The Evangelical Lutheran Synod of Missouri, Ohio, and Other States. Held at Concordia Teachers College, River Forest, IL, 1937.

Proceedings of the 22nd Convention of the English District of The Evangelical Lutheran Synod of Missouri, Ohio. And Other States. Held at the Evangelical Lutheran Institute for the Deaf, Detroit, MI, 1945.

Proceedings of the 32nd Convention of the English District of The Lutheran Church—Missouri Synod. Assembled at Concordia College, Milwaukee, WI, June 14-17, 1960.

Proceedings of the Golden Anniversary Convention of the English District of The Lutheran Church—Missouri Synod. Assembled at Concordia Teachers College, River Forest, IL, June 13-16, 1961.

Proceedings of the 34th Convention of the English District of The Lutheran Church—Missouri Synod. Assembled at Concordia Teachers College, River Forest, IL, June 4-7, 1963.

Proceedings of the 37th Convention of the English District of The Lutheran Church—Missouri Synod, Concordia Lutheran College, Ann Arbor, MI, 1968.

Proceedings of the 38th Convention of the English District of The Lutheran Church—Missouri Synod, Concordia Lutheran College, Ann Arbor, MI, 1970

Proceedings of the 39th Convention of the English District of The Lutheran Church—Missouri Synod, Concordia Teachers College, River Forest, IL, 1972.

Proceedings of the 40th Convention of the English District of The Lutheran Church—Missouri Synod, Concordia Teachers College, River Forest, IL, 1974.

Proceedings, "Special Convention" of the English District of The Lutheran Church—Missouri Synod, "Position Statement," Northlake Center, Northlake, IL, 1975.

Proceedings of the 41st Convention of the English District of The Lutheran Church—Missouri Synod, Concordia Teachers College, River Forest, IL, 1976.

Proceedings of the 42nd Convention of the English District of The Lutheran Church—Missouri Synod, Concordia College, Milwaukee, WI, 1978.

Proceedings of the 43rd Convention of the English District of The Lutheran Church—Missouri Synod, Concordia College, Ann Arbor, MI. 1980.

Proceedings of the 44th Convention of the English District of The Lutheran Church—Missouri Synod, Concordia College, Milwaukee, WI, 1982.

Proceedings of the 45th Convention of the English District of The Lutheran Church—Missouri Synod, Concordia College, River Forest, IL, 1985.

Proceedings of the 46th Convention of the English District of The Lutheran Church—Missouri Synod, Concordia College, River Forest, IL, 1988.

Proceedings of the 47th Convention of the English District of The Lutheran Church—Missouri Synod, Concordia College (University), River Forest, IL, 1991.

Proceedings of the 48th Convention of the English District of The Lutheran Church—Missouri Synod, Concordia University, River Forest, IL, 1994.

Proceedings of the 49th Convention of the English District of The Lutheran Church—Missouri Synod, Concordia University, River Forest, IL, 1997.

Proceedings of the 50th Convention of the English District of The Lutheran Church—Missouri Synod, Concordia University, River Forest, IL, 2000.

Proceedings of the 51st Convention of the English District of The Lutheran Church—Missouri Synod, Concordia University, River Forest, IL, 2003.

Proceedings of the 52nd Convention of the English District of The Lutheran Church—Missouri Synod, Hyatt Regency Hotel, Schaumburg, IL, 2006.

Proceedings of the 53rd Convention of the English District of The Lutheran Church—Missouri Synod, Hales Corners Lutheran Church & School, Hales Corners, WI, 2009.

Proceedings of the 54th Convention of the English District of The Lutheran Church—Missouri Synod, Concordia Seminary, St. Louis and the Sheraton Westport Lakeside Chalet, MO, WI, 2012.

Proceedings of the 55th Convention of the English District of The Lutheran Church—Missouri Synod, Concordia University, Ann Arbor, MI, 2015.

Proceedings of the 56th Convention of the English District of The Lutheran Church—Missouri Synod, Concordia University, Ann Arbor, MI, 2018.

English District—LCMS, Board of Directors

"Minutes" of the Board of Directors, English District-LCMS, Schiller Park, IL, June 25th, 1976.

"Minutes"'' of the Board of Directors, English District-LCMS, at Schiller Park, IL, February 12th & 13th, 1978.

Minutes"'' of the Board of Directors, English District-LCMS, at Chicago, IL, August 22nd & 23rd, 1988.

"Minutes," Board of Directors, English District-LCMS, at Romulus (Detroit Metro International Airport), IL, May 15th-16th, 1990, p. 7-8.

"Minutes" of the Board of Directors, English District-LCMS, at Romulus, MI, September 20th & 21st, 1994.

"Minutes" of the Board of Directors, English District-LCMS, tele-conference, October 13th, 1994.

"Minutes" of the Board of Directors, English District-LCMS, at Romulus, MI, January 15th-16th, 1995.

"Minutes" of the Board of Directors, English District-LCMS, at Romulus, MI, January 16th-17th, 1996.

"Minutes" of the Board of Directors, English District-LCMS, at Romulus, MI, April 16th-17th, 1996.

"Minutes" of the Board of Directors, English District-LCMS, at Romulus, MI, September 8th-10th, 1997.

"Minutes" of the Board of Directors, English District-LCMS, at Romulus, MI, November 11th-12th, 1997.

"Minutes" of the Board of Directors, English District-LCMS, at Romulus, MI, January 13th-14th, 1998.

"Minutes" of the Board of Directors, English District-LCMS, at Romulus, MI, August 11th-12th, 1998.

"Minutes" of the Board of Directors, English District-LCMS, at Romulus, MI, January, 9th-10th, 1999.

"Minutes" of the Board of Directors, English District-LCMS, at Romulus, MI, May 9th-10th, 2000.

"Minutes" of the Board of Directors, English District-LCMS, at Romulus, MI, November 6th-7th, 2001.

"Minutes" of the Board of Directors, English District-LCMS, at Romulus, MI, January 22nd-23rd, 2002.

"Minutes" of the Board of Directors, English District-LCMS, at Romulus, MI, May 6th-7th, 2002.

"Minutes" of the Board of Directors, English District-LCMS, at Trinity Evangelical Lutheran Church, Villa Park, and New Hope Lutheran Ministries, Chicago, August 12th-13th, 2002.

"Minutes" of the Board of Directors, English District-LCMS, at Romulus, MI, April 29th-30th, 2003.

"Minutes" of the Board of Directors, English District-LCMS, at Romulus, MI, May 3rd-4th, 2004.

"Minutes" of the Board of Directors, English District-LCMS, at Romulus (airport) and Farmington, MI (English District office), August 9th-10th, 2004.

"Minutes" of the Board of Directors, English District-LCMS, at Martin Luther Chapel, Pennsauken, NJ, August 8th-10th, 2005.

"Minutes" of the Board of Directors, English District-LCMS, at Romulus, MI, January 17th-18th, 2006.

The English District Bulletin, Vol. LXVI. *The Lutheran Witness – Part II*. St. Louis: Concordia Publishing House, July 15th, 1947.

"English District Remains Together as Convention Avoids Dissolution," *Lutheran Witness Reporter*. St. Louis: The Lutheran Church—Missouri Synod, July 20th, 1975.

The English District Story. Reprinted from the English District Witness, Supplement No. 5, "How the English Synod Became Missouri's Expandable District." March 7, 1961.

English Evangelical Lutheran Synod of Missouri and Other States. *Proceedings* of the 6th Convention of the English Evangelical Lutheran Synod of Missouri and Other States. Held at Detroit, MI (printed by American Lutheran Publication Board, Pittsburg[h], PA), July 5th-11th, 1899.

Evangelical Lutheran Hymnbook (ELHB). St. Louis: Concordia Publishing House, 1912.

First English Evangelical Lutheran Church 50th Anniversary, 1888-1938. New Orleans: Published by Louis T. Duckert Print, 1938.

Forty Years of LCMS District Statistics: Based on Lutheran Annual data for years 1970-2011. Prepared by LCMS Research Services: St. Louis, March, 2013.

Forster, Walter P. *Zion on the Mississippi*. St. Louis: Concordia Publishing House, 1953.

Free English Lutheran Conference, *Proceedings* of a Free English Lutheran Conference, held in the Town of Gravelton, Wayne Co., MO, August 17-20, A.D. 1872. Published in Columbus, OH, by John Gassmann, Printer, 1872.

Fry, C. George and Kurz, Joel R., eds. *Lively Stone: The Autobiography of Berthold von Schenk*. Delhi, NY: American Lutheran Publicity Bureau, 2006.

Granquist, Mark. *A New History: Lutherans in America*. Minneapolis: Fortress Press, 2015.

Grimm, Harold J. *The Reformation Era: 1500-1650*, second edition. New York: Macmillan Publishing Co., Inc., 1973.

Hamm, Dick. "The Resurrection of Middle Judicatories," Columbia Partnership (online), 2010.

Harrison, Matthew. Letter to the LCMS concerning COVID-19 Vaccines and CTCR sheet on "The LCMS and COVID-19 Vaccines: Facts and Considerations," online, January 21, 2021.

Hemmeter, H.B. "The Missouri Synod and English Work," *Concordia Theological Monthly*, Vol. XVII, May 1946, No. 5.

Henkel, Socrates. *History of the Evangelical Lutheran Tennessee Synod*. Henkel Press: New Market, VA., 1890.

Interviews (phone or face-to-face or via e-mail), March-August, 2020, with the Revs. Paul Bacon, Randy Boelter, Joe Fabry, William Fackler, Ron Farah, Frank Pies, Roger Pittelko, David Ritt, John Stieve, Jon Vieker, Larry Vogel, Brian Westgate, current pastors of the Detroit Circuits of the English District including the author's own Pastor, the Rev. Father Mark Braden, and the Rev. Tim Halboth, who allowed the author to delve into the files of his late father, the Rev. Dr. Victor Halboth, Jr.

Kidner, Derek. *Psalms 73-150*. Tyndale Old Testament Commentaries. London: Inter-Varsity Press, 1975.

Kretzmann, Karl. *The Atlantic District and Its Antecedents*. (Also known as: *The Atlantic District of the Evangelical Lutheran Synod of Missouri, Ohio, and Other States and Its Antecedents*). Published by Resolution of the District in the Year of its 25th Anniversary, 1931. Erie, PA: The Erie Printing Co., 1932.

Kurth, Erwin. *Catechetical Helps: Revised and Expanded*. St. Louis: Concordia Publishing House, 1941, 1997.

Lehman, Helmut T., General Editor; Wentz, Abdel Ross. *Luther's Works: Volume 36, Word and Sacrament II*. Philadelphia, Fortress Press, 1959.

Lueker, Erwin L., ed. *Lutheran Cyclopedia*. St. Louis: Concordia Publishing House, 1975.

Lueker, Erwin L.; Poellot, Luther; Jackson, Paul, eds. (2000). *Christian Cyclopedia* (Online ed.). St. Louis: Concordia Publishing House, Retrieved September 23rd, 2013. Information found in the online history of the Tennessee Synod in *Christian Cyclopedia*.

"Lutheran Accent," Vol. 2, No. 7 and Vol. 2, No. 8, July and August, 1976 (Editor, the Rev. Omar Stuenkel), published by the English District-LCMS.

The Lutheran Annual 2020 of The Lutheran Church—Missouri Synod. Compiled by the LCMS Office of the Secretary and Rosters, Statistics, and Research Services. St. Louis: Concordia Publishing House, 2020.

The Lutheran Church—Missouri Synod. *Statistical Yearbooks* of The Lutheran Church—Missouri Synod, 1934-1994. St. Louis: Concordia Publishing House, 1934-1994.

The Lutheran Hymnal. Authorized by the Synods Constituting The Evangelical Lutheran Synodical Conference of North America. St. Louis: Concordia Publishing House, 1941.

Lutheran Service Book. Prepared by The Commission on Worship of The Lutheran Church—Missouri Synod. St. Louis: Concordia Publishing House, 2006.

The Lutheran Study Bible. English Standard Version (ESV). St. Louis: Concordia Publishing House, 2009.

Marquart, Kurt E. *Anatomy of an Explosion: Missouri in Lutheran Perspective.* Fort Wayne, IN: Concordia Theological Seminary Press, 1977.

Marty, Martin E. Address to the English Synod, *"A New Song for a New People"* p. 18. English District Office, Archival files in the Museum Room.

McCain, Paul T. ed. *Concordia: The Lutheran Confessions: A Reader's edition of the Book of Concord.* Second Edition. Concordia Publishing House: St. Louis, 2005.

Meyer, Carl S. ed. *Moving Frontiers: Readings in the History of the Lutheran Church—Missouri Synod.* St. Louis: Concordia Publishing House, 1964.

Mueller, Martin W. *Amazing Comeback: Survey of English District History.* An English District 75th-Anniversary Publication, 1986.

Mundinger, Carl S. *Before The Beginning: A Biography of John Peter Baden.* Winfield, KS: Serialized manuscript in the April 1967 through May 1968 issues of the *St. John's Report.*

Nelson, E. Clifford, ed. *The Lutherans in North America.* Philadelphia: Fortress Press, 1975.

Nafzger, Samuel H. *An Introduction to The Lutheran Church—Missouri Synod.* (pamphlet) St. Louis: Concordia Publishing House, 2007.

Nissen, Eugene W. *The Bonnets From Strasburg.* Self-published book, 2010.

----------------- *The Bonnets From Zanesville.* Self-published book, 2009.

Patten, Howard J. *Concordia: "Hope Is Remembering With Praise."* Conover, NC: Concordia Lutheran Church, 1980.

Pearce, E. Geo. "The Story of the Lutheran Church in Britain Through Four Centuries of History." Published by The Evangelical Lutheran Church of England (ELCE), 1969.

Petersen, David H. "Bishop, Pastor, Deacon," *Gottesdienst*, Trinity 2020, Vol. 28, No. 2, published quarterly by the Evangelical Lutheran Liturgical Press of St. Paul Evangelical Lutheran Church, Kewanee, IL, 2020.

Predoehl, Theodore C. "Prelude," in *Zion Lutheran Church: 150th Anniversary, 1857-2007.* Unpublished church history, 1972.

Rast, Larry. *Nineteenth-Century Lutheranism in the American South and West: Ministry and Mission,* STM Thesis. Fort Wayne: Concordia Theological Seminary, 1995.

Reed, Luther Dotterer. *The Lutheran Liturgy.* Philadelphia: Fortress Press, 1947.

Scaer, David P. "Letter" to the Rev. David P. Stechholz, in English District archive files, May 10th, 1994.

Schumacher, William W. Convention Essay: "Why Us? Remembering to Understand," 54th Convention of the English District-LCMS. Westport Lakeside Chapel, MO, 2012.

"Sing a New Song," Convention packet for the First Convention of the English Synod Of the Evangelical Lutheran Church. Held at Arlington Heights, IL, pp. 1-23, and Constitution: November 12th-13th, 1976.

Sorrells, Nancy. "Huge family left mark on Augusta Co. history," "News Leader" (part of the USA Today Network) – On-line, February 20th, 2015.

Stapelton, A., Editor and Publisher. *The Henkel Memorial: Historical, Geographical, and Biographical.* A Serial Publication. York, PA: The Henkel Memorial Association, 1910.

Stechholz, David P. *Faith-Driven---Future Focused: The English District Celebrates 100 Years (Centennial Year 2011-2012).* St. Louis: *Concordia Historical Institute Quarterly,* Vol. 85, No. 1, Spring 2012.

-------------- *Love, Hope, and Faith: Anecdotes from the Building Programs of Three Churches.* Lulu Publishing Services, 2019.

Steffens, D.H. *Doctor Carl Ferdinand Wilhelm Walther.* Philadelphia: The Lutheran Publication Society, 1917.

Stein, Fred C. and Lieske, H. William. "Old Gravelton Revisited," *Concordia Historical Institute Quarterly,* Vol. XX, No. 4, January, 1948. Official Organ of the Concordia Historical Institute. St. Louis, MO: 1948.

-------------- "A Description of the Cradle of the English District After 100 Years," *The Lutheran Witness: The English District Edition,* Vol. XCI, No. 4. Concordia Publishing House: St. Louis, March 10, 1972.

Suelflow, August R. *The Heart of Missouri.* (A History of the Western District of The Lutheran Church—Missouri Synod). St. Louis: Concordia Publishing House, 1954.

Sunday School Hymnal. Published by Authority of The English Evangelical Lutheran Synod of Missouri and Other States. St. Louis: Concordia Publishing House, 1901.

Todd, Mary. *Authority Vested: A Story of Identity and Change in the Lutheran Church—Missouri Synod.* Grand Rapids, MI: Wm. B. Eerdmans Publishing Co., 2000.

Vieker, Jon D. *The Father's Faith, the Children's Song: Missouri Synod Lutheranism Encounters American Evangelicalism in Its Hymnals, Hymn Writers, and Hymns, 1889-1912.* Dissertation. St. Louis: Concordia Seminary, 2014.

Wikipedia, the Free On-line Encyclopedia, "Concordia College (North Carolina)".

Wilson, Donn. *The Word-of-God Conflict in the Lutheran Church Missouri Synod in the 20th Century,* (Master of Theology Thesis). Luther Seminary, Digital Commons @ Luther Seminary, Spring, 2018.

Young, Rosa. *Light in the Dark Belt: The Story of Rosa Young As Told By Herself.* St. Louis: Concordia Publishing House, 1950; revised edition 1914.

Endnotes

[1] "The English District Story," *"How the English Synod Became Missouri's Expandable District,"* Reprint from the English District Witness Supplement #5 of *The Lutheran Witness*, March 7, 1961, English District Dateline. Further dates are from the author's own personal files, 2015 Convention Workbook, and English District office files.

Chapter 1

[2] Alfred Faulstick, *"Martin Luther, His Life and Work,"* found in Catechetical Helps, by Erwin Kurth. St. Louis: Concordia Publishing House, 1961, revised and expanded, 1970, 1997, pp. 186-193.

[3] Introduction and Preface, Concordia: *The Lutheran Confessions* (A Reader's edition of the Book of Concord). Second Edition. Concordia Publishing House: St. Louis, 2005.

[4] Ibid.

[5] Frederick Bente, *American Lutheranism, Vol. 1*, Concordia Publishing House: St. Louis, 1919, pp. 70-82.

[6] Dr. A. Stapelton, D.D., Editor and Publisher, *The Henkel Memorial: Historical, Geographical, and Biographical.* A Serial Publication. The Henkel Memorial Association: York, PA, 1910, p. 83 (165). *The Henkel Memorial* preserves the history of the Rev. Anthony Jacob Henkel (known in history as Rev. Gerhart Henkel). Also, Frederick Bente, *American Lutheranism, Vol. 1*, pp. 138-139.

[7] E. Clifford Nelson, Editor, *The Lutherans in North America.* Fortress Press: Philadelphia, 1975, p. 51.

[8] Ibid., p. 56.

[9]Frederick Bente, *Historical Introductions to the Symbolical Books of the Evangelical Lutheran Church. Concordia Triglotta.* Concordia Publishing House, St. Louis: 1921, pp. 102-103.

Chapter 2

[10]Lawrence Rast, *Nineteenth-Century Lutheranism in the American South and West: Ministry and Mission* (STM Thesis). Concordia Theological Seminary: Fort Wayne, IN, 1995, p. 2. Dr. Rast, current president of Concordia Theological Seminary, Fort Wayne, has been a frequent presenter at English District Fall Regional Pastoral Conferences.

[11] Ibid., p. 208.

[12] H.P. Eckhardt, *The English District: A Historical Sketch.* Published by the English District of the Synod of Missouri, Ohio, and Other States, pp. 6-7.

[13] Ibid., pp. 6-7.

[14] Ibid., p. 7.

[15] Ibid., p. 8.

[16] Ibid., p. 9. Also Eckhardt cites Dr. Socrates Henkel's *History of the Tennessee Synod,* pp. 119-120, 139-140. But as noted in the text, Dr. Eckhardt would have gained huge historical and anecdotal knowledge of the Henkel family and Tennessee Synod from his close friendship with Rev. Frederic Kuegele.

[17] *Proceedings* of the 16th Convention of the English District of the Evangelical Lutheran Synod of Missouri, Ohio, and Other States, held at Concordia Teachers College, River Forest, IL, 1936, pp. 10-11.

[18] Luther Poellot, Editor, *Lutheran Cyclopedia,* Concordia Publishing House: St. Louis, 1954, revised, 1975; p. 325.

[19] Information found in the online history of the Tennessee Synod and cited from the following: Lueker, Erwin L.; Poellot, Luther; Jackson, Paul, eds. (2000). *Christian Cyclopedia* (Online Edition). Concordia Publishing House: St. Louis, Retrieved September 23rd, 2013.

[20] Socrates Henkel, *History of the Evangelical Lutheran Tennessee Synod.* Henkel Press: New Market, VA., 1890, p. 52.

[21] H.B. Hemmeter, *"The Missouri Synod and English Work,"* Concordia Theological Monthly, Vol. XVII, May 1946, No. 5, p. 322.

[22] Socrates Henkel, pp. 1-6.

[23] Ibid., pp. 7-11.

[24] Ibid., pp. 11-13.

[25] Ibid., pp. 24-25.

[26] Ibid., p. 25.

[27] Ibid., p. 26.

[28] Ibid., pp. 38-39.

[29] Ibid., p. 41.

[30] Ibid., p. 41.

[31] Ibid., p. 55.

Excursus: Koiner's Church

[32]Nancy Sorrells, Reporter, *"News Leader"* (Part of the USA Today Network) – online, Feb. 20, 2015. *"Huge family left mark on Augusta Co. history."*

[33] Ibid., Feb. 20, 2015.

[34] Ibid., Book review, online, *"The Amazon Book Review,"* An Historical Visit to *Michael Keinadt's Virginia*, by Lewis Coiner (paperback).

Excursus: Psalm 84

[35] Derek Kidner. *Psalms 73-150*. Tyndale Old Testament Commentaries. London: Inter-Varsity Press, 1975, p. 307.

[36]Study Note for 84:9 (Psalm 84), *The Lutheran Study Bible*, Concordia Publishing House: St. Louis, 2009, p. 929.

Chapter 3

[37] *Confessional Lutheran Migrations to America, 150th Anniversary*, published by the Eastern District of the Lutheran Church—Missouri Synod, 1988, pp. 26 & 47.

[38] Frederick Bente, *American Lutheranism, Vol. 1*, p. 218.

[39] This is listed in *The Lutheran Annual 2020* as 1855. Before the LCMS became its current 35 districts, also known as synodical districts or "district synod," it had four districts, with the following districts being the earliest in   branching off: Northwestern District (1874),   Illinois District (1875, from Western),   Iowa District (1879, from Western), Canada [Ontario] District (1879, from Northern), Kansas District (1888, from Western),   Southern District (1882, from Western District), Michigan District (1882, from Northern), Minnesota-Dakota (1882, from Northern), Wisconsin District (1882, from Northwestern), Nebraska District (1882, from Western), California-Oregon District (1899, from Western), Texas District (1906, from Southern), and Atlantic District (1907, from Eastern). *The Lutheran Annual 2020*. Concordia Publishing House: St. Louis, 2020, p. 793.

[40] *Proceedings* of a Free English Lutheran Conference Held in the Town of Gravelton, Wayne Co., MO, August 17-20, A.D. 1872. Also, Walter A. Baepler, *A Century of Grace*, Concordia Publishing House: St. Louis, 1947, p. 191.

[41] H.P. Eckhardt, pp. 13-14.

Excursus: "Old Gravelton Revisited"

[42] Fred C. Stein and H. William Lieske, "A Description of the Cradle of the English District After 100 Years, *The Lutheran Witness, The English District Edition*, Vol. XCI, No. 4, St. Louis, March 19th, 1972, p. 1.

[43]Fred C. Stein and H. William Lieske, *"Old Gravelton Revisited,"* Concordia Historical Institute Quarterly, Vol. XX, No. 4, January, 1948. Official Organ of Concordia Historical Institute, St. Louis, MO: 1948. Also, see FindAGrave.com. It would appear there's a discrepency with regard to the place of birth for Rev. F. Kuegele, and yet online records indicate his birthplace not as Germany, but as Ohio.

Chapter 4

[44] *Proceedings* of the 16th Convention of the English District..., p. 15.

[45] William Dallmann, *My Life*, Concordia Publishing House: St. Louis, 1945, p. 37.

[46] H.P. Eckhardt, p. 14.

[47] The German Missouri Synod's North American mission efforts are noted in the following: Rosa Young, *Light in the Dark Belt*, Concordia Publishing House: St. Louis, 1950; and, Mark Granquist, *Lutherans in America, A New History*, Fortress Press: Minneapolis, 2015.

[48] August R. Suelflow, *The Heart of Missouri*, Concordia Publishing House: St. Louis, 1954, p. 111.

[49] Eckhardt), p. 16.

[50] Dallmann, p. 37.

[51] *Proceedings* of the 16th Convention of the English District…, p. 18.

[52] Eckhardt, p. 17.

[53] Website, Bethany Lutheran Church, Waynesboro, VA. See History listing under their website.

[54] Dallmann, p. 51. It should also be noted that the General Evangelical English Lutheran Conference of Missouri and Other States (English Missouri Conference/Synod) is not to be confused with the Evangelical Lutheran General Synod of the United States formed in 1820 and headed by Samuel S. Schmucker.

[55] Eckhardt, pp. 20-21.

[56] The Rev. D.H. Steffens, *Doctor Carl Ferdinand Wilhelm Walther*, The Lutheran Publication Society, Philadelphia, 1917, p. 332.

[57] The Church of Our Saviour – Evangelical Lutheran, 75th Anniversary (Diamond Jubilee) Service Folder. Baltimore, MD: 1967. Founded (organized) by Pastor Dallmann in 1892 with 12 active members of Immanuel Lutheran Church. The fledgling congregation purchased a church building from Jackson Square Centennial Methodist Congregation right after the calling and installation of Rev. Henry B. Hemmeter as the first pastor, installed by Rev. Dallmann. The congregation then took the name Jackson Square Evangelical Lutheran Church, changing its name in 1919 to "The Evangelical Lutheran Church of Our Saviour." This first building was sold in 1919 and the congregation moved into a wooden chapel which had been built just north of where the present church building now stands. This building was constructed in 1929/1930 and dedicated on September 7, 1930. Pastor William Dallman preached at the morning service of dedication. In 1919, the old church building became Holy Trinity Russian Orthodox Church, which in 2019 celebrated its centennial, at which celebration, Our Saviour's pastor was an honored guest.

[58] One of the author's dearest friends is a former parishioner living with his family in Pleasanton, California, Mr. Rick Duemling, and a member of the English District's Messiah Lutheran Church in Danville, CA. Rick's great-great grandfather was the Rev. Herman Duemling (1845-1913), who was a professor of Mathematics and Science at the Gymnasium-College, 1874-1899 (a pastoral preparation academy, very common in the German Missouri Synod) at Fort Wayne in the late 1800s. Dr. Dallmann as a young boy attended the Gymnasium and Jr. College and had Professor Duemling as one of his teachers. Apparently Prof. Duemling had a little fun with young William Dallmann around 1877,

teasing him in front of the class. It did not seem to bother Dallmann, as he notes in his autobiography, *My Life.*

[59] Eckhardt, p. 21.

[60] Ibid., p. 23.

[61] William Dallmann, p. 58.

[62] Eckhardt, pp. 27-28.

[63] The LCMS hymnal, *Lutheran Service Book* (LSB, 2006), has 14 hymns which Professor August Crull translated from German into English.

[64] Luther D. Reed, *The Lutheran Liturgy*, Fortress Press: Philadelphia, 1947, pp. 182-199

[65] Jon D. Vieker, *The Fathers' Faith, the Children's Song: Missouri Lutheranism Encounters American Evangelicalism in Its Hymnals, Hymn Writers, and Hymns, 1889-1912*. Dissertation. Concordia Seminary: St. Louis, 2014, p. 38.

[66] Eckhardt, pp. 30-31.

[67] Ibid., p. 32.

[68] Ibid., pp. 31-33.

Excursus: Rev. Dr. William Dallmann

[69] Vieker, p. 107.

[70] William Dallmann, *"A Look Backward,"* The English District Bulletin, The Lutheran Witness – Part II, Vol. LXVI, Concordia Publishing House, July 15th, 1947, p. 2.

[71] Dallmann, *My Life*, pp. 93 & 91.

[72] Vieker, p. 107.

Chapter 5

[73] Eckhardt, pp. 33-37.

[74] The Reverend Howard J. Patten, *Concordia: Hope Is Remembering With Praise,* published by Concordia Lutheran Church, Conover, North Carolina, Chapter IX.

[75] Eckhardt, pp. 33-38; and Wikipedia, the Free On-line Encyclopedia, Concordia College (North Carolina).

Excursus: Early 20th Century Less Known Servants of the Lord

[76] Patten, Chapter XI.

[77] "The English District Story, p. 4.

Chapter 5 continued

[78] Eckhardt, pp. 38-40.

[79] Adam Catlin, "Wellington Daily News" (On-line), "Thirty-two years after closure, St. John's College still brings back its alumni," posted June 6th, 2018; and, Wikipedia, The Free Encyclopedia, St. John's College, Winfield, KS.

[80] Dr. Carl S. Mundinger, *"Before the Beginning: A Biography of John Peter Baden,"* A Manuscript serialized in the April 1967 through May 1968 issues of the St. John Reporter, p. 16.

[81] Wallace Behrhorst, *"St John's College, 1893-1986,"* St. John's College Alumni Association: Winfield, KS, pp. 8-46.

Chapter 6

[82] Eckhardt, p. 40.

[83] Ibid., pp. 41-42.

[84] Ibid., pp. 42-43.

[85] Ibid., p. 43.

[86] Ibid., p. 43.

[87] Everette Meier and Herbert T. Mayer, *"The Process of Americanization,"* in *Moving Frontiers: Readings in the History of the Lutheran Church—Missouri Synod*, edited by Carl S. Meyer, Concordia Publishing House: St. Louis, 1964, p. 361.

[88] Eckhardt, pg. 44. Also, *Proceedings* of the 6th Convention of the English Evangelical Lutheran Synod of Missouri and Other States, held at Detroit, MI (printed by American Lutheran Publication Board, Pittsburg(h), PA), July 5th-11th, 1899, p. 53. In the same Convention *Proceedings* of 1899, the author of this book's great-grandfather, H. Stechholz (Rev. Herman Stechholz) was noted as one of the assisting pastors at the Installation of the Rev, William Dallmann, previous of Emmanuel, Baltimore, MD, as pastor of Church of the Redeemer, New York City, on February 20, 1898; p. 13.

[89] Ibid., pp. 44-46.

[90] Ibid., pp. 46-47. Also, *Proceedings* of the 11th Convention of the (English) Evangelical Lutheran Synod of Missouri and Other States, held at Cleveland, OH, July 7th-13th, 1909, pp. 82-83. Also found in the German Missouri Synod Convention *Proceedings (Delegatensynode von Missouri, Ohio, und Andern Staaten,* 1911, pp. 31-40).

[91] *Ibid.,* p. 47.

[92] Eugene W. Nissen, The Bonnets From Zanesville, self-published family history, 2009, pg. 70.

[93] Eugene W. Nissen, *The Bonnets From Strasburg*, self-published family history, 2010, pp. 49-51.

[94] David P. Stechholz, *"Faith Driven—Future Focused" The English District Celebrates 100 Year,"* *"Concordia Historical Institute Quarterly,"* Spring 2012, Vol. 85, No. 1, St. Louis: Concordia Historical Institute, pp. 8-9. The context of this quote was the presentation of the Rev. Dr. Cameron MacKenzie of Concordia Theological Seminary, Fort Wayne, IN, at the Spring Processional Church Workers Conference of the English District, May, 2011. Dr. MacKenzie provided these insights of acculturation.

[95] "The English District Story," 1961, p. 1

[96] Ibid., p. 1.

[97] Eckhardt, p. 49. This author is going with Eckhardt's tally. Note, though, that in "The English District Story," p. 2, reported a vote that "40½ congregations were in favor, 12½ opposed. Thus the vote to unite had a 75% backing." Was this a second vote? Perhaps. The historical record is unclear.

[98] Eckhardt, pp. 47-54.

[99] Ibid., pp. 54-56.

[100] Ibid. p. 77.

[101] Ibid., pp. 54-56.

[102] Stechholz, p. 13.

[103] Eckhardt, p. 59.

[104] Ibid., p. 60.

[105] "The English District Story," p. 5 (Quotation of Kuegele in Historical Repast text box).

[106] "The English Work of the Missouri Synod," pg. 107, Concordia Historical Institute Quarterly, CHI, St. Louis, Fall, 1997. This same article is found in Ebenezer, edited by W.H.T. Dau, Concordia Publishing House, St. Louis, 1922. (Quotation of Dallmann in Historical Repast text box.)

Chapter 7

[107] Martin W. Mueller, *Amazing Comeback: Survey of English District History*, An English District 75th Anniversary Publication, 1986, pp. 6-7.

[108] Eckhardt, pp. 83-84. One may wonder why the English District was not 100% English. But during the time of growth as a new non-geographic district in Synod, the English District did receive congregations which were Latvian and Polish-speaking. Later in her history, the English District as a "mission district" would take in several ethnic groups speaking a number of African, Asian, and Latin American languages.

[109] Ibid., p. 60. See also *Proceedings* of the Thirty-Second Regular Meeting of the Ev. Luth. Synod of Missouri, Ohio, and Other States, Assembled at Fort Wayne, Indiana, June 20—29, 1923, pp. 45-46.

[110] Ibid., pp. 60 & 62. See also *Proceedings* of the Thirty-Third Regular Convention of the Ev. Luth. Synod of Missouri, Ohio, and Other States, Assembled at Holy Cross Ev. Luth. Church, St. Louis, Mo., June 9—18, 1926, pp. 151-153.

[111] Discussions on amalgamation by the Synod can be read in *Proceedings* of the Thirty-Fifth Regular Convention of the Ev. Luth. Synod of Missouri, Ohio, and Other States, Assembled at Milwaukee, Wisconsin, June 15—24, 1932, pp. 162-164. Response from the English District can be read in *Proceedings* of the Fourteenth Convention of the English District of the Synod of Missouri, Ohio, and Other States, Held at River Forest, Illinois, June 20—23, 1933, pp. 78-81.

[112] Ibid., pp. 63-64.

[113] Ibid., Mueller, p. 8.

[114] Mueller, p. 7.

[115] Karl Kretzmann, *The Atlantic District and Its Antecedents*, Erie Printing Company, Erie, PA, 1932, p. 153. In the Rev. Karl Kretzmann's book, *The Atlantic District and Its Antecedents*, he acknowledged brother English District pastors who had served or were currently serving (in italics) in English District congregations "in the territory of the Atlantic District." For the historian, this list of names is noteworthy.

[116] Dallmann, p. 91

[117] Mark E. Braun, *A Tale of Two Synods*, Northwestern Publishing House: Milwaukee, 2003, see Footnote 165, p. 57.

[118] Eckhardt, p. 55.

[119] *First English Evangelical Lutheran Church 50th Anniversary, 1888-1938*, published by Louis T. Duckert Print: New Orleans, 1938, p. 10. The document that includes the statistical information during Pastor Franke's ministry. The information was supplied by the Rev. John Ramsey, current pastor of First English, which is now located in Metairie, LA, a New Orleans suburb. Franke was very gifted as an English-speaking, but a German Missouri Synod-trained pastor. Additional information is also from a booklet entitled: *A Centennial of Grace 1888-1988 First English Lutheran Church*. No publisher is listed. The booklet is dated July 17, 1988, p. 38.

[120] Erwin L. Lueker, Editor, *Lutheran Cyclopedia*, pp. 110-111.

[121] Carl S. Meyer, *Moving Frontiers*, p. 418.

Excursus: The English Evangelical Lutheran Church of the Redeemer,   St. Albans, Queen Borough, New York

[122] David P. Scaer, Letter to the Rev. David P. Stechholz, in English District archive files, May 10th, 1994.

[123] This anecdotal information is from the author, who personally knew Pastor Kulow and was in his Study as he encouraged my father, the Rev. Erwin H.F. Stechholz, one of his first "youth workers" and then assistant pastor (1945-1947). Erwin Stechholz was one of those men whom Kulow took under his wing.

Excursus: Presidents and Bishop/Presidents of the English District, and Notably in the Early to Mid-20th Century

[124] Martin S. Sommer, *Prayers* (12th Edition), Rudolph Volkening & Sons, B. & S., Co.: St. Louis, 1929.

[125] Only during the COVID-19 Pandemic of 2020 was the unemployment rate in the United States higher than the extended era of the Great Depression. However, the coronavirus had an impact that lasted a much shorter time, and most Americans were able to get government financial assistance.

[126] This was an anecdotal piece of history shared with the author by his predecessor as English District Archivist, the Rev. Dr. Victor ("Vic") Halboth, Jr. (1934-2018). Apparently Pastor Schuessler was in tears at not being re-elected English District president.

Chapter 8

[127] Eckhardt, pp. 1-3.

[128] Mueller, p. 42.

[129] An explanation called "Why the Sycamore Tree?" was often printed in at least one of the daily information sheets (*"EDNA"* – *English District News and Announcements*) printed and later posted at English District Convention. *EDNA* died in the digital age by the 2012 English District Convention.

[130] The bishop's ring, used during the times of Drs. Pittelko, Ritt, and Stechholz, have the Latin inscription: SIGILIUM PRAESIDIS ET EPISCOPI ANGLICANA

DIOCECIS ECCLESIA LUTHERANA (Seal of the President and Bishop, English Diocese [District] Lutheran Church). Bishop Hardy's ring is of a different type.

[131] Bertwin L. Frey, "Helping to Keep Missouri Lutheran," in A Tree Grows in Missouri, edited by John W. Baumgaertner, Agape Publishers, Inc., 1974, p. 122.

Chapter 9

[132] Kurt E. Marquart, *Anatomy of an Explosion: Missouri in Lutheran Perspective*, Concordia Theological Seminary Press: Fort Wayne, IN, 1977, p. 49.

[133] Marquart, p. 51.

[134] Ibid., pp.51-52.

[135] The author can state this from personal experience. Not only personal recollections, but also the comments of other "PKs" (preachers' kids) indicated the desire of the parents to be pro-American in every way, including the exclusive use of English and abandoning the heritage tongue.

[136] *1948 Statistical Yearbook* of the Lutheran Church—Missouri Synod, Concordia Publishing House: St. Louis, p. 37.

[137] Granquist, p. 290.

[138] Mueller, *Amazing Comeback*, p. 11.

[139] This information was from a phone conversation that Bishop Roger Pittelko had with Rev. O.T. McRee on June 1, 1988. Already Dr. Pittelko was looking toward relocating the District Office within the Detroit area. 60% of the English District congregations were within 300 miles, as the crow flies, and noting that around 12 congregations were and still are in Ontario, Canada.

[140] *Proceedings* of the 32nd Convention of the English District of The Lutheran Church—Missouri Synod. Assembled at Concordia College, Milwaukee, WI, June 17-20, 1960, p. 123. How times changed. Over the course of decades, synodical districts were expected to do more as Synod dollars became tighter, resulting in a cycle of districts remitting less and less funds and percentage of funds for "missions" from the congregations, while congregations were remitting less and less to the districts. The result was that by 1978 the percentage of the English District's annual giving to Synod had fallen to $470,000 or 32% of funds received from the congregations. By 2020 in the English that amount had fallen to less than $200,000, and the Synod budget was more dependent on direct gifts from parishioners, investments, and other sources and less unrestricted dollars from synodical districts.

[141] "The English District Story," p. 5.

[142] Ibid., p. 5.

[143] *Proceedings* of the Golden Anniversary Convention of the English District of The Lutheran Church—Missouri Synod. Assembled at Concordia Teachers College, River Forest, IL, June 13-16, 1961, p. 23.

[144] Ibid., p. 26.

[145] Ibid., p. 36.

[146] Ibid., p. 38, Resolution No. 9.

[147] Ibid., p. 112.

[148] Ibid., p. 123.

Chapter 10

[149] *Proceedings* of the Forty-Fourth Regular Convention of the Lutheran Church—Missouri Synod, Assembled at San Francisco, California as the Twenty-Ninth Delegate Synod, June 17—26, 1959, pp. 191-192.

[150] Bertwin Frey, from *A Tree Grows in Missouri*, pg. 120.

[151] Carl S. Meyer, *Moving Frontiers*, p. 432.

[152] *Proceedings* of the Forty-Fifth Regular Convention of the Lutheran Church—Missouri Synod, Cleveland, Ohio, June 20—29, 1962, pp. 54-55.

[153] Meyer, *Moving Frontiers*, p. 432.

[154] Ibid., p. 434.

[155] Ibid., p. 435.

[156] James C. Burkee, *Power, Politics, and the Missouri Synod: A Conflict That Changed American Christianity*, Fortress Press: Minneapolis, 2011, p. 24

[157] *Proceedings* of the 37th Convention of the English District of the Lutheran Church—Missouri Synod, Assembled at Concordia Lutheran College, Ann Arbor, MI, 1968, p.19. These statistics are slightly exaggerated and different than those of the LCMS *Statistical Yearbook*s for 1967 and 1968. However, that comment in the 1968 *Proceedings* could be correct, since the District Convention was in mid-year, and Synod's *Statistical Yearbook*s are based on the data submitted the next year with the cut-off dates always being December 31.

[158] Mary Todd, *Authority Vested: A Story off Identity and Change in the Lutheran Church—Missouri Synod*, Wm. B. Eerdmans Publishing Co.: Grand Rapids, MI, 2000. Mary (née Ludwig) and this author attended Valparaiso University at the same time and became well acquainted with each other in the same Pittsburgh Circuit of the English District where the author and Mary's brother both served as pastors. Dr. Todd at one time served as president of the English District LWML. Though the author and Dr. Todd would take strongly opposite views on the ordination of women and other theological doctrines, her well-researched book had not received a through, needed rebuttal, other than a brief one at the time of the book's publication. At that date, Dr. Todd was a history professor at Concordia University-River Forest. She is currently a professor in the Honors College of Marshall University, Huntington, West Virginia.

[159] *Proceedings* of the Forty-Fifth Regular Convention of The Lutheran Church—Missouri Synod, Cleveland, Ohio, June 20—29, 1962, p. 8.

[160] Todd, *Authority Vested*, p. 54.

[161] This was personally told to the author by Rev. Dr. Ewald Mueller in 1976 at Bethlehem Evangelical Lutheran Church, Ridgewood, New Jersey, where Mueller was the long-time pastor and a New Jersey District vice president. The author vicared under Ewald Mueller, 1976-1977, with ample stories not shared in this work. Dr. Mueller was solidly conservative in doctrine and well-connected in Synod. He expressed the views of many who were hoping that Dr. Harms could right the ship of the Missouri Synod.

[162] Erwin L. Lueker, Editor, *Lutheran Cyclopedia*, p. 549.

[163] Marquart, *Anatomy of an Explosion*, p. 63.

[164] Dr. Samuel H. Nafzger, *An Introduction to The Lutheran Church—Missouri Synod*, Concordia Publishing House: St. Louis, 2007, p. 5.

[165] Martin W. Mueller, *Amazing Comeback*, p. 14.

[166] *Proceedings* of the 34th Convention of the English District of The Lutheran Church—Missouri Synod, Assembled at Concordia Teachers College, River Forest, IL, 1963, pp. 23ff.

[167] The English District had five regions, often referred to as "conferences." The fifth region, called the Southwest Region, including churches in greater St. Louis, MO, Lincoln, NE., southern Illinois and Indiana. After 1978, that region was merged together with the Midwest Region, and from 1978 on the English District had four regions.

[168] Ibid., p. 128.

[169] *Proceedings* of the 35th Convention of the English District of The Lutheran Church—Missouri Synod, Assembled at Concordia Lutheran Junior College, Ann Arbor, MI, 1964, p. 30.

[170] Ibid., p. 30.

[171] Ibid., p. 162.

[172] Ibid., pp. 141, 161.

[173] *Proceedings* – 37th Convention, pp. 48-55.

[174] Ibid., p. 19.

[175] *Convention Workbook* of the 39th Convention of the English District of The Lutheran Church—Missouri Synod, Assembled at Concordia Teachers College, River Forest, IL, June 23-25, 1972, pp. 24-25.

Chapter 11

[176] The author recalls Dr. Armin Moellering make this quip. It was confirmed by the Rev. Robert Tauscher, also an English District pastor who grew up in New Jersey as a PK and served English District parishes and uniquely as Circuit Visitor in all three circuits in New York-New Jersey, Philadelphia, and Cleveland East-Akron.

[177] Author's note - Not only was the English District and its congregations often labelled as "soft" on opposition to Lodge membership and to certain aspects of the Boy Scouts (Order of the Arrow, Scout Oath, etc.), it was often revealing itself in ecumenical gatherings, local pastoral ministry meetings and civic events, and other activities to be a bit "too liberal." Even more conservative pastors who stayed with Synod after the "split" admitted that they performed marriages with clergy of other denominations.

[178] *Proceedings* of the 38th Convention of the English District of The Lutheran Church—Missouri Synod, Assembled at Concordia Lutheran College, Ann Arbor, MI, June 22-25, 1970, pp. 20-21.

[179179] Ibid., p. 15.

[180] Ibid., pp. 20-21.

[181] Marquart, *Anatomy of an Explosion*, p. 62.

[182] Burkee, *Power, Politics, and the Missouri Synod*, p. 121.

[183] Marquart, *Anatomy of an Explosion*, p. 63.

[184] Ibid., p. 63.

[185] *"English Accent in the Lutheran Church/Missouri Synod"* (brochure), Office of the English District LC—MS, Detroit, MI, 1972, p. 7.

[186] Ibid., p. 3.

[187] *Convention Workbook,* 39th Convention of the English District, pp. 9-10. See *Proceedings* of the 39th Convention of the English District of The Lutheran Church—Missouri Synod, Assembled at Concordia Teachers College, River Forest, IL, June 23-25, 1972, p. 47.

[188] Ibid, pp. 15-22.

[189] Ibid., p. 14. In addition to Rev. Drs. John S. Damm and John Tietjen, were, among still others who were prominent leaders in opposition to the conservative direction of Synod under Dr. J.A.O. Preus: Richard H. Feucht, Charles D. Froelich, A. Lorenz Grumm, Harold Hecht, Bernard H. Hemmeter, Richard Jungkuntz, Carl H. Krekeler, Martin L. Kretzmann, George Hans Liebenow, Richard Luecke, Martin E. Marty, Edward C. May, J.J. Pelikan Sr., Wayne Saffen, Karl Schuessler, Ruben E. Spannaus, O.H. Trinklein, Paul Volz, Elmer N. Witt, and William Woldt.

[190] Ibid., pp. 50-56.

[191] Ibid., pp. 67-79.

[192] *Proceedings* of the 39th Convention of the English District.

[193] *Proceedings* of the 39th Convention of the English District, p. 34.

[194] Burkee, *Power, Politics, and the Missouri Synod,* p. 123.

[195] Todd, *Authority Vested,* p. 226.

[196] *Proceedings* of the 40th Convention of the English District of The Lutheran Church—Missouri Synod, Assembled at Concordia Teachers College, River Forest, IL, 1974, p. 5.

[197] Ibid., p. 6.

[198] Ibid., p. 7.

[199] Ibid., p. 7.

[200] Ibid., pp. 3-10.

[201] Ibid., pp. 14-15.

[202] Ibid., pp. 39-52. In the *Convention Proceedings,* 19 previously unprinted overtures were printed, not found in the preceding *Convention Workbook.* Many of these were incorporated into the 67 Resolutions that came before the District in Convention. Many of the resolutions did not deal with the synodical strife, but were of a ministry, mission, and affirming nature.

[203] Ibid, p. 46.

[204] *"English District Notes & Agenda,"* Official District Convention Publication authorized and produced under the direction of the president and the secretary of the District, 1974.

[205] *A Tree Grows in Missouri,* front and back inside of covers, and ix-xiv.

Chapter 12

[206] This was the case with this book's author, having a letter of acceptance to Concordia Seminary, St. Louis, and then having an unsolicited letter of acceptance to Seminex. The author elected to apply to and enroll in Concordia Theological Seminary, Springfield, IL, in the fall of 1974. It appears that letters

of acceptance were photocopied by Seminex officials with the hopes that many in-coming students would be lured away from Concordia Seminary.

[207] From Martin W. Mueller's *Amazing Comeback*, pg. 15, it should be noted: "A total of 45 Seminex graduates…found sanctuary in the English District, whose president [Dr. Harold Hecht] authorized their ordination and installation."

[208] Mueller, *Amazing Comeback*, p. 13.

[209] In the fall of 1974, this author visited his friends who elected to go to Seminex and sat in on classes with them, including a systematics class led by the Rev. Dr. Ted Schroeder, who had formerly been at Valparaiso University when the author was a student there. Dr. Schroeder was forthright that there was a deep underlying hermeneutic difference on how Scripture was to be interpreted, a theological difference between the Seminex Faculty (and the prior "faculty majority" at Concordia Seminary) and the LCMS and its two seminaries. This was a shock to the authors' friends, who had thought the underlying problem in the Synod was merely political and personalities. Sadly, the author's friends did not return the "favor" and then visit him at Concordia Theological Seminary, Springfield. Included in this difference was the question of women's ordination. Dr. Mary Todd in her *Authority Vested* notes that the Rev. Dr. Robert Bertram (a faculty "majority" member) was actually in agreement with the Rev. Dr. Martin Scharlemann (who changed his previous position in the late 50s and early 60s to be in agreement with and heading up the "faculty minority."). She asserts that "the ordaining of women was a precipitant in the real blowup in the Missouri Synod over…the issue of the authority of Scripture" (p. 215).

[210] Granquist, *Lutherans in America*, pp. 303-304.

[211] *"English District Remains Together As Convention Avoids Dissolution,"* *Lutheran Witness Reporter*, July 20, 1975, p. 4. See also *Proceedings* of the Fifty-First Regular Convention of The Lutheran Church—Missouri Synod, Anaheim, California, July 4-11, 1975, pp. 33, 109-111.

[212] *"Christ Frees, Christ Unites,"* a booklet for a "Special Convention of the English District of the Lutheran Church—Missouri Synod," Chicago, IL, assembled at Northlake Center, Northlake, Illinois, September 19-21, 1975, p. 26.

[213] In June 6, 2020 telephone interviews with Rev. Drs. Roger Pittelko of Villa Park, IL, and Joseph Fabry of Livonia, MI, both retired pastors in the English District at that time, information was shared that they thought that this Convention never occurred. However, it was confirmed in a same day phone call to Rev. Dr. Paul Bacon, a former secretary and first vice president of the English District, who was at that Special Convention, very near to where he was serving an English District congregation in Maywood, IL. The place where the Convention occurred is no longer the Northlake Center, which was also a hotel, but is called Concord Place, a senior retirement facility.

[214] In telephone interview with Rev. Dr. Paul Bacon, long-term pastor of both Trinity, New Lenox, and Bethesda, Chicago, IL, respectively, on June 7, 2020, the author was able to substantiate that the Special Convention occurred. It was also noted in the *Convention Proceedings* of the 1976 English District Convention, and a Convention Proceedings of the "Special Convention," 1975, was located at the English District Office. A June 8, 2020, telephone interview

with the Rev. Dr. Frank J. Pies, pastor emeritus of Our Savior Evangelical Lutheran Church & School, Hartland, MI, revealed that some pastors chose not to attend what was viewed as a rump convention and not the official, regular convention of the District.

215 *Convention Proceedings, "Special Convention"* of the English District of the Lutheran Church—Missouri Synod, Northlake Center, Northlake, IL, pp. 26-28.

216 Ibid., pp. 26-28.

217 Ibid., p. 6.

218 Ibid., p. 28.

219 Ibid., p. 28.

220 English District Office, personnel files of the Rev. Dr. George Bornemann.

221 English District Office, Archival files in the Museum Room, Dr. Martin E. Marty's Address to the English Synod, *"A New Song for a New People,"* p. 18.

222 This anecdote was shared with this book's author by Mr. Glenn Kittilsby. He was the lay delegate to the 1976 English District Convention from Christ Evangelical Lutheran Church, San Francisco. When Christ Church pulled out of the LCMS to join the AELC's English Synod, Mr. Kittilsby and his extended family transferred their church memberships to West Portal Evangelical Lutheran Church and School, San Francisco. West Portal had been a member of the CNH District but in 1978 became a member congregation of the English District. The author was later pastor (1991-2006) of West Portal Congregation. In West Portal Evangelical Lutheran Church and School, Kittilsby served in several capacities, including treasurer, vice president, and board of directors member. His pastor at the time of West Portal's transfer to the English District was Rev. Dr. Ihno Janssen, a popular, conservative pastor who had served at the English District's Redeemer Evangelical Lutheran Church & School in Philadelphia and as the English District Evangelism and Stewardship Counselor. Janssen had a major conflict with the CNH District president Jacob, one of the eight District presidents under discipline by Synod president Jack Preus. Glenn Kittilsby and his extended family had previously been active members at Christ Evangelical Lutheran Church, San Francisco, when Rev. Dr. Bertram Dallmann had served as their pastor.

223 *Proceedings* of the 41st Convention of the English District of the Lutheran Church—Missouri Synod, Assembled at Concordia Teachers College, River Forest, IL, 1976, pp. 17-18.

224 Ibid., p. 19.

225 *English District Notes and Agenda,* 41st Convention of the English District, June 17-20, 1976, River Forest, Illinois, p. 54.

226 Ibid., p. 20.

227 Ibid., p. 21.

228 *"Lutheran Accent,"* Vol. 2, No. 7, July 1976 (Editor, the Rev. Omar Stuenkel), published by the English District-LCMS, p. 1

229 *Proceedings* of the 41st Convention of the English District, p. 57.

230 Ibid., p. 46.

231 Ibid., p. 47. The author of this book is a resident of Livonia, and long after Faith Evangelical Lutheran Church closed its School and declined in membership

but before it eventually closed its doors, the author visited Faith Church and was shared information concerning its serving as the English Synod Office.

[232] *Proceedings* of the 41st Convention of the English District of The Lutheran Church—Missouri Synod, p. 22.

[233] Grace Evangelical Lutheran Church & School, River Forest, Illinois, was a prominent church in the forefront of the liberal/moderate wing of the LCMS. It left the Synod in 1977. However, because of a 1929 land contract with the LCMS and complex legal stipulations concerning Grace Congregation and its land and buildings, Grace was not able to affiliate with the AELC and later with ELCA. The Congregation had many Concordia University professors as members, creating an awkward situation. It remained an independent congregation, but was and is clearly aligned with the ELCA. The contract with the LCMS expires on January 1, 2028. Only time will tell as to the continued presence of this large congregation that sits at the corner of the LCMS' Concordia University-Chicago at River Forest. However, English District conventions held at Concordia University-Chicago have had no relations with Grace Church, and District convention Divines Services and essay presentations were held in the University's Chapel-auditorium.

[234] Ibid., p. 23.

[235] Ibid., pp. 23-24.

[236] Correspondence is found at the English District Office Archives (Museum Room) documenting letters of Pastor Nauss and vice versa with Rev. Drs. John Damm, Harold Hecht, John Baumgaertner, James Manz, Sam Roth, J.A.O. Preus, Robert Smith, et. al., mostly in 1974.

[237] Donn Wilson, *"The Word-of-God Conflict in the Lutheran Church Missouri Synod in the 20th Century,"* (Master of Theology Thesis). Luther Seminary, Digital Commons @ Luther Seminary, Spring, 2018, p. 91.

[238] *"Sing a New Song,"* Convention packet for the First Convention of the English Synod Of The Evangelical Lutheran Church, held at Arlington Heights, IL, November 12-13, 1976, pp. 1-23, and Constitution.

[239] Ibid., pp. 1-2 of the Preamble of the Constitution of The English Synod Of The Evangelical Lutheran Church.

[240] Granquist, *Lutherans in America*, p. 303.

[241] Ibid., p. 304.

Chapter 13

[242] *"Minutes"* of the Board of Directors, English District-LCMS, Schiller Park, IL, June 25, 1976. Also recorded in *"Lutheran Accent"* Vol. 2, No. 8, August, 1976 (the Rev. Omar Stuenkel, Editor), in an article entitled *"Seminex Policy,"* p. 2. This encouragement of President/Bishop Bornemann by the board of directors to postpone authorizing Seminex graduates' ordinations represented a major shift from former English District policy.

[243] *A Tree Grows in Missouri, p. 133.*

[244] Granquist, *Lutherans in America*, p. 304.

[245] Marquart, *Anatomy of an Explosion*, p. 79.

[246] Ibid., p. 99.

[247] Mueller, *Amazing Comeback*, p. 16.

[248] Ibid., p. 16.

[249] Ibid., p. 15.

[250] It should be noted that those removed were given the opportunity to first resign rather than to try to remain as members of two different synods, something the Dallas 1975 Convention of the LCMS stated was not possible. It should also be noted that in the English District Office Personal file of the Rev. Dr. John Tietjen is a letter to President George Bornemann, dated May 22, 1978, from LCMS President J.A.O. Preus that on September 24, 1977, Dr. Tietjen's name had been removed for cause from the LCMS clergy roster.

[251] *Convention Workbook* of the 42nd Convention of the English District-LCMS, Concordia College, Milwaukee, WI, 1978, pp. 25-27, 51.

[252] "Minutes" of the Board of Directors, English District-LCMS, at Schiller Park, IL, February 12th & 13th, 1978, p. 3.

[253] This comment was shared by Bishop George Bornemann on a number of occasions, including when he helped mediate a pastoral dispute in the Pittsburgh Circuit Winkel in early 1979 at Hope Church, Upper St. Clair, at which this author was in attendance. Bornemann's churchmanship, gentle admonition, and kind but firm encouragement resulted in the pastors pulling together in the same direction to plan, develop, and execute a highly successful Parish Christian Education Seminar for the Greater Pittsburgh Area LCMS Congregations from the English, Eastern, and SELC Districts.

[254] *Convention Workbook* of the 42nd Convention, p. 53.

[255] Ibid., pp. 63-64.

[256] *Proceedings* of the 42nd Convention of the English District of The Lutheran Church—Missouri Synod, Concordia College, Milwaukee, Wisconsin, June 18-21, 1978, pp.73-88. Dr. Bornemann was having a little fun with the District in calling his newsletter, *Monatsblatt*. Some pastors, this author included, enjoyed the humor of the English District having a newsletter called "*Monatsblatt*." Not every pastor seemed to be of that opinion.

[257] *Proceedings* of the 43rd Convention of the English District of The Lutheran Church—Missouri Synod, Concordia College, Ann Arbor, MI, 1980, pp. 40-41.

[258] Ibid., p. 41.

[259] Ibid., p. 42.

[260] Ibid., pp. 89-96.

[261] The Floor committee work of Dr. Ken Korby, 22 years a Professor of Theology at Valparaiso University and then pastor of the English District's almost all-African-American congregation of Chatham Fields Evangelical Lutheran Church on the south side of Chicago, was brilliant. Even though there was an effort to remove the last whereas of Resolution 7-01 that recognized differences among the members that some were convinced that there was no clear Scriptural prohibition against ordaining women to the pastoral ministry, that motion was defeated, 110-89. (The Floor Committee majority, of which this author was a member, was opposed to the ordination of women to the pastoral office.) The resolution, having then been tabled, was approved in the Wednesday, June 18 afternoon session (*Proceedings* of the 43rd Convention of the English District of The Lutheran

Church—Missouri Synod, Concordia College, Ann Arbor, MI, 1980, Minutes, p. 27.)

[262] Ibid., p. 32.

[263] *Proceedings* of 44th Convention of the English District of The Lutheran Church—Missouri Synod, Concordia College, Milwaukee, WI, 1982, Minutes, p. 50.

[264] *Proceedings* of 44th Convention of the English District of The Lutheran Church—Missouri Synod, Concordia College, Milwaukee, WI, 1982, Minutes, p. 15.

[265] *EDNA*, Monday, June 14, 1982, p. 2.

[266] This book's author was privy to some of the concerns. The tensions were to a large measure the result of different management styles and philosophies of leadership.

[267] Letter to the Board of Directors, English District-LCMS from District President Rev. George W. Bornemann, 7 September 1983 (from English District office files).

[268] *Convention Workbook* of the 44th Convention of the English District-LCMS, Concordia College, River Forest, Illinois, 1985, p. 65.

[269] Ibid., p. 65.

[270] Ibid, p. 65.

Excursus: George Washington Bornemann

[271] The author keenly remembers Bishop George Bornemann's comments on the day of the Dedication of the hew House of Worship of Redeemer Lutheran Church, Oakmont, PA, Sunday, November 16, 1980. Also serving along with the author (pastor of the congregation) and Bishop Bornemann was Rev. Alfred Faulstick, pastor emeritus of the Congregation.

[272] Bornemann file, English District Office Archives.

[273] In Rotary, there are one-year terms as a Club president, District Governor, or president of Rotary International, a world-wide service organization.

[274] "Historical Notes" section of the Parish Register, Redeemer Lutheran Church, Oakmont, PA, February 1984.

[275] Dr. George Bornemann's younger brother, Norman (1924-2015), and his wife Alvera Bornemann, were very active members of Grace Evangelical Lutheran Church, Universal, Penn Hills, PA, the nearest congregation to Redeemer Church, Oakmont, and were close friends of the author.

Chapter 13 continued

[276] *Convention Workbook* of the 45th Convention of the English District-LCMS, Concordia College, River Forest, IL, 1985, p. 30.

[277] *Proceedings* of the 45th Convention of the English District-LCMS, Concordia College, River Forest, IL, 1985, pp. 52 & 55. The author of this book was the original author of the overture to the Fall Eastern Regional Pastoral Conference, approved in the Fall of 1984, and then was submitted by the floor committee and approved by the District. The intent was to try to take Synodical Conventions out

of St. Louis and across the breadth of the United States in cities with large convention sites and lower in cost than holding LCMS Conventions in St. Louis.
[278] Ibid., p. 62.
[279] Mueller, *Amazing Comeback*, p. 18.
[280] *Proceedings* of the 46th Convention of the English District-LCMS, Concordia College, River Forest, IL, June 13-16, 1986, pp. 52.

Chapter 14
[281] *Convention Workbook* of the English District of The Lutheran Church—Missouri Synod, Concordia College, River Forest, IL, 1986, p. 52.
[282] Ibid., pp. 52-53.
[283] *Proceedings* of the 46th Convention of the English District of The Lutheran Church—Missouri Synod, Concordia College, River Forest, IL, 1988, pp. 3-6
[284] Ibid., pp. 7-45.
[285] Ibid., pp. 54-104. In *Convention Proceedings*, different Secretaries over the years would handle the resolutions in different ways, either incorporating them into the Minutes or simply listing the resolution voting results in the Minutes and printing out the Resolutions separately in their entirety.
[286] *"Minutes,"* Board of Directors, English District-LCMS, at Chicago, IL, August 22-23, 1988, p. 7.
[287] *"Minutes,"* Board of Directors, English District-LCMS, at Romulus, IL, May 15-16, 1990, pp. 7-8. Board of directors' meetings had now switched to various airport hotels at the Detroit Metro International Airport in suburban Romulus, MI. The joke was that after the Board had "eaten through the menu" at a given hotel, the Board switched to a different hotel, never an exclusive one.

Excursus: Robert Barnes
[288] It should be noted that there was actually a Scottish Lutheran martyr prior to Dr. Robert Barnes. Barnes was martyred July 30, 1540, and he was English. However, Patrick Hamilton was one who embraced the Lutheran faith and was burned at the stake in Scotland in 1528. This is noted in passing in "The Story of the Lutheran Church in Britain Through Four Centuries of History," written and compiled by the Rev. Dr. E. George Pearce, published by the ELCE, London, 1969, p. 4.
[289] Rev. Bruce W. Adams, "Robert Barnes: Luther's Ambassador to the English" (pamphlet), LLL "Life At Best," Adelaide, Australia, 1986, p. 6.
[290] Rev. Bruce W. Adams, "An English Prior and Reformer Speaks to Our Times: Dr. Robert Barnes (1495-1540), *The Lutheran*, February 10th, 1986, p. 40.
[291] Ibid., p. 11 (back cover).

Chapter 14 continued
[292] *Convention Workbook* of the 47th Convention of the English District of The Lutheran Church—Missouri Synod, Concordia College (University), River Forest, IL, 1991, p. 1.
[293] *Proceedings* of the 47th Convention of the English District of The Lutheran Church—Missouri Synod, Concordia College University), River Forest, IL, 1991, p. 15.

[294] Ibid., p. 33.

Excursus: Herman Noodix

[295] *A Tree Grows in Missouri*, xvii.

[296] Frederic W. Baue, *The Epistles of Herman Noodix*, Pergola Press LLC: St. Louis, 2011, xxiii. This correspondence from Noodix began when Baue was Pastor of Messiah Lutheran Church, Tucson, in the Arizona-South Circuit. There is also an Arizona-North circuit. In between was a single congregation of the (factious) Mid-Arizona Circuit which Noodix pastored called St. Urho's Lutheran Church. St. Urho was a factious saint who chased the grasshoppers out of Finland and whose saint day is March 16th, the day before St. Patrick's Day, Patrick, who "cast" the snakes out of Ireland.

[297] Ibid., pp. 42-43.

Excursus: JEDP

[298] Paul Bacon, Editor. *Journal of English District Pastors (JEDP)*, An unofficial journal of theological opinion and scholarship. Vol. 1, No. 1—Vol. 13, No. 1. Published at Bethesda Lutheran Church, 6803 N. Campbell Ave., Chicago, IL, 1988-2001.

Chapter 14 continued

[299] *Convention Workbook* of the 48th Convention of the English District of The Lutheran Church—Missouri Synod, Concordia University, River Forest, IL, 1994, pp. 1-6.

[300] Ibid., p. 5.

[301] *Proceedings* of the 48th Convention of the English District of The Lutheran Church—Missouri Synod, Concordia University, River Forest, IL, 1994, p. 14-17.

[302] Ibid., p. 29.

[303] Ibid., pp. 41-50.

[304] *"Minutes,"* Board of Directors, English District-LCMS, at Detroit (Romulus), MI, September 20-21, 1994, pp. 1-2.

[305] The city of Detroit was and still is the English District's "hub." However, a major decline in population and Caucasian percentage, second only to St. Louis in the United States, began in the 1950s. The issues were rooted in the mistreatment of African-Americans over the course of centuries of slavery and segregation began to erupt in the 1950s and resulted in the race riots of the 1960s. Detroit took the biggest overall lose in population among major American cities. Even now while Detroit is emerging as a "comeback city," the following information chronicles Detroit's decline (rounded figures):

Year	Overall population	White % of pop.	Black % of pop.
1940	1,620,000	91%	9%
1950	1,850,000	84%	16%
1960	1,670,000	71%	29%
1970	1,510,000	56%	44%
1980	1,200,000	34%	63%

1990	1,003,000	22%	76%
2000	957,000	12%	82%
2010	714,000	11%	83%
2020 (est.)	667,000	15%	79%

Estimated Detroit metropolitan area population – 4,280,000.

These figures are available online from www.census.gov, and www.worldpopulationreview.com.

[306] *"Minutes,"* Board of Directors, English District-LCMS, teleconference. October 13, 1994, p. 1. The Minutes state that the vote was unanimous.

[307] *"Minutes,"* Board of Directors, English District-LCMS, at St. Louis, MO, January 15-16, 1995, p. 1. The vote this time was not unanimous, though the resolution was ratified. The author of this book did not vote in favor. It was his stated view, though not recorded, that abandoning the city, the historic place of greatest work for the English District, was simply capitulating to what was the case with most church bodies, namely that safety issues, though extremely important, had become the sole determinate for such moves out of major U.S. cities.

[308] *"Minutes,"* Board of Directors, English District-LCMS, at Detroit (Romulus), MI, January 16-17, 1996, p. 33.

[309] *Convention Workbook* of the 49th Convention of the English District of The Lutheran Church—Missouri Synod, Concordia College University, River Forest, IL, 1997, p. 37.

[310] Ibid., p. 5.

[311] Ibid., pp. 1-7.

[312] At the time of that election during the 1997 District Convention, Stechholz was standing next to the other candidate, his good friend, Rev. Dr. Arnie Frank of Phoenix. Since he is the author of this book, he remembers well that election of being "un-elected" well, and so it goes in the English District!

[313] *Proceedings* of the 49th Convention of the English District of The Lutheran Church—Missouri Synod, Concordia University, River Forest, IL, Convention *Minutes,* 1997, pp. 49-72.

[314] Ibid., pp. 65-66.

[315] Ibid., p. 61.

[316] Frederic W. Baue, John W. Fenton, Eric C. Forss, Frank J. Pies, and John T. Pless, *Shepherd the Church: Essays in Pastoral Theology Honoring Bishop Roger D. Pittelko*, Concordia Theological Seminary Press: Fort Wayne, IN, 2002.

Excursus: Nomenclature Matters

[317] David H. Petersen, "Bishop, Pastor, Deacon," *Gottesdienst*, Trinity 2020, Vol. 28, No. 2, published quarterly by the Evangelical Lutheran Liturgical Press of St. Paul Evangelical Lutheran Church, Kewanee, IL, 2020, pp. 14-16.

[318] *"Minutes,"* Board of Directors, English District-LCMS, at Detroit, September 20-21, 1994, p. 1.

[319] The information on the "Symbols of The Office of Bishop" were taken and added from the Installation Service on the occasion of the Installation of The Rev. David P. Stechholz as Bishop/President of the English District-LCMS on Sunday,

374

September 10, A.D. 2006, at West Portal Evangelical Lutheran Church and School, San Francisco, CA.

Chapter 15

[320] *"Minutes,"* Board of Directors, English District-LCMS, at Detroit (Romulus), MI, September 8-10, 1997, pp. 1-15.

[321] *"Minutes,"* Board of Directors, English District-LCMS, at Detroit (Romulus), MI, November 11-12, 1997, pp. 1-6.

[322] *"Minutes,"* Board of Directors, English District-LCMS, at Detroit (Romulus), MI, January 13-14, 1998, p. 3.

[323] *"Minutes,"* Board of Directors, English District-LCMS, at Detroit (Romulus), MI, August 11-12, 1998, pp. 5-6.

[324] *"Minutes,"* Board of Directors, English District-LCMS, at Detroit (Romulus), MI, May 9-10, 2000, p. 2.

[325] *"Minutes,"* Board of Directors, English District-LCMS, at Detroit (Romulus), MI, November 10-11, 1998, pp. 1-20.

[326] *"Minutes,"* Board of Directors, English District-LCMS, at Detroit (Romulus), MI, November 9-10, 1999, p. 4.

[327] *Convention Workbook* of the 50th Convention of the English District of The Lutheran Church—Missouri Synod, Concordia College University, River Forest, IL, 2000, pp. 1-4.

[328] *Proceedings* of the 50th Convention of the English District of The Lutheran Church—Missouri Synod, Concordia University, River Forest, IL, 2000, pp. 1-7.

[329] Ibid., pp. 23-45.

[330] Bishop Stechholz of the English District-LCMS reached out to local pastors and congregations of the Detroit area and the senior pastor of Upper Arlington Lutheran Church, suburban Columbus, Ohio. These pastors and their congregations were deeply troubled by the drift in the ELCA from biblical teachings. Though none joined The LCMS and instead helped to form the NALC, they expressed appreciation for the sympathetic ears of LCMS leaders and pastors.

[331] *"Minutes,"* Board of Directors, English District-LCMS, at Detroit (Romulus), MI, November 6-7, 2001, p. 6.

[332] *"Minutes,"* Board of Directors, English District-LCMS, at Detroit (Romulus), MI, May 6-7, 2002, p. 5.

[333] *"Minutes,"* Board of Directors, English District-LCMS, at Detroit (Romulus), MI, January 22-23, 2002, pg. 3; and, *"Minutes,"* Board of Directors, English District-LCMS, at Trinity Evangelical Lutheran Church, Villa Park, IL, and New Hope Lutheran Ministries, Chicago, August 12-13, 2002, pp. 4-5.

[334] *Convention Workbook* of the 51st Convention of the English District of The Lutheran Church—Missouri Synod, Concordia College University, River Forest, IL, 2003, pp. 1-36; and *Proceedings* of the 51st Convention of the English District of The Lutheran Church—Missouri Synod, Concordia University, River Forest, IL, 2003, pp. 18-22.

[335] Ibid., pp. 9-28

[336] Ibid., pp. 29-36.

[337] *Proceedings* of the 51st Convention of the English District of The Lutheran Church—Missouri Synod, Concordia College University, River Forest, IL, 2003, p. 22.

[338] Ibid., pp. 1-52.

[339] Ibid., p. 80.

[340] Ibid., p. 98.

[341] *"Minutes,"* Board of Directors, English District-LCMS, at Detroit (Romulus), MI, April 29-30, 2003, pp. 2 & 5.

[342] "Minutes," Board of Directors, English District-LCMS, at Detroit (Romulus), MI, May 3-4, 2004, p. 5.

[343] *"Minutes,"* Board of Directors, English District-LCMS, at Detroit (Romulus) and Farmington, MI (English District office), August 8-9, 2004, p. 4.

[344] *"Minutes,"* Board of Directors, English District-LCMS, at Martin Luther Chapel, Pennsauken, NJ, August 8-10, 2005, p. 6.

[345] *"Minutes,"* Board of Directors, English District-LCMS, at Detroit (Romulus), MI, January 17-18, 2006, pp. 7-8.

[346] *Convention Workbook* of the 52nd Convention of the English District of The Lutheran Church—Missouri Synod, Hyatt Regency Hotel, Schaumburg, IL. pp. 1-7.

[347] *Proceedings* of the 52nd Convention of the English District of The Lutheran Church—Missouri Synod, Hyatt Regency Hotel, Schaumburg, IL, 2006, p. 25.

[348] The father of Rev. John Wm. Stieve was the Rev. William Stieve, Jr. (1915-1971). The father of Rev. David Stechholz was the Rev. Erwin H.F. Stechholz (1913-2000). Both served for a time in New York City, and both in institutional ministry. Both fathers were role models of pastoral care for their sons. Available from the Rev. John Wm. Stieve, *"A Faithful Chaplain under the 'Chief of Chaplains: The Life and Ministry of Pastor 'Bill Stieve',"* Green Valley, AZ, 1997.

[349] *Proceedings* of the 52nd Convention..., p. 28.

[350] Ibid., p. 30

[351] Ibid., pp. 38-40.

[352] In May 2007, Bishop David & Janet Stechholz were part of a mission trip to South Africa, joining two groups from Redeemer Church, Sarnia, Ontario, led by their pastor, Dr. Roger Ellis, and Christ Church-Lutheran, Phoenix, led by Mr. Bob Funk. Arranged with Bishop Tswaedi, this was a mission trip in a partnership "build" with Habitat for Humanity, Thrivent Financial for Lutherans, both church groups, the English District, and the Lutheran Church of Southern Africa in Shongweni, South Africa's the "land of a thousand hills." Bishop Stechholz preached in English at Bishop Tswaedi's Zulu and English-speaking congregation in Soweto, a suburb larger than its city, Johannesburg. With Bishop & Mrs. Tswaedi, they also visited the LCMS partner seminary in Pretoria, having brought books as gifts for the Seminary. Two homes were built and dedicated, and Sunday worship was at the partner church body's Shongweni congregation. Though the close friendships and partnership did not result in an English District-adopted ministry, such as the later Dominican Republic Lutheran Mission, the relationship proved endearing.

[353] *Proceedings* of the 52nd Convention, p. 56.

Excursus: Fall Regional Pastoral Conferences

[354] The author of this book remembers well that episode, both having been the first of two pastors to challenge in a brotherly way the pastor who persisted in false doctrine in the context of daily devotions at the Western Regional Fall Pastoral Conference and then years later having to do the "dirty work" of a Bishop by removing that pastor from the LCMS. This was done fairly and correctly, upholding biblical doctrine and the Christian faith.

Chapter 15 continued

[355] *"Minutes,"* Board of Directors, English District-LCMS, at Detroit (Romulus), MI, May, 6-7, 2007.

[356] *"Minutes,"* Board of Directors, English District-LCMS, at St. Luke's, North York (Toronto), ON, August 12-13, 2008.

[357] Convention *Workbook* of the 53rd Convention of the English District of The Lutheran Church—Missouri Synod, Hales Corners Lutheran Church, Hales Corners, WI, 2009, p. 3-1.

[358] Though he took flack for it, Bishop Stechholz made sure that over 50,000 Ablaze! Cards, encouraging LCMS congregational members to be ablaze with sharing their faith in Jesus Christ, were distributed to each congregation of the English District following Divine Services at which he was in attendance.

[359] Ibid., pp. 3-5.

[360] C. George Fry and Joel R. Kurz, editors, *Lively Stone: The Autobiography of Berthold von Schenk*, American Lutheran Publicity Bureau: Delhi, NY, 2006.

[361] *Proceedings* of the 53rd Convention of the English District of The Lutheran Church—Missouri Synod, Hales Corners Lutheran Church, Hales Corners, WI, 2009, pp.17-24.

[362] *Convention Workbook* of the 53rd Convention, 2009, pp. 3-1--3-83. A few highlights of the 2009 *Convention Workbook* are here noted. Rev. David Thiele in his Missions report emphasized the four-legged stool of support for congregational revitalization including coaching, learning, local connections, and financial resources. In the Regional Vice President reports, Dr. Larry Vogel (Eastern Region) noted the passing of pianist/organist and mainstay in the Region, Rev. Mark Sallach, Pastor of Trinity Evangelical Lutheran Church, Erie, Pennsylvania. Dr. Roger Ellis (Lake Erie Region) reported on the active involvement of the District's Canada Corporation (CCEF) in mission development, loans, and investments. Dr. Martin Bangert (Midwest Region), a Seminary classmate of Bishop Emeritus Pittelko and Dr. Vic Halboth, noted the passing of the former First Vice President of the English District, Rev. Mel Tassler of Lincoln, Nebraska, at whose funeral he represented the English District and Bishop Stechholz. First Vice President Dr. John Stieve (Western Region) in his report pointed out the uniqueness of Region like a five-pointed star (the five major cities) and the formation of a new LCMS campus ministry at the University of Arizona in Tucson, ALCMS (Arizona Lutheran Campus Ministry Society).

[363] Ibid., pp. 25-27. It should be noted that Bishop/President Emeritus David Ritt brought greetings to the Convention, providing a challenge and a blessing to the Convention. Bishop Emeritus Roger Pittelko was unable to attend but sent greetings.

[364] Ibid., pg. 37.

[365] *"Minutes,"* Board of Directors, English District-LCMS, at Detroit (Romulus), MI, November 8th-10th, 2010, pp. 1-3.

[366] Convention *Workbook* of the 54th Convention of the English District of The Lutheran Church—Missouri Synod, Concordia Seminary, St. Louis, and the Sheraton Westport Lakeside Chalet, MO, 2012, p. 3-1.

[367] *An Historical Sketch/Bible Study* booklet was authorized by the 100th Anniversary Committee. However, it was not produced.

[368] Convention *Workbook*...54th Convention, p. 3-7.

[369] *Proceedings* of the 54th Convention of the English District of The Lutheran Church—Missouri Synod, Concordia Seminary, St. Louis and the Sheraton Westport Lakeside Chalet, MO, WI, 2012, pp.15 & 16.

[370] William W. Schumacher, Convention Essay: "Why Us? Remembering to Understand," 54th Convention of the English District-LCMS, Westport Lakeside Chapel, MO, 2012, p. 2.

[371] Ibid., p. 5.

[372] Ibid., p. 6.

[373] Ibid., pp. 7-10.

[374] *"Minutes,"* Board of Directors, English District-LCMS, at Concordia Theological Seminary, Fort Wayne, IN, August 2-4, 2014, p. 3.

[375] *"Minutes,"* Board of Directors, English District-LCMS, at Detroit (Romulus), MI, November 5-7, 2014, p. 5.

Excursus: The English District LWML

[376] *The Great Potluck From Across The English District, A Collection of Recipes, 100th Anniversary*, Morris Press Cookbooks, Kearney, NE, 2011, inside cover page.

Chapter 15 continued

[377] *"Minutes,"* Board of Directors, English District-LCMS, at the Sheraton Hotel, Ann Arbor, MI, May 6-7, 2013, pg. 3. – Note: The Board approved the DRLM but with no funding coming from the District Budget. Such funds would have to be raised in a minimum two-year commitment over and above congregational District support. And it was!

[378] Convention *Workbook* of the 55th Convention of the English District of The Lutheran Church—Missouri Synod, Concordia University, Ann Arbor, Michigan, 2015, pp. 3-5—3-8.

[379] Bishop Stechholz was deeply grateful for the honorary Doctor of Divinity. Concordia University-Ann Arbor had now become a significant part of his life, along with that of his wife Janet, who graduated from Concordia in 1973 when it was still a two-year college of the LCMS.

[380] *Proceedings* of the 55th Convention of the English District of The Lutheran Church—Missouri Synod, Concordia University, Ann Arbor, Michigan, 2015, p. 13

[381] *Workbook* of the 55th Convention, p. 3-9.

[382] *Proceedings* of the 55th Convention, p. 15.

[383] Ibid., p. 48.

[384] Ibid., p. 59.

Chapter 16

[385] "Minutes," Board of Directors, English District-LCMS, at Angelica Evangelical Lutheran Church, Allen Park, MI, August 10–12, 2015, p. 2.

[386] *Proceedings* of the 56th Convention of the English District of The Lutheran Church—Missouri Synod, held at Concordia University, Ann Arbor, MI, pp. 15-16, 20.

Excursus: District Communications

[387] Copies of the printed communications of the English District are archived at the English District Office in Farmington, MI.

Chapter 17

[388] Martin W. Mueller, *"Amazing Comeback,"* p. 43.

[389] H.P. Eckhardt, *The English District: A Historical Sketch*, p. 64.

Chapter 18

[390] Dick Hamm, "The Resurrection of Middle Judicatories," Columbia Partnership (online), 2010, pg. 1.

[391] David P. Stechholz, *Love, Hope, and Faith: Anecdotes from the Building Programs of Three Churches*, self-published, 2019, pp. 10-11.

[392] Among our missionaries who had to rapidly exit China were the Rev. Will Holt and his family (to Hong Kong) and the Rev. Paul & Carol Kreyling through Shanghai, and then re-assigned by the LCMS Mission Board to Japan. Pastor Holt was a missionary in Hong Kong till 1963, and then as a founding pastor of a Chinese congregation in San Francisco, California.

[393] *"The Lutheran Witness,"* June/July, 2020, published 11 times a year by Concordia Publishing House: St. Louis, pp. 1-29.

[394] Ibid., pp. 13-14.

[395] Matthew Harrison, Letter to the LCMS concerning COVID-19 Vaccines and CTCR sheet on "The LCMS and COVID-19 Vaccines: Facts and Considerations," online, January 21, 2021.

[396] Telephone interview with Dr. Roger Pittelko on Monday, May 4, 2020, from his home in Elk Grove Village, IL. Other telephone interviews in May, June, and July were with Dr. Paul Bacon, Dr. Joe Fabry, the Dr. Frank Pies, Jr., Rev. Brian Westgate, Dr. Larry Vogel, Dr. John Stieve, and Rev. Luke Zimmerman.

[397] The seasoned pastor, whose name remains in confidentiality, played a significant role in the life and ministry of the English District over the course of over 30 years. He also noted how Zoom meetings, whether of the District or Bible

classes during the COVID pandemic, have been good but impersonal. His desire would be for the English District brethren to work hard at being alive and practicing intense care for one another and fellowship (from a phone interview, July 26, 2020).

Statistics

[398] *Proceedings*, 17th Convention of the English District of the Evangelical Lutheran Synod of Missouri, Ohio, and Other States, held at Concordia Teachers College, 1937, pg. 91.

[399] *Proceedings*, 22nd Convention of the English District of the Evangelical Lutheran Synod of Missouri, Ohio, and Other States, held at the Evangelical Lutheran School for the Deaf, Detroit, MI, 1945, pg. 117.

Index